ADVANCE PRAISE FOR
APPREHENSIONS & CONVICTIONS

"Part police procedural, part contemplative memoir, Mark Johnson's *Apprehensions & Convictions* is all true, and a revelation. His story is by turns hair-raising, hilarious, and heartfelt. It should take its rightful place in the colorful Southern tradition of storytelling."

—**Winston Groom**, author of *Forrest Gump*, *Kearny's March*, and *The Aviators*

"This unique and entertaining memoir by a former national charity executive, who finds himself policing dangerous inner-city streets as a 50-year-old rookie cop, is exciting, absorbing and unflinchingly honest."

—**Joseph Wambaugh**, author of *The New Centurions*, *The Blue Knight*, the *Hollywood Station* series, and numerous other crime novels

"Gritty, thoughtful, and authentic. Johnson gives you unvarnished insight into a world in which few dare to tread. He's the real deal and so is this book."

—**Adam Plantinga**, author of *400 Things Cops Know*

"F. Scott Fitzgerald claimed there were no second acts in America. He was wrong. Mark Johnson proves it. He's into his third act now, from social worker to cop, and now to writer, and in *Apprehensions & Convictions* he leaves little doubt that he's mastered that third incarnation. You'll be grabbed by the seat of your pants on the first page and he won't let go till the very last word."

—**Charles Salzberg**, Shamus-nominated author of *Devil in the Hole* and *Swann's Lake of Despair*

"*Apprehensions & Convictions* is a thoroughly enjoyable and compelling read, chock-full of authenticity and soul. Mark Johnson's book is not only motivational, but, in a way, an excellent anthropological study of police culture and human behavior. Definitely essential reading."

—**David Swinson**, author of *The Second Girl*

APPREHENSIONS & CONVICTIONS

Adventures of a 50-Year-Old Rookie Cop

Mark Johnson

Fresno, California

Apprehensions & Convictions: Adventures of a 50-Year-Old Rookie Cop
Copyright © 2016 by Mark Johnson. All rights reserved.

Published by Quill Driver Books
An imprint of Linden Publishing
2006 South Mary Street, Fresno, California 93721
(559) 233-6633 / (800) 345-4447
QuillDriverBooks.com

Quill Driver Books and colophon are trademarks of
Linden Publishing, Inc.

ISBN 978-1-61035-264-2

135798642

Printed in the United States of America
on acid-free paper.

Library of Congress Cataloging-in-Publication Data on file

Contents

For Nancy, and Pete and Kate.
And in memory of Margaret and Stan.

Preface

I'm not a career cop, nor a natural warrior. But cops have always been among my heroes. Looking at the downside of fifty, it seemed time was running out. More than two decades of social service philanthropy (the majority as CEO) in three distinct cities had left me feeling restless and out of touch. Instead of trying to effect community-wide change, I thought maybe I could be more effective—more *useful*—to a few neighborhoods, even to just a few families or individuals at a time. I wanted to make a more tangible difference, in a more hands-on way. Not many jobs are more hands-on than policing. It seemed like a good idea at the time. It still does.

The names, nicknames, and aliases of all those portrayed in this book—police, suspects, arrestees, witnesses, informants, victims, public defenders, prosecutors, magistrates, and judges—have been changed, with the exceptions of Officer Steven Green and Lawrence Wallace, Jr. (both deceased, and a matter of public record), my immediate family, me, and good ol' Ernie.

All events herein are from my own first-hand experience. My memory of them is supported by my dispatch notes, case files, official reports and narratives, conversations with others at the scene, and, in a few cases, news accounts.

Spoken words are necessarily recreated as closely as memory allows. In the absence of recorded transcripts, every effort has been made to convey the essential truth—the intention, inflection, and meaning—of the speaker and the words spoken. This includes colloquialisms, slang, and dialect, sometimes requiring improper grammar, profanity, and phonetic spellings. Some of the slang is racially unique, some is just southern. Mobile's population is roughly half African American, half Caucasian, but my police beats were in primarily African American neighborhoods. I wrote the way the people in those neighborhoods talk. It's not exaggerated or distorted. It's different from the way people talk in Denver, Milwaukee, or St. Louis. In fact, understanding the local black dialect was a significant challenge in my early days as a cop. I had to ask people to repeat themselves multiple times, sometimes needing them to spell out what they were saying. I even had to do this on the air with police radio dispatchers—and this after having lived in Mobile for seven years. It's a thick accent, a dense and colorful jargon, and it takes a while to fully comprehend.

At several points in my story, I use strong terms to refer to people encountered on the job. Some may take offense at words like "feral" or "savages." I make no apology. Words mean things, and the people I refer to match the meanings of the words, and it has nothing to do with race or class and I don't speak for all cops, anyway.

I have met cops from all over the U.S. and from a dozen foreign countries, and have found an uncommon commonality between us, stemming from the unique perspective and shared experience that the work bestows upon us. It's scary, disturbing, dangerous work, mostly a plodding grind, occasionally thrilling, usually for scandalously low pay, but offering unsurpassed rewards. It's the best job I ever had.

1

What *Are* You?

Men sleep peacefully in their beds at night only because rough men stand ready to do violence on their behalf.
—attributed to George Orwell

I'm just a few days out of Mobile's Police Academy, my third night in the Third Precinct riding with my FTO, Porter. Sarge had just dismissed us from roll call, and we were in the precinct parking lot loading and fueling up Porter's squad car. It was 1815 hours on a sweltering mid-September evening.

Porter had told me the first night, "Get this straight, up front: I don't know you and don't wanna know you. Don't give a damn about you, your life's story, your wife and kids, what you did before this, and why you wanted to work in this fucked-up department, especially at your age, Grampa. You're not my buddy, and you won't be after this month is up." He had punctuated this declaration by slamming the squad car trunk, where I'd just stowed my shotgun.

"I never volunteered to be a field training officer and don't get paid any extra for all the goddamn paperwork. I hate rookies. Even though you're old enough to be my pawpaw and you look like Clint fucking Eastwood— in *Blood Work*, not *Dirty Harry*, have you seen that yet? Then you know what I'm talkin' about: he's so old, he has a heart attack in the first scene— you're just another goddamn rookie to me. All I ask is that you don't bug me, don't try to talk to me, or ask a million stupid-ass rookie questions. Just stay the fuck outta my way and don't do anything to embarrass me."

"Yes sir," I'd said that first night, an academy reflex. I'd been told before of my resemblance to Clint but without Porter's specificity. This time it kinda stung. I had just seen *Blood Work*. After the opening-scene foot chase ends with Clint's heart attack, for the rest of the movie everybody tells him how bad, how sick he looks. Wasn't Eastwood like seventy-five? I had just turned fifty.

"Jeee-zus," Porter had said, blowing smoke and shaking his head in disgust. He'd then thrust his plump round face into mine, his sneer exposing teeth crying out for orthodonture. He barely has whiskers, I'd noticed, and a sparse, utterly pathetic mustache darkened his upper lip. I'd gotten a pungent whiff of coffee and nicotine from his breath but resisted pulling my head back.

"You see any fucking stripes on my sleeve, Pawpaw?" He'd raised a thick bicep, pulling at the sleeve. "First rule: Don't call me 'sir'!"

I'd felt my mouth forming the *y* of yessir but aborted it, leaving my chin slightly jutting, in what I'd hoped might be taken as defiance, or determination. It was taken as neither. Porter wasn't even looking at me as we'd pulled out of the precinct and into the night. He was on a roll.

"Second rule," he had announced. "Forget all that crap they taught you in the academy. It's useless. Horseshit. Has nothing to do with how it really is out here on the streets. Just watch what I do, and the other guys on the squad. Except that worthless piece of shit Whatley. Do exactly the opposite of anything he does." I had wondered, what makes Whatley a piece of shit? So much for the "brothers-in-blue" thing.

But Portly Porter droned on, his self-importance reminiscent of Deputy Barney Fife condescending to deputize Gomer Pyle in Mayberry. "Keep your mouth shut, your eyes and ears open, then maybe, just mayyybe, we'll get along and you'll survive this month." He grabbed the radio mike and put us 10-8 (in service), as a *one*-man training unit. I didn't count—even as a man, much less a cop—and wouldn't for another ninety days.

I remember thinking, you fat fool, you're a walking cliché, giving me that tired, world-weary-veteran-to-recruit spiel. You're maybe half my age. Former Marine? Big whup. Do you really think I haven't watched that scene you're playacting, in maybe a million movies, most of 'em made before you could even talk?

But I was used to rookie disdain as the default setting of department veterans by now, having been razzed and lorded over and called crazy for the past six months by old cops, young cops, female cops, fellow recruits, academy instructors, my wife, and most of our family and friends ever since I'd abruptly quit my old job heading up Mobile's United Way for a 75 percent pay cut and hired on with the department. I just sucked it up and held my tongue. I'm not one for much conversation, anyway. And if I ever do come up with a snappy comeback, it's several days late.

Porter liked to write tickets. Traffic enforcement is my least favorite part of policing. But for Porter, it justifies parking the squad car on the road-side behind some bushes and just sitting there until the radar whines. I'd sat in obedient silence for two twelve-hour shifts, trying to focus on the radio, listening for our unit number to be called. Porter had mostly chain-smoked Marlboro Lights and talked for hours on his cell to some female in Arkansas he'd met online: "What's your favorite thing at Taco Bell? Dontcha love those new Gorditas, with extra sour cream!" I was begin-ning to believe that old saying about police work: 90 percent boredom and 10 percent terror. I was craving the terror. And thinking maybe this was a really dumb career move, after all.

But third night out, as the day's thick heat slowly rose up out of the asphalt while the blazing Alabama sun eased beyond the horizon, we finally get dispatched to a hot call, a domestic: white female caller, assaulted by known white male subject armed with a knife. Both parties still on scene. At last! I think. We get to rescue a damsel in distress!

Dubovitch will back us. (A reminder to me that even to the dispatcher, I don't exist, at least not as sufficient backing for Porter.) I try to picture Dubovitch. From what little I've gathered, if he's the guy I'm thinking of, he seems pretty squared away, based on his bearing at roll call and how the others regard him. A little cocky, maybe, but (I'm beginning to think) who of these guys isn't? Dubovitch has been on about as long as Porter, seven or eight years, and is about the same age, late twenties, maybe thirty. At least he's not fat and loud like Portly.

We pull into the rundown motor court, a place that charges by the week and month (and probably by the hour). That old jukebox chorus pops unbidden into my head: "I'll even tell you that I love you if you want me to. Third rate romance, low rent rendezvous." The Amazing Rhythm Aces.

The dozen-room Bama Pride motel's neon sign has a nearly burnt-out, flickering *P* and so alternately reads "Bama ride." It's a long, sad-looking, one-story cinder-block building with peeling lime-green paint, sagging eaves, missing shingles, and broken windows held together with duct-taped cardboard. Room numbers are nailed all cattywampus to the splintered, scarred doors. Its weedy, cracked, and heaving parking lot is littered with cigarette butts, flattened malt liquor cans, broken glass. There's a lone, battered, and rusty eighties-model Ford pickup, mostly faded blue but with a primer-gray door, parked at the far end of the lot. Evidently, most of this motel's guests don't own vehicles.

Dubovitch is already there, leaning against his squad car smoking a cigarette next to an agitated, anorexic, bedraggled, hard-looking woman talking fast and loud. Our damsel could be the "Bama ride" herself. She had likely been attractive, in a lascivious sort of way, in a previous incarnation. A large near-empty wine bottle is on the ground next to her.

She's carrying on about how "the thum-bitch came at me with a knife! A goddamn knife!" She seems more pissed off than scared or hurt. She's maybe mid-forties, her lisp the result of gaps in her frightfully discolored teeth. Strands of greasy, sweat-soaked hair stick randomly to her forehead, cheeks, and neck; she's wearing a soiled, stretched wifebeater (barely containing her drooping, braless breasts), neon-pink short-shorts with white piping, no shoes, filthy bare feet. Tattoos, mosquito bites, scratches, scabs, and welts adorn her arms and legs. Dubo's not even looking at her while she rants on with punching and parrying motions and points to the door of room number five. As Porter and I approach, I can smell her. It's not a pleasant scent: a yeasty, sour odor similar to dirty sweat socks but sharper.

Dubovitch smiles and says, "Hey Porter, check out her tattoo. Show him your tat, darlin'." The woman stops mid-sentence and proudly displays her upper right arm.

Porter reads aloud the faded greenish lettering, "FUCK MEN," then grins.

"Is that your attitude, ma'am, or your job description?" Good one, Porter, I concede, grudgingly. He's still a pompous ass, but I'll grant him points for wit.

"I don't need no thit from you, ath-hole!" our complainant spits through her gaping teeth. "I want him arrethted! Prothecuted to the fulleth exthtent of the law! I know my rightth!" A devotee of TV court dramas.

"No injuries," Dubo says, ignoring her, "but those two over there witnessed the whole thing." He nods toward a couple of gray-haired black men sitting on lawn chairs at the end of the parking lot, under the generous cool shade of a massive, moss-dripping live oak, whose roots are responsible for the crumbling, upheaved asphalt. "Guy did have a knife, they say, and he started it. It's her old man. They both been drinking and fighting all day, according to the witnesses, and she confirms it." He gestures to the wine bottle at her feet. When I look their way, the witnesses nod in affirmation. I swell up slightly and nod back with my most serious countenance: a man on a mission. At least *they* think I'm a cop. "He retreated to the room when she smacked him upside the head with the bottle."

"You got her information, Dubo?" Porter asks.

Dubovitch nods. "I just gotta get her signature on the DV* form, and the witness statements. Why don't you and your rookie go fetch him. He's still in the room. No backdoor. Still has the blade on him."

"C'mon, Pawpaw," Porter says. "Let's go get Mr. Slingblade." He strides toward the door, which is partially open, to room number five. I notice he unsnaps the holster of his Glock and do likewise. My heart is pounding and my hand is trembling and I'm relieved nobody seems to notice. We stand on each side of the door. Porter gingerly pushes on it, calling out "MPD" as it swings open. We peer inside.

Naked except for darkly stained shorts, a man sits on a bed, propped against the wall. Blood covers him from a gash on his swollen forehead. He's bald, except for long wisps of gray hair around the ears, bound into a ponytail behind his ruined face. The tangled sheets around him are soaked with gore.

Spying us, he snarls, "Arrest that bitch! She damn-near killed me! Looka me! I want that bitch chained down in Metro!"

"Settle down, Pops," Porter says, waving off his demands as we enter. My eyes are popping at the sight of him. Porter's eyes sweep the room, and mine follow. It's all torn up. A nightstand next to the bed has been knocked over, its lamp shattered on the floor. A chrome-and-plastic chair lies on its side among broken dishes, scattered French fries, half-eaten hamburgers, and Sonic Drive-In wrappers swept off an overturned kitchenette table. Beer cans, wine bottles, and dirty clothes cover the floor.

"Where's the blade?" Porter demands.

"What blade?!" Mr. Bloodyface snaps. "Wha'd that bitch tell you? She fuckin' conked me with a bottle! I want her arrested!"

---

* Domestic violence.

The poor bastard clearly got the worst of it. Who's the real victim here, I'm wondering. Porter approaches him. "Get up and put your hands behind your back," he orders, unsnapping his cuffs from his duty belt. The bloody man is outraged and bellows, "I'm barely fucking conscious! You put that *bitch* in cuffs, not *me*! Why are you idiots taking me? What's the charge? I have a right to know the charge! I demand you arrest her! Get me a motherfucking ambulance!"

Unfazed, Porter jerks him upright from the bed and quickly cuffs him despite his twisting and shouting.

"You started it, Pops. Got witnesses. You're the primary aggressor, so shut the fuck up and quit buckin' on me or I'll bloody you some more." Then with equal contempt for me, mute and immobilized at the tableau, "Don't just stand there with your mouth open, rookie. Search his pockets!"

The man is still attempting to jerk free, despite Porter's firm grasp of his cuffed wrists. "Careful of the blood, rookie. He might have AIDS. You got the Bug, Numbnuts?"

I pull a small folding knife from a pocket of the blood-sticky shorts. "Hang on to that, Pawpaw. Evidence." Porter marches our arrested subject out the door to the squad car. He's dog-cussing us, calling us pigs, calling her a nasty dogfucking whore. His victim returns the barrage, taunting, "Yeah, motherfucker! Who'th the tough guy now?" Dubo has to restrain her from lunging at him as Porter stuffs the bloody man into the cage. He's demanding our badge numbers, demanding justice. I drop the knife into my breast pocket and follow like a heeling pup.

At the hospital, bloody Lester Puckett shouts and struggles all the way into the ER intake bay, where Porter plops him down in front of a desk occupied by a soft-spoken matronly administrator. (Metro won't accept anybody in Lester's condition without a medical release. A doctor has to deem him fit for incarceration, so Metro doesn't get sued if he croaks in its custody.) Regular people, seated in the room awaiting loved ones, feign averting their eyes from the spectacle. One woman actually covers her kid's ears and turns his head away.

The intake specialist asks Puckett for his information, calling him Mr. and Sir. After a thoughtful pause, Lester grunts, "I ain't gotta talk to no nigger bitch." She seems remarkably unperturbed, but Porter apologizes for him anyway and provides her Lester's info, gathered by Dubo from the FUCK MEN tat lady, and from his squad car's mobile display terminal when he'd pulled up Lester's rap sheet. Dubo had cleared from backing us and returned to his own beat.

Once she enters all Lester's data into her computer, the lady explains to Lester that she will need him to sign the treatment authorization form. Porter unlocks the cuff on Lester's right wrist so he can sign the form, warning him not to try anything stupid. He keeps a firm hold of the freed cuff, still attached to Lester's left wrist. Lester calmly, tenderly rubs his freed right wrist.

Then he explodes, rising up and pounding the desk. Paper clips bounce, knickknacks dancing. "I ain't signin' nothin'!" he screams. The startled administrator pushes back away from him in her chair. Porter jerks Lester backward with the loose handcuff, knocking Lester's chair into me. With his other arm, he hooks Lester around the throat from behind, sweeps him up off his feet, and slams him down hard on the floor. You can hear the thud as the back of Lester's skull and shoulders hit the tile. The wind's knocked out of Lester, he's gasping for air, eyes bugging out. Porter pins Lester to the floor by the throat. Lester's feet are kicking, arms flailing away like he's drowning. The normal citizens clear the room.

"Yer gonna sign the fucking form, shitbag!" Porter growls.

Lester's sucking air, sputtering, and grunts, "No . . . I . . . ain't!" He keeps kicking.

Porter tightens his choke hold. Lester's turning purple. Making gurgling noises. Porter puts his full (considerable) weight on Lester with a knee to the chest. Still Lester fights.

Porter shouts over his shoulder to me. "Grab an arm! We're gonna cuff him to a gurney and sedate the motherfucker!" We each lift him by an armpit as he kicks and wheels his feet like those cartoon characters in midair when they've run off a cliff. Lester's shorts fall to the floor. He writhes and curses, buck-naked, as we carry him down the hall to the trauma bays, nurses and orderlies scattering in our wake. We slam him on the first empty bed and cuff a wrist to each rail. Lester keeps kicking and fighting as Porter orders a nurse to give him a shot. With the sedative pumping into him, he quits resisting. Porter tells the nurse to go fetch the intake lady's paperwork. Lester's fading fast. Nurse comes back with a form on a clipboard, and Porter puts a pen in Lester's limp fist, passes it over the treatment authorization form, inking an illegible scrawl on the appropriate line. Then he barks, "Keep an eye on this piece of shit, Pawpaw. I'm gonna grab a smoke."

When I see Porter exit the building, I slink down the hall and retrieve Lester's blood-caked shorts. Delicately (for my own sake) I slip the crusty, stinking drawers up his bruised, bony legs, under his skeletal trunk, and over his shriveled genitalia. He nods at me. Moments later, Lester's out cold, but at least he possesses a shred of modesty, if utterly lacking in dignity. Later a nurse's aide wipes the dried blood off his face and head as he snoozes fitfully. Then a doctor examines the gash in his head. A few butterfly bandages close the wound. Lester snores and shivers, covered with goose bumps. I find a blanket on a closet shelf and put it over him. His shivering stops but not his snoring. I sit at his bedside, awaiting Porter's return. Nearly an hour passes. I figure he's yammering on his cell to his Arkansas taco belle.

I remember the knife I'd taken from Lester and fish it out of my shirt pocket. I can't believe what I see. Just then, Lester stirs, snorts, and opens his eyes a slit. His cuffs clank against the bed rails, startling him. He blinks hard and groggily studies his shackled wrists, then the blanket, then me, with no apparent comprehension. "Thanks," he murmurs, falls silent again, and closes his eyes.

Still no Porter. I study the knife's familiar fleur-de-lis emblem and work the blades. They've got a good edge to them, well honed. The knife is clean, oiled, maintained. I wonder . . .

Finally, I clear my throat loudly. "You awake, Lester?" He rouses and grunts. "Mind if I ask you a question?" Another grunt I take to mean "okay."

"Your knife, here, the one I took off you? For evidence?" Lester nods, eyes still shut, silent.

"Did you know it's a Boy Scout knife?"

"'Course I do," he says hoarsely. "'Smy knife, ain't it?"

"Just wondered if it was actually yours, or you just found it somewhere." Silence.

"You ever a Boy Scout, Lester? 'Cause I was, long time ago."

"Yeah," Lester croaks. "Long, long time ago an' a long ways from here."

"Really! How far'd you get up the ranks?"

"Eagle. I'm a Eagle fuckin' Scout."

I'm speechless. After a long silence, I declare, utterly amazed: "Me, too! And my son—he's grown now—made Eagle, too."

"Yeah? My daddy was the goddamn scoutmaster." Lester's eyelids flutter to a squint, as if he's straining to pull up a distant memory. Or maybe he's just wincing in pain. But there seems to be a faint trace of interest stirring him. "He was also a deputy sheriff in Manatee County, Florida, 'fyou can belee' dat," he says, punctuating it with a sneer and a faint head shake.

I'm struck mute for another long moment. My jaw drops, brows arch. "What? No," I snort, shaking my head. "No, a deputy?" I trail off. Lester offers nothing further. Minutes pass in silence.

Finally, in the most amicable tone I can muster, I say, "So tell me, Lester, if ya don't mind my asking, how the hell did you go from Boy Scout, Eagle Scout, son of a deputy, to—" I turn my palms up, gesturing toward him: beaten, battered, shackled.

"To this sorry fucked-up mess?" Lester's eyes are open and he's looking right into mine. "Zat whatcha wanna know?"

I don't reply. Just hold his gaze.

"I ask myself that." Lester pauses, sighs. He takes a long, deep breath. "This is how it went: I graduate from high school, right? Daddy helps me get a small fishin' boat. Work hard, eventually put something down on a little trawler, makin' pretty decent coin. 'Nuff ta hire me a couple crew. They even called me Skipper." A hint of pride.

"Then one day somebody says to me, 'Lester,' he says. 'This is chump change. You could be pullin' down serious bank if you was to dee-versify,' he says. All I gotta do is pick up a little cargo fer 'im from time ta time. So I start tran-sportin instead a trawlin." He pauses, frowning. "Hell, it was smugglin' is what it was, straight up. Sometime it's weed, usually it's flake, sometime guns and wetbacks. Coupla times, all a that in one load. I'm makin' more fuckin' money in a run than my ole Daddy makes in a whole month. But then, a course, I start samplin' the goods." He shakes his head. "Stupid as shit, I know. Like a bad fuckin' movie. But here I am: a lowlife cokehead. A fuckin' loser, who gets his ass kicked by a dirtyass coke whore and then gets locked up for it."

Long silence. We both look elsewhere. Then:

"Hey, Lester. Y'ever try to kick? Listen, I know a guy, personal friend, runs a rehab. Twelve-step program, you know? Live-in, set you up in outside day jobs, stay there as long's it takes."

Lester's silent. Shaking his head.

"Seriously, man, the guy's a buddy of mine. A real professional. Lots of support, just pay what you can, when you can. He's recovered himself, and I know he'd open up a spot for you if I asked."

Porter steps in the door. He takes in the scene, his eyes passing from Lester to me and back to Lester. He must have been eavesdropping outside the room. He fixes his accusing gaze on me at Lester's bedside. Porter's lip curls into a look of horrified revulsion, eyes narrowed, shaking his head in disbelief. "Wha . . . what *are* you, some kinda fucking *social worker?*"

I shrink back in my chair, eyes dropping to the floor. I have no retort. I can't deny it. But I can't really own up to it, either. I force my eyes to meet Porter's and thrust my jaw out in defiance. Still unable to speak, I just hurl mean thoughts at him: Yeah, I was a kind of social worker, Porter, but you didn't want to hear about any of that, I recall. So fuck you, Portly, you fat ignorant oaf. Fuck you and the horse you rode in on. Porter turns and marches down the hallway. I mobilize and fall quickly in step behind him.

A month later I rotate to the Second Precinct and a new FTO. I never saw Lester Puckett or his FUCK MEN gal again, not even in court. Both failed to appear; the tatted coke-whore "victim" no doubt ignored her subpoena because she had subsequent active warrants for sordid assaults on human dignity and public decency. A fresh bench warrant was issued for Lester for bail skipping.

Skip on, Skipper, like the wind across the Gulf.

2

The Turd in the Punch Bowl

You don't hafta be drunk to be useless.
—Anonymous (heard at a Twelve Step meeting)

Some two decades earlier, the lights are dimmed and the slide show begins in the crowded hotel banquet hall. The narrator's voice sets the scene as the pictures and music tell the story.

"It was a day like any other. Manny Gonzalez and his Colorado Power crew were doing routine maintenance on the power lines in a quiet Manitou Springs neighborhood," the voice-over intones.

The screen shows Manny, a barrel-chested, middle-aged lineman in coveralls, hard hat, and the elbow-length insulated gloves of electrical workers. He's thirty feet up in a brilliant blue Colorado sky, working at the top of a power pole in his bucket truck on a sunny spring afternoon. The majestic Rocky Mountains tower in the background.

The slides show Manny distracted from his work on the lines. His attention is drawn to something on the ground, in a backyard below, several houses away. The camera zooms in on Manny as he leans out of his high bucket, transfixed by something puzzling, offscreen. We see his gloved hand pushing back the brim of his hard hat, then another, tighter shot of his weathered, lined face, his eyes straining to grasp the scene on the ground, and then a wide-eyed realization, a look of alarm on Manny's face.

The point of view switches to a couple of shots from Manny's perspective downward. From on high we see a quiet working-class neighborhood, a series of modest homes with fenced-in backyards. The camera zooms to one backyard, where children are playing on a swing set. A closer shot reveals what Manny has spied: seven-year-old Lupita Rivera has gotten herself tangled in the chains of her swing. She's struggling to free herself from the tightening loops around her neck as her feet kick in the air, several feet off the ground.

The screen flashes rapid-fire shots of Manny lowering his bucket, jumping from the truck to the ground, and shouting at his crew to call 911, intercut with shots of the struggling Lupita flailing and kicking. The beefy lineman is seen sprinting down the sidewalk, then bounding over the chain-link fence enclosing Lupita's backyard. The scene cuts to a young Hispanic woman looking in utter panic out her kitchen window. It's Lupita's mother, alerted by the shouts of Lupita's playmates in the backyard. She flings open the backdoor and reaches her struggling child just as big old Manny Gonzalez scoops her up in his arms, putting slack in the chains. Mrs. Rivera untangles the chains from around her daughter's neck, her face contorted in terror as Lupita's head flops, her body limp in Manny's arms.

"Lucky for everyone, Manny knows CPR," the narrator says, as the screenshots show Manny kneeling, laying the lifeless body of little Lupita in the grass, Mrs. Rivera kneeling beside the large lineman, tears streaming down her stricken face, desperately holding her daughter's hand.

"He had learned it through a lifesaving class provided free to Power Company workers by an agency of your Pikes Peak United Way," continues the voice-over as the screen is filled with Manny's huge hands doing chest compressions on little Lupita, then Manny's whiskered, leathery face breathing life into her. "The American Red Cross trains thousands of county residents each year in lifesaving and emergency first-aid," the narrator declares. "It wasn't just luck that saved Lupita Rivera's life that day last spring. It was your fair-share gifts to United Way, which fund Red Cross programs like Manny's CPR training."

The music swells as we see a revived Lupita being lifted up from the ground by the burly Manuel Gonzalez, his big lineman's arms tenderly passing the child to her mother, the child hugged tightly by her grateful mom, then several closing shots of the three of them in the Riveras' backyard, Lupita and Mrs. Rivera kissing a smiling Manny on each cheek, a couple of shots from the Annual Red Cross Heroes Banquet with the three of them onstage, Manny looking a little abashed and uncomfortable in a Sunday suit as he's presented a medal and a framed proclamation of his heroism.

The audio track of the slide show switches from the familiar narrator's voice to Mrs. Rivera's. "I truly feel God was looking down on my little Lupita that day, through the eyes of Manny Gonzalez. He was an angel sent to us by God."

"I'm so glad I knew what to do," says Manny. "Without the Red Cross training, it could of been a tragedy."

Music swells. The final face on the screen is a smiling little Lupita Rivera, as we hear her say, "Thanks to Mr. Gonzalez, thanks to Red Cross, thanks to *you*, it works for all of us, the United Way."

Little Lupita's smiling face fades into the United Way's multihued rainbow of hope over the support-offering hand of charity, holding in its palm the human figure with its upstretched arms simultaneously signifying supplication and triumph.

I switch off the synchronized projector and sound track and cue the stage lights. Vic Jackson, president of First National Bank of Colorado Springs and chairman of the 1983 campaign of the Pikes Peak United Way, is center stage.

"With us here today are Lupita Rivera, her mom, and our hero, Manny Gonzalez."

The thunderous applause is immediate, the crowd comes to its feet, shouting, cheering. I look around in awe from my projection post at the rear of the hall; the room's reaction makes my eyes well up, gives me goose bumps.

Campaign chairman Vic Jackson shares the mike for some brief, upbeat banter with the slide show's stars. Mrs. Rivera and Lupita reiterate their gratitude, not just to Manny but to everyone in the room. Manny is modest, self-effacing, nervous, and utterly genuine. "I'm no hero, I just did what anybody in this room woulda done, if you woulda had the training like I did. And I wouldn' of had the training, if it wasn't for everyone giving to United Way, so I just wanna say thanks to *you*."

Following my script with perfect poise and timing, Vic Jackson then calls to the stage Hugh Woolsey, southern regional vice president of Colorado Power, who presents Jackson with the first Pacesetter corporate gift to the campaign, a giant-size mock-up of a check for $103,223, which, Woolsey explains, is the first-ever dollar-for-dollar corporate match of employee pledges, meaning that Colorado Power's total gift to the campaign will be $206,446. More thunderous applause. Vic thanks Hugh for the check, and

Hugh says they were all inspired by their coworker, Manny Gonzalez, who exemplifies the Colorado Power spirit of caring.

Vic then closes the kickoff luncheon with an exhortation to "give till it *helps*, to this year's United Way campaign."

Then he departs from the script.

"And before we leave, I'd like to recognize Mark Johnson, United Way's campaign and public relations director. Mark put together this wonderful audiovisual presentation. Isn't it great?" More applause. "I think he did a heckuva job. Maybe the best I've ever seen, and I've been volunteering for United Way my whole career. Mark, stand up! He's in the back by the projector. Stand up, Mark. Wave so we can all see you." The crowd turns to look at me, and the applause increases. My eyes well up with emotion, as they do still, decades later, at the mere memory of it.

I had always dreamed of being a hero, just like the heroes I watched each week on the family TV of my childhood: *Roy Rogers, Sky King, Sea Hunt, Dragnet*. As an adolescent, my favorites were *77 Sunset Strip, Peter Gunn*, and *Adam-12*. In my early teens I loved Vic Morrow's Sergeant Saunders in *Combat!* and wished I had been a part of World War II.

Eventually, of course, I outgrew childish dreams of heroics. Realizing the long odds of saving lives as a cowboy, a cop, or in combat, I settled for the more modest aspiration of just "making a difference." As a Boy Scout, I had earned the God and Country Award, which required service work in the church. I became president of my church youth group and was elected a deacon at age sixteen. I got to know my pastor, Mr. Huey, and began giving thought to following in his footsteps. At his suggestion I became an inner-city Head Start volunteer at a program housed in an urban church, and through friends I made there, I visited other downtown congregations. I was transported by the fiery, rhythmic delivery of the Word by black preachers and by the spontaneous, joyful response in the pews. I loved clapping and swaying with the choirs.

As I advanced into my later teen years, however, I encountered a major stumbling block to making a difference by aspiring to the clergy: sin. Lust, to be specific: the temptations of the flesh.

As a college freshman majoring in architecture, I dreamed of making a difference in the blighted neighborhoods I had come to know in my Sunday morning sojourns to the rough neighborhoods of north St. Louis: I would redesign urban housing. The infamous Pruitt-Igoe towers in the worst part of the St. Louis ghetto were nationally reviled for their filth, crime, and spirit-deadening uninhabitability. I knew people who lived there. Through outreach, citizen input, sensitive active listening, and revolutionary design, I would make a difference in the inner city by transforming urban housing, thereby restoring community, dignity, and civility, and probably eradicate poverty and racial strife in the process.

However, in the second semester of my sophomore year in the School of Environmental Design, I encountered a major stumbling block to my dreams of urban renewal through architecture: calculus.

Although I eventually passed calculus, I gave up architecture. Discouraged, disoriented, despairing, and by then utterly dissolute (having discovered the instant ease and comfort produced by a cold pitcher of Coors and a bag of weed), I informed my folks that I would no longer waste their money on tuition and instead would join the Marines to serve my country in the jungles of Viet Nam. I secretly hoped the corps would turn me into a hero, or at least a man (if not a casualty).

Alas, I encountered yet another stumbling block to my dreams of battle-field sacrifice and glory: Dad. He insisted that I carry on, at least until I earned a diploma in *something*, and then if I still wanted to join the Marines, fine. With a degree, I could be more useful to the corps and make a greater *difference*, as an officer. I switched majors to English Lit (which had been my favorite subject and in which I'd always excelled) and justified it with vague dreams of "making a difference" by touching the hearts and minds of men through authoring the next great American novel.

By the time I had graduated, Viet Nam was over. With no sense of direction, I stumbled into a series of jobs that offered little sense of mission, usefulness, satisfaction, or pride (especially to one of such grandiose and narcissistic aspiration), and my drinking accelerated. The drinking, of course, steadily degraded my job performance and undermined my young marriage to Nancy, who was really the only one who had any remaining hope for me.

In my fourth job since graduating (after six months in Brussels, Belgium, at a corporate-kickback job arranged for me by Dad, then six months driving a cab and a year as a short-haul delivery trucker in Denver), I wrecked a company car in the Oklahoma Panhandle, which wasn't even in my sales territory. I wiggled my way out of that mess with the help of an understanding (and equally alcoholic) boss, then switched jobs and got fired from that one six months later, when Nancy was just weeks away from delivering our first child. I wrote freelance stories for the *Rodeo Sports News*, and Nancy got me some assignments at the weekend magazine of the *Colorado Springs Gazette Telegraph*, where she worked as a full-time reporter. Together, we made just enough to stay above water.

Then I got a break, just a month before the birth of our first child, Peter. The Pikes Peak United Way needed a PR director—mostly, just someone who could write brochure copy, speeches, and press releases with a decent command of grammar and a willingness to work for $14,000 a year. I had minimal knowledge of United Way: a vague notion that it ran an annual campaign for nonprofits like the Boy Scouts and the Red Cross. But I had always assumed (mistakenly—as do many) that all nonprofits were by definition run by volunteers.

At last, I had found a way to *make a difference.* The phrase was at the heart of the United Way mission and permeated the corporate culture. I was meeting real-life, everyday heroes, like Manny Gonzalez. It was my job to give the Mannys of the world the recognition they deserve, and to inspire others to emulate them, and to support their heroism.

My life turned around, my sense of purpose, my sense of myself, restored. I even stopped drinking, so grateful was I to be useful to something good, something important, something greater than myself.

It had been a good run, for more than two decades. But then I found myself looking at fifty, and it didn't seem to be working any more. Pete was grown and gone, as was my daughter, Kate, born just eighteen months after Pete. United Way seemed neither *united* nor the *way* to make a meaningful difference, in my life or anyone else's, much less in the wider community.

After seven years of steady growth and success at the Pikes Peak United Way, I had been pushed out of the nest by my boss and mentor to become an executive director of my own local United Way. I had landed in Waukesha, Wisconsin, a wealthy suburb of Milwaukee. Eight more successful years passed, as my little family grew and my annual campaigns reached ever-higher goals.

But I grew restless. I had lived the first five years of my life in a little Mississippi River town just outside New Orleans. Sweet, tender memories of Gulf Coast life in Luling, Louisiana, beckoned. After suffering through seven brutal Wisconsin winters, I longed for warmer climes, more diversity, and the simple, gentle rhythms of the Deep South. Several interviews for exec director openings in other communities around the country (including a disastrous one with the United Way in Baton Rouge) eventually resulted in an offer that seemed made for me. Despite Nancy's lengthy crying jag, we decided we would decamp from the suburbs of the upper Midwest for Mobile, Alabama.

"Isn't that a really backward place?" all our friends had asked. For me, it was a calling, a mission. For Nancy, it was foolhardy, and very scary. Her first instinct was to call the synagogue in Mobile.

"Is it okay being Jewish in the Deep South?" she inquired.

"Sure," they'd said, amused. So south we came.

Now after eight years at the helm of the United Way of Southwest Alabama, I'm sitting in my executive office, seething. My face is red, heart pounding, hands trembling with rage. I've just returned from the monthly meeting of United Way's board of directors. And I've got issues.

The reason Mobile's United Way doesn't work like the one in Wisconsin, or my first one in Colorado Springs, is that it's a larger community, with larger problems, and more intractable ones: race, poverty, ignorance. I've been grinding my way through the past eight years here, and we've grown the campaign totals by nearly 40 percent, to more than $7 million, but there ain't *nobody* happy about it, and the community's toughest challenges have grown rather than diminished. The givers are feeling as though their pockets have been picked; the agencies are pissed off at United Way because of our requirements for more accountability, higher performance, and true unity.

At the board meeting I had produced prima facie evidence of an agency's violation of its contract with United Way, grounds for expelling the agency and withholding further allocations from the annual United Way campaign. The violating member agency? Boy Scouts of America.

A nonprofit agency seeking a piece of United Way's multimillion-dollar annual campaign pie signs a contract. A key condition of the contract is the agency's agreement to refrain from its own fund-raising during the United Way campaign from September through mid-November of each year, to avoid cannibalizing the united appeal. The Boy Scouts had flagrantly violated this rule repeatedly, holding big special events and broad, public fund drives for Scouting every fall, even conducting corporate solicitations and a few limited workplace payroll deduction campaigns (the inviolable sanctum sanctorum of United Way). Compounding the injury, the BSA had ignored our repeated requests to improve and increase programming for underserved—especially inner-city, minority—youth.

"We do character building," they'd sniff. "Our experience has shown us that the Scouting model has limited appeal to certain demographics. You run a great community chest appeal. With all due respect, stick to fundraising and leave youth programming to us."

Those damn Boy Scouts. Scouting might have been the reason I went into charity work in the first place. And now the Boy Scouts is the reason I'm getting out: the damn Scout exec, in my opinion a corpulent, complacent careerist making the highest salary of all member–agency execs, named Doug Stout—Smug Doug, the Stout Scout—lording over a diminishing fiefdom of white middle-class boys and supported by the southern white aristocracy of Mobile.

The BSA wasn't alone in thumbing its nose at United Way. In other communities, the Salvation Army and the Red Cross, the other two agencies with the strongest brand recognition (and the strongest boards) occasionally colluded with the Scouts to challenge United Way. But it was most often the Scouts, and always started by the Scouts. I had reported this to my board. The extent to which these big, well-known agencies, which already get the lion's share of the campaign pot anyway, compete with the united appeal is exactly the extent to which our revenues are diminished and our ability to address underserved and emerging needs is limited.

"In a tangible, measureable way," I had concluded to the board, "they are impeding our very mission!" I had expected the usual, idealistic argument that "philanthropy is not a zero-sum game, blah-zay, blah, blah," but there came not even that in response. There was no response. Nothing.

Instead, silence engulfed the boardroom, broken only by the clearing of throats, the shuffling of papers. Brows furrowed. People of lesser influence gauged the reactions of those with greater influence. I had expected my case to provoke a lively debate, which I'd hoped would develop into a call to arms; it's met instead with a call to table the issue and adjourn. A chorus of relieved voices seconds the motion. I feel like the turd in the punch bowl.

So I'm sitting in my office, unable to shut off the loop in my head replaying the meeting. I see the writing on the wall, and I'm wishing I had a pint of Beam in my bottom drawer.

Several months later I had done all of the things I knew to do: kept all controversy off the board agenda, hit the punching bag in my garage for hours, been solicitous and self-effacing with the executive committee of the board, hit lots and lots of my Living Sober group meetings, worked the heck out of my 12 steps to recovery. I had talked and argued with my recovery mentor and at his direction written a fearless and thorough moral inventory of myself, looking for where I was the problem, and talked and argued endlessly with Nancy.

"Let's just get the hell out of Dodge," she'd say. "Get on with another United Way, someplace where they value education and they change as they need to and they move forward. Someplace with more Jews. You wanted to go where the problems are toughest, and this is what you've got."

We had moved before, but things had seemed to work out better. Not this time. I knew the "geographic cure" wouldn't work any better for a career in crisis than it does for chronic alcoholism. I had reflected deeply on twenty-three years of United Way work: literally, a hundred million dollars' worth of campaigns in three different communities. Hundreds of speeches made, meetings convened, interviews given, editorials and slogans and films produced, agencies funded, programs created. Tens of thousands of pledge cards and brochures printed, contributions collected and allocated, and needy people served. What did it all add up to? Were these communities any better off for these efforts? In the last twenty-three years, in all three communities where I'd been the United Way guy, poverty had increased, as had teen pregnancy and illiteracy and divorce and disease and drug abuse and child neglect and high school dropouts and juvenile delinquents and wife beatings and homelessness and mentally ill zombies walking the streets and frail, elderly homebound folks needing wheelchair ramps and … especially here, in Mobile. But (God knows why) I like it here.

Clearly, though, other than raising more money and volunteers every year, I wasn't making much of a difference with United Way. And United Way wasn't making much of a difference in the community.

I interviewed with a couple of other United Ways. Got a nice offer to join the staff in New Orleans, one of my all-time favorite places in the world. But I knew I was getting stale, and the boardroom maneuverings, politics, and personalities would be part of the job at every United Way. Getting out of town was not the answer. I knew I was just one step ahead of the United Way lynch mob; it would catch up to me no matter where I went. Instead of growing healthy communities, effective services and programs, and hope,

I had grown frustrated, hopeless, and bitter. A change of scenery wouldn't change the problem. The problem was me.

As ol' Red, my recovery sponsor, would say, "The problem with the geographic cure is, no matter where ya go, there y'are."

The truth was, I had become as strident, unbending, and self-righteous as Smug Doug. I could try to dial it back, disengage, become a caretaker of the organization rather than a champion of it, but I knew that would just sicken, embitter, and eventually cripple me (to say nothing of the damage to the organization). No, it had become my way or the highway, and all indications were that my board was about to invite me to take I-65 northbound, back to the Yankee ways from whence I came.

My sponsor Red—a guy who hasn't taken a drink for more than thirty-five years, a retired railroad brakeman whose judgment I trust more than my oldest best friends, more than my United Way mentors and colleagues around the country, more even than my wife (who is well intentioned but hardly objective in matters this close to home)—had observed a pattern emerging in me during the years since we'd been going to meetings together.

"Let's see if I got this right," Red said. "You've come to me with gripes about the Boy Scouts, the Sally, the Red Cross, the beat-up-wives place, the Cancer Society, the mayor and city council, the old-money Mardi Gras societies, the Chamber of Commerce, mosta the doctors and lawyers in town, several bank presidents, the newspaper, and the TV newspeople. Left anybody out?"

I shook my head.

"Oh, now wait, I remember a few more," Red declared. He had run out of fingers, so he started over with his first hand to enumerate the next batch of enemies. "The environmentals. The save-the-whales-and-puppies folks. The starving kids in Africa. The goddamn hospitals and universities who can name buildings after people who give 'em money. Oh yeah! And the public schools. The state mental health board and department of human services. And let's not forget those chintzy foundations who just hoard their money!"

I nodded and heaved a big hopeless sigh. I had ranted against them all, over and over.

"See anything in common?" Red asked. "This is one helluva resentment list. Beats any I ever saw!" Red shook his head slowly in grinning wonderment. "Now, other'n you, what do all these enemies have in common? What ties 'em all together?"

I was at a loss. Red was silent for a long time, letting me puzzle it out. I shrugged, utterly clueless, despairing.

Finally, Red said, "It's your job, is what it is. It's what you *do* that ties all this mess up together. Now I'm just an old railroader, and I don't know much about boardrooms, or politics, or charity. But I know this: your job is gonna get you drunk."

3

Psychic Payne

I'd rather have a bottle in fronta me than a frontal lobotomy.
—variously attributed to Tom Waits, Dorothy Parker, and Jerry Jeff Walker

So give a guy with a messiah complex and a three-page enemies list a firearm and the authority to use lethal force. Might could work.

I quit my job. Ended my twenty-three-year career. It was September 2002. I filled out applications for the Mobile and Prichard Police Departments and, as a backup, traveled to Albuquerque, New Mexico, where Nancy and I both have cousins, to apply for the APD and the Bernalillo County Sheriff's Office.

"Trading campaign and cajole for command and control," I wrote an old buddy, a guy I've known since kindergarten. Ernie thought it sounded like a cool idea.

"Replacing cadge & dun with a badge and a gun," I added. My kids, Pete and Kate, thought it was an awesome idea.

When you tie it up in a cute little ditty or two like that, it might even seem, like, inspired. Destiny, even.

Unless maybe you're my wife. What I might consider destiny, Nancy's inclined to label "magical thinking." She's a hard-boiled type, a skeptic by nature. Green eyed, petite, and pretty, Nancy's pretty tough and disarmingly forthright. The first-generation daughter of German Holocaust survivors, Nancy had an already-excellent, built-in bullshit detector that she finely tuned while working as a reporter for over two decades, with the *Rocky Mountain News* and the *Denver Post*, then with the *Milwaukee Journal Sentinel*.

She accepted the interruptions and setbacks to her career that came with two children and with the necessary geographic dislocations of my own career path. But as she sees it, now I'm not keeping up my end of the bargain—that of being the primary breadwinner—because of a little discouragement and dissatisfaction with my career.

And the 75 percent cut in pay is the least of my betrayal. After I run the numbers and demonstrate to her that we can take the financial cut without jeopardizing our retirement, there remains the cut in status, which is irreversible. No more blue-ribbon committees, no more mingling with elected officials, captains of industry, pillars of the community. She'll be married to a cop. Most cops are not college educated; if they are, they advance through the ranks to command staff, but I've told her I have no desire to supervise or manage anyone anymore, *especially* cops. I've had a belly full of management, and the politics and power games of managing a 500-man police department are no doubt even more brutal and nauseating than managing a multimillion-dollar nonprofit. This will leave me among the lower ranks, who will be half my age, with less than half my higher education and work experience.

I accuse her of snobbery, but that's worse than a cheap shot: it's a lie. I quickly abandon that line of defense.

I argue there are things of value, lessons and challenges and goals, that cannot be found in classrooms or boardrooms or council chambers.

"Like what? Learning to shoot a gun? Learning how to fight a thug? You're fifty years old, and don't take this wrong, but you're not a natural warrior. They'll hand your ass to you."

I retreat to my last ditch. "I can't expect you to get it, I guess. It's a guy thing: facing fears, overcoming doubts, dealing with the *real* world, the grit, the blood and guts, there's something to be said for that."

"What about making a difference? The real, long-lasting, quality-of-life kind of difference in a community that you've been preaching for years with United Way? Was that all just part of a script, just an abstraction?"

"Cops make a difference!" I declaim. "They save lives . . . they . . . they protect and serve!" Sheesh, Mark: a tad derivative, y'think? Not to say weak? "They're useful, necessary, in a tangible way."

Nancy rolls her eyes. "You're copping out," she says, shaking her head, without even a hint of a pun. "You're smart. You have talents. You're artistic, and creative. You can write, and speak, and motivate and even inspire people. But you're squandering all that, to indulge yourself in some boyhood adventure. Lots of men have tough times in their careers, and they man up, they hang in there. But you're just taking the easy way out."

There it is. That's the nut of it, the kernel. What nobody else will tell me, though they may think it. Not my buddies, who say it's cool, not my kids, who say it's awesome. I don't have an answer for this, though I knew it was coming. I guess that's why I married her: she's fearless when it comes to truth.

But her truth and my truth are not necessarily the same thing, not this time. Nor are they mutually exclusive. It certainly requires courage and smarts to "hang in there," but in this case it seems even more courage is required of me to change. And smarts is not the same as wisdom.

I wonder what my father would think. He'd say, "Don't be foolish. Don't be a quitter." In other words, don't manifest your utter lack of both wisdom and courage. He always said I was "impetuous" and "impulsive." And I know I always disappointed him in the Manliness Department, probably owing to my not being flesh of his flesh, blood of his blood. He once described my employment in the nonprofit field as "women's work."

But . . . might he just think law enforcement would be . . .? Nah. Who'm I kidding? My dad? Stan the Man? Iron Man Stan? Approving this? Magical thinking indeed!

As if reading my mind, Nancy says, "I wonder what your father would think of this? You know it's only because of what he left us that you even have the luxury of considering it."

I'm surprised it took her so long to get here, but I'm ready for her. If she's gonna pull the Stan card, so can I.

"I know one thing for sure about Stan the Man: he damn sure wouldn't be bullied by his wife when it came to making a decision like this!" The discussion is over.

Still, I wonder—is this path the way of wisdom? Of courage? I won't know until I take it. But I do know that the path I've been on for the last two decades won't get me there.

If it's up to the contract psychologist who does the testing and screening for Albuquerque Police Department and Bernalillo County Sheriff's Office recruits, however, I won't be getting on the path. She ain't buying my story any more than Nancy is. And she has her own set of truths. Ms. Payne, the psychologist, has always resented the annual strong-arming for United Way by her boss. And she objects to United Way's failure to fund Planned Parenthood and to the gross disparity between United Way funding to the Girl Scouts and the Boy Scouts (favoring the boys by a factor of three). And Ms. Payne comes from a family riddled with chronic alcoholism and drug addiction. To her, self-help, "12-step" recovery programs appear to be little more than bogus, ineffectual autosuggestion.

Don't get me wrong. I have the utmost respect for the psychotherapeutic arts and have benefited greatly from capable, dedicated practitioners at several critical points in my life. A patient and kind psychologist helped guide me through some turbulence during my early college years; a few visits with an insightful shrink afforded me much-needed clarity through the intense confusion produced by meeting, in my late twenties, the woman who had given me up for adoption shortly after giving birth to me; and a wise, no-nonsense marriage counselor deserves much credit for keeping Nancy and me together through our rocky times as young working parents with demanding careers.

But Ms. Payne displayed none of these characteristics in my forty-minute meeting with her. It seemed she had made up her mind about me before I walked in the door.

After passing the written basic competency exam (kid stuff), the health screen (a little more challenging for a fifty-year-old with a "frozen shoulder" from a long-neglected high school football injury and bad habits ranging from daily bacon cheeseburgers to a pack a day of unfiltered Camels), the financial and criminal background check (I'm neither broke nor in debt, but the arrest history could be a liability if they go back more than twenty-five years; they do, but I'm credited for lengthy straight time), the poly-graph (hope they don't ask about all the stuff from that prolonged, trou-bled adolescence; they do, but because decades have passed, and I didn't lie about it, and the department is desperate for recruits willing to risk their lives for a little over twelve bucks an hour, all is—tentatively—forgiven), and the physical stamina test (nothing that can't be fixed by a few months of daily agony, doing push-ups and sit-ups and running sprints and miles in the sodden Mobile summer as well as the lung-searing thin air of the New Mexico mountains), and the worst part, the insensate, inscrutable plodding of the County Personnel Board, which offers no indication, for months on end, about recruits' scores, relative standing, prospects for hire, the department's vacancies or needs or timetable for hire—after all this, I'm bounced by the contract psychologist, Ms. Payne.

She starts by flattering me: "You are way overqualified, both in education and especially in work experience." We then exchange pleasant collegial banter as fellow human-service professionals about community needs, mental health care, United Way's role in same, and the aforementioned "issues" she takes with funding to particular agencies. My account of fighting the good fight at United Way makes no apparent impact on Ms. Payne.

Instead, firmly in control of the discussion, Ms. Payne describes her task as it relates to the department and me. Her contractual and ethical obligation to the department is unique. All previous tests are statutorily administered by the County Personnel Board for all law enforcement agencies in the county: sheriff's deputies, municipal police, village constables, probation officers, jail guards. There's no redress for failure on any one of those, which are standardized, objective. Her contract, by contrast, is directly with the hiring agency, not the Personnel Board. The nature of her expertise being somewhat subjective (as I could no doubt ascertain from the battery of aptitudes and values tests she has just administered to me), her recommendations are acted on at the discretion of the hiring department's command staff.

That being said, Ms Payne explains, the high cost of training good police officers compels her first to screen for employees who are most likely to make a long-term commitment to the department.

"We need to recoup our investment in recruits, and that takes time—almost three years, at currently budgeted training rates. Having extensive management experience as you do, I'm sure you understand cost recovery and ROI fundamentals, which is why I'm sure it will come as no great surprise to you that I cannot in good conscience recommend your placement in the next academy class. At your age, and with your background, you'll be bored to tears and quit in months. This is a young man's job. The typical recruit is half your age, no college, usually with military service, which I noted from your CV appears to be the one common qualification you lack. Not that it's an insurmountable deficit, but I'm sure you'll agree there's a world of, shall we say, cultural difference between the military and the not-for-profit sector, Mr. Johnson. The police department is a paramilitary organization."

I try to object, but she waves me off. "I've been in clinical and private practice for over two decades, Mr. Johnson," she continues. "You're an educated man. You've no doubt heard of the male midlife crisis. This looks to me like a classic example, except maybe your little red sports car is a blue uniform." She leans forward, her hands open, her head tilted, a wistful, indulgent smile crossing her lips, her fixed gaze that of a principal trying to get little Johnny to admit he was the one who wrote naughty things on the boys' room wall.

Naughty thoughts flash: she's not actually too bad looking . . . she's one of those women of a certain age, intellect, and pear shape who eschew cosmetics, cut their hair short and sort of spikey, drape themselves in shapeless earth-tone sacks and unflattering but pricey Eileen Fisher ponchos, and wear thick socks or leggings with their Birkenstocks . . . poor woman probably hasn't been laid in months.

I take a breath, smile slightly back at her in the same way she smiles at me, and arch an eyebrow, gazing vaguely past and above her, as if giving serious consideration to her theory of my motivations. After an appropriately respectful pause, I make my opening argument: This is no impulsive, pathetic attempt to regain lost youth. I have concluded my former career, one that I was quite successful in for, like you, more than two decades. I won't be going back. I am committed to doing this, to being a cop, what I have wanted to do since I was a boy, before it's too late. This is no passing whim. And there will be no "culture shock." I am motivated by service. By helping people in need. That's what kept me going in United Way for so long. Law enforcement is just another way to serve, to help people. A more hands-on way. Instead of raising money for the Women's Shelter, I will lock up the wifebeaters who force them to seek the shelter. (I figure this angle, in particular, will appeal to Ms. Payne, no doubt an ardent feminist.)

She's unmoved. "All of that is very noble, Mr. Johnson, but dangerously naïve. Police work is not social work. I've seen numerous studies showing that the cops who view their work as primarily service are three times more likely to be injured or killed on the job than those who see their duty as primarily enforcement. Let me just give you a hypothetical. Say you're in a hostage situation. Bad guy's got a gun to the head of a pretty young female, says to you, 'Give me your gun or the dame gets it!' She poses like the bad guy, one arm around the girl's throat, the pointing finger and upright thumb of the other hand a gun to the head of the hostage. "Quick! What do you do, Officer Johnson?"

"Heck, that's a no-brainer," I say. "I just keep him talking till backup arrives."

"No, you're changing the scenario," she says. "No backup's coming, your radio broke, no snipers on the roof who can pick him off. He's serious, you can't stall him, he wants your gun or the girl is toast, what do you do? Quick!"

Never really thought about something like this. How do they do it in the movies? The hero always bravely puts down his weapon and talks his way close enough to the bad guy to get the jump on him, disarm him, save the girl. I tell Ms. Payne I'd start moving slowly toward him, talking all the time to develop trust, and when I get close enough, I'd put down my gun and—

"Bang. You're dead," says Ms. Payne, pointing her finger gun at me. She blows the smoke from her finger and points it sideways. "Bang. The bitch dies, too. Cop 101: *Never* surrender your weapon. Case closed. You don't have the instincts."

"Wait a minute! I, I've got a backup piece, strapped to my ankle! I pull it out and—"

"You're already dead," she says, shaking her head at me. "He's blown your head off while you're bending over, pulling up your pants leg." She's laughing now. "You can't quick-draw a backup pistol."

The laughing stops abruptly. She points her finger gun threateningly at me. "Actually, he doesn't shoot the girl after killing you. He brutally rapes, tortures, and sodomizes her first. Or, just as likely, he doesn't kill you. He makes you handcuff yourself to a pipe and watch, helpless, as he assaults her sexually to death. Six weeks later you blow your own brains out."

I think, jeez, what a sicko! Talk about your morbid ideation! But I'm beat. No comeback. No shots left. I opt for whining.

"But I have always wanted to be a policeman," I complain. "Your scenario—they teach you what to do! In the academy! That's just tactics, not instincts! I've always wanted to be a cop, Ms. Payne! I don't think you get that. And I know I'd be a good one! I'd be thrilled to do nothing else for the next ten to fifteen years. I won't get bored and quit!"

She shakes her head. "If you've always wanted to be a cop, you'd have been one long before now."

"But I couldn't afford to be a cop! Not with a family, kids to raise and educate. But now they're grown and gone, working, married; the house is paid for. I can finally take the cut."

Her lips tighten, impassive. I switch to charm.

"Besides, I had to wait for some distance from my misspent youth." A winsome, mischievous grin: little Johnny admitting to the principal that he had, indeed, once been the naughty boy.

"I'm glad you acknowledge that," she says, not charmed. "That's my second concern, and actually the one I can't overlook: your alcoholism and 'recovery.'" She uses the au-(so)-courant-two-fingered-double-handed-quotation-marks gesture as she refers to my two decades of "recovery." Citing her extensive clinical work with alcoholics, she then confides her family's personal struggles with addiction, which has afflicted them for at least three generations, including the youngest, the generation that includes her own offspring. There is no cure, she declares. Periods of remission, yes, but nobody ever recovers. And certainly you can understand the risks and the liabilities for the department—nay, for law-abiding citizens—of one so afflicted, in a position of armed, uniformed authority!

I nod but point out that I've already passed the polygraph, which had included numerous questions regarding my drinking and drugging history and how long it had been since either had passed my lips, or nose.

She smiles disdainfully, in a way that says, "Silly you!" and informs me that the polygraph is so unreliable as to be inadmissible in court and that denial and deception are key hallmarks of addiction. "Remember that old Seinfeld episode where George says, 'It's not really a lie if you actually believe it'? That bit holds a lot of insight when it comes to addicts. They seem especially gifted at deception. It's my theory that they're so good at deceiving others—and perhaps even polygraphs—because they've been lying to themselves for years."

I slump back in my chair, cup my chin in one hand, and battle the urge to lunge across the desk at her throat. She drones on about the misery of her mother at the hands of her alcoholic father, her brother's three unsuccessful attempts at rehab, her divorce from an alcoholic husband, and the heartbreak of a teenaged son with two DUIs, numerous wrecks, and minor-in-possession citations already. Slowly the heat rises, my throat constricts; a finger at my temple confirms the acceleration of my pulse. I struggle for composure, my eyes roaming her office, her bookshelf, her desktop, her window overlooking a strip mall parking lot, focusing on anything but the source of this pathetic, vindictive tale of woe and doom.

"We pause when agitated, and ask for direction," I think, from my daily recovery meditation book. "When we are disturbed, the problem is within us." Then a tiny, wheedling voice from deep within me: a slash of Beam would sure go good about now.

I absently activate the little swinging-ball desk toy in front of me. The one where four or five chrome balls are suspended by strings in a line, you pull back one at the end, release it, it slaps the others, and sends the one at the other end flying, click, click, click.

I'm pissed. I could sue: age discrimination! Or violation of the Americans with Disabilities Act! (Alcoholism is surely a certified disability.) Nah. I'm not really one for litigation. More recovery lessons come to me: "Accept the things you cannot change, have courage to change the things you can, and pray for the wisdom to know the difference." Sure can't change Ms. Psychic Payne here. Her mind's made up. But I'll be goddamned if I just roll over. I'm not gonna let this bitch, or Smug Doug, or the conflict-averse cronies on my old board of trustees pull my string and send my balls flying.

Ms. Psychic Payne washed me out of both the Albuquerque PD and the BCSO. It was a long, discouraged drive back to Mobile.

But a few weeks after my return, I met with MPD's shrink. Sitting across from him at his desk, I struggled to control my nerves, my breathing. He was an utterly ordinary-looking, slightly balding, middle-aged guy like me, who studied my test results and résumé in silence for a few moments as I awaited his pronouncement on my fate.

Finally, he looked up and spoke, his poker face offering me no clue of his decision.

"In my considered opinion," he said, "you're crazy."

He shook his head slightly but could not suppress the hint of a grin. "Why on earth you want to be a cop escapes me. The cut in pay, the shift work. You know they say it's 90 percent boredom and 10 percent terror, right? Don't you think it'll bore you to death?"

I insisted, of course, that I had given due consideration to all aspects of policing and was firm in the conviction that not only would the work suit me, but that I could bring a lot to the work, that I would make a good cop.

An eyebrow arched slightly as he looked at me, then looked down to sign off on the form that cleared me for academy enrollment. "Good luck, Mr. Johnson. Be careful."

Clearing the last hurdle and getting hired doesn't put you, necessarily, right into the academy. They only do academies when the budget allows, when there are sufficient vacancies in the department to justify one, and when they round up enough qualified recruits to compose a class sufficient in size to fill those vacancies and to make the effort cost effective. So, your hire date may be as long as six months away from the start of your academy class. They put you in a sort of holding pattern, on the payroll, require you to shave your head and wear a white button-down shirt and navy blue Dickies slacks, and assign you as an unskilled factotum in various areas around the department where you're not likely to cause any damage or be in harm's way, like filing clerk in records, or intake clerk at the impound lot or property or evidence, or gofer at the radio shop.

I worked as a groundskeeper at the firing range for six months before my class started.

I was the envy of my fellow recruits for this, the choicest of pre-academy assignments. Mostly, the job entailed picking up expended brass casings at the firing lines, cutting the grass, and routine painting and maintenance on the target mechanisms and buildings. But the range master, a grizzled, garrulous, white-handlebar-mustachioed old sergeant with a million cop stories from his thirty years on the job, was generous with me, providing much one-on-one firearm instruction and virtually unlimited rounds of target-load ammo to practice shooting when my chores were done.

Still, I had a lot of time on my hands and spent hours closely observing the cops who would come out to the range in twos and threes when they were off duty to keep up their skills. They would shoot up to fifty or a hundred rounds at the stationary paper targets, ignoring me entirely, then would smoke and joke among themselves (within earshot of me) about how the department is getting so desperate for recruits it's accepting senior citizens. Then they would depart, not to return for a month or more. A few would come out more frequently and pop off a few rounds with their shotguns and backup pistols as well as their Glocks, and maybe even sight in their military-style Ruger Mini-14s or Bushmaster AR-15 assault rifles, if they were authorized to carry them on duty (sergeants and above).

But there was one guy who was out at the range every week, and sometimes more often. He was older than most—probably just a few years my junior—and always came by himself and kept to himself. He had a rough, ruddy face, a chiseled physique, and a permanent frown. He would do something different almost every time, using a variety of handguns and long guns. Sometimes he'd shoot paper targets on the regulation range, but not standing still—he'd run and dive and roll while firing; sometimes he'd set up elaborate scenarios in the steel knock-down target area, where he'd run forward and backward from barrel to drum, using them as cover, firing all the while at multiple targets as if he were in a firefight; sometimes he'd go room to room in the heavy-timbered "shooting house" kicking in doors and clearing rooms, shouting all the while to imaginary fellow officers. He would even drive his squad car onto the range and fire at targets while driving.

After I had been there several months, I asked the range master, "What's up with that guy?" nodding to the frequent visitor, dressed that day in camo fatigues and a dirty T-shirt, loading scrap lumber into the trunk of his squad car.

The range master chuckled and said he was surprised it had taken me so long to ask.

"That's the legendary Tom McCall, our one-man SWAT team. Been in more firefights than anybody in the department. Wounded more times than I can remember. He once commandeered an ambulance and drove it straight into live fire to rescue another cop who'd been hit. They say he even carries an American flag in his trunk so we can wrap his body in it when he gets killed in action. Y'oughtta get to know him, and today's a good day to do it, because he could use a hand. He's out here to rehang some doors he busted up in the shootin' house last time he was here. Take the Gator and load it up with hammers, coupla power drills, coupla coffee tins of wood screws and 16-penny nails, and meet him down there. Tell him I sent you to help him."

I did as he directed. "Sarge sent me down here to give you a hand."

McCall nodded and looked me up and down. "Just gimme stuff I ask for." Then, over his shoulder, "And try to stay outta my way."

We worked without even breaking for a drink of water, in near silence for more than two hours, shoring up door frames, replacing hinges, hanging doors, slapping mosquitoes. When we were done we gathered up our tools and scrap and tossed them in the bed of the Gator and sat in the cab, feet up on the dash, and drank from liter bottles of water, in silence. McCall pulled some beef jerky out of a cargo pocket of his fatigues and wordlessly offered me some. I accepted, nodding my thanks.

"How old are you?" he asked, not looking at me. It was the first complete sentence I'd heard him utter since we began.

"Fifty."

He nodded. After waiting a respectful moment for him to comment, I realized more was not likely forthcoming. After a while, I ventured, "You?"

"Not far behind you," he said. We returned to chewing our jerky thoughtfully, gazing at the shooting house. Then he observed, "Comin' to the game a mite late."

I let the silence hang for what seemed the requisite rhythm of our exchange, then said, "Ya think?"

He looked at me, expressionless. Thinking he might have taken me as glib, I elaborate.

"Late bloomer."

There appeared the faintest flicker of a grin.

"You're that guy from the United Fund." The flicker faded, if it was ever really there.

I nodded wordlessly in the affirmative. He directed his gaze back to the shooting house.

Then, "I been at this awhile. I don't know about your line a work, but in this one there's only two kinds: sheep and wolves. If you're gonna survive, you *got* to be a wolf. But not just any wolf; the kind that preys on other wolves."

I nodded solemnly.

He faced me, smiled slightly, and shook my hand with a thick rough paw, then got up and walked to his squad car. As he got in, he said, "Thanks for the help, buddy. See you on the streets."

So after about six months of applications and testing, then six more at the range as a recruit, I finally joined Class 31 of the Mobile Police Department's academy. And by September 2003, almost a year to the day after my departure from more than two decades of nonprofit management and development, I'm delivering the graduating speech as president of my class at a midday ceremony. My whole family, including my cousins and seventy-eight-year-old Aunt Billye from Albuquerque, is in attendance. Hours later that same day, I will hit the streets of Mobile's Third Precinct on night shift as a uniformed rookie patrol officer.

Already scheduled for my first day off is the surgery I've been needing for a double hernia I've suffered since before the academy began, incurred while working at the range. (I had attempted to move a fifty-gallon drum full of spent brass casings by myself and felt the tearing in my groin but told no one. To delay my entry into the academy for any reason, including medical, would have meant a complete redo of the entire application and testing process and waiting for the department to call for the next class of candidates to be assembled, a price I was unwilling to pay.)

Incidentally—and perhaps portentously—signal 31 is police radio code for a subject with "mental problems." Perhaps fitting for the so-diagnosed fifty-year-old president of MPD's Class 31.

4

The Christmas Gift

Blessed be the Lord my strength, which teacheth my hands to war, and my fingers to fight.
—Psalm 144:1

I'm rolling around with my windows down, the sharp cold air helping to fight off the sleepiness. It's that last, drowsy hour before dawn and the end of another twelve-hour night shift. The streets are dead, and I'm dead, too. It's Christmas morning, my second as a policeman on patrol. The first holiday season I was so pumped up at the idea of guarding the public while children everywhere were snug in their beds, I had been in a heightened state of vigilance all night. I had felt as if I were St. Nick with a Glock. St. Glockolas. But that was last year, my rookie year. Tonight, all I want to do is go home and sleep.

Despite the fatigue, I actually prefer night shift. More crimes, more hot calls occur at night, and there's far less traffic to worry about when running code to a hot one. But the excitement typically tapers off around 3 a.m. That's when cops gather in Waffle Houses and IHOPs to rehash the night's events, flirt with the waitresses, and drink lots and lots of coffee to fortify us for the next three slow, sleepy hours of patrol. Some of us, exhausted from working daytime "extra jobs" before coming in for night shift, will need to "forty up" (rendezvous) with a partner in a secluded "hidey-hole," cruisers parked close, driver door to driver door, facing opposite directions. We work our beats solo: one-man units, unless we're a car short or we're training a rookie. We don't have the luxury of snoozing in the passenger seat while a partner drives. And it's way too dangerous to simply pull up behind a building somewhere to catch a quick nap, alone. We've seen the horror stories in the academy, video footage of dead cops in their patrol cars, engines idling, blood and brains oozing from their heads. The official account is always the same: officer writing up reports at night, his interior lights blinding him to the approach of somebody with a gun and a hate-on for cops. Never see it coming. The lesson is to write up your reports at night in well-lit places, backed up to a building to cover your Six*, and keep scanning so nobody can approach without your knowing about it. What was unsaid in the training videos, but told to us by old timers, was that some of these dead cops probably weren't writing reports, they were sleeping. And the real lesson is, sometimes you just gotta sleep, for whatever reason. But it can be deadly, so don't do it alone! It can kill you.

Or get you fired. Two old-timers also told us about solo snoozers who didn't wake up when called by Dispatch. One said he was so dog tired he had nodded off while stopped at a red light. He's not responding to repeated calls on the radio. His buddy in the next beat (who is still in the department today, way up in the senior command ranks now) rolls up on the sleeping cop and lays on the horn.

"Get on the radio, now!" he yells. "They been calling you for five minutes!"

The groggy patrolman jerks awake and keys his radio mike. "Two-thirty-seven to Dispatch, do you copy? Unit 237, come back! Can you read me now, Dispatch?" When the dispatcher replies, the officer affects an exasperated tone. "Be advised I'm having transmission problems with this mike. I'll be en route to precinct."

Both old-timers had been far more concerned about the fireable offenses of failure to respond to the radio, or sleeping while on duty, than the fact that one had been so tired he'd dozed off behind the wheel of a department vehicle on a city street, the car in drive and his foot balanced on the brake pedal. Nowadays, you can't get away with that, the old-timers warned. Each patrol car is equipped with a tracking device that indicates the car's location. "They tell us it's for our own safety, so they can find us if we get into trouble, but we all know it's really to get us into trouble when they find us. So when you gotta sleep, don't do it alone!" Typical of so much police training. It's a coping mechanism, I think. One minute, murdered cops in color close-ups with gunshot wounds to the face and head, next minute knee-slapping stories about outsmarting captains.

---

* Your six o'clock position (behind your back)

I'd been shocked at the notion of cops sleeping on the job, quite aside from the safety issue. It angered me as a taxpayer, made me think less of the noble guardian in blue. But a couple of things changed my mind on that. The first was the challenge of supporting a family on $12 an hour—the lot of my squad mates. These guys, in their twenties and thirties, married, with kids, were struggling. If they could work an "extra job" (in uniform, while off duty, sanctioned, coordinated, and encouraged by the department), they were gonna do it, even if it meant getting by on two or three hours of sleep and napping on duty when the call volume slows down at night. The holidays are the prime extra-job season, because it's also the prime shoplifting and thievery season, especially at the malls and other retailers, where the pay for cops to supplement "loss prevention" staff, and to beef up parking lot security, usually starts at $25 per hour.

The other thing was the chief. Clearly a qualified, experienced professional, respected by his peers, his men, his community. I had made his acquaintance back in my United Way days, when he volunteered in the campaign leadership. In the bleak final days of my old life, the chief had enthusiastically encouraged my interest in a career change. When I ran into the chief after my first few months on the streets, his opening question, after confirming my enthusiasm for the work, was "Have ya learned how to sleep sitting up yet, Mark?"

So probably half my twelve-man squad is fortied up, taking turns sleeping, and the rest of us (who hadn't worked an extra job that day) are patrolling the entire precinct. I am grateful that I don't need the extra-job income and glad to "cover" for my squad members who do. But eager for this damn shift to end so I can go to bed.

The radio has been silent for at least an hour. I've been driving around and around, covering three beats, in a rundown section of town. Lots of boarded-up storefronts between barbershops featuring artistic patterns shaved onto the scalp, or hair treatments called twists and 'rows, "urban fashion" boutiques where they charge over $100 for baggy jeans with brands like Coogi and FUBU, cell phone discounters, Dollar stores, and nail parlors. Everything is closed, even the Circle Ks and the 24/7 tat 'n' pierce parlor. Not a creature is stirring, not even a mouse. I've caught myself snapping awake a couple of times while driving, not certain how long I had dozed, hoping it was only for a split second, relieved the car was still between the lines. I can't take any more coffee, but I sure could stand to off-load some of the six or seven cups I drank at the Waffle House, and it would do me good to get out and stretch my legs in the cold air, maybe wake me up a little. I pull into the alley behind a cut-rate grocery, at the end of a rundown strip mall composed of a beauty supply shop, a secondhand-goods store, and a boarded-up coin-operated laundry. The grocery, P & H Market, is the "anchor" retailer of the strip. Cops call it the Pimp & Hoes Market. They employ a security guard there who's the Pimp. He's gotta be in his sixties. His gray hair is heavily pomaded. He wears purple suits, complete with a matching purple Dobbs bowler. The hat has a cloisonné pin in its crown proclaiming "Mack Daddy." On a chain around his neck hangs a large, gold, official-looking badge. If you look closely, it reads "Security Officer." On his hip, in a holster hanging on a purple alligator-look belt (matching his purple alligator-look shoes, polished to a high gloss), is a chrome Smith & Wesson .38. The Pimp usually posts up by the front door of the P & H when he's not helping pretty ladies to the car with their groceries. His presence may actually deter theft at the store to some degree: we get fewer calls to the P & H for shoplifting than we do for domestic disputes in the parking lot. The domestics usually arise from jealousy and betrayal between lovers. Hence the "Hoes" part of the P & H.

I cut my headlights, turn off the AM-FM radio (sick to death of Christmas music), step out, and take in the silent darkness. I had thought I'd gaze at the stars for a moment and imagine peace on earth, goodwill toward men. But, hell, it's friggin' freezing out here! In Mobile Alabama! How the hell do people in Wisconsin survive the winter? I'm shivering as I urinate next to my squad car and jump back in as soon as I'm done, glad I had left the engine running with the heater pumping hot inside. I decide to contemplate Christmas from inside the cruiser and sit a few minutes in the darkness. The jolt of cold air had been bracing, and my drowsiness has dissipated. It's quarter to five: another hour to go before I can head to the precinct. I review in my mind the items under the Christmas tree at home, anticipating my family's pleasure in opening them. Life is good. I'm a lucky man.

Slipping the Crown Vic into drive, I creep down the littered, graffiti-adorned alley from behind the P & H, past the rear of the Dis 'N' Dat secondhand store, the Phlawless Hair Plus Beauty Supply, and the boarded-up Bright Spot Coin Laundry. As I round the back of the laundry, I see a man trying to open the door of a parked car. A car I know had been in that spot for weeks. A car whose tag I had run to check for stolen but had turned out to be just the object of a dispute between warring spouses. The guy halts abruptly when he sees me and turns to walk away from the car, away from me. I hit him with the spot and roll closer.

He stops and faces me. He's tall—easily 6 foot 3 or more—and thin and bedraggled. Week's stubble on his face, shoulder-length dirty blond hair coming out from under a black knit cap. Torn, dirty, ill-fitting navy peacoat, blue jean cargo pants. Gloves with the fingers cut off. He's holding his coat closed, hugging himself in the cold, shivering.

"Merry Christmas. 'S goin' on, Bub?" I lower the spotlight a little below his nose so he's not totally blinded by it.

"Locked myself out of my car," he says.

"Bummer. You got spare keys at home? Or you want me to call Pop-A-Lock?"

"I got spares at home. I was just gonna go get 'em," he says, and starts to step away.

"Hang on. Where ya live? I could give you a ride. Too damn cold to be walking."

He pauses, looking from side to side. He eyes my backseat cage, shakes his head. "Thanks, man," he says, a friendly, grateful smile, "but I'm just over at the Howard Johnson's. It's not too far to walk," he says, though it's a good mile, at least. He takes a couple of steps in the opposite direction of the Howard Johnson's Motel, which is a nest of prostitutes, drug peddlers, and lowlifes on the I-65 beltline.

I roll up alongside him. "Hang on a minute. That's not the way to the HoJoMo. And anyway, if you're staying there, what's your car doing all the way over here, parked by a boarded-up laundromat on Christmas morning?"

He grins. Shrugs. Stops hugging his peacoat to raise his palms up in a "beats me" gesture. As he does so, a metal bar about two feet long clanks to the ground from inside his jacket.

"Hold it right there," I say, fixing the spotlight back in his eyes. He complies, standing still except to shade his eyes from my light. I key the mike. "Three-twelve to radio, I'm out with a 63 subject, by the old laundromat next to P & H Market, P'Valley and Halls Mill." She dispatches Claggett to back me. Claggett's fortying with Anderson, way down the parkway. They're probably both asleep.

I sigh. "What's that?" I say, spotlighting the pry bar by his feet. He looks down, mute in discovery, acting surprised, bewildered. And then embarrassed.

I climb out of the cruiser. The kid's definitely got a few inches on me, but he's a string bean, maybe 160, 170 tops. "Step over here to my car. Put your hands on the hood, spread your feet apart. You know the drill." He assumes the position. I'm thinking, dammit! This could tie me up past the end of shift. "What's your name, date of birth?"

"Carl Weatherby. February 11, 1980."

"Got warrants, Carl? Anything else in this coat? In your pockets? Anything that could stick me? Any contraband?" I step in behind him, my foot between his legs, and pat him down, checking both inside and outside coat pockets, shirt, waistband front and back. Nothing so far, except that familiar sour smell of decay. "That's not really your car, is it, Carl?"

"No, sir," Weatherby mumbles. "I-I'm sorry. I was just cold."

Yeah. Right, Carl. I start down his right pant leg, with special attention to the cargo pocket on his lower thigh, which does not appear empty. "Was your plan to steal the car, or just whatever's in it, Carl?" He doesn't answer. "What's the bulge in this pocket, Carl?" Still no answer. I bend down to tug on the cargo pocket's Velcro flap.

Bam! Flashes swirl, I'm tasting pennies.

Carl has bashed me hard in the face with the full force of his elbow. Blood gushes from my nose, and I stagger backward, stunned, sharp pain stabbing me between the eyes, knees wobbly. And he's on me, fists pounding my face, my neck snapping side to side, my boxed ears reverbing like feedback at a Santana concert. I raise my right forearm to fend him off, my left hand struggling to key the radio mike clipped to my jacket collar. "Got. One. Resisting! Stepitup!" I grunt, not sure if I'm even getting out over the air. Heck with the radio, I've gotta use both hands just to block the flurry of blows pummeling me.

Carl is still advancing, I'm still backing up, reeling off balance but keeping on my feet. I attempt to return a punch or two. He's a skinny dope boy, but Carl's reach exceeds mine. I'm swinging wildly, but nothing's connecting. My fists are just bouncing off his arms and shoulders while his are splitting my eyebrow, my lip, each concussion a blinding flash of hurt, and the edges of my vision are darkening. I seem to have lost my peripheral vision, can't catch my breath, my balance, and can't get inside, to his face or belly.

I think: just minimize the damage he's doing till you can get steady, get squared off. He's gonna get tired, turn and run. He just wants to get away. I raise my forearms to protect my face and feel him striking at my belly. The body armor diffuses the impact of his gut punches. As he's going low, I get lucky and pop him a good one to the face. It rocks him a bit, stopping his advance but not his punches. My own clearheadedness surprises me. I'm actually thinking! I'm considering the tools on my belt: which would be best to deploy? The pepper spray? The nightstick? The Taser? And where the hell is my backup?

I can count on one hand the number of actual fights I've been in. My first one, on the fifth-grade playground, I won. But my opponent, who had started it, was just an obnoxious, nerdy weakling, and when I had him down, choking him as he turned purple, I felt sorry for him and stopped without really beating him much. The next one, just a year later, still shames me after forty years. It had been in my own front yard, my father watching from the house, with an older kid who was nevertheless no bigger then I was. Just tougher, and not the least bit intimidated by my home yard advantage and parental observer. It had started with a dispute over a pickup ball game, then name calling and taunts, culminating in kicks and punches. It had not lasted long. David Hammond landed a roundhouse to my mouth, breaking off a front tooth and cutting the hell out of my lip. Shocked, I spit a bloody chunk of incisor into my cupped hands and cried out, "My tooth!" From the front porch, my dad yelled, "Hit 'im back!" But instead I ran, horrified, into the house to look in the mirror. The injury to my vanity was far worse than whatever pain the blow had inflicted. Worse still was the look in my father's eyes as I ran past him.

The next three battles had been in college, each of them pathetic defeats (despite being highly intoxicated and feeling no pain) due to (1) being grossly outmatched (against a starting defensive linebacker), (2) being outnumbered by two Air Force Academy "zoomies" who thought I was making moves on one of their girls; they ambushed me in the men's room of a Denver disco, and (3) being both outmatched and outnumbered by three of Boulder's finest who had teargassed me before throwing me to the ground during a Vietnam War protest (at which I was really an observer, not a participant, but they just wouldn't listen). One could rationalize that I lost so many fights because of unfair disadvantages. But I knew the truth.

Since then there had been several confrontations that, if I'd had more confidence, or courage, or character, or Coors, could have easily escalated to fisticuffs. But I had backed down before the first punch had been thrown, scared and humiliated. One time in particular still haunts me. I was riding on a Mexican bus from Nogales to Puerto Vallarta with my then-girlfriend, on spring break. The rest of the passengers were Mexicans, except for three other Americans, obviously on spring break, too. One was particularly drunk, loud, and obnoxious, and he began an obscene flirtation with a couple of Mexican girls in the back of the bus. Their discomfort grew to fear, but he would not be discouraged, neither by the girls nor by his own traveling companions who urged him to "cool out" and leave the girls alone. I studied him dispassionately: not any bigger than me but definitely better built. However, I reasoned, his judgment—and likely his reflexes, as well—were clearly impaired by tequila, which could work to my advantage. The deciding factor, that which propelled me to action, was the certainty that I had right, if not might, on my side (and could therefore probably count on backup from other male passengers, possibly even from the bully's own buddies, who clearly wanted to avoid a scene). I walked down the aisle of the bus, his back to me as he leaned down leering into the girls' faces. I put a hand on his shoulder. Before I could even announce my defense of the young damsels in distress, he turned on me, grabbed me in a choke hold, and pulled my face within an inch of his own. "Back off or I'll hurt you, bad," he had said in a low snarl. The look in his eyes made me feel the urge to urinate. He released me and I slunk back to my seat. I'm not a natural warrior.

But I'm now remembering what they drilled into us at the academy: *cops can't lose fights.* It's not just a matter of pride, or of enforcement. It simply must not happen. My arms are still up, defending my face from Carl's rain of fists, and I'm wondering why he hasn't figured "This old cop will be easy to outrun" and simply turned and fled. Then I feel a tug on the right side of my duty belt. With a jolt I realize: my gun! This fucker's trying to get my gun! He doesn't just want to stun me and flee, he wants to shoot me! This is why cops can't lose fights. There's always a firearm on the scene of a fight with a cop. For a cop, losing a fight is not just humiliating. It's death.

Something inside me uncoils. To my surprise (and Carl's), I land a solid one to Carl's eye. It rocks him back. I step in and land another, and he's staggering, falling, down on the blacktop. I step in, and he kicks me hard on the side of my knee. My leg buckles and I tumble on top of him. I feel him tugging again at my Glock, and I twist my right side back and away, putting my left forearm across his throat. But he pushes up with his legs and grabs a handful of my shirt with his right hand and rides my twisting momentum over and now I'm on my back, on the bottom, on the pavement. He's straddling me, still tugging at the Glock with his left hand, clawing at my eyes with his right. Thank God for double-retention holsters! Carl doesn't know the snap-and-rock motion required to draw the Glock, and he's at the wrong angle to do it even if he knows. He raises his left leg to get better leverage on the Glock, and I knee him hard in the groin and he crumples. I thrust a thumb into his eye socket and we roll again on the asphalt and now I'm on top and I drive a knee into his solar plexus, raise up, and draw and fire my Taser, hoping deployment at such close range won't diminish its effect. It doesn't. Carl screams, immobilized as one prong strikes him in the throat, the other just under his left rib cage. I let him take the full five-second, 50,000-volt ride, then hear myself bark "Stop resisting!" without irony. Carl wants no more of it. I snap a cuff on his right wrist, jerk him over onto his face, and put my full weight on a knee between his shoulder blades. Carl is fully compliant. I holster my Taser, cartridge still attached, and drop my other knee onto his neck, grinding his face into the asphalt as I jerk his left arm back and complete the cuffing.

I rise to my feet and put a boot to Carl's neck just as Claggett and Anderson screech into the parking lot of the P & H, lights flashing, sirens whoop-whooping. Harry Claggett is out of his car and dropping a knee into Carl's back with all of his 220 pounds. "Three-nineteen, start medical to our location. One tased, with abrasions and lacerations about the face and head. Subject is conscious and alert." Tyrone Anderson puts his arm around my shoulders and walks me over to lean against the push bumper on the front of my cruiser. "You a'ight, Johnson?" he inquires, steadying me, studying me. "Ya look like shit, man!"

I'm suddenly weak, trembly, short of breath. But giddily grateful to be sitting on the bumper, grateful for Anderson's steadying hand, grateful for the relentless whoop-whooping and the sparkly blue strobes of their Crown Vics. "I'm fine, 'Rone. What the hell took you guys, anyway? Did I not get out on the radio?"

Tyrone pulls out his flashlight and points it at me, eyeing my bloody face more closely. "Pull out that do-rag a yours. You need to wipe off your face before the medics get here, or they'll be sayin' you need to be, like, examined or whatever." Sleepy, laid-back, slow-talking 'Rone: just twenty-three years old, already unflappable. I pull the bandana from my back pocket and dab gingerly where it hurts.

"Alls we could hear was a lotta gruntin' and yellin'," Tyrone continues. "It was real, like, garbledy." He pauses, considers. Grins. "But we could tell was it you gruntin' and yellin' and garblin'. We just didn't know was it you puttin' the beatdown on somebody, or you gettin' a whuppin'." He glances over at Carl, immobilized by Harry's mass. "Guess we shoulda known."

Sarge arrives at the same time as the paramedics, who busy themselves with Carl Weatherby, removing the Taser prongs, swabbing his asphalt-torn cheeks. Sarge surveys Weatherby and the collection of pharmaceuticals, weed, and meth or crack rocks Harry has removed from Weatherby's right cargo pocket. Harry has also run Weatherby's ID, and Dispatch advises he's got an active bench warrant for Failure to Appear on a (surprise!) Possession, Controlled Substance case. Sarge approaches me and Tyrone.

He's a big man, Sarge is: barrel chested, thick everywhere, 6 foot 4, 265. The stereotypical Irish cop, in his mid-forties, policing since his mid-twenties, when he got out of the service. He lips out a Camel Light and offers it to me. I tear the filter off and light it from Sarge's Bic.

"Merry Christmas, Mark," Sarge says, grinning, thoughtful. He shakes his head once. "We may be a coupla old farts to these young'uns, but ain't it great to know ya still got it?" I take a deep draw on the Camel. I can't help but smile broadly (though painfully) to Sarge and Tyrone.

"Yes," I say, nodding. "Yes it is," thinking: especially when you never knew ya had it.

It's chilly and mists rise from the earth as the sun starts to shed light on Christmas morning. As I do after every night shift, I stop by the police barn on Virginia Street to feed Nancy's horse, Prince. In her typical, in-your-face, tough-broad manner, she had joined the volunteer auxiliary of the department's Mounted Unit shortly after I joined the department, without so much as telling me until after it was done. As a member of the Mounted Unit Auxiliary, she wears a uniform similar to mine but carries no weapon or power of arrest. In other words, sitting in the saddle above a churning, chaotic crowd, she makes a very nice target for a cop hater, who'd fail to notice the subtle distinctions in her uniform, or her lack of authority; who'd fail to realize she's a wife and mother and a journalist by trade, not a cop. At least the department issues her a bulletproof vest.

I take great comfort in the fact that her horse, Prince, is a veteran with the department. A sixteen-hand, twenty-year-old Tennessee walker, he's been doing parade duty, crowd control, and project patrol for more than a decade. I rely on Prince to keep Nancy as safe as she can be, given the circumstances she rides in. We acquired Prince from a retiring auxiliary member and board him at the police barn. The stall space is free, but auxiliary volunteers are responsible for the care and feeding of their own mounts.

One night of Nancy's mounted duty during my third Mardi Gras, I got a little taste of the kind of worry she had to endure every time I went out the door. A post-parade, open-air rap concert had been scheduled, but for reasons unknown, the rapper was a no-show. The restive crowd was refusing to disperse. I had just gotten off my parade assignment and was headed home when I heard radio chatter dispatching all crowd-control, Ranger, SWAT, and Mounted units to the concert location. I made a U-turn and called Nancy to find out where, exactly, she was headed. The background noise drowned out her voice, and then the phone went dead. I hit my lights and headed for the park, frantically redialing her number, getting her voice mail. I worked my siren's yelp button and swept the crowd with my spotlight to ford the torrents of revelers in the streets. The radio traffic was nonstop with reports of fights, shots fired, and calls for backup, but that's not unusual for post-parade mayhem. Without knowing Nancy's exact location relative to the radio reports, though, my concern escalated to alarm as I imagined Nancy and Prince in the center of a maelstrom. When finally she answered, she yelled out her location, said her sergeant was ordering her off the phone, and abruptly clicked off.

Within minutes I was close enough to pick her out of a line of mounts holding the west perimeter of the sea of angry rap fans in the park. I pulled up and parked behind a traffic unit posted there. Jack was sitting calmly on the push bumper of his squad car, watching the spectacle. He wasn't even wearing his riot helmet. I approached him wearing mine, carrying my shotgun, prepared to wade in and pluck Nancy off Prince, and lead them both to safety.

"Whoa, cowboy. You can put that away," Jack said, nodding at my 12 gauge. "Unless you know something I don't know. It's not as bad as it sounds on the radio."

"My wife's out there," I said. "She's Mounted Auxiliary, on that tall one, about the fourth from the left."

"Ain't no big thang," Jack said. "Chill."

Just then a Hungry Howie's Pizza delivery car arrived. Jack got up from his push bumper, reaching for his wallet. As he paid the delivery guy, he said to me, "Hungry? I got a whole pie here. It's way more than I can eat."

Dumbfounded, mouth agape, I slung the 12 gauge over my shoulder and shook my head, looking from Nancy, a stone's throw away on Prince, above the noisy, menacing crowd, back to Jack opening up the pizza box on the hood of his squad car. He pulled out a large steamy slice and offered it to me.

The aroma awakened my appetite. Keeping an eye on my wife and Prince, and the shotgun at the ready, I gratefully accepted and noshed contentedly with Jack as Nancy and Prince maintained law and order. Eventually, the crowd dispersed and the Mounts headed off to horse trailers at their staging area several blocks away.

Later, at home, I let Nancy tell me about the crazy danger of her post-parade riot duty at the canceled concert before I confessed to her that I'd had her back from a distance of fifteen yards the whole time. And later still, I even admitted that I had done so while splitting a pizza with Jack.

Though usually dog tired and eager to collapse into bed after twelve hours of night shift, I look forward to a visit with Prince at the police barn on my way home. I work my way down the row of stalls, feeding every horse a slice of the apples I've brought. I save a whole apple just for Prince. I love to feed him slice after slice, as much as he loves to eat them. His big rubbery lips are so supple they seem almost prehensile in their ability to get every last morsel of the grain that I scoop into his box, even from the corners.

I always stay until he's done with the apple and the grain and often stick around just to watch him munch his hay with gratitude and contentment. It's contagious, his gratitude and contentment. A distinct calm always settles over me there, no matter how brutal or terrifying the previous hours have been. I'll sit on his comfortable bed of straw, lean back against the wooden stall, breathe in deeply the rich, loamy scents, the quiet stillness, and admire him: his towering strength, his gentleness, his humble obedience and his guilelessness, his trustfulness and trustworthiness. Invariably, being there brings to mind the childlike delight in Nancy's face when he prances for her.

I love being here with him. The earthy simplicity and beauty of it always move me. It's an unworldly peace, at dawn, with the Prince. As a manger should be.

Five months later I was dispatched to a domestic in progress in that same parking lot, in front of the P & H Market. A white male was slapping around a white female. After we got them separated and put the bully in the cage, I was getting his information for the arrest form. He identified himself as Merle Weatherby.

"Any chance you're related to Carl Weatherby?"

"Yeah, he's my brother" came the sullen reply. "Or *was*. He died about six weeks ago."

Carl had bonded out from his Christmas morning arrest. While awaiting trial, he had overdosed on heroin. At this news, my only thought was good riddance.

5

Cops 'n' Corpses

Dying should come easy, like a freight train you don't hear when your back is turned.
—Charles Bukowski

We'd been dispatched to an audible burglar alarm at a funeral home, Tyrone and me. We found the door ajar. Tyrone, usually the picture of deadpan cool, advised me I was on my own, that stiffs give him the creeps, and anybody who broke into a building full of stiffs had to be even creepier. I teased him about being a scaredy-cat and entered the building alone while he waited outside and lit a Newport. Always eager to find a live burglar I drew my gun and swept the rooms with my flashlight, creeping from chapel to chapel, office to office, finding nothing amiss and nobody there.

A letdown. The caretaker had probably just failed to properly secure the door when he left. I slowly made my way to the backrooms, eventually coming to what appeared to be the cadaver prep area. I eased open a creaking, swinging door and a jolt like a Taser shot down my spine. My beam had swept a steel table in the center of the room on which a motionless human form laid. The shock of the corpse weakened me at the knees, churned my stomach. Goose bumps coursed across my shoulders, down my arms, my back and calves. I regulated my breathing and circled the slab, studying him. A sheet across his midsection maintained his modesty but none of his dignity. I paused, mentally noting his characteristics as I might a fleeing suspect: white male, early to mid-sixties (not much older than I am), 5 foot 8 or 9, 200–210, probably forty pounds overweight. Blotchy complexion, balding gray hair, unshaven, stiff brushes of gray hair protruding from his ears and nostrils, a slack jaw revealing uneven, discolored teeth, large working-man's hands, scarred and unadorned, dirty fingernails, a rounded mound of beer belly, big feet with gnarled overgrown yellow toenails. I sniffed the air. There was none of that fabled "scent of death," just an antiseptic, chemical smell: maybe Pine-Sol, with a hint of something sharper. It occurred to me that maybe this guy's already been embalmed. I considered lifting the sheet for a peek at the mortician's handiwork but decided against it. As the goose bumps faded from my arms I chuckled at myself, thinking, what did you expect? You're in a funeral home, doofus. When I regained my composure, I rejoined Tyrone outside and teased him a little more. "Nobody's talkin' in there," I said. I didn't tell him that the corpse had made me jump out of my skin.

Many times I had backed other officers on signal 26s (dead bodies), but the primary units had always been simply responding to a dispatch initiated by the call to police from a discovering party—usually a family member, or a hospice worker—who had found the body first. We knew what to expect. The deceased had always been elderly and bedridden, and there was usually the odor of soiled bedclothes and linens (from the involuntary evacuation of bladder and bowels) mingled with a more subtle though unmistakable scent of decay. These deaths had always been relatively recent, however, and invariably peaceful and tidy; the discovering spouse or caregiver, though clearly saddened, was in control (or simply muted), often having been calmed and comforted by close relatives whose arrival had preceded ours.

But one time I was searching abandoned houses for stolen flat screens and other booty stashed from recent burglaries in the area. I was alone at dusk and pulled up the gravel driveway of a dilapidated shack nearly obscured from the road by waist-high weeds and overgrown shrubbery. The front door was half open, and it was dark and silent within. I entered, knocking, and announced myself: "Police!" Silence. I peered around the front room, the waning light sufficient to see that the house had been stripped of everything but random broken furniture and piles of old clothing, fast-food wrappers, and decades-old periodicals and newspapers littering the floor, which was an exposed concrete slab, absent of flooring or carpet. Insulation hung in fuzzy garlands like moss on a live oak, from gaping holes in the ceiling through which the attic's electrical wiring had been ripped. The kitchen cabinets, counters, and sink had been violently jerked from the wall, its copper piping cut and pried out from behind the ravaged sheetrock. I walked down a darkened hallway stepping carefully over debris, then froze at what sounded like a television or a radio coming from behind a bedroom door. Could there still be electricity in this ruin? None of the light switches had worked.

I rattled the doorknob: stuck. I stepped to the side of the door, then reached to pound on it, yelling "Police!" louder. No response. I drew my weapon and considered kicking it in, but something made me hesitate.

Sometimes places like these, despite their complete devastation, are still inhabited. Usually by squatters, or crack whores doing five-buck blow jobs—either being arrestable trespassers—but every now and then, an ancient, frail homeowner somehow stubbornly clings to a place like this, though it's literally falling down around him. I exited the front door, holstered my gun, and checked the mailbox. Nothing but yellowed fliers addressed to Occupant. I waded through the weeds to the window of the room I'd heard the audio coming from. Cupping my hands and face to the glass, I let my eyes adjust to the room's dark interior and shined my flashlight through the filthy panes and battered window blinds sagging inside. There was a flickering TV across the squalid room. I thought, no plumbing, no water, no lights, heat or air, but by God they've got the boob tube wired!

My eyes fell to what appeared to be a cot or narrow single bed, snug up against the window, right before me. I shined the flashlight up and down the length of the bedding, which was a lumpy mass of tangled dirty sheets and a thin, ratty blue blanket. It looked like it might be occupied, but it was motionless, and I couldn't make out a head, feet, or limbs. I banged on the glass and yelled "Police" again. No stirring, no sound, save the incessant chatter from the TV. I redrew my Glock, went back in the front door, down the hall, kicked on the bedroom door and jerked the knob both ways. To my surprise, it swung open. A familiar stench greeted me, a signal 26 stench. Damn, I thought. A stiff.

Across the room was the lumpy blanketed bed I'd glimpsed from outside the window. Next to the bed was a battered wheelchair and a nightstand crowded with medicines and pill bottles and medical-looking equipment with wires and tubes leading to the bed. I followed a tube with my eyes from the nightstand to where it snaked in under the sheets and made out its end point, covered in white adhesive tape, buried in a patch of pasty flesh: an arm, or a leg. I couldn't tell which.

Damn, I muttered, thinking I'm due to get off in a half hour and processing this corpse could last well through end of shift and suppertime.

I considered just leaving, letting a neighbor or next of kin find the stiff and phone it in for the next squad to handle. But duty—or the chance of having been observed going in, and then getting reported for not doing my duty—drove me to confirm my discovery. With the tip of my boot I tapped gently on the bed's metal frame. Nothing. Just to be safe, I raised my Glock. I've seen them play possum, then come up fighting. But they don't usually stink like this one. I addressed the stiff, barking, "Let me see your hands!" then kicked the bed, hard.

Suddenly a head pops out from under the sheets and I nearly crap my pants. A contorted, blanched face squeals at me, his eyes popping at me as mine are at him. "I'm deaf! I'm sick! I'm deaf!" The bald-headed baby-faced old man is convulsing in terror. My own tremors nearly shake the gun from my hand. I holster it, catch my breath, and put up both hands. "S-s-sorry," I stammer, backpedaling. "I-I thought you . . . you. . . . Sssorry, mister!" I back out the door and pull it shut, steady myself on the wall down the hallway, and escape to the safe comfort of my Crown Vic, spraying the house with gravel as I drop it into gear and spin away.

The next day, feeling guilty, I checked with the neighbors of the bedridden deaf guy and learned that he wasn't just wasting away all by his lonesome in that wreck of a house. The neighbors assured me that a county human services caseworker checks in on him every week or so, and a hospice worker stops in daily to change his dressings, monitor his fluids, and check his equipment. And the old man's only local relative, a daughter who works as a nurse's aide at a local assisted-living facility, visits him at about once a month.

What a relief.

The only thing worse than discovering a stiff that turns out to be alive is to come upon a really, really dead one. A ripe one, still at home, unprepped by the undertaker. It's not that spooky. Just wretched, stinky, and often unbearably sad. The neighbors, alerted by the smell emanating from the house and fierce swarms of buzzing flies at its screened windows, had called the old man's daughter. When she arrived from across town and smelled the smell, she called police, afraid of what she knew was inside. Her daddy, Mose Battles, was in his late eighties, she said. Lived alone, except for his little old dog, Sweets, named after the Swisher cigars the old man loved to chew on. She wondered why Sweets wasn't barking. Daddy was diabetic, she said—he'd already lost part of a foot—and had a heart condition, but he was too stubborn to move in with her or to a nursing home. She hadn't seen him since the Fourth of July. It was mid-August, in Mobile, Alabama. The house wasn't air conditioned.

Batting flies, I opened the front door with the daughter's key as she and gathering neighbors waited at the curb. The distinct smell of something dead and rotting made me gag, and made the daughter and neighbors cover their mouths and noses with hands and kerchiefs. Inside, I called out "Mr. Battles? Sweets? Mobile PD." I could hear a television on in the bedroom and headed that way, down the hall. As I passed the bathroom, there he was. The old man had died while defecating (not uncommon) and had fallen off his toilet. He lay crumpled on the tile, between the tub and the toilet, his pajama pants still down around his ankles, his feces still in the bowl. The room sweltered. He had been slowly basting in his own juices for weeks. A small, old, overweight pit bull mix—Sweets—lay at his master's feet, also dead. I guessed the dog had died from starvation after the old guy had fallen off the toilet. The dog's fur had begun to fall away from its flesh in tufts on the tile around him. The old man was swollen and discolored on the bottom half of his body: his left cheek, shoulder, buttocks, and legs were a dark eggplant color from livor mortis, the hypostasis of blood settling to the body's lowermost points. At several places along the darkened lower half of his face and trunk the swollen skin had split like overripe fruit, oozed organic matter, and crusted. The smell of their vacated bowels (the dog's crap littered the bathroom floor) combined with the putrefaction of their flesh made for a staggering stench. But my eyes welled up at the tender, sad sight of Sweets. What had he thought, these last weeks, slowly failing, growing weaker, starving, as Mose lay immobile and unresponsive to his whimpers and wags, sniffs and pawings?

Outside, the histrionics had begun, like a live performance of James Brown (I've seen him five times) but without the spangley cape they drape over his shoulders to usher him, weak from sharing too much soul, offstage. As siblings, children, nephews, nieces, and in-laws arrived, each had his or her moment of bawling, chest-pounding, hair-pulling anguish. People fell to their knees in the street, shouted their disbelief, implored the mercy of Jesus, proclaimed their loss. Others shoved and pushed (though not convincingly) my partners, who arrived to gawk at the stiff and to keep order.

Some of the bereaved were apparently driven to enter the house. By what? Spirits?

For what? To rescue or anoint the deceased? To demonstrate the depth of their loss? To say good-bye, to gaze once, last, upon the dearly departed's earthly vessel? Would Mose—or anyone—want to be seen stinking, stiff, discolored, suppurating, and defiled, with his pants around his ankles? Others held them back as if to say you dare not look this way, asserting their control of the scene, their protection of the deceased from the living—or the living from the deceased. Teens and young children took their cues from their elders, intently studying with wide eyes the adults' writhings and weepings, then spontaneously erupting with their own outcries and gyrations of grief, or panic. Was it genuine? There were actual tears shed, yes. But was it theater? A cultural response? A social expectation? I was as troubled by my own coldly skeptical response to this most human scene as I was by my sole urge to weep only at the discovery of the stilled, loyal canine at Mose's feet.

Fortunately for me, there were official duties to divert me from crowd control, grief assessments, and searing doubts of my own compassion: radio for Fire & Rescue paramedics to confirm the death, rule out any question of foul play, inventory and seize the contents of the medicine cabinet, determine the names of the decedent's physicians, get one of them by phone to speculate on the cause of death and to agree to sign the death certificate, report all this to County Department of Forensics, arrange for the transport of the body to the mortician.

As the ambulance team wheeled Mose out the front door and muscled the gurney down the steps, I took my leave of the family. It had not been too many years since I had lost my own parents, and I purposely thought of them as I expressed my condolences to the bereaved Battles clan for the loss of their elder. To my relief, my throat tightened and a tear trickled. The grievers seemed genuinely touched, grateful for my empathy. I was glad to know I could still at least summon these somatic signals of humanity, even though they had failed to arise naturally.

But emotional subtleties and skepticism play no role when dispatched to a death scene that's not the result of natural causes. Mangled, twisted, severed corpses at interstate wrecks provoke the ghoulish, irresistible pull of a freak show. The Backwards Man remains vivid in my mind and appears from time to time in frightening dreams: broken and twisted at the waist a full 180 degrees, so that he faced the opposite direction that his feet pointed in. The Faceless Biker, struck by a car, catapulted through the air, whose visage was no more than a protracted smear on the asphalt, the only vestige of human countenance the few broken teeth in his dangling jaw. Even more compelling are the criminal death scenes, like that of the executed thug, Melted Man, felled by a close-range shot to the head from a rival, then doused with fuel and set ablaze from the neck up. And of course, the gore-smeared, bedridden old Mama, whose crack-addled fifty-two-year-old son had bludgeoned her to a lifeless crimson pulp with a brick-filled pillowcase, slung repeatedly against her skull. He departed with a bounty of $47 cash from her purse in her battered nineteen-year-old Taurus, headed for the casinos in Biloxi, leaving Mama's tender-loving brains splattering the bed, headboard, and walls. Mama's seven-year-old granddaughter had discovered the brutal scene. She had been screaming with hysteria for fifteen minutes before I arrived. (Forty minutes later the brick slinger had been taken into custody by Mississippi troopers alongside I-10, where Mama's car had run out of gas.)

I was at once repelled and relieved by the utter absence of the emotions I had expected would sweep over me: revulsion or horror or anguish or grief or rage. And this cold calm wasn't gradual, the result of a series of numbing, deadening exposures to savagery. It had arrived with the very first murdered stiff and has remained, unvarying, through dozens of mutilating, desecrating deaths of young and old, innocent and otherwise, at the hands of others.

I once arrived at a shooting, first at the scene, and the victim, a mid-teen gangbanger, lay dying on his mother's front lawn. The rest of the family was still inside, cowering from the automatic gunfire that had sprayed the house. The shooters were nowhere to be seen. I rushed up to the boy and knelt beside him. He was gasping for air and choking on his own blood. Lifting his head slightly, I wiped some blood from his lips and demanded he tell me who shot him. He struggled mightily to speak, looking earnestly into my eyes. His eyes bespoke surprise, fear, and intense longing. I leaned in close to his face in an effort to understand the words he mouthed. He gurgled and choked and expelled his final wet breath on my cheek as backup arrived, and his screaming family came streaming from out of the house. I stood up to stop them and only then noticed the 9 mm semiauto still clenched in dead boy's hand. Another youth about the same age— the victim's brother? a fellow gangbanger?—bounded up and reached for the weapon. I stepped on the victim's clenched pistol and clotheslined the rushing kid, his feet flying out from under him. "Get back!" I heard myself growl, startled at my own voice and my gun hand brandishing my own Glock in a wide arc toward all comers. I was startled, as well, by their abrupt compliance. "He's gone!" I declared. "You can't help him now!" Then, flatly into my radio, "Three-twelve to Dispatch, start medical for one down, gunshots to the chest and throat. Advise 1 Sam 3 to start ID and Homicide."

I remember thinking, it'll probably hit me later, the panic, confusion, and emotions, but for now: protect the scene, contain the evidence, keep the family back (but don't let them leave), scan the gathering crowd for weapons and suspects, string the yellow tape, look for shell casings and other dropped or discarded weapons. But as my squad secured the scene's perimeter, controlled the crowd, and began identifying and questioning witnesses, and as I reported both orally and in writing what I had seen and found to my sergeant, then to Homicide detectives, there was still no nerve-jangling shock or even an inkling of dismay at what I'd just experienced. In fact, it felt more like the opposite: thrilling!

And finally, hours after the completion of all duties, reluctantly peeling off my duty belt and vest and collapsing on the couch at home, I wondered and marveled at myself, replaying the scenes in my mind. Had all that training and drilling, seemingly so insipid and obvious at the time, really been effective? Had it changed me? Made me so coolly efficient? Or is it just the gun, the badge, the uniform, the body armor that has this effect, on anyone? Did I just rise to this particular occasion, drawing on unknown wells of resolve and focus? Is this a fluke? Is this really me, or have I become somebody else? If I still get choked up by lonesome, loyal dogs, orphaned and lost children, grieving widows and grandmas, and even corny romantic comedies, how does that square with the guy commanding the murder scene? Why aren't I weeping for fifteen-year-old Demetrius "Meechie" Creyton who died in my arms? Or at least for his stricken, hysterical mama and kid sisters? Or vowing to see justice brought to his shooter?

Instead, I just feel nothing, save exhaustion. But I'm aware of a tiny, tingly sneaky hope for more shifts like tonight. As I drift off, I allow myself to peel it back slowly. Man! That was the Shit! The Real Deal! You were there! The sweet dreamless slumber of a newborn embraces me. No night sweats, terrors or tremors, no shock or dread or rage. Nothing. Wow. That's cool. Isn't it?

6

Baby-Mamas and Bastards

My job is to save your ass, not kiss it.
—attributed to Officer Jack Balzer

Sharon Brown was almost four months along when I first met her—just starting to show, although it depended on what she was wearing. She mostly wore loose-fitting tops and baggy blue jeans. There was no mistaking that she was a mother, however: her three previous children occupied most of her time, energy, and attention. They were Lucy (fifteen months), James (twenty-eight months), and Rayford (three and a half years); Sharon was just twenty-three.

She resided in a "transitional living" apartment for single moms, a program run by a United Way agency. The agency's director had suggested Sharon as a success story worthy of a campaign video. The hardest part of producing a campaign video is to find a good subject—someone whose misfortune resulted from circumstances beyond her control, to which no blame could be attached. (This rules out the lazy, the addicted, the self-indulgent, and all the blamers, schemers, demanders, and dramatizers.) You need a hard-luck case with integrity, humility, and strength, someone who had lived by the rules, worked hard, stayed true, but found herself nevertheless in impossible circumstances. Someone who would make you think, "There, but for the grace of God, go I." Someone who, with just the right break, could overcome her dilemma and live happily ever after. And if you can find those qualities in someone who's reasonably articulate and attractive, you've got a winner. It seldom happens.

Sharon was that winner, a fund-raiser's dream. She possessed an uncommon beauty, seen immediately in her deep brown almond-shaped eyes, clear and guileless yet shyly averted. If she returned your gaze even for the briefest of moments, you could get lost in those eyes. Her long lashes, perfectly arched brows, creamy caramel complexion, full tender lips, and silky black mane were free of all artifice and cosmetics. Frequent smiles flashed pearly perfection worthy of a Crest commercial, yet her countenance conveyed a modesty and simplicity unmarred by vanity.

She had joined the army right out of high school but had been released when she became pregnant the first time. The return to her hometown and junior college had produced an associate's degree in mechanical drafting and a brief marriage, from which her second child was born. Her husband had turned out to be an abuser. "He had a temper that would just take ahold a him; he couldn't help it. But neither could I. Seem like it never was nu'n I could do right for him." She shook her head dolefully. "Mama warned me he had the rage in him, she saw it, but I didn't listen. Thought I could just love it away, or the babies would soften him, but . . ."

Rather than live in fear and raise her babies in violence, Sharon left him. His stalking was relentless until she left town altogether and, babies in tow, moved in with her older sister in Atlanta. There she fell in love with her employer, a successful older man, a city alderman who had built his own insurance agency and had promised to leave his wife for her. Her naïveté had resulted in a third child. "He was my boss, a big public man, and I believed him," she said, embarrassed. The alderman provided generous child support in exchange for her silence.

"I will say, he's good about that. I couldn't have made it without his checks every month—or almost every month. There's been some lapses." Sharon paused with a downcast look but shook it off with a deep breath and a bright smile. "But that's why I'm so thankful to the Women's Center for this place. We are truly blessed. We'd be out on a park bench, and that ain't no place for babies, is it Ray Ray?" She bent to hug little Rayford, who tugged on her knee.

I didn't ask about the father of the unborn child she carried now. I didn't want to know. I was enthralled by the matter-of-fact candor with which she spoke of her life. There was no trace of bitterness, blame, or self-pity. No despair. Sharon's full and boundless heart was plain in her delight with her firstborn, as she gave Rayford a tender squeeze and set him toddling off to resume play with his brother, a gap-toothed grin stretching ear to ear. Sharon spoke on of her gratitude to the center, unfazed moments later by the interruption of Lucy's plaintive whimpers from the crib. The infant quieted as soon as Sharon scooped her up and nuzzled her to a breast with a practiced, efficient modesty. "This place has other mamas like me, and when the center helps us find work, we're able to fix our schedules so we can help each other watch the kids. I've met some really good people here, people who've had it way worse than me, but they're still such good, nice people. They're even gonna help me move into my own place, soon's I can find somebody with a truck."

Despite the seeming chaos of squallers and crawlers, Sharon's tiny apartment was tidy and clean, if sparse. The children were content and healthy. There was a noisy, cozy harmony to the household, and it emanated from Sharon. I got some great footage, and Sharon's spontaneous audio would require minimal editing.

"I've got an old pickup," I told her. "When do we start the moving?"

"Why are you doing so much for that woman?" Nancy inquired after I'd spent the better part of a weekend getting Sharon and all her babies settled in her new place. "I don't get your endless compassion for her, anyway. She keeps making the same mistake, over and over, and doesn't seem to learn from it. Hasn't she ever heard of birth control?"

"She has shared her story, basically exposing herself to everybody who's gonna see the video, with no expectation of payback in any way," I reply. "And it's gonna be my best, strongest work yet. It's the least I could do."

"But hasn't she heard of birth control? She's in her twenties, had some college. The pill's been around now, for what? Two, three decades?"

I feel myself getting defensive, like my video lacks credibility or my compassion is misplaced. Or both. "She just falls in love easy . . . she's from a small town, never with more than one man at a time . . . she's a real good mama, and working her ass off to provide for all those babies." I can hear myself getting louder, strident. "Working twenty hours a week, taking two college classes, doing child care for the other women at the center almost every day, and nurturing her own kids around the clock!" I'm forgetting to take a breath, my face is reddening. "And she's so grateful for everything! Says she's 'blessed,' of all things!"

"Whoa! I'm sure she's very kind and a good mother and hardworking," Nancy replies, calmly earnest. "I'm just saying, I don't get it. What's her problem?"

"Don't you see? She has a compulsion. It's got nothing do with education, or culture, or even logic," I say. "Everybody has their own blind spot. Some people, it's alcohol or drugs. Other people, it's status or the corporate ladder or getting rich and powerful. It's just their . . . their thing-that-trips-them-up, that consumes them, something they think they're good at, and they think is a good thing, or at least good for them, but they don't even see what it's costing them. They just can't help it. With Sharon, it's babies. Or maybe certain men. Or both. But mainly babies." I had just articulated something I hadn't really thought through myself and doubted Nancy would get it. Or buy it.

To my surprise, she sort of tilted her head, pondering, and began nodding. "Yeah, I guess that could be it. Never thought of it that way."

I won several local and regional United Way and PR association awards for my campaign video that year, and we had one of our most successful fund-raising efforts ever. We even introduced Sharon and her kids at the post-campaign awards banquet. Sharon's second daughter, fatherless child no. 4, Felicity, was with us by then, along with Rayford, James, and Lucy, all of whom were very well behaved and cute as speckled pups. Sharon thanked everyone on behalf of her family and the other single moms at the Women's Center and announced that if all went according to plan she would receive her BA from the university by next May, which would mean a bright future for her and her kids. She received a standing ovation.

The following year I moved to the United Way in Waukesha County, Wisconsin, a larger community, halfway across the country, and lost touch with Sharon. She sent me a long, newsy upbeat letter a few months after I got settled in there, wished me good luck in the new job, and asked me to write back. Months passed; I had my own struggles in the new job and didn't keep up my end of the correspondence. One afternoon I came across her letter and called the Women's Center, asking for her. She was no longer there, they said. Sharon had met someone, a man who had a good job on the Alaskan pipeline, and she had packed up all her babies and gone off with him. She had managed to complete her BA before she left, they said, but had taken up with the oil man before starting a career. The last they had heard, she was expecting again.

Years later in Mobile, at my third United Way, I had been asked to join the Quality Assurance Committee of the local office of the Alabama Department of Human Services. It's one of many such committees and task forces that a local United Way guy is asked to join. Among my duties on this committee were quarterly home visits with caseworkers to DHS clients. We were to monitor the professionalism of the DHS staff and acquaint ourselves firsthand with the often daunting challenges presented by the DHS caseload.

I'll never forget the visit to a rundown Section 8 project house in Prichard, Alabama. Prichard is the shame of Mobile, if not of the state of Alabama and the entire Gulf Coast. Half the housing units are vacant, burned-out hulks, set ablaze accidentally or otherwise by cracked-out, homeless squatters. The occupied units intersperse the charred, collapsing wrecks and the weedy vacant lots with nothing but heaving sidewalks to orphaned steps to bare foundations strewn with broken glass, used condoms, syringes, and soiled Pampers. Prichard is worse than the worst of Detroit or Chicago or New Orleans. Prichard's Alabama Village looks worse than anything in Beirut or Baghdad. It looks like the end of civilization.

On my DHS Quality Assurance home visit to Alabama Village I met the Fannie Dortch family of twelve who reside in a three-bedroom home with one bath, a small kitchen, and a living room. The packed-dirt yard was strewn with trash. Underneath the house, mangy pit bull mongrels snarled menacingly among mounds of their own flyblown feces. The wretched curs were restrained with stout chains looped around the cinder blocks supporting the house. Inside the house was even worse than outside. The floors sagged. The furniture was ripped and broken. Bare mattresses on the floor served as beds for three or more. Plastic garbage bags overflowing with sour clothing served as chests of drawers. The kitchen sink was piled high with greasy, crusty pots, pans, and dishes. The stench would gag a goat. The floors, cabinets, and countertops were alive with vermin. I didn't want to stand still for too long and damn sure wasn't gonna sit down anywhere. I felt itchy after just minutes.

The lone adult in the home was Fannie Dortch, twenty-nine, mother of all except the newborn, who was the child of Fannie's fifteen-year-old daughter, Shermekya, who (according to Fannie) was at school. Fannie was clearly not right in the head. She alternated between aggression, terror, and vacant wordless stares in her responses to the checklist of questions the cheery caseworker posed from her notes in the case file. ("I don't see any green leafy vegetables in your salad crisper. Remember what we talked about last time, about proper nutrition?" "How's Keisha doing with her asthma? Have you gotten her prescriptions filled? Where's her inhaler?"

"And Jamarcus—why isn't Jamarcus at school today? We haven't been suspended again, have we?") Children ranging in age from Shermekya's infant to eleven or twelve years old were everywhere, in all stages of undress and varying degrees of filth: crusty eyes, running noses, scabby and sore-ridden cheeks and arms, stained underclothes. Some would stare sullenly or smile shyly at the caseworker and me. Some would chase each other screaming right between us as we attempted to converse with mama in the kitchen, or crawl underfoot as the caseworker gingerly checked the refrigerator, the pantry, and the medicine cabinet.

As we drove back to the DHS office, the caseworker (a dispassionate, orderly, relentlessly professional MSW* in her eighth year with DHS) explained the Dortch family to me: all the children had different fathers, some of whom paid child support, most of whom did not. Fannie has been diagnosed as bipolar and learning disabled and did not progress past the fourth grade. The home is a frequent scene of domestic violence between the various fathers, sometimes between the older children themselves, and between Fannie and all of them. I asked why the children had not been removed from the home, adopted or parceled out to foster care, or even institutionalized. "We're about keeping families intact, flooding them with resources and supportive programming aimed at building on their strengths, not focusing on their deficits, breaking them up and scattering them to the four winds. We're all about family, for the obvious societal, moral, and legal reasons."

I nodded thoughtfully at her words, thinking, this is no family. This is a multigenerational train wreck. How many more like this are out there? No amount of state, federal, or United Way funding, or DHS casework, is going to make any difference to Fannie Dortch and her brood.

A couple years into policing, I'm dispatched to back Jack Balzer on a domestic. Balzer is an eight-year veteran, mid-thirties, with a quick, irreverent wit, lots of swaggering trash talk. ("My Balzer bigger'n yours!") He's the kind of quirky, mischievous guy who will wander around your home at a Christmas squad party, notice you have the word NOEL in decorative, wooden block letters nestled in holly on your piano top, next to the Christmas tree, and surreptitiously rearrange them to spell LEON. You discover the rearrangement and move the letters back to spell NOEL, only to find them ten minutes later changed back to LEON. You leave them

---

* A holder of a Master in Social Work degree.

unchanged. A half hour later, he confesses, snickering. You look at him blankly for some kind of explanation.

"Who the fuck is Leon?"

"Santa Claus, in the 'hood," he replies with a broad grin. "He's a dope slinger in my beat. Everybody knows him and likes him. We shouldn't forget the Leons of the world in this season of goodwill to men."

I still don't get it. But that's Balzer's off-kilter sense of humor. He's always playing the smart-ass for laughs with Sarge at roll call, always the center of outrageous storytelling at squad keggers. Sometimes when he's been drinking (which is frequent) his mouth writes checks his fists can't cash, and he gets cut down to size. One night at a squad party, Balzer got into a shouting match with our corporal, a big bear of a guy, 6 foot 3, 300 pounds, who wouldn't hurt a fly. His size made it rarely necessary for the Bear to even raise his voice. But Balzer had gotten carried away, teasing the Bear about being out of shape. They stood nose to nose shouting taunts at each other, until Balzer made an unfortunate remark about losing all respect for the Bear, at which point Bear, with one lightning-fast stiff-arm to the chest, launched Balzer airborne over a table and into a flower planter on the opposite wall. It was a sight to behold, like out of a movie, one that was described many times over at subsequent squad socials, often by Balzer and the Bear together.

One time Balzer and a few of his buddies were drinking at Legends Lounge, a low-rent bar down Dauphin Island Parkway favored by outlaw bikers and loose women. A brawl erupted, with Balzer right in the thick of it. When a heaved chair shattered the back-bar's mirror and its proud display of whiskeys, the barmaid screamed, "Somebody call the law!" Balzer looked up from the hapless brawler he was beating senseless in the midst of the fray, raised a bloodied fist, and bellowed, "I *am* the Law!"

Always in debt—largely due to his several ex-wives and hefty child support obligations—Balzer would use up all his vacation days, comp time, and sick days as soon as he earned them, to work extra jobs and do mechanic work to make ends meet. Gifted with a wrench, he always managed to keep his Harley and his truck roadworthy, as well as those of his loyal customers (mostly cops and bikers). In a scheme to get ahead of his debt once and for all, Balzer quit the department to go to Iraq to do contract policing or quasi-military work for one of those hired-gun outfits employed by the Pentagon. The promise was six figures, tax free, for a nine-month tour of duty. He returned to the department in about two months, reporting that it was totally FUBAR and the promises were bogus. The experience cost him all the time he had built up in his PD pension and did nothing to improve his bank balance.

But for all his reckless, errant ways, hare-brained schemes, and imprudence with women, Balzer was pretty 10-8 when on duty, the kind of guy you were glad to have backing you.

He didn't suffer fools or would-be heroes (often one and the same) on the job. I had a squad party at my home once, and some of the guys started teasing me about responding to calls before backup arrived. My wife and daughter were in attendance, and I didn't need them getting all worried about my taking unnecessary chances, so I poo-pooed the criticism by dishing it back, accusing my accusers of laziness or jadedness or driving like little old ladies. Balzer, who had not even been part of the conversation, exploded.

"It ain't no joking matter, and I'll tell you why. You walk into a scene you think is just a garden-variety domestic or something, you think you can handle it without backup, and all of a sudden you're outnumbered and you're fighting for your life, screaming like a girl on the radio. Not only is your own life in danger, but now you have endangered me and everybody else who's running code to get to you, risking a wreck on the way. And when I get there, it's a goddamn fight going on that probably never woulda started if *two* cops had walked up, and so I'm bustin' my knuckles on some assholes that probably woulda complied if you hadn't thought you were Dirty fuckin' Harry or something!"

There's that damn Clint Eastwood thing again, I'm thinking. All the joking and the trash talk ceased. Balzer had the floor.

"And the biggest risk is when they've already whipped your elderly ass before any of us even gets there, and *they've taken your gun!* Now me and everybody else is comin' into a whole new scene, and if one of us gets popped with your gun, *it's on you, motherfucker!*"

I can see the stricken look in the eyes of my wife and daughter to this day. It comes to me when I get the urge to respond without backup.

For all his bluster, Balzer could laugh at himself, and some of us knew Balzer was really kind of mushy on the inside. He once had asked me if I would kick in some cash for a down-on-their-luck father and son he had found sleeping in their truck one night on patrol. All they needed was a couple hundred to get the dad's toolbox out of the pawnshop and Balzer had arranged for a good construction job for him, one that could put him and his teenage son in a decent apartment.

It had sounded to me like a bullshit scam, one I'd heard (and fallen for) too many times at United Way. I had learned the hard way to leave these kinds of cases to pros. "Why don't they go to the Sally or the Waterfront Mission?" I'd asked Balzer. "They got real caseworkers, three hots and a cot, and they even have short-term cash loans for just this kinda thing."

Balzer would hear nothing of it. This was his project. The damn Sally and Rescue Mission were just flophouses for mooches, winos, and manipulators. He was a cop, not a bleeding-heart social worker. He could tell when people were bullshitting or not, and this case was the genuine article: a bona-fide workin' man, down on his luck, just trying to be strong for his son. I told Balzer I was still unconvinced, but I'd match whatever he was willing to give them. We each put in a hundred. A week later, I asked him how his father-son rescue project was going. He grew sheepish and admitted the two had skipped town the next day. "The shitheads probably scored a flask a Wild Irish Rose 'n' a fistfulla Lortabs 'n' headed for the boats in Biloxi to blow the rest of our cash," Balzer said. "I shoulda listened to you. From now on it's strictly cuffin' and stuffin' for me. I'm leavin' the social work to the professionals."

So Balzer and I forty up a couple of doors down from the domestic. "Ever been here?" he asks. I shake my head, so he briefs me. "I'm here once or twice a month. I can tell you what's going on. It's always the same. Grandma's good people. Mama Ruthie, she works in the kitchen at the Tiny Diney and supports the whole bunch. Problem is her crazy-bitch crack-whore daughter, Shaletha or Shabetha or Bathsheba, something like that, who keeps poppin' out babies and dumpin' 'em on Mama so she can be rippin' and runnin' with dope slingers and gangbangers for days at a time. Then she comes home all tweaked out and tells Mama she ain't raisin' her babies right." Balzer flicked away his half-smoked Marlboro. "You ready? Taser charged? I ain't kiddin', she's a handful when she's been flyin' about three days nonstop."

Balzer and I mount the front porch and listen to the crashing and breaking of furniture inside, the screeching of women's voices and the wailing of children. We pound on the door and yell "Police!" to no avail. I keep pounding on the metal door while Balzer steps back to his cruiser, hits the yelp siren, then repeats "Mobile Police Department, open the door now!" over his PA system. A kitchen chair crashes through a pane of the front picture window as Mama Ruth comes ducking out the front door.

"She crazier'n' ever dis time, Officer!" grandma cries, her eyes pleading. "Y'all gotta stop her 'fore she hurts one a dem babies!" Balzer and I enter the fray.

The house is a shambles, or "ramshacked" as they say in the 'hood (and in many police report narratives). A fifty-inch flat screen has been shattered. Chairs are overturned, kids' toys and treasured knicknacks scattered and broken everywhere. Grandma's framed portraits of Dr. King and an African Jesus have been ripped from the wall and impaled on the plastic handlebars of a child's tipped-over Big Wheel trike. We can hear smashing dishes and a woman's incomprehensible growling in the kitchen. Terrified toddlers are shrieking. A boy about fourteen emerges sobbing from a hallway, his contorted face a spasm of anguish. Balzer and I scoop up the younger ones in our arms and herd the others out the front door. There are five of them, all but the teenager preschoolers, all crying and trembling and clutching at us. It breaks my heart. A boy in diapers who's maybe three or four is bleeding from a pretty deep cut to his palm. One of the others has blood smears on him but apparently not his own. I wrap the wounded toddler's hand in my bandana as Balzer radios to start medical. We tell Mama Ruth to keep pressure on the hand and to make sure they all stay safe out here in the yard till the paramedics arrive. I pull out my pepper spray and Balzer unsnaps his Taser. Together we reenter the fray.

A young woman is slinging glassware and dishes against the refrigerator in the kitchen, her eyes fierce, inhuman, her voice a low moaning keen over the devastation she wreaks. She has the visage of a horror-flick fiend, a she-devil. She's outfitted in shiny, knee-high red vinyl boots with stiletto heels, torn fishnet stockings, a skintight skirt barely covering her buttocks, and a spangly T-shirt pulled tight into a knot above her bejeweled navel. The straps of her G-string ride her hips above the waist of her skirt and the T-shirt's neckline plunges so low that half her lacey red brassiere hangs out. A florid script proclaiming "hug Love" is inked across her cleavage. (The *T* that I assume precedes "hug" tatted on her left breast is obscured from view.) Platinum tresses, an outrageous contrast to her deep chocolate complexion, have become caught and twisted in the tangle of bling around her neck and have pulled the entire wig askew. Both eyelids are painted with some kind of neon sparkle; one eye has inch-long false lashes. At first

I think it's a spider perched on her brow. The other eye's lashes have, apparently, been lost in the fray.

When she spies Balzer and me, she shrieks and launches a volley of saucers at us. We duck and dodge, and they smash against the overturned kitchen furniture and walls.

"Shaletha! Stop it now!" Balzer commands.

"Get on the ground, now!" I bellow. "Don't make us put hands on you!"

She fires another plate at us, hissing, "Fffuck you honkey muhfuckas!" and makes for the backdoor through the adjoining laundry room. Balzer leaps and grabs her by the hair, and the tangled blonde mass slips completely off her head. But the ringlets knotted into the tangle of golden chains around her neck form a noose in Balzer's grasp that tightens around her throat and jerks her off her feet. With a loud thud, the house shakes and Shaletha's on her ass. We're both on her, yelling "Stop resisting! Give us your hands!"

For a nineteen-year-old girl no more than 120 pounds, Shaletha's strength surprises both of us, and she's scratching and squealing and biting like a wounded panther. Her claws slash at my throat, and she sinks her teeth into one of Balzer's hands.

"Sheee-it!" Balzer yelps. "Fuckin' bitch *bit* me!"

I blast her with the pepper spray, less than a foot from her face. The problem with pepper spray in a fight is it gets all up in everybody's face. In an instant the fight's out of all three of us, but mostly it's Shaletha who's blinded and choking for breath. Balzer and I manage to flip her and cuff her before we stagger away coughing, leaving Shaletha in a snarling writhing mess on the laundry room floor. We catch our breath in the living room, spitting and slinging stinging strings of snot from our noses.

I squint out the window and see the paramedics out in the yard with Grandma and the kids.

"You go on out and let them look at your bit hand," I sputter. "I got her."

Balzer exits through the front door and I direct my attention back to Shaletha. She's still twisting and straining against the cuffs, kicking at the washer and dryer that ring out with loud metallic clangs from her stiletto heels, but mainly she's just heaving around trying to breathe and spewing vicious, incomprehensible obscenities at me. I go grab her by the arms, hoist her to her feet, and wipe the pepper spray from her face with a dish towel.

"Settle down and the breathing won't hurt so much," I tell her. She tries to twist away from my grasp, which I tighten.

"Owww! You're hurting me!" I ignore her.

Outside, the children have become distracted by the big shiny red fire engine and the ministrations of the paramedics—all but the older boy, the teenager, who still weeps openly. It occurs to me that he's too old to be Shaletha's child; maybe a younger brother. Is he weeping out of shame, because he failed as the "man" of the house to stop his big sister? Or does he see in Shaletha his own dreaded future?

Shaletha resumes her bucking. I'm always a bit puzzled by this, from cuffed prisoners. If they break free, is their plan to run down the street with their hands behind their backs until some sympathetic thug with a cuff key or a hacksaw rescues them?

"Just settle the fuck down, Shaletha! It's over! None a this shit was even necessary!"

"You don't know!" she shrieks. "You don't feel me!" Then, "Necessary!" she sneers. "How you know what be 'necessary' to me! An' dis shit ain't over! It never gon' be over! 'Less'n I'm dead, or dey be gone! Y'on't know shit, y'ole honky muhfucka!"

We make our way to Balzer and the paramedics. Shaletha screams "Balzer! You know! You feel me, bruh! Take my babies! Take 'em away from me, please! I can't do it no mo'! Please take my babies, please, Balzer!" I'm disgusted and wishing the babies were out of earshot.

Balzer turns his attention from the paramedic swabbing antiseptic on his Shaletha-bit hand. He gets right up in Shaletha's face. Tears are still streaming from all our pepper-sprayed eyes. Shaletha's mascara has run down her cheeks in long smeary black stripes highlighted with the glittery sparkles from her lids. We're all blurry to each other, but the situation is very clear to Balzer, and he speaks for me, too.

"First off, I ain't your 'bruh,' bitch. You self-centered little cunt! I don't want your babies! Don't you get that? Why should I, or Officer Johnson, or these firefighters, or even your poor old mama have to take care of your babies? We have our own babies! We take care of 'em, like grown-up human beings are supposed to! When are you gonna grow the fuck up, Shaletha, and stop letting your gangbangin' dope boys put dick all up in you?"

Shaletha is seething, quivering with rage. But mute.

"Huh, Shaletha? Will you ever grow up? Do you ever think about anybody but yourself? Or is dope boy dick and partying all you care about, Shaletha? You are one sick, twisted fuckin' crack ho!" Balzer turns to me and mutters, "Put her in the fucking cage where she belongs." That I do and shut the door with a satisfying slam.

When I return, Balzer is apologizing to Mama Ruth for his profanity and advising her to call DHS to get the custody of the kids transferred to her, and to get a restraining order against Shaletha, and *not* to bail her out, no matter what she promises when she calls from Metro or how much she blubbers about being sorry. "Don't even accept her calls," Balzer instructs, and explains that Shaletha will be jailed for DV assault, child endangerment/neglect, resisting arrest, and assaulting a police officer. Mama Ruth is so apologetic for Shaletha's behavior and grateful for Balzer's coarse, rough compassion, I feel like weeping.

I want to suggest to Mama Ruth that she put the kids up for adoption, give them a chance at a decent life. But I know it'll fall on deaf ears, or likely offend her. And worse, I know that even if she chose adoption as the best option, DHS would put the kids through an endless bureaucratic shuffle of paper and temporary placements in foster homes (where the caregivers are indifferent at best) until they age-out of the optimum adoptable years and begin bouncing between juvenile detention and the state reform school, eventually becoming no more than crime or death statistics.

In the back of my mind is the small whisper "There, but for the grace of God . . . ," but I disregard it. I just don't have the heart to tell her (or Balzer) that the bureaucratic, brainless, heartless twin threshers of Human Services and Justice doom Mama Ruth's grandbabies to a destiny of unrelenting, mind-grinding, soul-slaying misery, to be repeated generation after generation.

Several weeks later, Nancy and I are at a small dinner gathering of the smart set—people whose acquaintances I had made in my previous life and who (largely for Nancy's sake, I figure) had not yet dropped us from their social rosters.

The event is hosted by the manager of a German petrochemical plant down Rangeline Road and his wife. We know Heinz and Ilse Schultz from serving on the symphony board together. At the party I overhear Nancy speaking with Heinz.

"So Heinz, what do you think of my husband's new career?"

I listen closely (though surreptitiously) and brace myself, knowing Heinz's answer will be ammo for Nancy in some future argument between us. Being of German descent herself, Nancy admires the often-bruising candor of Germanic opinion. Heinz takes a moment to consider his response.

"Only in America is it possible," he says, with a gee-whiz kind of tone. "Only in America is it possible for one to make such a change, to reinvent oneself so completely. You know, I think it's just great! It's a noble thing your husband chooses to do. I admire him for it."

Whoa! Take that, Nancy! I'm putting that nugget in my own clip.

The gathering comprises educators, a psychologist, a journalist, a federal administrator, an investment broker, a civil litigator, a medical researcher, and a geneticist—professional, learned, progressive thinkers all. After dinner, while we're all still gathered at the table, the question is posed to me: Since your, er, shall we say, unorthodox (chuckle) career change, Mark, you've sort of seen the world from both sides now, from the social work view and now from the rather, um, rough-and-tumble perspective (heh, heh, har, har) of law enforcement; how have your opinions changed (if indeed they have) vis-à-vis social problems and solutions?

For the first time in a long while, I have the floor, and I'm not at a loss for words. I pause, for effect. "Great question! One I've given some thought to, actually, because I do sense some subtle changes in me." Another momentary pause. Knowing looks, titters around the table, sympathetic glances from the women to Nancy. "A career cop I know told me early on, 'Us cops have the rare privilege of confronting evil, face to face, and the ability to do something about it.' That was his word: privilege. That really struck me. He wasn't talking about campaigning to raise money or taxes to start more programs, or making speeches, or rallying and marching to 'stop the violence.' He was talking about doing something tangible, right now. Cops have the unique ability—the duty—to act. To act *at once*, in the face of evil: to stop it, contain it, even eliminate it, destroy it, if necessary. It's really an awesome privilege.

"But confronting pure, living, coldhearted, dead-eyed evil is rare, even for cops. What really gets to me is what we encounter way more often, what some of us call feral youth. Kids, born to older kids, all on drugs, raising themselves with no responsible adult supervision or example, with absolutely no sense of right and wrong, never even heard of the golden rule, absolutely no direction, discipline, ambition, or integrity, utterly bereft of any moral sense. They don't go to church, or school, or to any kind of job. They're not in Scouting, or the Boys & Girls Club, or on the football team. They steal from each other, abuse and assault and kill each other, often as not their own flesh and blood: mothers, brothers, cousins, baby-mamas, babies, uncles, grandmas. They're not evil, really. They're barely sentient or capable of reason or abstract thought. They're animals. Not even domesticated. Feral. And they're armed. I arrest twelve- and thirteen-year-olds with Glocks in their pockets, over and over. The same ones, from the same families—but not 'families' like anything any of us know. I've put three generations, all related, into Metro at the same time, more than once.

"So the solution has become real clear to me, for these litters of feral youth running our streets: adoption or foster care. We need to break up these destructive, chronic clusters of criminal parasites. They're not really families—there's no social unit to save. Adopt 'em out to real families ideally, though that seems to be out of fashion these days.

"For the life of me I don't know why. Some of you know, I'm a bastard, myself. A love child, put up for adoption as an infant. There was too much stigma back in the fifties for unmarried girls to keep their kids. Today, the middle schools have special parenting classes for thirteen-year-olds! Where's the shame? We need to put the stigma back on pregnant girls and snatch their little bastards up for adoption.

"And if there aren't enough adopting families, we build orphanages. Run by professionals, usually affiliated with churches. They're a thing of the past, too, because it's fashionable to be a single mother, and Uncle Sam subsidizes it. We build either more orphanages or more prisons."

I'm undeterred by the open mouths and wide eyes around the table. I let the other shoe drop: "That's the treatment. But to break the cycle, to prevent it, we should require monthly drug screenings and contraceptive injections as a qualifying condition for any and all government or charitable aid.

"There you have it: state-mandated adoption, orphanages, drug testing, sterilization."

Silence.

I can talk a good game, despite private doubts. Besides, being the turd in the punch bowl can be fun, when your career isn't threatened.

7

My Parents *Never* Did *That!*

"You bastard!"
"Yessir, in my case, an accident of birth. But you, sir, you're a self-made man."
—Lee Marvin's reply to Lee J. Cobb in *The Professionals*

Ernie and I and the others huddled in our tent, our flashlights focused on the cosmic wonders revealed in Ernie's older brother's smuggled copy of the holy grail. These amazing women, with their boobs exposed, smiled shamelessly, alluringly at us from the dog-eared pages of the *Playboy* magazine. We were maybe eleven or twelve years old, on the annual Boy Scout Troop 68 Spring Camporee, at Round Spring in the Ozarks.

The glossy anatomical catalog naturally led to a discussion of "the birds and the bees," or "the facts of life": the Talk that we were all awaiting from our fathers, the one about how babies are made. We knew it had something to do with our penises and the mysterious (and unseen) private parts of the female of the species. For well over a year now, about the time since we'd all graduated from Cub Scouts to Boy Scouts, what was to be revealed to us in that imminent Talk was a matter of relentless speculation and conjecture, hopes and fears, discussed and imagined in minute detail every time we got together for a troop activity. Occasional reporting back from second- and thirdhand sources—usually somebody's friend's older brother or cousin, who'd received the Talk already—provided us with tantalizing, shocking, unbelievable details.

After our meticulous examination of female anatomy as revealed in *Playboy*, the mystery (and the sheer *power* of the mystery) of Woman struck awe and terror into my heart. Simple images, poses, skin, triggered murky thoughts that caused alarming physical stirrings and thickenings over which I had no control. What was going on?

Ernie and I retired to our own tent, and that's when Ernie confided that he had discovered the Facts of Life in a book he had found hidden away in his older brother Chip's closet. This didn't have pictures, like *Playboy*—it was like a textbook, and it had diagrams. He had committed a key one to memory and re-created it for me. He drew a picture of a female from the waist down (actually, from the boobs down) and a male from the waist down. With arrows, he indicated what went where. I was horrified and demanded to see the original text. Ernie swore this is what he had seen in Chip's textbook.

"Chip would beat me up if he looked in his closet and the book was gone!" Ernie said. "There's no way I could sneak it out without him finding out! But I'm tellin' ya, this is what it shows! I memorized it! *This* is what happens. Our parents did this to have us!"

I bowed up. My hands balled into fists, ready to go to blows with my best friend.

"Not *my* parents! They *never* did that!" I declared.

"Everybody's parents do this! Mine, yours—it's how the sperm gets to the egg! It's in the book! And they do it sometimes even if they don't want babies!"

"What? *Why?*"

"Because it feels good!" Ernie explained, as if it made perfect sense to him. "There's 'pleasure,' the book said."

"I don't care *how* good something feels, it's not good enough to do *that!* My parents *never* did *that!*"

"Yes they did," Ernie declared, assured, crossing his arms, triumphant. "Or else how did you get born?"

He thought he had me there. But he didn't know what I knew. I was "special." My own parents had told me this, as long as I could remember. I had been "chosen" by them. At a hospital. I told Ernie so.

"But . . . well . . . ," Ernie pondered, stammered. He didn't question my account of my origins, but for him it still didn't explain everything. "But how did you get to the hospital?"

This I had never considered. Never asked. Never been told. I was surprised at my own lack of curiosity and was utterly stumped by Ernie's question.

There had to be an explanation. My mind raced. I was losing credibility with Ernie as the seconds passed. Finally, I hit upon it. Of course!

I shook my head as if Ernie was just an imbecile.

"I just came straight down from heaven. I'm *adopted*."

Ernie considered this. "Oh." He climbed onto his cot, saying no more. We switched off our flashlights. Ernie seemed to buy it.

But I had my doubts.

By the end of the next day, most of the guys in the troop had learned that I was special. Chosen. *Adopted*. Ernie may have bought it, but there were some older kids who knew better. One of them, Stephen Huntsinger, informed me of this. Huntsinger was fifteen and smoked cigarettes on our campouts. Purloined Chesterfields from his father. He acted like a hood and easily intimidated—if not outright bullied—us younger scouts.

Huntsinger called me over to the older guys' campfire. This could be considered an honor, or a trial by fire. I steeled myself for the latter.

"So you're adopted, eh Mark?" Huntsinger said with a menacing smile.

"Uh-huh."

"Do you know what that means, Mark?" His smile broadened, as he faced his audience of fourteen- to seventeen-year-olds.

"Y-yeah," I said. "'Course I know what it means. My parents told me."

"Yeah, we heard what your parents told you, didn't we, guys?" The older guys all smiled conspiratorially, and I braced myself, for I knew not what. "But we're gonna tell you the Truth." He paused for effect, again taking in his audience, building anticipation. "Adopted means you're a bastard."

My face must have indicated confusion. The audience snickered. Huntsinger elaborated.

"It means your mama was a *whore*."

I had heard that word before, applied to older girls at school, who had already "developed" (had budding breasts) and were known to have on occasion allowed one or more boys to look at them, or—in one alleged account—*touch them*. But I still wasn't clear on how that applied to adoption, or my mama.

Judging from the laughter of the audience, I realized that this was evidently meant to be an insult of some kind.

"You don't know anything, Huntsinger! Just go to hell!" I declared, affecting a pathetic swagger as I quickly walked away from the guffaws of the onlookers.

When I returned home from the Spring Camporee, the first thing I did was to ask my parents what a bastard is. My dad looked angry, my mother sad. They asked where I'd heard it, and why I wanted to know.

"Steve Huntsinger says adopted means I'm a bastard, and—" I paused, considered sparing them the rest, then decided to go ahead and unload it. "And it means my mama's a whore."

Their mouths dropped. Mama hugged me, and I think she was crying a little. They composed themselves, then told me the rest of the story, the part that preceded choosing me at the hospital.

There had been another mama and daddy, they said. Before us. But the other mama and daddy were poor and couldn't afford to pay for everything a baby needs. And they loved me and didn't want me to be hungry or cold or sad, so they decided the best thing for me was to give me to another mama and daddy who could afford a baby but couldn't have one of their own. They were very sad to give me away, but they loved me so much they did what was right for me, even though it made them sad. And of course, it made us very, very happy. So don't pay any attention to those boys and their bad words. Your mama was not a whore and you are not a bastard, and we don't want to hear you use those words ever again.

I was immensely relieved that this exempted my mama and daddy from having engaged in that repulsive act that Ernie had diagrammed for me. But a little wiggling worm of wonder and worry was now implanted deep in my heart, and it continued to wiggle and grow for the next two decades: who were those other parents?

"I don't think you're a loser, Mark. Or an outlaw. Or even an alcoholic," Dr. Cohen said, with soothing tones of assurance. I was eighteen and seeing the psychiatrist weekly. In the past year I had transformed from the high school senior Academic Honor Roll, Eagle Scout, Presbyterian Deacon, and Football Letterman to the freshman on academic and disciplinary probation, who had been arrested twice for brawling and disorderly behavior and was drunk almost daily.

From Wally Cleaver to Eddie Haskell, and worse. From Dr. Jekyll to Mr. Hyde. I was in my second semester at the University of Colorado, Boulder.

I had disappointed my parents' hopes for me of an Ivy League education by picking Boulder. I told them it was because of the architecture school there and the outdoor opportunities in the Rockies. But it was really to get as far away from St. Louis as my parents would allow. Dad had vetoed anything in California.

And it was for the Coors. The drinking age for beer was eighteen in Colorado.

Which is what finally brought me to Dr. Cohen, who had accepted my referral from the university's Student Health Center.

"This is nothing more than identity confusion, Mark. You told me in our first meeting that you're adopted. 'I'm a real bastard' is the way you put it, remember? Your first words at our first meeting. And you told me the little you know from asking your parents about your biological parents: 'My father was a Marine, and my mother was one of the whores he knocked up on his way to Korea,' you said. Then you admitted your mother was really a college freshman at some fancy East Coast college for women. She's Presbyterian and an accomplished pianist. And that you even found out that your original name wasn't Mark Johnson. It was Russell Culkin, wasn't it?

"All these episodes, these misadventures you've been having since you left home for college, are nothing unusual, except maybe by degree in your case. But all freshmen, or any young adult who moves out of his parents' home, whether he goes to college, or joins the navy, or gets a job, everybody goes through a process of individuation, whereby they separate from their parents and become their own persons. It's normal for the process to be a little scary, and a little painful, and there are lots of missteps, but everybody goes through it."

"Yeah, but nobody I know has dumped his high school girlfriend, fought with cops, and almost got kicked out of school in just a semester and a half. And nobody drinks like me."

"Exactly," Dr. Cohen said. He was unflappable. Calmest grown-up I'd ever met, even when I had described to him the depths of my depravity. "But how many of your friends are adopted? See, I think you've known for a while that what pleases Mr. and Mrs. Johnson doesn't necessarily feel right for Mark Johnson, to say nothing of how it might feel for Russell Culkin—whoever he is, or was. Does that make sense to you?"

I nodded.

"I think all of your uncharacteristic behaviors are just a kind of research, it's how you are trying out different ways of being, seeing what fits best. Unfortunately, some of the personalities you've tried on are not healthy or productive ones. You've been taking a sort of trial and error, experimental approach, and I don't think it's getting you any closer to who you really are, do you, Mark? In fact I think you'd agree it's getting you farther away."

I nodded again.

"Let me suggest a more effective way of solving the Mark/Russell riddle: instead of this sort of random, sometimes dangerous experimentation, why don't you seek out the truth? Go directly to the source?"

"The records are sealed, if you're talking about the original parents."

"They can be found and opened," Dr. Cohen asserted. "Russell Culkin's roots can be discovered and examined, and your questions, your doubts and fears, can be put to rest, and then you won't need to wonder and to try on all these other personalities. You can just be you."

Thus began my first taste of detective work.

Being an unschooled amateur, and utterly without resources, I was clueless about how to proceed. I asked my parents what it would take to find out the identities of my biological parents. As usual, my dad got mad and mom got sad.

"What do you want to know for? The records are sealed," Dad reminded me. "But even if they weren't, there's nothing good that would come from it. Who put this idea in your head? I bet it was some sociology professor." (Dad had little regard for most of my elective courses.)

"Dr. Cohen. He said he thought it would help."

"I shoulda known!" Dad said, shaking his head. He was building up a good rage, though he'd always been pretty adept at keeping it from blowing his cool. "Margaret, I don't know why we're paying for that psychology business. He's not even Christian! We don't know anything about his credentials."

"Why does Dr. Cohen think it would help?" Mom asked, ignoring Dad's rant, her moist eyes focused on me.

I explained to them about "individuation" and getting questions about identity resolved.

Dad walked off in disgust.

"We've told you everything we know, and your father's right about the records being sealed."

I asked Mom if she could just show me any paperwork they might have, like my birth certificate, or any legal adoption papers. She went to the filing cabinet and brought out a folder full of yellowed papers that they had showed me once before. "The name was a mistake," she explained, pulling out the certificate of adoption. "They were supposed to put Mark Johnson, our name for you, there," she said, pointing to a blank on the form that had the words "Russell Culkin, white male infant, age 6 weeks" typed in. "The agency said we could have the adoption certificate amended, but since they got it right on the birth certificate, we just never bothered. We were so excited to bring you home!"

"What 'agency'? I always thought you got me at a hospital. You said I was born at Tulane Hospital."

"You were. But before the delivery, the girls usually stay at a home for expecting mothers. And the home arranges the adoption. It was called The Willows. Our doctor recommended it to us. He said it had an excellent reputation and was known nationally for good placements. But I think it's been closed for years. I don't remember what I heard about why it went out of business. There wasn't any trouble or scandal, but I do recall hearing about its not being around anymore. So as your father said, even if legally somehow the records could be unsealed, which they told us could never happen, I'm not sure you could even find the records, with The Willows closed for so long. I'm not sure you had even started kindergarten when I heard it closed, it's been that long."

"Well, do you know anything about the name? Culkin? Was that her name, or his?"

"There's no way of telling, and what damn difference would it make if you knew?" snapped Dad. He had returned in time to hear my question, and his rage had simmered to a peevish disdain. I noticed he had poured himself a drink, although it was only midafternoon.

"Stan!" Mom scolded. "There's no need for that language!"

"I just don't see the point of him runnin' off down some rabbit hole that's not gonna lead him anywhere, Margaret! What he needs to do is buckle down to his studies!" He turned to me. "You need to just straighten up, get on an even keel. You're not in college to 'discover yourself.' Or to learn how to drink beer! You're there to get an education so you can start a career.

This is nothing but a distraction from your studies, a waste of time! And your time is running out, do you understand me? The school's about had it with you, and we're about out of patience, too. Do you understand?"

"Yes."

"Yes what?"

"Yes, sir."

"Stan! I don't see what harm if Dr. Cohen thinks it could help."

"Margaret, don't make me spell it out," Dad said, his eyes flashing again. "You know, and I know, he'll never find out. And you also know that if he did, it likely would not be good. This matter is settled." He then turned back to me, gravely serious. "Agreed?"

"Yes, sir."

When I got back to school I contacted a free lawyer at Boulder Legal Services, who told me that I would need to hire an attorney in New Orleans, and that I would need to have a compelling medical reason on which to base a legal argument for a court order to open the records containing the identifying information about the relinquishing biological parents.

"I think my shrink would certify that my 'compelling medical reason' would be lunacy, likely of genetic origin," I said, testily.

The legal aid lawyer was unfazed. That might suffice, he said, but with the placement agency closed for so long, chances were slim I'd be able to locate the records, even with a court order to open them. And in the unlikely event that the records could be found, and opened, he continued, the father's name would probably not be included, and the mother's name would most likely be a maiden name that would have changed over the years due to marriage. Rather than legal action, he said, I might want to consider hiring a private detective. But, he cautioned, that could easily be even more expensive than hiring an attorney, adding (with a chuckle) it's even harder to find an honest, reliable detective than an honest, reliable lawyer.

"So Mr. Johnson," he summarized, "I don't want to discourage you, but I don't want to give you false hope, either. You just need to recognize the fact that the whole enterprise could be quite costly and time consuming, with little prospect of success."

It was a no-brainer. I would simply take the matter into my own hands.

8

Runnin' Code

By grace alone are ye saved, not works, lest any man should boast.
—Ephesians 2:8, 9

Some of the best fun you can have as a cop is driving fast, lights ablaze and sirens yelping. Of course it's fun just to drive fast as a civilian in, say, the family Caravan, but it's also a little nerve wracking because of maybe getting a big fat speeding ticket, or causing a wreck. But driving fast as a cop is really nothing at all like driving fast as a civilian, for a number of reasons. Sure, it's scary, too, as a cop, because you can get into wrecks, and those wrecks can be your fault and can really fuck up your career (to say nothing of your health or that of the people you collide with). In fact, cops get into lots of wrecks. Compared to the civilian population, my guess is most cops routinely drive 20 to 25 miles per hour faster (and civilians routinely drive 10 to 15 over the limit) and cops probably wreck way more often than civilians. I've had more than my share. More cops are injured or killed in car wrecks than any other way, on or off the job.

But as a cop you don't have to worry about speeding tickets, or points on your license, or hikes to your insurance premiums, which takes a lot of the dread out of driving fast, leaving mostly just exhilaration. And even without my lights or siren on, it's always a pleasure to see the traffic in front of me brake and peel off, parting like the Red Sea for Moses, as I cruise down the interstate on my way to, oh, anywhere: to a nuisance dog-barking call, or to get a cup of coffee and piece of pie at Denny's, or to take a dump at the precinct.

The thing is, the tension and worry of civilian speeding that is absent from cop speeding is often replaced by chest-pounding adrenaline mixed with a series of terror jolts, when the cop speeding is legitimate and purposeful, as in a hot call or a vehicle pursuit. The sheer volume of drivers who don't hear or see an emergency vehicle, or don't know that they're supposed to yield, or get confused and unpredictable and yield first to the left and then to the right, or just don't give a damn at all, produces little tingling nanoseconds of shock several times a minute. You swerve and screech and slam the brake to the floor spilling all your gear everywhere because of some oblivious idiot, then watch the bad guy pull away. You want to jump out and choke the jerk who made you lose visual of the bad guy, and you'll be damned if you radio that you've lost visual because your chase will be canceled, so you shake your fist at granny in her Studebaker, put the pedal to the floor and your Crown Vic seems to growl and rear back and *leap* anew into pursuit, your wheels smoking and squealing, and as the terror jolt subsides, you've got a fresh boost of fury powering you through rush-hour-choked intersections, scanning for the bad guy and hoping a pedestrian doesn't step out into the crosswalk.

If you're lucky, though, your hot call or your chase will be in the dead of night when the streets are empty and headlights indicate cross traffic a block away. You scream down Springhill Avenue under the canopy of live oaks, the fine old mansions blurring past you on both sides, you and your buddies going 90 behind some desperate schmuck dumping dope and guns out his window, and you know this will end when he either wrecks or bails, and you're hoping he bails so you can jump out and run him down and maybe tase him as he tries to clear a fence. There's nothing like it.

My first and perhaps most memorable such chase was with ol' Portly Porter, my first FTO. He may have been a pedantic blowhard at times, but in a car chase he had NASCAR skills. One night well past midnight we found ourselves behind a stolen vehicle. "Three-thirty-seven, we got a gold Monte Carlo, tag 2B-boy, 4-2, A-Adam, 6-1, refusing to stop, tag comes back stolen." Porter lights him up. The chase is on. But after just a few blocks, our quarry manages to slip across some railroad tracks seconds before a freight train blocks our path. Before I can even tell Dispatch that we have lost visual due to the train, Porter jerks us 90 degrees to the left and stomps the gas. We're paralleling the train and I'm thinking to myself, surely he doesn't think he can get ahead of it at the next crossing, but when we make another 90-degree turn to the right in a four-wheel drift, I brace myself for impact until, to my shock and relief, we dip into an underpass and glide beneath a trestle as the lumbering freight groans and clanks overhead. Porter hardly lets off the gas as he cranks another hard right, rockets us back a block to our original route, and slices the corner by bouncing us to the left through a gas station's parking lot, and we're back in the chase in time to catch a glimpse of our fleeing felon's taillights. Our suspect is turning east onto Springhill Avenue's wide five lanes and blazes his way toward downtown.

Porter calmly advises Dispatch that we're still in pursuit, now eastbound on Springhill approaching Broad, approximate speeds 75. I steal a glimpse of the speedometer and it's well to the right of 90. Other units are on Broad, approaching its intersection with Springhill. When our thug spies the flashing blues of the other units on Broad, he spins a 180 and comes screaming back at us. Not just in our direction, but *aiming right at us*. Porter doesn't brake, doesn't swerve. Once again I'm bracing for impact, arms covering my head. The gap is closing fast for a horrific head-on when the bad guy loses his nerve at the last second and jerks it to the left. He blows by in a blur just inches from my door as Porter expertly steers us between two oncoming units in pursuit of the bad guy. The chase ends when Mr. Car Thief, who had oversteered his last-second break from the head-on, jumps a curb and wraps his headlights around the trunk of a huge old live oak. Much laughter at my expense was enjoyed around the check-off desk at shift change, as Porter reenacted my cringes and wide-eyed terror.

A good chase is even more exhilarating when you know your bad guy has active warrants for really serious crimes, wrecks, and then bails out on foot. (Our train-dodging, high-speed chicken-match loser was too stunned to run.) When they jump out on foot, you know they're really desperate, and they may be armed as well as dangerous, but the adrenaline goes through the roof and you know you have free reign to pull out all the stops and rain all kinds of hurt down on them because they've got it coming and it's your job (and your *privilege*) to bring them to justice. The danger and risk, if you think about it at all, make it all the more exhilarating. But you probably don't even think about it. You just want to be in on it, you want to get there before they're cuffed or dead and it's all over.

Those are the chases you live for. But most of them aren't that pure. Most of them are complicated with uncertain justification or dangerous conditions or both. If it's dark and rainy, or you're nearing a school zone in midafternoon, or the fleeing suspect has children in his car, it's probably not worth a high-speed chase, especially if you only lit him up for an expired tag or failure to signal, in the first place. You'll get your chase canceled by most sergeants, and for good reason. Unless of course you minimize the speeds and the risky conditions when you go over the radio with the pursuit. But if you do that, and then you wreck, or run over some kid on a bike, you'll have to live with that for the rest of your life.

One spring morning I'm sitting at a Circle K sipping a cup of coffee and finishing up a report when a bounty hunter comes up to my patrol car window and says he's just seen a bail jumper he's been hunting down the road at the Superfoods grocery. He says the guy has active warrants for drugs and domestics and other felony warrants in next-door Baldwin County, describes the car the guy's in, and says he'd appreciate some help since his fugitive has a companion and he doesn't want to be outnumbered. Off we go, the skip tracer leading the way, but I vaguely recollect something in the General Orders forbidding us from getting involved in the "fugitive recovery" operations of bail bondsmen. I call Sarge on my cell and tell him what I'm doing, and he says I shouldn't be doing it because we can't get all tangled up in bounty hunter bullshit.

We roll into the parking lot and the bounty hunter points to the car. One guy's in the driver's seat and his buddy is coming out of the Superfoods with a grocery bag and opening the passenger door. I figure I better roll up beside the bounty hunter and tell him I've been dispatched to another call and can't help him, but Bad Guy sees my blue and white and slams it in reverse, the open passenger door sweeping his buddy off his feet and directly into my approach path. I nearly run the guy over before I jerk into reverse, do a hard J-hook, and the chase is on. Without thinking I hit the lights and the siren and start calling my chase, describing location, direction of travel, the vehicle and its tag number, and what little description of the driver that I could glimpse. We're northbound on five-lane Dauphin Island Parkway from the Superfoods, and my fugitive is pulling away, weaving in and out of traffic, running mostly in the center turn lane at about 70 (which I lowball at "about 50") in a 40 zone, and I don't know who he is, have no probable cause, don't really know for sure if he's even got active warrants, and I'm doing all this based on unconfirmed—and probably unreliable—information from a gray-area operative on the fringes of the justice system with whom I'm forbidden to cooperate by my own General Orders—no doubt to prevent exactly this kind of circumstance. Uh-oh.

Dispatch asks me the reason for the pursuit. I got none (but, dammit, he's running from me for some reason!) and I sure don't want to quit. He must be a desperado to've burned out of the Superfoods lot with his door flapping like that. I know Sarge knows what's going on 'cause I just told him on my cell phone. The radio code for telephone traffic is 10-21. In response to Dispatch's query about the reason for the pursuit, I say, "Previous 21, per 1Sam3." I'm figuring Sarge will cancel me, but it doesn't happen right away so I fill the radio with location, direction, and speed updates. Nobody cancels me, and I'm starting to gain on him, but he blows right through the red light at Old Military Road, and I've gotta slow down to avoid T-boning some idiot who doesn't hear my siren or see my blue strobes (or doesn't care), and by the time I clear the intersection the bad guy's cresting the I-10 overpass and I have no visual.

I should report that I've lost visual, but I'm hoping I can make the crest of the overpass in time to get a glimpse of him, so I step on it and keep mum on the radio. Still no cancellation, and other units crowd the radio traffic to report they're heading my way and I'm hoping somebody else will see him before he disappears and the chase is stopped.

I top the overpass in time to see Bad Guy try to make a 90-degree right turn onto Delta Street and wrap himself around a telephone pole at 70 miles an hour. It's a doozy. I report the location of the wreck and slow down, thanking God that he didn't hit another car or one of several pedestrians in the parking lot of the Dollar General, just steps away from the wreck. I'm about to tell Dispatch to start medical because the guy's gotta be all mangled up inside when, Shit! He climbs out of the steaming twisted hulk and begins limping off around the corner of the Dollar General. I can't believe it.

"Subject has bailed, running eastbound on Maryvale."

Now my heart's really pounding and I'm like a 'coon hound with the scent of blood. I stomp down and round the corner of Maryvale in a four-wheel drift just in time to see the guy disappear down the alley behind the Dollar General. I try to make the turn into the alley with every intention of running the shitbag over, but it's just too tight a turn at my speed and I take out about thirty feet of wooden fence between the alley and a fire station. The Crown Vic stalls. I can't back up and renegotiate the turn. I can't even open the goddamn door because the collision has jammed my front left quarter panel back into my door. I yell into the radio that I've just had a 1-car signal 7 with the damn fire station fence and I climb over my center console and out the passenger side door just as the asshole rounds the corner at the south end of the alley and disappears.

Now I'm really pissed, and I know I'm in deep shit. I've caused one wreck with a telephone pole, damaged and disabled my own cruiser, destroyed the Fire Department's fence, and the sumbitch is about to get away. I'm blind with rage and dread and adrenaline, and I'm running after this asshole whom I have no probable cause to pursue and don't know who he is or why he's running, all because I took the bait of a damn "fugitive recovery agent." I'm screwed and I know it, but at least I can catch this dickhead and make him suffer along with me. I round the corner at the end of the alley in time to see him running east through a backyard at Delta and Brook. He either is starting to get winded or is hurting from his wreck, or both. He slows and I get within Taser range and I really want to give this bastard the electric ride, but he drops to his knees and puts his hands up. I gallop up behind him and plant a boot in his back and he hits the ground and I put a knee between his shoulder blades and cuff him.

Whew. I'm praying he's really got warrants as I search his pockets and pull out a fist-size bag of cocaine. Without warrants there's no probable cause and even the dope does me no good—it's merely "the fruit of the poison tree" and I can't even make a possession case on him.

Sarge arrives just as the bail bondsman does, too. Bail bondsman's all excited, saying, "Great job, Officer!" and I give him a "Get lost, mother-fucker" glare, which he gets, and he melts away into the gathering crowd. "Sorry, Sarge. I screwed up bigtime, I know. It all just sorta got on a roll, y'know?"

Sarge, to my amazement, dismisses my whining. "What you said on the radio about the reason for the pursuit? Something about a 21?"

"Yeah, I said 'previous 21, per 1Sam3.' I didn't mean to get you all caught up in this mess, too. I was referring to the 21 with you on my cell, right before all this shit started."

"No you weren't," Sarge says, a stern look on his face. "You were referring to a previous *signal* 21, right? A *concerned citizen* tipped you to a guy with warrants for dope and a previous assault. *Signal* 21, not 10-21." He put a firm grip on my shoulder and waited for me to comprehend.

"Yes sir!" I reply. It's nu'n but grace, pure and simple.

The following week at roll call I was surprised to receive the following Commander's Citation, signed by Sarge, and my lieutenant, and my captain:

"On October 14, 2006, a citizen advised you that a subject wanted on outstanding warrants was in a nearby parking lot. You located the wanted subject in the parking lot and as you approached he sped off in a vehicle leading you and other officers on a pursuit. Being tenacious and persistent, you pursued the subject in your patrol car until he abandoned his car and fled. You then chased the subject on foot, eventually apprehending him. The subject was not only wanted on two felony warrants for narcotics, he was also in possession of narcotics at the time of his arrest. Further investigation determined he was an unregistered sex offender.

"Your dedication to the police profession removed this criminal from the streets of Mobile. Your actions, which led to the arrest of this subject, are a credit to you and bring great honor to the Mobile Police Department. Therefore, your supervisors and I proudly present you this Commander's Citation for a job well done."

The squad whooped and hollered and made lots of wisecracks about my driving like a senior citizen, endangering the public, and the mess I'd made of my car and the fire station's fence.

"In regard to that matter," Sarge said, interrupting the chatter, "I have a performance observation for you as well." Mercifully, he didn't read that one aloud, although most of the squad seemed to regard the performance observation as the real badge of honor. It reads:

"On October 14, 2006, you were involved in a traffic accident while operating your assigned vehicle. A subsequent investigation determined the cause of the accident was driver not in control. This is your second at fault accident within a 2-year period. Your actions placed you in violation of Rule 26.30.05 of the Mobile Police Department General Orders.

"While you are to be commended for your actions in the apprehension of a felon, you cannot overlook your responsibility to operate your vehicle in a manner that does not endanger yourself or the citizens of Mobile. While this accident only resulted in property damage (in the amount of $1,674.00) your failure to maintain control of your vehicle could have resulted in far greater consequences. While in the pursuit of a suspect or vehicle you must maintain your situational awareness, constantly scanning for danger and innocent bystanders."

Sometimes, at least in the Police Department, you can have it both ways.

9

A Pot to Piss In

Love makes your soul crawl out from its hiding place.
— Zora Neale Hurston

. . . Or into it
—Addendum mine.

I'm on the way to Metro with a domestic-violence offender in my cage.
He's a raging bully who had been threatening the mother of his children
with a foot-long kitchen knife (in the kids' presence) because she had "disrespected" him. While my backup partner had written up the specifics of the
incident, I had offered the still-trembling victim the opportunity to accept
or decline immediate escort to "the beat-up wives place" as my sponsor
Red referred to Penelope House, a United Way agency providing secret and
secure housing for victims of domestic violence (per MPD protocol for DV
calls). She declined. I had then, on my own initiative, taken the opportunity to offer the offender a referral to Lifelines, a United Way agency that
offers anger management and family counseling on a sliding-fee scale. He
also declined. Or rather, made no response but to stare wordlessly, fixing
me with a look of incredulity that slowly morphed into palpable contempt.

Now from the cage behind me, I hear a low snarl, a warning.

"You best be watchin' your back when I bond out. A man could follow
you home from work some night, follow you right up into your driveway,
and slit your throat befo' you even get outta your car, befo' you even see it
comin'. Uh-huh, be easy to do. And then a man could go knock on your
door, call out all your family—your wife, alla your chilluns—so they could

watch you bleed to death, right there in y'own driveway. Yeah, a man could do dat. It'd be real easy."

"Just to clarify: is that a threat?"

"Hell, ain't no threat. It's a promise," he says.

"Well, that's not very nice."

There comes no retort to my rapier-like repartee, and we continue to Metro in blessed silence.

Signal 39—domestic violence: our most frequent type of call. I used to get all psyched up when I got dispatched to one, because it seemed like it would be a great opportunity to be heroic. There would actually be a damsel in distress at my destination, and I could arrive like a blue knight in a shiny squad car, eradicate the brute, and save the day for the ever-grateful fair maiden and her frightened, innocent cherubs. I would almost always run code to the call, my imagination conjuring hysterical toddlers trying to pull a savage off their bloodied mother. The cavalier attitude toward domestics of my more experienced squad mates baffled and bothered me. Far from getting excited and hurrying to a domestic, most would groan. Some seemed to dawdle. Though we were trained—and ordered—to never enter a scene before our backup arrived, especially a domestic with "disorderly background, both parties still on scene," I could not simply sit a block away from the mayhem awaiting the arrival of a pokey partner. I had to ride to the rescue, and if backup was slow to arrive, then let the chips fall, I figured.

The problem, of course, is that it almost never plays out the way I imagine it while speeding to the scene. Domestics are usually messy, illogical, chaotic, and crowded with multiple parties, twisted in their own ways with alcohol, drugs, jealousy, and rage, who are shouting their versions of who should be arrested and why. An extremely high-bullshit level distinguishes most domestics. The arrival of police is often unwelcome by the supposed victim, who may have simply made the call hoping the aggressor would get scared, stop the beating, and flee, but whom the caller has absolutely no desire to see actually arrested. Such callers often turn on police as soon as we put hands on the boyfriend/baby-daddy/husband, will deny ever making the call, or say it's really all their own fault, or actually become combative with police. Or the caller may not be the victim but instead one of the other parties on the scene, whose motives are unclear and whose allegiances are uncertain and changing depending on what stories are being shouted to police by whom. These might be adult children of the disputing parties, or parents, aunts, or uncles of either side, or current or previous boyfriends or girlfriends, or neighbors from the next apartment. There are multiple accounts of what happened, who should go to jail, who saw what, and who's lying. Physical evidence—injuries, blood, bruises—is often ambiguous, mutual, subtle, faked, self-inflicted, denied, or nonexistent. A woman with a black eye and a fat lip will tell us she's clumsy and walked into a door. A man will have scratches, a ripped shirt, and bite marks on him that a "witness" swears he did to himself just before our arrival. Children—usually honest witnesses—are often mute or hysterical with trauma, or have clearly been coached. Domestics rarely offer the opportunity to be the good guy, much less the hero. Instead it's more like being the high school principal breaking up a slap fest in the girls' room, or the parent wading into a tussle between squabbling siblings. You want to just say, "You're all grounded! Go to your rooms! No TV for a week!" and drive away.

But every now and then a domestic is different. It's real, and violent, and tragic. Or really creepy. LaDarius Jones and I responded to a call from a woman who had fled her house to a nearby fire station (the same one whose fence I had taken out in a pursuit) because her ex, against whom she'd filed a protection order, had popped up in her driveway as she loaded her kids in the car for school one warm April morning. As she drove her kid-laden Navigator across the street to the fire station, she saw him run behind the house, but she had not seen him emerge from there.

She has kept watch on the house from the fire station until we arrive and is convinced he's gotten inside, although she says she changed the locks when she threw him out months ago, and all the doors are locked.

"He mighta kicked in the backdoor or busted a window," she says, trembling. "The last time we was together, he 'bout kilt me to death!" Her three young ones in the backseat giggle and wiggle among themselves, oblivious to mama's fears and the unfolding drama. "He pult my hair right outta my head, hit me all up in my face with his fistses, choked me. I like t'a died, I ain't lyin'!"

LD and I circle the house on foot. No sign of forced entry. We check all the bushes and hiding places in the backyard and the exterior laundry room in the attached carport. Nothing. We return to the lady across the street and report our findings. She pushes the front door key into LD's hand

and orders us to check inside. Mumbling to each other about this being a goddamn waste of time, LD and I cross the street again and enter the front door. We clear the house, guns drawn, checking every room, every closet, under all the beds, behind the couch, behind the huge fifty-inch TV in the living room. No wifebeater jumps out at us. Back at the fire station driveway we report to the woman that her home is secure. She insists it's not and demands to know if we checked behind the shower curtain. We assure her we checked everywhere, and there's nobody lurking in her house.

"You check the attic? I betcha ain't look up there!" I start to tell her we did, but LD says, "No ma'am. But if he ain't got inside the house—which he ain't—then how he gone be in the attic?"

"He tole one of my boys once about a secret way he can get up in there th'oo the carport laundry some kine a way. I don't know, I just ain't goin' back inside till you check it, an if you ain't, I'll call for some other police dat will!"

We cross the street for a third time, muttering about this paranoid bitch. In the kitchen there's a pull-down trapdoor with a fold-out ladder to the attic. I go on up while LD steadies the rickety ladder for me. The attic is low slung—the only standing room is at the center, where the roof peaks, but even there, cross struts will require a crouch. It's hot, which all attics are, and the air is thick, with an unexpected whiff of locker room to it. The entrance to the attic is ringed with the typical jumble of stored boxes, Christmas decorations, old luggage, unused toys and the like, balanced on rafters and blocking easy access. I climb up the ladder just enough to peer over the top of the clutter, quickly scanning all four corners with my flash-light. Just as I'm about to climb back down, I light up what appears to be a couple raggedy pieces of plywood propped up or nailed to vertical two-by-fours, blocking a clear view of the eastern gable. I climb to the top step and train my light on the gaps between the vertical pieces of plywood and see, beyond the barricade, what appears to be a platform lying on the rafters, no bigger than a single four-by-eight sheet of plywood. On the platform is a pile of blankets or sleeping bags. Alongside the bedroll, lining the edge of the platform, folded clothes are neatly stacked, next to a couple pairs of men's sneakers. Some coke cans, beer bottles, and jars are lined up like little soldiers, and a few bags of pork rinds, beef jerky, and potato chips are scattered nearby in the insulation between the rafters. I push a couple boxes of Christmas decorations out of the way, step up into the attic, balancing in a crouch on a rafter, and play my beam over the pile of blankets and sleeping bags some ten yards away. The edge of a pillow is visible at the far end of the platform, mostly obscured by the thick, lumpy pile of blankets and the plywood barricade. Then I spot the toe of a white sock sticking out the end of the blanket nearest to me. I step a rafter closer and study the sock. It appears to be occupied by a foot. It dawns on me that I've discovered a crude pallet on which somebody's lying, perfectly still and silent, beneath the pile of blankets. I jerk upright, bonking my head on a crossbeam, and draw my weapon.

"Let me see your hands!"

The bundle of blankets remains motionless.

"Y'a'ight, Johnson?" LD yells from the below. "Whatcha got?"

With one hand full of flashlight, the other full of Glock, and my chest full of pounding, I advance toward the pile on the pallet, carefully stepping from rafter to rafter. The adrenalin rush is in full force; I have no free hand to steady myself on the overhead struts as I pick my way across the two-by-sixes and cannot, dare not, even for a second, interrupt my fixed gaze on the pile of blankets twenty feet away. Then the white-socked foot disappears under the pile of blankets, which begins moving. Still no hands or head visible; I quicken my steps, my chest heaving.

"Show me your hands!" I bark. My right foot slips off a rafter and crashes through sheetrock. I sink balls-deep, my right leg dangling, kicking in thin air, my left knee hitting hard on a rafter when I drop. The sharp pain of my knee and wrenched left leg is nothing compared to the shock to my 'nads. I'm straddling a two-by-six, dizzied and doubled up in sick testicular agony, madly swinging my leg in the room below. I hear LD below, yelling again, "Y'a'ight?" and I wonder, does it sound like I'm a'ight, LD?

I prop my foot-long Streamlight in the direction of my target and push down hard on a rafter to take the weight off my battered crotch, wriggling and kicking my leg up through the sheetrock and out of the room below, all the while yelling, "Hands! Hands up, motherfucker!"

A pair of palms and a head with bugged eyes poke from beneath the bedding. I holster up, scramble on my knees and shins across the remaining rafters, gain purchase on the pallet, and jerk the bedding off the terrified man in a T-shirt, boxer shorts, and white socks. I flip him on his belly and cuff him as he whines "I ain't did nuthin'! Whuzzis all about, sir? Sir? Whuzz gwine on? I ain't did nothin'!"

I walk the attic dweller across the rafters, down the ladder, and turn him over to LD in the kitchen to take out to his backseat cage. Returning to the attic dweller's pallet to check for weapons and contraband, I sit to catch my breath and wait for the wave of smashed testicle pain to subside. As the throbbing eases, I examine my surroundings. Among the neat piles of folded jeans, shirts, and underwear, and the cans, bottles, and snack sacks lining the edge of the platform I observe a flashlight, a pocket-size New Testament, a half-empty pack of Newports with a Bic lighter tucked in among the smokes, a jar-lid ashtray full of butts. I help myself to a smoke and continue the inventory: a toothbrush, stick of Axe deodorant, wads of used Kleenex, a skin mag full of split black beavers, and a wide-mouthed jar half full of urine. I feel a fleeting pang of pity for my quarry, then heave myself up to retrieve my Streamlight. Before leaving the attic I peer through the hole my leg had made and observe the living room below. Downstairs, I pace the distance and the direction of the pallet from the hole in the living room ceiling; the attic dweller had made his nest directly above his ex's bed. I return to the living room and estimate the ceiling damage in the hundreds of dollars.

Outside, our victim is telling LD how she knew he'd been up there, because he would call her on the phone sometimes, demanding explanations for things she had said that he had no way of knowing about. "An' y'know, they was times I be layin' in bed at night, when I'd swear I could smell 'im! I know his smell, y'know'm sayin'? An I could smell his smell an I couldn't get how I could be smellin' him when he ain't be in my house fuh months! He a sick mothafucka, you feel me?"

Sarge arrives, looks quizzically at the white sheetrock powder covering one leg of my uniform, and I confess my misstep into the living room. Our victim overhears me and goes inside to look for herself. Sarge is telling me not to worry about it, asking if I'm okay, and assuring me I won't hafta pay, and neither will the City if he has any say in the matter, when Miss Victim comes striding out, wagging her finger, doing that ghetto-girl side-to-side head-nod thing, and demands my name and badge number for when she sends the bill to "da Chief, or da muthafuckin Mayah" for her ceiling. "What I'm gone tell da rent man? I be damn if I gone pay fuh dat shit! Dey's a hole as big's his ass in my ceiling! Po-lice gone be payin' fuh dat, or Mobile, or somemuthafuckinbody, but it sho' ain't gone be me!"

Sarge tilts his head to her and in calming, measured tones says, "No ma'am. The one responsible will be the one who pays the damages. That would appear to be your baby-daddy there." He points to the attic dweller, slumped in LD's cage. Miss Victim is outraged. "Him? How dat worf'less muhfucka gone pay? He ain't got a pot to piss in!"

"Oh, but you're mistaken," I hear myself say. "It's a jar, actually, and it's in your attic, ma'am." Sarge shakes his head to silence me, waves her off, and turns back to LD and me as I stub out the attic dweller's Newport in the driveway.

"Switched brands?" Then, before I can answer, he addresses LD. "Draw a case number for burglary and violation of protection order, and take him on to Metro." Then he puts a steadying hand on my shoulder.

"Go home. Change your pants." He nods at my hand, which I discover has been cradling my scrotum. "And while you're at it, check your balls. I'll handle this."

En route to Metro another day, with another prisoner, from another signal 39, who taunts me from the cage. (Some hands-on persuasion, and eventually tasing, had been necessary to peel him off of his bloodied beloved and bring him into custody. His girlfriend was taken by ambulance to the ER, her jaw likely broken, her hair ripped out of her head in big hanks.)

My charge speaks to me in a singsong falsetto from the backseat. "Punk-ass bitch. You think you're so tough. You fuckin' pigs ain't nothing but punk-ass bitches. Without that badge you ain't jack shit." Then he switches to a low-register menacing growl: "In a fair fight I'd break you in half. I'd make you my bitch in less'n a minute. Y'ain't nuthin' but a weak-ass, limp-dick, gray-haired old bitch. Hear me, old man? 'Thout a gun, you just a weak-ass pussy bitch."

I pull off on a quiet side street and remove my duty belt. "'Sa matter, you gotta stop and pee, old man? 'Fraid you might piss your pants? Ha! I done scared the piss outta you, man! Yeah, you better stop and dribble out some old-man pee, so's you don't hafta change your Depends before we get to Metro, you punk-ass old bitch."

I step out of the car and lock the front seat with my weapons inside, then open the backdoor. "Turn around so I can take off your cuffs," I say calmly. He sits mute, motionless.

"Turn around. Let me uncuff you, you sorry shit stain."

He doesn't move, or speak.

"C'mon, motherfucker! You want a piece of this? Fair fight: no cuffs, no backup, no gun, no Taser. Step on out. Step out, you pussy! Come on!"

He won't even look at me. I bend over and scream into his ear, "Just what I thought, you fucking half-wit: all talk. You're all badass when you're fighting a hundred-pound female, or you're safe in this cage. One more word and I'll drag your sorry ass out and stomp it into the dirt! Then I'll take out my old man pecker and dribble some old-man piss right into your crooked, rotten trailer-park teeth, motherfucker!" I slam the door and we proceed to Metro in blessed silence.

There comes no smart-ass retort this time either, although I remain enraged and twitching with adrenalin long after depositing Mr. Shit Stain in Metro.

10

Love and Anger Management

Love is a perky elf dancing a merry little jig and then suddenly he turns on you with a miniature machine-gun.
—Matt Groening

It's a predawn domestic and I'm backing LD. The caller's location is in one of the Woodlawn Apartments off Dauphin Island Parkway. Woodlawn is a cluster of half-vacant, ruined, and uninhabitable hulks that have been stripped of all plumbing fixtures, piping, and electrical wiring for their scrap value, currently around three bucks a pound at any of a dozen local scrap yards who never question the origin of perfectly good plumbing and copper cable delivered to their scales daily by hundreds of crack addicts and other petty thieves. The few remaining occupied apartments in Woodlawn, rundown roach-crawling Section 8 federally subsidized hovels, are inhabited almost exclusively by baby-mamas and their babies, which means they are frequented by their alternately robbing, ripping, and raping baby-daddies. Hence, Woodlawn Apartments is visited several times a day by police responding to domestic violence calls, with your occasional running gun battle between feuding baby-daddies over cuckold/cocksman conflicts. Often you get a combination of both types: the genesis of a baby-daddy versus baby-mama drama will have been some kind of gunplay with a would-be suitor who got away, leaving the aggrieved baby-daddy no satisfaction until he takes it out of his cheating baby-mama's hide.

It was just such a call that LD and I were dispatched to on a cold gray February morning, and we were both worn out from the extra parade duty we'd been pulling due to Mardi Gras. Dispatch tells us while we're en route that earlier that night police had been called to the same address by the same caller who reported two black males fighting, both of them brandishing firearms, but both males were gone by the time officers arrived. Now seven hours later, at about 5 a.m., the complainant is awakened by breaking glass, to be confronted by her baby-daddy, gun in hand, reaching through the broken window of the kitchen door demanding to be let inside or he'd shoot her and their child. "Both parties still on the scene, shots fired, very disorderly background," Dispatch cautions. Subject black male Finest Odom, twenty-three years of age, dark "skinded," approximately 5 foot 7, 150 pounds, wearing a black hoodie, drives an older blue Cutlass Supreme with fancy rims. Caller's in a bedroom, and subject has not yet made entry.

LD is closer than me and puts himself at the scene when I'm still a few seconds out. It's cold enough to see your breath in the first light as I roll up to see LD's idling cruiser parked at the curb, exhaust fumes curling up from his tailpipe. LD advises over the radio that he's attempting to contact the subject, whom he spotted in the blue Cutlass parked just in front of his own Crown Vic. I put myself 10-23 (at the scene) with Dispatch and stop next to LD's cruiser just as LD begins yelling and beating on the driver's side window of the Cutlass. Evidently, Mr. Odom had heard his baby-mama talking on the phone to Dispatch and was trying to dip on us. Unfortunately for Mr. Odom, when he had arrived to terrorize his baby-mama, he had parked his big ole ghetto sled a little too tightly behind a big ole Expedition, and now LD had hemmed him in by pulling up real tight behind him. Parallel parking makes quick getaways a bitch.

Mr. Finest Odom is not about to be defeated by a tight parking spot, however. He reverses his Cutlass hard into the grill of LD's Crown Vic, shoving it back a foot or so, then shoots forward, crumpling his own grill into the rear bumper of the Expedition in front of him, skidding the heavy SUV forward a few inches. Finest's escape plan clearly is to simply bumper-car his way to freedom. He pops it into reverse again and jolts LD's cruiser back another few inches, prompting LD to draw and point his Glock and yell, "Stop fuckin' up my car man!" which falls on deaf ears with Mr. Odom. Finest cranks his wheels hard to the left but still lacks the space needed to exit the slot he's in, and gets the right headlight of his beloved Cutlass all up into the Exped's left taillight. Tires screech again into reverse, a cloud of pungent rubber smoke rises as Finest disengages from the Expedition and rams LD's Crown Vic back a few more inches, despite LD's pointed Glock and commands to "Stop! Halt! Freeze, Muhfucka!" Finest was having none of it.

I had started to get out of my car to assist LD but thought better of it; LD wasn't meeting with much success persuading Finest to un-ass his Cutlass, even with the point-blank threat of lethal force in the face. In fact, it appears now to me that Mr. Odom might have just demo-derbied enough space to squeal away on us this time. LD realizes simultaneously that the gate to the corral has now swung open. In a last-ditch effort to keep the pony in the pen, LD jumps from the side of Finest's Cutlass to the space directly in front of it, in the hard-won spot just created by Mr. Odom's beyond-Bondo, body-shop wet dream. I'm thinking, jeez, LD, you gonna stop all that Detroit horsepower with just your "Command Presence"? LD assumes his most fearsome stance, about a pace from the hood ornament of the battered Cutlass, the stance we practice at the firing range: feet planted squarely on the pavement, bent slightly at the knees, leaning a little forward at the waist, weapon gripped with both hands, pushed out at full arm extension directly from the chest, pointed at the center mass of Finest Odom, seated behind the steering wheel. For a long moment they simply glare at each other.

"Stop or I'll shoot!" LD barks.

Then a bunch of things happen at once: Finest Odom shifts his Cutlass from reverse to drive and stomps it, LD jumps two giant steps backward while maintaining his fierce firing stance, I pop my Crown Vic from park to drive and stomp it, my push bar and grill caving in Odom's driver door and driving the front right quarter panel of his Cutlass into the hapless Expedition, immobilizing everybody. Despite (or because of?) nearly being mowed down by the Cutlass, LD remains frozen in "ready-fire" position; Finest Odom's desperate, still-spinning wheels let out a deafening, piercing shriek but get him nowhere, and my own wheels join in the howling chorus, my foot to the floor pushing my cruiser ever tighter into the Cutlass, the Cutlass ever harder into the Expedition, all in a tenuous effort to keep Odom pinned and LD whole.

For another long moment it's just a ridiculous standoff, with LD pointing and bellowing, acrid rubber smoke billowing from four tires screeching. I'm not sure how long I can keep the Cutlass stopped. With no plan other than to somehow extract Finest from the squealing, shimmying Cutlass before it flattens LD, I jam my shifter into park, stomp on the parking brake, jump out with my gun drawn. There's no way to pull him out through the driver's door, which is full of my Crown Vic's push bar. The only access to him is through his passenger door on the other side. I pick the quickest, most direct route and clamber up onto the hood of my cruiser, then to the roof of the straining Cutlass, and jump down on the passenger side between the Cutlass and the wrecked Expedition. Miraculously, Odom's passenger door is unlocked; I won't have to shoot out its window. I jerk it open and lean inside, Glock extended, the barrel little more than a foot from Finest Odom's right ear.

"Shut it down, shitbag!" I scream over the keening of the tires.

Odom's eyes dart from me to LD and back to me, but still he stands on the pedal, his hands gripping the wheel, the banshee howl of his tires driving us all insane. Odom is as frozen at the wheel as LD is out in front. With my free hand I reach in to pull the key from his ignition, and a visible electric tremor hits me when I spot a silver .38 lying in Odom's lap. I snatch the gun and jerk the key all in one strike, then stuff them both into the front of my pants.

An abrupt silence washes over us, over the wreckage, over all of Woodlawn Apartments, in a soothing wave of quietude, giving all three of us permission to exhale.

"Hands up. Both hands off the wheel. Let me see 'em," I instruct. "Now reach your right hand this way toward me." Odom, just moments ago a crazed, cornered animal, is calmly compliant now. I snap a cuff onto Odom's right wrist and, backing up out of the Cutlass, drag him across the front seat with the other cuff as LD climbs over the hood of the Cutlass to join me. I pass the prisoner off to LD to finish the cuffing and pat-down, and slump against the trunk of the Cutlass, holster my Glock, and light a Camel.

The radio crackles, "Three-thirteen?"

"Three-twelve for 313," I answer.

"Checking on your situation."

"Subject in custody, so far?"

"So far."

"Start 1 Sam 3 to our location, along with Traffic Investigators. We have a four-car signal 7 involving two police vehicles. Also, start the Impound wrecker for a Blue Cutlass."

"Ten-four. Copy, Sam 3?"

I hear the groan in Sarge's reply, "Ten-four, en route from Precinct," and look at my watch. The sun has just climbed over the eastern horizon:

0630, end of shift. I survey the wreckage and am filled with dread: hours of paperwork await us.

"I'll go see if I can find the victim, get her statement," I tell LD as he inserts Finest Odom into the cage of his ruined Crown Vic.

It may be end of shift, but we're still a long way from quitting time.

Finest Odom's mama arrived on the scene even before the Impound wrecker; she had been called by Finest Odom's baby-mama, who was having second thoughts about having called the police in the first place. The neighbor whose Expedition's rear end had been smashed, her whole family, and most of her neighbors (now claiming to have witnessed the entire incident) were outraged, demanding the city pay for the Expedition's damages; Finest's mama furiously demanded an explanation for her son's captivity and to know when the city would pay to fix her battered Cutlass. When Sarge informed her that not only would the city not repair her Cutlass, but that the city was seizing it as evidence in an attempted assault on an officer, to say nothing of the original domestic complaint involving menacing with a firearm, the gloves came off. Or rather, the cell cameras came out. "We recordin' dis. Gettin'us a record a e'rthang y'all do!" "Yeah! We callin' 'Ternal Affairs raght nah. We gon have all y'all officers brought up on charges!" Additional units had to be called to disperse the crowd. Finest's mama bonded him out after his mandatory twelve-hour lockup for the domestic complaint—at about the same time LD and I were reporting to roll call for another twelve-hour night shift.

Three months later, there was a bench warrant for Finest Odom for failing to appear on a previous domestic charge involving the same baby-mama. LD received a tip from Odom's probation officer that despite dipping out on his court date, Odom had been religiously attending the weekly Wednesday night anger management classes that were among the conditions of his probation. "He probably takes those classes a lot more seriously than he does me, or the judge, because they're the key to baby-mama's good graces," the PO observed, speaking as one who had seen it all too often before. When LD had suggested to her that the anger class might provide us an opportunity to pick Odom up on the bench warrant, the PO had enthusiastically supplied him with dates, times, location, and contact information for the instructor.

LD set it up with the instructor. One of us would arrive at the class early, in scruffy plain clothes, and sit in the back of the classroom posing as a newly sentenced domestic violator attending his first anger class. The other would be in uniform, waiting in a blacked-out marked unit behind a building two doors down. When Finest arrived, the inside guy would punch his cell speed-dial to the outside guy, who would pull around and enter the building and the classroom from the front, as the inside guy closed off any attempt by Odom to flee out the backdoor. We'd simply scoop him up and whisk him off to Metro.

We debated who should be the inside guy and who should be the outside guy. We both wanted to have the pleasure of cuffing Finest once again, which would most likely be done by the outside guy. But we worried Finest might recognize the inside guy, turn and run out the front before the outside guy could respond to the speed-dial signal, so LD decided that since "all you white guys look alike," I would be best suited as the under-cover inside guy.

It worked like a charm, except not exactly as planned. I'm a real Luddite when it comes to anything techie, including even the humble cell phone (which we purchase and pay monthly charges on out of our own meager earnings). I carry only the simplest, cheapest twelve-buck Walmart version, having ruined one in a foot chase that ended in a creek, cracked the screen on another when it slipped its holster and I stepped on it while aiding a fellow officer with one resisting arrest, and drowned a third when I acci-dentally dropped it in a precinct urinal. (I'm not exactly a whiz at multi-tasking.) I don't text, I don't e-mail, I don't take pictures with my phone. It's all I can do to place and receive calls, and that's fine with me.

So when Finest entered the classroom and took a seat two rows in front of me, I reached into the back pocket of my jeans to speed-dial LD but discovered I had somehow already butt-dialed my wife, who was loudly saying, "Hello? Hello?" Finest and several others seated around me turned to see what the disturbance was, and I decided I'd better just improvise. I jumped up with my Glock in one hand and cuffs in the other. Guys dived under their desks. Odom froze, just as he had the last time I'd had a Glock to his ear.

"Finest Odom, I have a warrant for your arrest. Remember me?" He was speechless, paralyzed. "Put these on," I said, handing him the cuffs. He snapped one on and I snapped the other one to the arm of his classroom desk. The instructor approached to help.

"Just make sure he doesn't try to run out the door with your desk while I'm trying to call my backup." As several of my anger classmates recovered their composure they encircled Finest, who remained seated and mute.

It was sweet.

I've learned to savor the sweetness when I can, because it's often short lived. At Finest's trial several months later, his baby-mama testified that they had since reconciled and she wished to drop the case. It was a joyful thing to see: they positively beamed at one another in court.

And several months after that, I was delighted to learn from other guys on my squad that my patrol buddy LD had received an "Excellent Police Conduct" medal, ribbon, and citation from the chief for his courage, initiative, and professionalism in the two arrests of convicted felon Finest Odom. I guess modesty had kept LD from telling me.

11

Mudbug

Pride goeth before the fall.
—Proverbs 16:18

She was probably no more than a hundred pounds, tops, barely 5 feet tall (her height was hard to judge while she rode her old beat-up, fat-tired one-speed bicycle). Though her size and mode of transportation were typical of adolescents and young teens, I knew she was probably closer to forty than fourteen, just from pacing my squad car slowly behind her for a block, before I ever saw her face. She wore dirty blue jeans and a stained white tank top. It was about an hour or so out of roll call, and the sun was bright and warm, but the night's chill still lingered on this bright, sunny March morning, just a few weeks past Mardi Gras. The sleeveless cyclist had to be cold. Her afro was shaggy and wild, not shaped or brushed, but shooting straight up from her head like a cluster of celery stalks. When she sensed me following behind her and stole a quick glance over her shoulder at me, I recognized the feral look of an addict.

What caught my attention was neither her clothes nor her hair but her cargo. A large purse dangled from a handlebar, bulging so full that the zipper remained open, and objects not resembling a cell phone or hair brush jutted out—they were pipes and odd-size hunks of metal. Even more suspicious was the filthy canvas sack, easily twice the size of her purse, propped horizontally across the handlebars. The rucksack could have accommodated a couple of sawed-off shotguns, a few tire irons, and enough baseball bats for a little league team.

She was attempting to hold the canvas sack in place with the thumb of each hand, but its weight and bulk were hard for her to manage, especially with the laden, clanking purse swinging from the handlebar, bumping her left knee with every downward stroke on the pedal. Her shifting load was unsecured and unevenly distributed, and the bicycle rocked and lurched precariously.

We were headed southbound on Pinehill, not far from the WhatABurger across from police headquarters, and approaching the bridge over Eslava Creek. She quickened her pedaling, despite the instability of her loads, after the quick, over-the-shoulder glance at me. The neighborhood comprises numerous abandoned or vacant homes. Soaring scrap metal prices made the wiring and plumbing fixtures of unoccupied houses prime targets of crackheads. My bushy-headed bike rider's load, if it was mostly copper, would probably fetch her more than enough to buy a day or two's supply of crack rocks for her and her boyfriend. What was unusual was that she was female. Most copper thieves are male; it's hard, dirty work to cut, pry, and wrench copper out from behind sheetrock walls, from filthy crawl spaces creeping with insects and vermin, and from sweltering attics. I figured her boyfriend did the wrecking, and she did the trekking, so he could lay low from the Po-po.

I continue to pace my quarry, who I'm guessing is headed to a nearby scrap recycler popular with copper thieves because he asks no questions, requires no photo ID of his scrappers, and keeps no records.

Over my PA speaker I inquire, "What's in the bag, ma'am?" She ignores me and pedals harder. I smile at her determination and intone "Ma'am? Ma'am? What's your hurry? Please pull to the side of the road." Not only does she fail to comply, her pedaling becomes a furious blur. I check my odometer: we're up to a blazing 7 mph.

I activate my blue lights and give her a couple "whoop-whoops" from the yelp setting on my siren. She's standing to pedal now, leaning forward over her handlebars like Lance Armstrong in a Tour de Maysville, nothing but elbows and butt bones from my perspective, and she's not looking back.

When she crosses the Eslava Creek bridge, she hooks a sharp left down a rutted, bumpy dirt road that parallels the creek. I follow, my Crown Vic rocking and scraping bottom on the uneven, unpaved surface, used by Water Board and Public Works trucks. "Three-twelve to radio, I'm following a signal 63 black female subject on a bicycle, refusing to stop.

We're eastbound on the dirt road just south of the Eslava Creek bridge on Pinehill, the utility road that comes out by Ward's Recycling at Halls Mill and Fairway."

"Ten-four, 312. We have no backing units at this time," Dispatch replies.

"No backing needed," I answer.

I'm familiar with—and fond of—this road, which runs through the heart of my beat. Eslava Creek is a typical urban waterway: largely neglected, unseen, obscured by residential backyards and the rear loading docks of strip malls. It often stinks, especially in the heat of August, of sharp chemical smells and sewage. Choked with discarded tires, the rusting hulks of long-abandoned cars, half-buried shopping carts from behind the Food World, floating plastic Faygo and Fanta soda bottles and soiled Huggies, the creek's course was long ago "stabilized" by the Corps of Engineers and Public Works, who lined its banks at the crooks and bends with chain-link-encased ric-rac rock and hunks of broken concrete to inhibit erosion when spring and summer rains turn its normal six inches into a swollen, churning brown torrent.

The levees along each side of the straight parts are a gently graded 30-degree slope covered with tall grasses and reeds, inhabited by at least one granddaddy-size 'gator and many graceful white and blue herons, who seem unperturbed by their habitat's scents and sights of decay.

I've recovered more than one stolen car from the banks of Eslava Creek. They are often torched by the carjackers before being pushed ablaze down the gentle slope to the water's edge. It's favored by carjackers because in many places the tall weeds and vines along the banks fully obscure the vehicles for weeks before neighborhood kids or the occasional fisherman will discover and report them.

The two-track down which I'm now in active pursuit is one I typically bounce along several times during a twelve-hour shift, when the radio traffic is slow. I may happen upon a drug transaction, or a stolen car, but mainly it's simply a welcome departure from the streets and from the watchful eyes of the public, a place that's quiet, and calm, where I can step out and take a pee, pick my nose, read the *Press Register*, ask an old fisherman what he's catching, and what he's using to catch it with, or just gaze at the waterfowl for ten or twenty minutes. It also provides me some strange small pleasure to take a road posted with signs at each end declaring "Authorized Vehicles Only."

So I know this little road at least as well as the bushy-haired bicyclist attempting to elude me. She probably didn't think I would follow her down this path, but I know where the holes and humps are and maneuver around them, staying right on her rear fender.

Over the PA again, I adopt a calm, conversational tone.

"Ma'am, this is a restricted road. Private. You're now trespassing." Her posture and effort remain Olympian. "Don't hurt yourself, just give it up. You can't outpedal me." For all her effort we're still at the 7 or 8 mph range. Either she's tiring or my avuncular reasoning is working on her: she slows down. But doesn't stop. "I've already got backing units en route to the other end of this road," I bluff.

This works, finally. She abruptly stops and dismounts, breathing heavy. I skid to a stop, and she drops the bike, the rucksack, and her purse to the ground. Without a command from me, she even assumes the position, leaning forward, hands on the hood of my car, legs spread, as I put it in park and get out.

"Three-twelve, subject detained, about halfway between Pinehill and Halls Mill, on the dirt road along the south bank of the creek," I advise Dispatch, trying hard to sound matter of fact, tamping down any hint of triumphal tone to my transmission. This is, after all, just a ninety-pound female suspected of being in possession of maybe thirty bucks worth of copper scrap that will be all but impossible to prove is stolen. Not exactly a major apprehension.

I come around the front of my car, and in the blink of an eye she bolts down the passenger side of my cruiser, back down the road we had just traveled, and then cuts down the levee through the tall weeds toward the creek as I run behind her, barking "Three-twelve! Subject's running down into the creek!" into my shoulder mike.

When she gets down the levee near the water's edge, the reeds are as tall as she is, and thick, and she slows. Right behind her, I discover why: it's a wet, thick, boot-sucking bog. She struggles, and I struggle, and then I'm on her with all my weight, tackling her, and we both go down into the oozing muck. She struggles, but not against me. She struggles as I do to keep from getting hopelessly tangled in weeds and sucked under the black muck. I manage to regain my feet and she reaches up to me. We're both soaked and slathered in a dark, thick, reeking ooze. I jerk her to her feet and we struggle together back up the levee, back to my idling cruiser.

I wipe the muck from my hand and key my shoulder mike. "Three-twelve, subject's in custody, everything's 10-4 here," again trying to sound calm, cool, and in control, though enraged at my mud-caked uniform and embarrassed that she played me after I said on the radio that I had her detained.

I open the backdoor to my car and sling her into the cage, slamming the door shut. I pop the trunk and pull a couple towels out and smear most of the thick muck from my face and clothes, but there's no way I can do this shift without a shower and a change of uniform. I'm dreading the ribbing I face from my squad and sergeant.

My prisoner pleads from the cage to roll down the window. "It ain't no aih up in here! Cain't breathe! Please, officer, I'm sorry, but I be suffercatin' up in dis mug!"

I don't reply because I'm too pissed at her to say anything without triggering a profane tirade I might regret, and I've got enough to regret already this morning. I lower her window from the control panel on my door's armrest and walk around the front of my cruiser to empty the contents of her purse on my hood and the rucksack on the road in front of my car. Freshly cut copper plumbing lines, faucets, and fixtures clank into the dust. Among the contents of her purse on the hood of my car are a pack of Newports containing a glass crack stem and a small baggie of weed and another containing three little crack rocks that look like broken baby teeth. I sigh with relief that at least I have something more than a misdemeanor to arrest the bitch for, and look up just in time to catch a glimpse of her with her skinny bone-thin hand reaching through the bars of the cage on the door with the window down, opening the door from the outside handle.

Oh, shit, I think, I didn't lock the backdoor! Who knew she was so skinny she could reach between the bars of my cage and let herself out? My thieving little mudbug has jumped out, escaped! I leap around the front of my car just in time for one of my outstretched hands to slither down her bog-slicked arm as she rounds the trunk and slips my grasp. My duty boots feel like they weigh a ton with the muck still clinging thickly to me from the knees down. She circles around my car and is off in a flash, scampering lickety-split down the road in the original direction I'd pursued her. I lumber along behind her, reporting her direction of travel and clothing description on the radio, hoping somebody's 10-8 to catch her at the end of the road, because I'm just not all that into this thing anymore.

I hear Tyrone on the radio report he has a visual on my subject just as I see him zooming toward my scampering Mudbug from the other end of the road where it ends at the back of the seafood place. I'm about "give-out," a half a football field from my fugitive and losing ground, when I see 'Rone jump out of his car and draw his Taser. Mudbug stops dead in her tracks, looks back at me huffing toward her, leaves the road and runs behind a clump of bushes and small trees. 'Rone pursues, and they run circles around the bush as if they're schoolkids playing ring around the rosie, till Balzer rolls up in a cloud of dust, jumps out, fires his Taser from three yards as the circling Mudbug comes 'round the bushes directly toward him, and drops her. One Taser prong strikes just below her left nipple, the other embeds in her neck. Balzer gives her the whole five-second ride, and she's screaming in satisfying agony as I drag myself to the scene wheezing, mud caked, and humiliated.

Yeah, back at the precinct, where they take Mudbug for questioning by a detective, I catch a ration of shit. Everybody comes in off their beats to get a look at me and Mudbug and yuck it up at my expense. But Mudbug is a changed, chastened woman. She's had an epiphany and wants to change her ways. She tells the detective where she and her ole man have been staying, and tells him about all the copper he's been stripping from houses in the neighborhood, which she's been taking to Ward's for him, several times a day. Mudbug recognizes now that she's been used by her boyfriend, she's been taking all the risk, and not even getting her fair share of the money, and she is more than happy to testify against him, if the detective could just see his way to overlook the paraphernalia, marijuana second, cocaine possession, receiving stolen property, failure to obey, escape, and eluding charges. She tells them right where they can find her old man, who's waiting for her to return from Ward's Recycling with the cash.

By the time I come back to the precinct in a fresh uniform, Mudbug has been sprung and her old man is in custody, charged with eleven felonies: eight counts of burglary, one receiving stolen second, possession of burglar tools, and possession of controlled substance. The detective thanks me for helping him to clear a backlog of cases. Four weeks later he gets Officer of the Month for his multiple case clearances through the arrest of one of Mobile's most prolific burglars.

12

Stranger in a Strange Land

I have an idea that some men are born out of their due place. Accident has cast them amid strangers in their birthplace . . . they may spend their whole lives aliens among their kindred.
—W. Somerset Maugham

In Waukesha, Wisconsin, in the early nineties, I was successful, prosperous, and well loved by friends, neighbors, employees, board members, donors, agency directors (even the Boy Scout exec!), the newspaper (where I wrote a weekly column), the pastor and my fellow elders at First Presbyterian, and the many earnest and sincere, sober members of the Badger Recovery Group. Ten years later, and three years into policing, I found myself asking how on earth did I end up here, on the meanest streets of Mobile?

Nancy has been asking that question in countless ways, verbal and otherwise, for nearly two decades now. She began asking well before I quit Mobile's United Way to become one of Mobile's finest, to tangle with thugs like Finest. And the longer I'm here, the more I find myself wondering the same thing. We have now lived in the Azalea City longer than either of us lived anywhere else, including St. Louis, Colorado, Wisconsin, and Louisiana (where I spent my first five blissful years in Luling, just upriver from New Orleans).

It's no great mystery, really, why I left Waukesha: I hated the Wisconsin weather. The cold was brutal: 20 below was not unusual. Hard even to breathe in that cold. A deep breath of frozen air burns in your lungs, freezes your snot, and makes your nose run when you get back indoors. But worse for me than the stinging freezes was the Great Gray. To me it was palpable.

It seeped into everything. The absence of sunlight, the short days and long nights, the six or more interminable months of winter, year in, year out. It hung on me, pulling me down, like heavy, damp, itchy wool. It demanded my attention to things I didn't want to think about: fabrics, and layers, and thermal insulation ratings and chill factors and hat hair and wet gloves and earmuffs and neck scarves and windshield scrapers and snow shovels and protecting my boots and my car's undercarriage from rock salt damage, and allowing time for battery charging, engine warming, tire chaining, defrosting, and icy creep-along low-viz-blizz road conditions complicating every simple outing to the grocery store for a quart of milk, or to a movie, or to visit a friend across town. There's not much spontaneity in Wisconsin in the winter. And in Wisconsin it's always winter.

Even worse for me than the burden and confinement of the cold gray was the chilling, plodding dullness of the visual gray and the human gray. It's the pale gray that is the universal color of all human activity and interaction, the absence of color spectra in people, in personality, in perspective. It's the absence of color, not just in the chromatic sense, but as you might read in a guidebook, in the phrase "colorful indigenous populations." Color that comes from difference, from eccentricity, variety, passion, and agitation. Wisconsin's dull gray is the color of sameness, uniformity, homogeneity in all measures: education, race, ethnicity, income. It's the dull grayness of the spirit, of the plodding upper-Midwest German/Norwegian culture of dogged duty, conformity, discipline, predictability, safety, planning, and good orderly progress in all things. The complete deliberate elimination of surprise, serendipity, risk, whimsy, color.

There was exactly one black guy in Waukesha: guy named Spraggins, head (and sole member?) of the Waukesha County NAACP. He lived around the corner from me, did something with the state board of education. (Coincidentally, he was a native of Whistler, Alabama, a village near Prichard, a suburb of Mobile.) When I told Spraggins I was thinking of moving to Mobile, he lit up. Told me with visible pride that Mobile had, unlike much of the South (especially in Alabama), avoided overt racial strife. The kind of thing that is synonymous with Selma, Montgomery, Birmingham. Spraggins was walking, talking proof of the Mobile difference: he was in the first integrated graduating class of a Deep South university—Mobile's own Spring Hill College—even as Governor George Wallace made his infamous schoolhouse stand. (It didn't dawn on me to ask Spraggins how or why he had ended up in the most lily-white dull gray Republican county in Wisconsin.)

Waukesha did have a small cluster of Hispanics—enough to warrant a United Way–funded agency, La Casa de Esperanza, and its doggedly pedantic executive director whose mission was to address the unique challenges and needs of the descendants of migrant farmworkers who had harvested the county's crops for generations before La Casa was established to harvest the county's Nordic guilt. As agricultural work became automated and corporatized and clusters of McMansions sprung up in the former rolling cornfields and tidy pastures that had been home to the contented bovines of stolid dairymen, I guess the Mexican workers had to learn new trades, and having brown skin and foreign accents and not much education or money, they had hardships in 95 percent white Waukesha County, where the median household income exceeds $70,000, the median price of a single-family home hovers around $300,000, and more than half the population has at least a few years of college.

All was not dark Lutheran bleakness: ice fishing, snowmobile racing, cross-country skiing, tailgating at Brewers and Packers games, Sven and Oley jokes—all good clean hardy, wholesome fun, to be sure. Proud community spirit was amply manifest in generous philanthropy, quality education and health care, extensive parks and recreation infrastructure, a history of progressive politics, strong family bonds and genuine neighborliness, a cozy tavern with Pabst on tap at every corner. Though you had to search hard as a charitable fund-raiser to find scenes of poverty and despair for the annual tug-at-your-heart-and-wallet campaign video, it was really a pretty easy gig. "Giving back" having long been such a big part of the upper Midwest culture, it's relatively easy there to raise ever-higher campaign totals, rust belt economies notwithstanding. The affluence, homogeneity, education, and universal values, while wholesome, and good for fund-raising and community building, are nevertheless mind-numbingly dull for a self-indulgent, somewhat decadent slacker like me. I was at once successful, somnambulant, and stricken with a deep ennui.

A mere twenty-minute jaunt to the east on I-94 lay the menacing black urban ghettos of Milwaukee, seething with crime and poverty, referred to in national media as among the top-three hyper-segregated communities in the nation, just behind Detroit and Chicago. Now that, I figured, would be something I could really sink my teeth into. Only on a smaller scale, and in a warmer clime, with a tastier cuisine, funkier music, and more eclectic cultural currents.

I had long nurtured idealized childhood memories of Luling and New Orleans: the warm, sunny, friendly, easygoing Deep South. Steeped as I was on Mama's sleepy-time readings of Uncle Remus stories, my own visions of moss-draped live oaks, the brassy jubilant sounds of the music and maskers of Mardi Gras, and the soothing soft singing of Essie, who cleaned our house and changed my diapers. The cliché about the difference in race relations between the North and the South must have been originated by someone from the Deep South: northern whites love the black race but hate the individual Negro (with whom they refuse to live), while southern whites love the individual Negro (with whom they live cheek by jowl) but hate the race. Which is worse? Both are deplorable, but to me it seemed that the southern attitude lacked the self-righteous hypocrisy of the North.

I do know what it means to miss New Orleans: I could still see fields of tall clover, almost waist high to a child, through which we'd make intricate mazes, all paths leading to the giant live oak with the vine-covered branches dripping thick coils of Spanish moss, branches that would hang so low they would nearly touch ground, like a father bending down to scoop you up in his arms. We'd construct multilevel, multichambered tree houses and forts in these live oaks. I remember Mama taking me into town, to Luling's sole barber, Claude, whose shop was in a converted boxcar on a side spur a block from the river road. There was a Kool cigarette penguin sign on the front door: "It's Kool inside," Mama would read to me each time from the penguin's word balloon. Blueish white icicles hung from "Kool." The small one-chair shop was frigid compared to the humid blanket of Louisiana summer. Claude was a garrulous older fella with a mustache, brown skin, and a funny—but common—accent that I would recognize years later as Cajun. He would set me on a special seat across the chair's armrests and pump the chair up high. The buzzing tickle of his shears around my ears would give me goose bumps. Then he'd set me up for what he called the "coo-day-grah," extolling the virtues of his famous Lilac Vegetal aftershave, which would give me a cold jolt as he slathered it on my neck before dusting me with a fragrant white-bristled brush. Then he'd pump the chair back down and sweep his barber's apron off me with a flourish to shake my shorn locks to the floor, declaring to my mother, "Dar he be, Miz Johnson: Eee-ree-sistable! De plu' beau p'ti' garcon dis side o' Noo Awwwlins!" Claude's shop was near the part of town where the colored people, including sweet Essie, lived. I knew even at that tender age—without ever entering their tiny, unpainted shotgun shacks—that they were way less fortunate than I, that they had somehow been screwed by somebody or something. It wasn't fair.

As for me, my early childhood was filled with nothing but happy sweet memories of the weekly shopping trips with Mama, starting with a car ferry ride across the expanse of the Mississippi, which looked to me like an endless flow of chocolate milk. The ferry boarded at a dock just over the levee across the River Road from the entrance to Daddy's plant, which was marked by a big sign on which the "Lynall doggie" resided—which was my description, never having seen a lion, of the mascot logo of the Lion Oil Company. After the ferry crossing, the next stop would be the Morning Call in the French Market: steaming, aromatic, chicory-laced café au lait for Mama, chilled orange juice for me, warm sweet powdery beignets for both of us. The houses in N'wolins were older, taller, all built up higher and narrower, but much fancier than the identical modern ranch homes in Luling built by the company for managers. In the city, the houses had hardly any yards, but they were enveloped by blazing jumbles of viney flora sprouting out of every window box, hanging from the arches of every gallery. Roots of towering palms and ancient live oaks heaved up sidewalks making even foot traffic, much less cycling, an adventure. In the late afternoons after a full day of shopping and visiting, Mama would always stop at the Frosty Top drive-in for root beer in chilled mugs. On the roof of the Frosty Top's kitchen was a giant rotating, illuminated frosty mug. Then we'd head back to Luling, requiring a return river crossing, this time not by car ferry but by the Herewego, which is what I called the Huey P. Long Bridge. It was high and scary and thrilling. Built tall enough to accommodate Mississippi River traffic, with a long gradual ascent and equally stretched-out descent to accommodate the shuddering, chugging freight-train level just beneath the automobile level, it was always choked with thundering truck traffic muscling its way over the river in its narrow lanes, which had low side railings and a view that gave me tingly shivers every time, a view that took in countless puffing smokestacks of trains, ships, and complicated chemical and oil refineries, the low-slung cityscape of all New Orleans, the snakey bayous and low-lying swamps flooding thick and tangled spooky spikey trees sticking up right out of the waters, waters in every direction, waters filled with alligators and garfish and slithering snakes and nutria and crabs and crawdads and Cajun men on long flat pirogues, still waters of Lake Pontchartrain on one side, the muddy, churning working waters of the mammoth industry-choked Mississippi beneath us, including the tall stacks and huge round tanks of the plant where Daddy worked in the distance, and finally the wide endless waters of the Gulf and then the ocean to the south. From the top of the Herewego I could see to the very edges of the world.

When I could stand the cold gray of the upper Midwest no longer, I interviewed for the top post at the United Way in Baton Rouge, and had there learned (the hard way) not to raise any questions about race relations or poverty. The search committee couldn't hustle me back to the airport fast enough.

I had approached Baton Rouge with the same tried-and-true technique that had worked for me before. In advance of the formal meetings with the search committee, I would plan enough time to do the following: hit a local recovery meeting and afterward talk to the folks about the town, visit a couple United Way-funded agencies (such as the Salvation Army and maybe an Urban League or women's shelter) where I could gather a little intel on local social services, and, if possible, look up any local acquaintances. Failing that, I would study the local newspaper in order to gather a few local names and pick up on current points of civic pride or contention. Then I would sort through all this and pick out the most interesting and obscure tidbits to sprinkle into the interview process. It had wowed the search committee in Waukesha when I had casually mentioned the mayor's name, praised them for their progressive public school system, which I had learned hosted recovery meetings for youthful addicts in local high schools, and demonstrated a decent grasp of the local racial, ethnic, and economic demographics.

Upon arrival I called the Baton Rouge recovery hotline and requested somebody to take me to a meeting. A rough-looking fella with missing teeth and a fine mullet flowing out of the back of his greasy tractor cap picked me up in his battered rebel flag-emblazoned GMC and took me to a meeting on the west side of the river, in what he called the "Free Republic of West Baton Rouge Parish," where a colorful collection of outlaw bikers and backwoods Cajuns shared their drunkalogs and stories of recovery. Then I looked up an elderly retired Lion Oil executive, a friend of my dad's, whose second trophy wife was mildly intoxicated when I got there and flirted with me, while he (apparently oblivious or indifferent to her coquetry) liberally (but apologetically) used the N word to describe the major challenges facing his beloved hometown.

I had a cab driver (who grilled me about Milwaukee's then-infamous homosexual cannibal serial murderer Jeffrey Dahmer, as if by coming from the same area I could explain it) take me to a United Way–funded homeless shelter in a rundown part of town, but the night manager there, speaking through a cautiously cracked door, eyed me suspiciously and denied me admission, refusing even to talk with me. He insisted I make an appointment with the director if I wanted to talk about the agency or its mission or its relationship with United Way.

In spite of this discouraging start, it had seemed to go really well with the search committee, in the beginning. They appeared to think I was a perfect fit. The local foundation exec, who was an ex officio member of the board and chair of the search committee, told me over lunch at the penthouse Petroleum Club that he personally had selected me as a finalist from among the numerous applicants because he recognized and appreciated my prep school education. He was a preppie as well, he confided, and, though not from the South, had found the prep school experience invaluable in grasping and navigating the sometimes tricky social subtleties that he had learned are so important in the Deep South. A matronly socialite, also a member of the search committee, whose assignment had been to drive me around the grandiosely pillared and galleried subdivisions from among which I would no doubt choose to quarter my family, was convinced I was a true son of the South.

"You really understand our little river town," she declared, beaming. I had just recited a florid declamation (not unlike the preceding) of fondness and longing for Luling, where "my daddy" (a consciously selected term) had been the plant manager of a petrochemical plant—the likes of which were of course the primary economic engine of Baton Rouge (after LSU).

"We really feel like you're one of us," she had declared midway through the final interview with the search committee. Other heads nodded in agreement around the table. The committee of about eight prominent business leaders, plant managers, bank presidents, and the like had been inquiring about my philosophy and experience in fund-raising, consensus building, community needs assessment, donor cultivation—the usual United Way stuff.

Having satisfactorily fielded the committee's questions, they then had invited me to ask any questions I might have about their United Way, their hometown, their way of life. All I did was to observe that the only black people I had met over the course of my visit to their ethnically fifty-fifty town had been the porters at the airport, the taxi driver, and the house-keeper at the hotel, and to wonder aloud why. There was confused silence in the room. I felt compelled to explain my question, though it should have been obvious they had understood it all too well. I pointed out that unlike their demographically diverse community, as far as I could tell there were no black United Way board members, or even agency executives, and there didn't appear to be any funding allocated to an Urban League or similar kind of minority-focused program or community center in the shamefully rundown parts of town I'd had my taxi driver show me, which were but a stone's throw from the proud and pristine campus of LSU. The matronly socialite's brow furrowed tragically, and the foundation exec, chair of the search committee, and fellow preppie had scowled and reddened, sput-tering, "I take issue with the implications of that question!" and gone on to point out that the Reverend So-and-so, a most outspoken and vigorous leader of "that community," is on the board, though he was unavailable to serve on the search committee, and that the chamber has been trying to clean up that part of town for decades but has been actively resisted by its residents, and we can certainly all agree that no understanding of any depth can be obtained by simple head counts and sweeping generalizations based on a few hours of sightseeing and conversations.

And bam! It was over. I was whisked directly to the airport, hours before my flight's departure.

I read in a trade newsletter a month later that they ended up hiring a black female. Go figure. At first flabbergasted, I quickly figured it out: my profound insight and the fearless probity with which it was delivered had so shaken and traumatized the search committee that its ultimate decision to select an African American female was an act of shame and contrition. I had done Baton Rouge a big favor.

So when I was invited to interview in Mobile, I was a lot more circum-spect and cautious. Arrived a full day early, at my own expense for the extra hotel night. Took my time. Rented my own car and drove around town myself, starting with an alternate route from the airport, not the way they had directed me to get to the downtown hotel. Arbitrarily picked Old Shell Road, instead of Airport Boulevard, to approach downtown Mobile, simply because the name conjured the white, oyster-shell-packed surface of the cul-de-sac of company housing I remembered from Luling. Starting way out west by the University of South Alabama, whose small, new, raw-looking campus bespoke earnestness, humility, unself-consciousness—and didn't even look like the same species as that shrine to southern pride, LSU—Old Shell took me through the heart of Spring Hill, the stately tree-lined neighborhoods of homes large and small, which I later learned were the homes of "Old Mobile" families—not at all like the starkly ostentatious, newly built, uniform subdivisions of the petro-plant oligarchy I had toured in Baton Rouge. These places were tasteful, lovely, gracious. And then, in the blink of an eye, Old Shell took me down a hill, under an interstate, and I emerged into block after block of shotgun houses. But nothing like the dilapidated, littered and peeling, dangerous-looking crack shacks of Red Stick's "colored town." These were almost Victorian in appearance. Gaily painted, some of them, most charmingly tidy albeit older, modest homes that appeared to be occupied by a mixture (!) of friendly middle-class black and white folk who cut their grass, kept up their cars, and swept their front porches.

I stopped and called the local recovery hotline, explaining I was from out of town, somewhere on Old Shell Road, and is there a nearby meeting anytime soon?

"Theyah sure is, honey" came the deliciously southern reply. "If ya hurry, you'll catch the bettah part a the 'leven o'clock Sunshine Group at the Old Shell clubhouse. It'll be ohn ya right if yuh comin' from the ayuhpoaht, a green house with the numbers ten-oh-fahv above the front poahch. Ya just go ohn 'round back to pahk, go ohn in the back doah, poah ya'self a cup and find yase'f a chayah, sugah. It's a goo-o-d meetin', the Sunshine Group is."

And it was. Black and white, male and female, young and old together. Jittery newcomers with tattoos, flitting eyes, and court papers to be signed, wise and wizened old-timers who spoke gentle truth and hard experience.

A block away from the Sunshine Group was the Salvation Army. As I had at the agency in Baton Rouge, I stopped in unannounced, explained I was visiting for a United Way interview, and asked if I could look around a little. A genial staffer gave me a quick tour of the busy facility, offered me lunch, which was just being served (generous portions of tasty red beans and rice among the offerings), and introduced me to clients, kitchen crew, and professional staffers alike, all of whom were friendly and treated me like some kind of visiting dignitary.

Wow! I was home! So I made damn sure not to blow the interview. I asked no accusatory questions. Instead I charmed and soothed and flattered and painted word pictures and told amusing anecdotes on myself. In the end, before I left town the search chair told me that I was her choice and confided that it had come down to a young man from United Way of America (the office of the national association of U'Ways in Alexandria, Virginia) who was about the same age as me and had the same number of years' experience, but his was mostly at the Alexandria headquarters rather than local United Ways. He had a broader view and a more analytical approach because of his perspective from the national office. "Ah told the committee, as Ah see it, it comes down to a choice between a technician and an artist. On the one hand we have a theoretician, a statistician, an expert in best practices from all across the country. But in you we have more of an artist, with soul and passion. And I made it cleah to them which of y'all I believe is right for our little Mobile."

The search committee's choice (though not unanimous, I was later told—local labor volunteers had received a less-than-unqualified endorsement of me from their union brethren in Wisconsin) was decidedly in my favor.

When they made the offer, it was a no-brainer for me, though Nancy took some convincing. A lunch with a local Jewish couple finally assured her she need not fear cross burnings on our front yard. We didn't learn until a few months after settling in that as recently as 1984 there had been a random lynching of a young black man on a street corner downtown. (Spraggins hadn't mentioned that.) Despite this unsettling discovery, when I came across the following a few weeks later, it seemed to speak for me:

> *Perhaps it is this sense of strangeness that sends men far and wide in search for something permanent, to which they may attach themselves. Perhaps some deep-rooted atavism urges the wanderer back to lands which his ancestors left in the dim beginnings of history. Sometimes a man hits upon a place to which he mysteriously feels that he belongs. Here is the home he sought, and he will settle . . . among men he has never known, as though they were familiar to him from his birth. Here at last he finds rest.*

—W. Somerset Maugham

Or did I just will it to speak for me?

13

Plainclothes and Provenance

I needed a drink, I needed a lot of life insurance, I needed a vacation, I needed a home in the country. What I had was a coat, a hat, and a gun. I put them on and went out of the room.
—Raymond Chandler, *Farewell, My Lovely*

In my third year of patrol, I was contacted by a detective in Domestic Violence. He said there was a vacancy opening up in their unit and thought I would be a good fit. I was flattered. Then I asked why me?

"You write good reports," he said. "You're one of the few who can write a complete sentence and spell." (Most cops are bright and witty and capable, but with spelling and grammar, not so much.)

I was no longer flattered but was still intrigued. I talked it over with Sarge, Roney, and Balzer. I was surprised at their unanimous rejection of the idea. Sarge warned that going to headquarters, for *any* assignment, was a bad idea.

"Nothing good happens at headquarters," Sarge warned. "Too much office politics, backstabbing, ass kissing. Too much brass, with not enough to do, all up in your business."

Roney and Balzer opposed the idea as well but on wholly different grounds.

"Domestic!? You goin' jankity on me, bruh?" Roney said, his eyes big. "You don't get enough 39s out here? All that lyin' and cryin' . . . think about doin' nu'n *but* domestics, all day, e'ry day!"

"Not only that, but it ain't even *real* police," Balzer opined. "It's a lotta paperwork, lotta court, lotta talkin' on the phone, ridin' a desk, wearin' a necktie." Balzer cocked his head and narrowed an eye, as if considering another perspective. "On second thought, that might be just right for an old fart like you."

I withdrew myself from consideration the same day.

A year later, I was invited to consider moving to Financial Crimes, the unit some consider the white-collar detail. FiCri covers employee theft, fraud, forgery, embezzling, and the like, although it's just as often more blue-collar theft by deception: the guy who says he just resurfaced your neighbor's driveway around the corner and happens to have enough hot tar and asphalt left over, and rather than just dump the excess product, for half the normal price, today only he'll do your driveway. You give him a few hundred dollars, only to find after the next rain that he did nothing more than paint your driveway black. And of course, by then he's long gone, back up to Clarke County or halfway across Mississippi.

Again I declined the offer. I was still having way too much fun in patrol.

But by my sixth year on the job, I was on my third captain, Sarge had made lieutenant and been transferred to the Third, the Bear was dead, Roney had become a jump-out boy with a street interdiction antidrug unit, and Balzer was riding a Harley in Traffic Enforcement. Few of my original squad were reporting to the First Precinct anymore. Even LD had gone to HQ, to become, of all things, a PIO*. He looked good on TV, as long as he didn't talk too much.

Meanwhile, I was in the same precinct, same squad, same beat. Beat 12 covers a lot of geography and comprises commercial businesses, single-family homes, and Section 8 houses and apartments. It has the second-highest call volume in the precinct, and it borders beat 13, which, comprising the Birdsville and RV Taylor projects, has the highest call volume, much of which bleeds over into 12.

I remembered a conversation from a couple of years back. It was at the checkoff desk one morning after a particularly active night shift. I had humped two dozen calls, made six arrests (three of which were felonies), and covered nearly two hundred miles in the preceding twelve hours. Sarge and the Bear, looking over my reports and my daily call log, had asked me why I never requested a different beat.

"Twelve is a young man's beat, Mark," the Bear said. "Don't get me wrong—you handle it fine, don't you agree, Sarge?"

---

* Public Information Officer.

"May be the best on the squad," Sarge confirmed.

"So why doncha work a swap and take it easy for a change?"

I mumbled something about us old guys being creatures of habit, and I didn't wanna hafta learn a whole new set of streets and thugs.

"Besides, I've grown kinda fond of my peeps in beat 12," I joked. "And they would no doubt miss me, too."

But now I'm beginning to think maybe a change would do me good. I had always gotten restless in previous jobs after about six years. I had moved on from each of my three United Way posts at around the seven-year mark.

And of course Nancy was still pissed off that I was even a cop at all, still getting into fights and chases every few weeks. Most of our non-cop friends were baffled by my refusal to advance up the ranks, if not for the reduced risks, then at least for the (slightly) higher wage, and to put my management skills to use. I had passed a reluctantly taken, not-studied-for corporal exam a while back, but I had been relieved to learn that my score had not been high enough to qualify for placement in one of the limited number of corporal slots; I then decided not to risk promotion again and never took another exam. (The tests are really mechanisms for culling morons—though they seem to fail often in that regard—because the two hours of multiple-choice questions require little more than rote memorization of inane, arcane details having little to do with street policing or supervision.)

I became a cop partly to escape management. Personnel problems were constant, aggravating, and among the least satisfying parts of any job I'd ever had, so why do it as a cop for a dollar more an hour and stripes on my sleeve?

Then, six years into the job, six years riding beat 12, six years as a no-rank slick sleeve, the captain calls me into his office one day and tells me that they're restructuring the Investigations Division, beefing up property crime investigations at the precinct level, putting more manpower where it can be more focused and effective on burglaries and thefts, and he wants me to be on a detective squad he's putting together. There's no test to take. There's virtually no training, either, other than OJT*. Nor is there any pay, rank, or even status change. Oh, I would get a $200-a-year clothing allowance, since I'll be going "plainclothes," wearing my own civilian duds on the job

---

* On-the-job training.

now. And when I'm on a scene, I control it, even if there are sergeants and lieutenants around. "But I doubt that'll go to your head," the captain says.

I ask the usual why me, and he answers with the usual: "You can write a good report. And you should make a good impression in court."

Then he presses for the close.

"You've had an unusually long run at one spot for this department, Mark. Six years in the same beat. You've seen how people get moved around. If you don't take this, pretty soon you'll just see your name on the transfer list anyway, and they won't be inviting you, they'll be ordering you, and who knows where you'll land? How'd you like to end up in some shit hole like Property, or the Impound Lot, or the Pawn detail?"

I don't respond immediately. I'm remembering the time at United Way that there had been some campaign donations missing from the fund drive among faculty and staff of the Mobile County Public School administration building. It was only a few thousand dollars, and I knew none of my staff had stolen it, but I needed to prove it to my board and to the school board. So I had asked for an investigation from MPD.

A guy in a cheap, ill-fitting rumpled suit, with a bad haircut—not unlike Peter Falk's Columbo—had appeared at the office one day. Except he had none of Columbo's wit, or charm, or even street smarts, so far as I could tell. I explained to him that my staff were exemplars of probity, but I simply needed the MPD's confirmation of that fact to remove all suspicion from our end of the money handling. While I certainly wanted him to be diligent and thorough in his investigation of my staff, it really amounted to a pro forma demonstration of our system's checks and balances and integrity. He proceeded to spend the better part of a week grilling and browbeating my staff, bringing several of them to tears (including the men) and enraging the rest, only to conclude that his investigation was inconclusive and to suggest I subject everyone to polygraph examinations. I thanked the idiot for his help and dismissed him.

If that's what it means to be a detective, I'm thinking I'd just as soon stay on the streets. But I don't share any of these misgivings with my captain.

I've known the captain since he was the sergeant running the academy and I was his oldest recruit. We'd had some candid talks about career trajectories and life lessons, and I respected and trusted him. He had given me good insight into police culture.

"Cops are often petty and real jealous of each other's success. Avoid calling attention to yourself if you can," he had counseled when the press had wanted to do a story on "old United Way guy becomes cop." (I had done it anyway and regretted it. I was immediately suspected to be a dabbler, a dilettante, a rich "hobby cop.") And the captain had provided pithy but profound counsel on other matters as well, such as the cop tendency to become suspicious of *everybody* ("When you're a hammer, everything looks like a nail") and how to deal with cop groupies (who exist, even for one of my advanced years). "Just remember: the badge'll get ya pussy, but that pussy'll get your badge."

The captain is a smart man, and an honest one. I know I can trust him not to give me a bum steer.

After a moment, I hear myself say, "Hell, Cap, I guess you've made me an offer I can't refuse."

So I became a detective, somewhat reluctantly. I knew that at least Nancy would be happy. (Or, more precisely, a little less worried.)

And, in the back of my mind, there was always this: I already had a little experience with investigation. Nearly three decades earlier, I had cracked a cold case that had spanned the globe and the better parts of three lifetimes, a case involving missing persons (one of whom had long been presumed dead).

It had been, in a manner of speaking, a case of identity theft: my own.

For ten years, from my eighteenth to my twenty-eighth year, my investigative efforts had consisted mostly of looking in phone books for Culkin listings whenever I went to a new town. Never found a one.

In the meantime, I (somehow) graduated from CU with a degree in English (a hard-driven bargain with my beleaguered dad, who allowed me to drop out of architecture and major in whatever I chose, on the condition that I at least stay in school until I graduated with a degree in *something*, so when I went to Viet Nam with the Marine Corps—as I had threatened to do—I'd at least have a shot at going in as an officer rather than as cannon fodder). I had also married my college sweetheart and, since 'Nam had ended by the time I graduated, had taken a series of soul-deadening sales jobs, despite having little if any interest or knack for selling, especially since my product lines ranged from soft drinks to condiments to cookbooks. The chief benefits of the work, as I saw it, were a company car and an expense account, little accountability due to management's distant location, and a five-state territory covering the Rockies. Roaming such a vast expanse of geography afforded ample opportunity to look in numerous phone books, as well as to introduce myself as Rusty Culkin to every bartender, barfly, and beat-down booze whore in every roadhouse, motel lounge, and honky-tonk in Colorado, Wyoming, New Mexico, Arizona, and Utah. Always looking for that flicker of recognition, never finding one, then luxuriating in the bizarre and twisted freedom of being, at least for that night, whoever Rusty Culkin might feel like being: an advance man for *60 Minutes*, in town to do preliminary research for a feature on western saloons that might well include *this very bar!* Or a columnist for the *ProRodeo Sports News*, in town to do a story on local cowboys and the rodeo groupies who worship them, or a skip tracer, hunting a guy who's wanted in three states for bail jumping on charges of embezzlement, or bigamy (that last one always played well in Utah).

Though my random, hit-or-miss investigative techniques were utterly futile, they were cheaper and a lot more fun than hiring some shady Sam Spade character (why hire one when, as Rusty Culkin, I could just *be* one?) or engaging a pricey New Orleans litigator to wage a court battle to unearth the Dead C Scrolls. (The C being for the whore-bitch Cunt who'd squeezed me out, abandoned me, then probably crawled off to die of syphilis in some skid row free clinic.)

And then, as fate would have it, my long-suffering wife, a working journalist, was assigned to do a feature story on a group called Adoptees In Search, which was holding some kind of confab in Colorado Springs. Nancy came home from work and mentioned some of the people she had interviewed for the article and the successful, heart-melting "reunions" they had helped arrange between "relinquishing mothers" and their long-lost illegitimate offspring. She urged me to contact them.

Eventually, I did but with little hope for any useful suggestions or resources. After all, what could a group of amateurs in Colorado do to unlock sealed adoption documents nearly three decades old from a home for unwed mothers a half a continent away in New Orleans that had been out of business since 1957? I had nailed down the date of The Willows' demise through some desultory research at the library (this was well before the Internet), where I had found a fairly recently microfilmed *New Orleans Times-Picayune* story that included a reference to The Willows' closing. The main story was on the general decline in adoption, owing to the legalized access and widespread availability of birth control and abortion and the fading stigma of unwed motherhood, which made it much easier for pregnant girls who chose not to abort to keep their children to raise themselves. The piece on The Willows was just a sidebar story to illustrate how, in contrast to today's open acceptance (if not fashionability) of unwed motherhood, the topic used to be spoken of in hushed tones with euphemistic language. From an old The Willows promotional brochure: "Long recognized as offering some of Nature's choicest products to America's finest families." The florid, fulsome snob appeal nauseated me. Why not just something on the order of Get your USDA Prime bastards here at the The Willows, folks! But the dated literature, as well as the *Picayune*'s story, did bear out Mom's recollection of The Willows' national reputation.

Still, no matter how well known or well regarded it had been, I had my doubts about the ability of Adoptees In Search to get me any closer to my phantom forebears.

O me of little faith! Within a week, the organization had hooked me up with a similar group called Louisiana Triad, which put me in contact with Betty (who preferred not to reveal her last name). Betty was a retired delivery-room nurse who had worked at Tulane University Medical School Hospital. She had dealt with searches for Willows clients many times before. She had "access" to sealed records, and if I agreed not to ask questions about the nature and legality of her access to such records, she would provide all the information she could gather if I would simply read her the specifics (dates, times, names of adopting parents, etc.) from my birth certificate and adoption papers.

Betty was shocked that I had an actual pre-adoption name, saying that this was very rare, a major clerical faux pas, and a major break for me, which would expedite her research.

A week later, Betty called me back with the name of my biological mother (Judith Anise Culkin), her age when I was born (nineteen), and her hometown in 1952 (Hampton, Virginia). She added that I was really lucky to have the somewhat uncommon surname Culkin, because if my mother had been a Smith or Jones (or Johnson), I might *still* never find her, even with this many solid leads.

"Holy shit, I can't believe it!" I blurted. "A name and hometown! Let me pay you something, Betty, please! You're way better than any gumshoe!

Wow! I'm catching the next flight to Hampton, Virginia! You have no idea what this means to me, what this feels like right now!"

"Oh, but I do," she replied. "I've been there, Mark. But you need to slow down. Take a breath."

Betty urged me to talk some more to the Adoptees In Search people who have completed their own searches and reunions before launching off on my hunt for Judy Culkin, because "even if the search is successful, the reunion may not be."

"Huh?"

"She could be dead. She could be sick. She could be in an asylum, or a prison, or somebody you just would rather not be related to. She could be in denial, and not want to be reminded of you, much less talk to you or meet you. She could be happily married and never have told her husband or kids about you and living in fear all these years that you'll show up and wreck her marriage. I've seen it play out in all these ways, and more. You need to give some sober, informed, prayerful consideration to how you will make your approach, and how you might handle the various outcomes, Mark. Promise me you'll do that."

My mind was reeling; I was speechless.

"Not all reunions are heartwarming and liberating," Betty continued. "It can just as likely be unsettling, frustrating, burdensome, and heartbreaking. Even tragic. Take it slow, Mark. Easy does it. Promise me."

I hadn't given any thought to most of the possibilities she had rattled off (except, naturally, my own lurid whore fantasy). And the shock of the breakthrough was making it almost impossible for me to process all the new possibilities and variables.

Finally, I found my voice.

"Yeah, sure, of course I will, Betty, I promise." It was a lie, naturally. Lying was second (maybe *first*) nature to me, anyway, as a son, as a student, as an alcoholic, as a salesman, as a husband, as a lifelong imposter.

And I had gotten my first taste of the hunt, that jolt of the adrenalin that fuels the chase, the momentum that years later would sustain me daily, as a bona-fide police detective. Forty-eight hours after I hung up with Betty I was en route cross-country to Judy Culkin's house.

14

Missing Persons

The road of excess leads to the palace of wisdom; prisons are built with stones of law, brothels with bricks of religion.
—William Blake, "Proverbs of Hell," from the poem "The Marriage of Heaven and Hell"

I left at night. Nothing's finer than a good long overnight cross-country ramble to clear the mind. An evening departure means less traffic, slack trooper enforcement, higher speeds, better time. Plus you can get good reception of the all-night nationwide truckers' radio show on KVOO out of Tulsa, and for variety you can pick up the Mexican stations out of Juarez.

A thermos of strong black coffee, a pocketful of speed and weed, and eight hours of white lines and starry night were just what I needed to contemplate what lay in store for me.

I reviewed what I knew so far. After hanging up with Betty, I had dialed directory assistance in Hampton, Virginia, requesting residential numbers for any and all Culkins.

"I have no listings, sir," the operator said. Undeterred, I asked her to check for Culkin in the business listings.

"I do have two: Culkin Memorial Hospital and the Culkin Branch of the Hampton Public Library, sir. Would you like those numbers?"

Hey, now! Whoa! A hospital and a library? These Culkins must be robber barons. Or sweepstakes winners.

"No thanks. But could you check for Culkin in Newport News, Norfolk, and Portsmouth?"

"One moment, sir. I find no residential or commercial listings for Culkin in any of those metro areas, sir."

I thought about just driving to Hampton and going to the hospital and the library and asking around about the family whose name graced their fine institutions. Surely some blue-haired librarian, filled with civic pride at the opportunity to share her knowledge of local history, would be delighted to tell me about the pillars of her community and what became of the Culkin clan. But I recalled Dr. Cohen's words from freshman year in Boulder a decade ago and decided a more focused, less impulsive investigation might be better.

I called directory assistance in Richmond. No Culkins. Then I tried Washington, D.C., and Baltimore. Pay dirt! In Baltimore, there was a listing for a Willard Culkin. When he answered the phone, it was clear from the timbre of his voice that he was up in age. I explained that my name, too, is Culkin, and as an amateur genealogist, I was working on my family tree, and my research had led me to a connection to the Hampton, Virginia, branch. Might you be familiar with them, Mr. Willard?

"Oh, yeah! You're not a Culkin if you haven't tried to find a link to the Hampton clan! That's the rich side of the family! But unfortunately, I'm not a part of it."

"Well, I kinda figured there had to be some wealth there, because of the hospital and the library. But I'm not after money, just information. I just want to fill out all the branches on my tree. It surprised me that the operator said there were no listings for any Culkins in the Hampton area. Do you know what became of them?"

"Well, as I say, that branch is pretty distant from my own, and it's been a number of years since I did my own research, but I do recall that the Culkin who donated the hospital and the library, the old man who made the original fortune—of course he's long since passed now—I think he made it in oil and commodities, back in the twenties and thirties. And in his later life he was a U.S. congressman, I believe, or maybe it was just the Virginia statehouse. I'm not sure, it's been so long. I'm an old man, you know. But I seem to recall his oldest son took over the family concerns and runs an oil outfit in Texas somewheres. The only first name I can remember is William, because it's similar to my own, and that was the politician's. Beyond that, I'm afraid I'm of little use to you, young man. Don't recall any others, or any locations, either. You might try Dallas, though, for William's son. If it's oil, in Texas, I believe I'd start with Dallas."

I had thanked ol' Willard Culkin for his help and expressed a sincere hope that we'd meet some day, then found a listing for Culkin Oil in Dallas; the adrenaline boosters fired anew.

A receptionist put me through to Ben Culkin, president of Culkin Oil, but only after I identified myself as Russell Culkin, from Colorado Springs, calling on a personal family matter.

Ben seemed like an affable if inquisitive fellow. When I went through the family tree spiel that had worked so well with ol' Willard in Baltimore, I could hear him warming to me and was encouraged.

"I'm a bit of a genealogy buff myself, Russell, and I gotta say I've never heard of any Colorado Culkins. This is intriguing! Hold on a second, do you mind?"

I could hear a rustling of papers in the background, and my encouragement morphed into panic.

"You there? Good. I've pulled out some of my charts here, and I'm trying to see how we might be related. What were your father's and grandfather's names on the Culkin side?"

Shit! I hadn't thought this through. I couldn't hem and haw; any delay at all, and he'd figure I was just bluffing, a fortune-hunting con artist.

"Stanley Byron Culkin, Junior and Senior," I replied, without hesitation. I just used what I knew: my Johnson family names.

"Stanley Junior and Senior, you say? Hmmm. Where were they born?"

"Well, my father was born in Oklahoma City, and his father was born in Mountain View, Arkansas." It was so much easier just to use the truth than to try to think up something on the fly.

"Oklahoma and Arkansas!" Ben exclaimed. "And all these years I thought I was the only one to ever leave the eastern seaboard! So much for my rugged pioneer pretensions! How old are you, Russell? And do you know your dad's and granddad's birthdays? I'm penciling in a new branch on my chart as we speak."

"Well, I'm twenty-eight, and my dad was born in 1919, but I don't have my chart with me right now, and I can't recall my grandfather's birthday. But let's see, he died in '73 at the age of eighty-one, so the year, at least, would be—"

"Eighteen ninety-two," Ben offered. "What line of work were they in, Russell?"

"My granddad was with the Frisco Railroad, in some management capacity. And Dad's a chemical engineer, been with Monsanto for almost forty years now. President of Monsanto International Engineering—oversees all the stuff they do outside the U.S."

"Fascinating!" Ben said. I could hear more papers rattling. I had to turn this conversation around, and fast.

"But Ben, tell me about your side. You were originally from Hampton, Virginia, am I right? You're the son of . . . let's see, was it William? I spoke with a Willard Culkin, in Baltimore, who told me a little about the Hampton side, your family."

"That's right. Yeah, I see Willard here on my chart. I think he would be a second or third cousin once removed of my dad's."

"Okay, so we're on the same page, it sounds like. But Willard's kinda old and couldn't recall much more than William's name and that he had a son in the oil business, which brought me to you. I just took a shot and called Dallas directory assistance and got Culkin Oil. So tell me a little about your family. Do you have any siblings, Ben?"

"I have an older brother, yes, Will Junior, who lives in Miami. He's in the music business, an entertainer. And two sisters, Kathy, who's married and lives in Vermont, and Judith [jackpot!], who recently moved here to Dallas, as a matter of fact. Wanted to be closer to family after her divorce [another lucky break: no pesky husband to muck things up!]. And my wife and I have a son and two daughters."

I was electrified. My hands trembled. Adrenaline rushed through my veins. My breathing came quick and shallow, and I could feel my own heart beating. I struggled to keep the excitement out of my voice, to sound more clerical than inquisitive, like the next questions were just mundane follow-up details. I must, at all costs, keep him from thinking I was zeroing in on Judith, or he'd circle the wagons and I'd be left, once again, outside the circle.

"And, let's see now . . . how old are you, Ben? Forty-nine, you say? And your brother, Will Junior? Okay, fifty-one, right, you said he's the oldest . . . and sister Kathy in Vermont? Forty-five, okay, and how about the other one, was it Judith? Um-hmm, forty-seven [bingo], okay. And, oh, by the way, did she take back her maiden name after the divorce, or . . . just for my notes, y'know, for the chart?"

"Understood. Actually she never let go of the family name. Did one a' those fancy hyphenated names. Probably an early sign that the marriage was doomed," he said with a laugh. "But I think she's dropped the hyphen part now and gone back to just plain ole Judy Culkin."

I stopped listening as Ben rambled on about his kids. It was all I could do not to just hang up on him and head for Dallas. Somehow, I managed to gracefully conclude the conversation. Ben and I expressed our earnest hopes that "we Culkins" could get together some day to compare notes in greater detail. I assured him that he'd be hearing more from me real soon.

I immediately redialed Dallas information and got Judy Culkin's phone number and address. I couldn't believe it. This was way better than the Dead C Scrolls. This was the goddamn holy grail!

To keep my promise to Betty—and more likely because I really just desperately needed to tell somebody who could fully appreciate the impact all this was having on me—I called a couple folks from Adoptees In Search with the news.

After all the congratulations and the way-to-gos, they told me that the consensus is that the telephone is the best way to make initial contact, based on much hard experience. A letter could be accidentally opened by a spouse who's completely ignorant of his wife's firstborn. And of course, you *can't* just knock on the door and introduce yourself—there's no telling what might be on the other side! It could be like a bombshell for both of you. No, the best way is with a discreet inquiry by phone, usually best done at midday, when everybody's off to school or work. This way, both of you can absorb it all gradually, and nobody's rushed or crowded or threatened. She can consider if, and when and where, a face-to-face meeting might be arranged, usually in a safe public place like a shopping mall or a restaurant. After all, she has no idea if you've turned out to be a serial rapist, and it allows her to preserve confidentiality, to protect her family from her past, if she feels that's necessary.

As for the benefits to me of this approach, it gives me time to ease into the reunion or even to decide not to proceed if I get a bad feeling from the telephone conversation. (I couldn't imagine anybody coming this far and then stopping for a "bad feeling.") Sometimes the mother will sort of leech onto the child, they explained, to expiate long-buried guilt or to exploit for financial support, or respond in less predictable, even worse ways, to a myriad of psychological and emotional impulses, depending on past and present particulars. I acted like I was giving thoughtful consideration to the Search folks' cautions. Yeah, that makes sense, I said. I hadn't thought of that, I said. Of course, I can see how that's important, I said. I indicated I'd follow their counsel and take the cautious, considerate, safe approach.

But I had no intention of giving Judy Culkin any opportunity to decline or stall a face-to-face meeting. What if she just hangs up on me? What if she says, "I don't know what you're talking about, you have the wrong person, and do *not* contact me again!"?

No. Better not even give her the option. I mainly want to just lay eyes on her, once, if only for a moment before she slams the door in my face. I want to see that flicker of recognition I've been looking for in all those honky-tonks for all those years. I want to see if she looks like me, or I look like her. I want to meet my blood, in the flesh, if only for an instant.

So I'm cruising at 80 across the wide open Oklahoma Panhandle on a moonlit southbound two-lane. I figure to be in Dallas, parked on Judy Culkin's street, in time to observe her leaving for work in the morning.

"Can I help you?"

She peers at me cautiously, the door opening only as wide as the security chain allows. I look intently at the inch-wide slice of Judy Culkin, my biological mother. No flicker of recognition in the one eye studying me through the cracked door. No, it's more like a flicker of suspicion, or even fear. I try to calm her with a warm smile.

"Yes, ma'am. Are you Judith Culkin? Judith Anise Culkin?"

"Who's asking?" The open space between the door and the jamb narrows slightly, as does her one eye, looking me up and down through the vertical slit.

"Oh I'm sorry, ma'am. Shoulda introduced myself. I'm Russell Culkin. I think we might be related."

Her lips part slightly, her brow furrows, but she makes no reply.

After what seems like a long silence, she says, "I've never heard of any Russell Culkin. This must be some kinda mistake."

Yep that's me, Ma. You nailed it: Russell Culkin, Mistake. I clear my throat, take a half-step back, hoping to seem less threatening. "But you *are* Judy Culkin, right?"

"Yes, but—"

"Good. I don't really expect you to *know* me. We've never met. I mean, wull, I guess we *did* actually meet, once, briefly, but it's been a long time, and I looked a lot different then."

Earlier that morning, I had observed Judy from a half block away. It was about 7:30 a.m., and she had appeared to be dressed for work. She and two male teenagers carrying book bags (half brothers to me?) had piled into the family van and driven right past me. Nobody else—no new boyfriend, ex-husband, or other kids—had left the house, and nobody had returned. After an hour or so of surveillance, I surmised that the place was unoccupied and checked into a nearby Motel 6. I called Nancy to assure her I'd arrived in Dallas safely around sunup and had found Judy's place with no problems.

"I couldn't get too good a look at her, or the boys," I said. "The house is more modest than I expected for somebody who's rich."

"Just 'cause she comes from money doesn't mean she has any," Nancy said, astutely. Then she made me promise to try to get some rest before just showing up and knocking on her door in a sleep-deprived frenzy.

But after gazing at the ceiling for an hour, I abandoned my effort to sleep. Who was I kidding? My mind raced through every scenario I could imagine, and the permutations were endless. I showered, shaved, put on a fresh pair of slacks, a clean white button-down shirt, and a navy blazer (deciding a tie was too formal for the occasion). Took a half tab of white cross just to keep my eyes open till lunchtime, then went to a Waffle House for a fresh hot refill of the thermos. For good measure, I choked down the All Star breakfast—two over easy, hash browns, bacon and sausage, toast, and the obligatory waffle—just to take the edge off (despite an utter absence of appetite). When the liquor stores opened at 10, I laid in a fifth of Jim Beam and iced down a case of longneck Buds in my motel bathtub (for later, whatever the outcome), then returned to my post a half block from Judy's house, to sip black coffee and smoke Camels while waiting and hoping she might come home for lunch, alone. It could be my only chance to snag her without the boys around.

And then I had gotten lucky, yet again.

Now there's another awkward silence as Judy considers my mysterious last words (about our first encounter, long ago) and I search for my next words.

She cocks her head for a moment, then shakes it.

"No, I'm certain we've never met. But you say you're a Culkin?"

She unhooks the security chain and opens the door a little wider, though still not enough to indicate welcome, much less an invitation to enter. But she eases into a friendly banter.

"There aren't too many of us, you know, especially out here in the Wild West. I've only been here in Texas for a few months now, myself . . . "

"Well, not to be presumptuous, ma'am, but I'm pretty certain we *have* met. It's just been a long time ago—like twenty-eight years." I study her eyes closely, for the flicker.

But all I see is confusion. Then she throws caution to the wind, opens the door all the way, takes a step out and looks beyond and around me with an uneasy smile. It's my first full, close-up look at her. She's attractive, in a cute, mid-to-late-forties kinda way. Trim figure, nice teeth, full breasted—I've always sorta fancied older women.

I catch myself with a start: Yikes, Johnson, you sick fuck! She's your mother, for Christ's sake!

"Is this some kinda *Candid Camera* stunt?" She's looking around for Allen Funt and his crew. "I mean, how old are you, anyway? Where could we possibly have met twenty-eight years ago? I woulda been just a teenager, and you . . . ?"

She really bears little if any resemblance to me. She has stubby fingers like me, and her coloring is similar, but otherwise, I just don't see it. Neither, apparently, does she.

"Well, it *was* kind of a unique circumstance. I don't actually remember anything more than the date, to tell the truth, and that's only because people have told me. I'm hoping maybe you'll remember more about it than I do. Does January 26, 1952, ring any bells?"

And there it is: the flicker.

She takes a stagger-step backward. Her mouth opens, but nothing comes out. She quits looking for the cameras in the background and fixes her gaze on me.

"It was New Orleans, Louisiana, they tell me. At Tulane Hospital. And there was a place you stayed at there, called The Willows."

Judy's eyes get big. There's white all around her pretty green pupils. She puts a trembling hand on the doorknob and leans against it to steady herself. My ears fill with what sounds like pounding surf, and I feel a little wobbly in the knees myself.

"Oh my God," she whispers, her face stricken, the blood draining from her face. "It can't be you. It can't be . . . God! They said you'd never . . . how did you . . . God! I need a cigarette."

She reaches for a pack of Marlboro Reds from a table in the foyer, tears at it with shaky fingers, torches the filter end with her Bic before realizing her mistake, relights it, and takes a deep pull on the proper end. I could use a smoke myself, and a slash of Beam to go with it, but hold off.

Exhaling as she looks me up and down once more, she finally says, more to herself than to me, "You're Russell? My little, sweet, baby boy Russell? Ohhh, you must be! How else could you know?"

Then the dam breaks, and the cradle must fall, and down floats the baby, cradle and all—on a river of maternal tears.

She opens her arms, reaching for me, sobbing.

That intense—in some ways, harrowing—first encounter with Judy had taken me a while to process. Despite (or because of?) her wealth and privilege, Judy's life had not been one of ease and comfort. In many ways her life and family stories reminded me of my own, and of several I had come to know from my classmates at the snooty St. Louis prep school I had attended (which had compelled my decision to get as far away from there as possible in search of a new persona as much as a higher education).

That long drunken night she had shared with me the intimate details of her struggles, her compulsions, escapes, and losses. With the kindest of intentions (but blurred boundaries) she had disclosed her life to me as a sort of cautionary tale, perhaps hoping at some instinctive, protective maternal level to steer me clear of the pains she'd suffered as the result of her own incautious behaviors. The reckless, impulsive behaviors that had drawn her as a teenager to a swaggering Marine only to be cast aside by him and cast out by her own family; that had later damaged her reputation and ruined her marriage to a kind and decent man from rural Michigan. Demons that had driven her to relocate and reinvent herself from the impossibly rich East Coast debutante to the frozen lockstep of upper Midwest domestic conformity, to the gay divorcee partying with the rowdy wildcatters and cowboys in Dallas.

Though I didn't look much like Judy, I identified with her far more than I'd anticipated—or would have liked.

At that first encounter, all three of Judy's kids welcomed me into the family with the same delight and enthusiasm that Judy had. Suddenly I had three half siblings. Such welcome had not been forthcoming from the rest of Judy's family, however. Her brother Ben was furious that my deception of him had been the key to locating Judy, and sister Kathy was certain I was just a gold digger after a piece of the family fortune. Notwithstanding their skepticism, my "reunion" had been about as successful as such reunions get, compared to the horror stories I'd heard from the adoption search people.

But I was troubled by the similarities between Judy's life and my own, particularly by the alternating patterns of profligacy and piety. Meeting Judy had answered many old questions, but it seemed to open up a bewildering array of new, scarier ones. How much of my destiny is predetermined by nature, how much by nurture? What must I do to forge my own path, independent of either?

And what of that other wild card, the mysterious Marine who impregnated then abandoned Judy thirty years ago, no doubt further scattering his seed from here to Korea?

I would replay in my mind that boozy, blubbery night when Judy told me the story of Tom Whitaker. He had been her first love, she said, "And they're always the most intense, you know." A crack marksman, he was a riflery coach at Parris Island. "And he looked like a movie star in his dress blues," she'd said, sounding like the teenager she'd once been. "You know the Marines have the best uniforms, with the brass buttons, the red piping, and the white belts and hats!" His hometown was Motown, his father some big exec in the auto industry. Though only a year older than Judy, he seemed (to her sheltered nineteen years) so worldly and dashing and "slightly dangerous"; he was simply irresistible.

"You look just like him: so handsome," she'd said, her eyes brimming.

But when she had shared the news of her pregnancy with him, he denied responsibility, saying "anybody in the barracks" could be the father, for all he knew. She insisted tearfully that he'd been her first, her only. But he had stormed off and then would not even take her frantic phone calls. A few months later, as my presence grew obvious, one of Tom's fellow Marines telephoned her with the news that Tom had requested duty in Korea and had shipped off to the 38th parallel to be a sniper behind enemy lines.

Her parents were furious with her. They plucked her out of Wright College for Women in Beaufort, South Carolina, and put her on a train to The Willows in New Orleans. There, all the other girls whispered that she must be the daughter of Howard Hughes because of all the trunks of fine clothes that had arrived with her. They were jealous, and they shunned her. She was miserable and unbearably lonesome for what seemed an interminable six months. Her parents would visit her not once in New Orleans.

On January 26, 1952, after a sleepless night of increasingly painful contractions, she delivered me at a little past midmorning. She was allowed to hold me for all of two hours at Tulane Hospital before she was shuttled back to The Willows. She never saw me again and was whisked off by her parents a few days later for a whirlwind tour of Paris. Not to cheer her up, or to begin a new life for her. The trip was solely for the purpose of buying enough French trinkets and souvenirs, taking a sufficient number of snapshots of her next to landmarks, to lend credibility to the great Culkin cover-up: Judith had spent a semester studying at the Sorbonne.

"I had absolutely no say in the matter, you understand. There was never any discussion of keeping you. My parents, especially my mother, they were proud people. And of course back then, it wasn't like it is now. It could have been a major, major scandal, a disgrace to the whole family, and my father had his businesses to think of and his political aspirations. If it had been like nowadays, I'd have probably just had an abor—" She caught herself but not quite soon enough. I must have blanched. "Oh, honey, I'm sorry! I didn't mean what that sounded like! If you only knew how I grieved for you, for years! Every January, I'd get so-o-o blue around your birthday, I'd just hafta drink my way through it!"

There's a comforting thought, I remember thinking, as I had downed another shot of Beam and chased it with a pull of Bud.

When she returned to Hampton, Virginia, a letter was waiting for her, from that same barracks buddy of Tom's who had told her of Tom's orders to Korea. He was writing, sadly, to inform her that Tom had been killed in action on one of the many frozen, barren, unnamed pork chop hills of this forsaken hellhole. Before Tom had shipped out, the guy wrote, "Tom made me promise that if anything happened to keep him from coming home, I would let you know. Tom was a brave warrior, a patriot, he gave his life for

141

his country, for our freedom, blah, blah, blah," Judy recited with a sneer, twin flumes of blue smoke streaming from her nostrils.

I was a little put off by her cynical telling of Tom's story, and saddened by the news, despite his less-than-honorable exit from their shared predicament.

"Weren't you devastated?"

"What? 'Devastated'? Oh, Hayelllll no!" she scoffed. "I thought, good riddance, you cowardly son of a bitch!" Evidently, some long-buried resentment still stirred. Judy took another gulp of Beam and a drag from her Marlboro. "I mean, the way he treated me? To hell with him! He got what was coming to him, courtesy of the corps and the commies!"

There was a long pause, and my throat constricted. "So, that's it for him then, huh Judy? Adiós, muchacho? I guess it's sorta the end of a road for me, too, in a way. Do you know . . . is he buried in Arlington?"

"Ohhh, honey, I'm sorry," Judy said, suddenly tender. "I did it again, didn't I? Oh, you're so sensitive. I knew you would be . . . I just assumed . . . I guess I thought . . . I guess I didn't think, did I? But since you found out everything about me, I guess I just thought you knew all about him, too. But of course, you couldn't. You didn't even know his name until you found me. Oh, I'm so sorry. And no, I don't have any idea where he's buried."

"Didn't you get some kind of official telegram or something from the Defense Department, or the Marines? A letter of condolence, at least?"

"Why would I? I wasn't next of kin. We were never married. They don't send that stuff to old girlfriends. I'm sure the Marines don't even know I exist."

No, of course not. A guy like Tom Whitaker probably had lots of girlfriends. No way the Corps could or would bother with any of them. No official communication for Judy Culkin or any of the countless other grieving jilted girlfriends left behind to deal with Tom's liberally scattered seed. How sad, how tragic, really, but (it struck me, out of nowhere) how very *convenient* for him.

15

Deception for Detection

"You want answers?"
"I want the truth!"
"You can't handle the truth!"
—Aaron Sorkin, *A Few Good Men*

So, yeah, it had been more than twenty-five years since I'd tracked down Judy Culkin, missing person. But that was enough for me to believe I have a knack for detective work, or at least a head start on becoming a detective. After all, it could not be said that I was a *total* rookie, like right out of the academy, that I didn't *know from* investigating. It's not like I had to learn from scratch how to dig and scour and pound the pavement to chase down the facts, how a little deception can aid detection. In addition to the lessons learned in the (dumb-luck-laden) search for Judy and Tom, my six years on the streets of beat 12 had given me the rudiments of interrogation, fact checking, and forensics.

And seeking "the facts, just the facts, ma'am" was something I had fancied since boyhood. Steeped as I am in *Dragnet* drama and the big-screen adventures of Dirty Harry Callahan, to become a detective is really the more perfect fulfillment of puerile fantasy than being a uniformed cop had been. Truth be told, I was now, finally, really, living the dream.

For in some primal way, it feels like I was made for this job. It fits like my favorite jeans. The fundamental paradox at the heart of detective work, the fact that an essential tool of the trade is the masterly use of *deception* in the dogged pursuit of "truth," is quite literally and specifically second (or first?) nature to me.

This is not to say that I don't miss uniformed patrol work. I do, intensely at times. I could have been happy riding a beat for many more years, if only I had started earlier. In just a quick half-dozen years on the job, I was already seeing my sunset on the horizon. The pulled muscles from fence-hopping foot chases and the cuts and bruises from cuffing "one resisting" hurt more and longer with the passing years. And despite my ability to outdistance most cops half my age, a good cop needs speed more than endurance. Thugs don't usually have endurance, anyway. (Most of them are chain smokers, after all.) But if you lose visual contact because of the gap they put behind them in the first sixty seconds, it doesn't matter how long or how far you can run—you won't find them. They've turned, doubled back, laid down somewhere. If you don't catch them quick, they're gone. Even in my youth, I had never been a sprinter.

Instinct—the lightning-fast ability to read and react—is even more crucial than physical conditioning to survival on the streets. It was becoming apparent to me that no amount of training or practice would quicken my ability to read the signs. I had lived too long in another world. My suburban, prep-school youth and nonprofit boardroom career taught me to take the measure of a man by the firmness of his handshake, the steadiness of his gaze, the cut of his suit, the shine of his shoes.

In a street cop's world, you don't shake hands, you watch them. Eyes don't tell you much, but hands can kill you; don't let anybody get within the six-foot zone of safety. The layers of FUBU jerseys and sagging Coogi jeans aren't studied for "cut" or fabric, but for the lumps and bulges that might conceal a firearm. The shine on the Air Jordans doesn't matter, it's the knives, cuff keys, and nickel bags inside them that do. Tats, do-rags, colors, and haircuts indicate ever-changing 'hoods, affiliations, and occupations: dope slinger, thief, street soldier, each with varying degrees of risk and threat, depending on location, time of day or night, and circumstances of police contact.

Hell, I need an interpreter sometimes, so foreign to me is the street dialect of the beat cop's milieu. It's not just a barrier of slang or racial dialect (y'feel me, brah?), it's a generational ignorance that keeps me at a disadvantage (and therefore a danger to myself and my partners). In my mid-fifties, I'm just too slow for the streets, too slow to pick up on who's who and what's what.

A detective needs instincts and street smarts, too, but in most investigative circumstances the consequences of an overlooked detail, or the missed tell, are not as dire, and certainly not as immediate. The pre-frisked suspects (usually cuffed to an eyehook bolted to the interrogation table), the often plodding pace, the dogged slog through the detail of investigation, and the bullshit of interrogation are much better suited to one my age than is patrol.

Patience, deliberation, and deception are essential for a detective; speed, strength, agility, not so much. I used to hate it when, as a uniform, I'd bring a suspect to headquarters for questioning, and it seemed like the damn detective was somnambulant, moving in slo-mo, just deliberately taking as long as possible to deal with the miscreant. I was eager to dump the guy at Metro and get back out on the streets. I figured the detective was either lazy or avaricious, deliberately stretching out the double-time hourly pay he was earning for after-hours callout. I later learned that while both descriptors may be accurate, it's also a fact (and therefore a tactic) that the longer the perpetrator sits isolated in custody, the more likely he is to confess. It's been measured, documented.

And the deception thing: a good detective is a creative master when it comes to lying to get to the truth. The basics are "I got three eyewitnesses who picked your mug out of a photo spread, put you at the scene," or "Your prints are all over the broken glass from that window you busted to get in," or "The neighbor's security cameras picked you up clear as day." Of course you have to be reasonably sure it's believable that witnesses might have been around, or that your perp wasn't wearing latex gloves, or that remote security video is plausible. But most perps are blessedly stupid, unless they're career types who've heard it all before and spent some time comparing notes at the crime academies we call the Department of Corrections.

Such seasoned criminals require advanced detective tactics, which in turn require deployment of advanced deceptive tactics. I got my first inkling of this when, as a uniform, I'd brought a robbery suspect to headquarters one night. The storekeeper who'd been robbed had not gotten a look at the robber's head or face, which had been covered by a hoodie and a bandana. The thug had fired a round into the shop's ceiling to show how serious he was, and the terrified victim had lain on the floor, eyes closed, and now couldn't even recall height, weight, age, or anything beyond the usual "black male, black sweatshirt, black baggy jeans, black sneakers." I had snatched this poor suspect up a block away because he matched the description—as did virtually everybody in a five-block radius—but he was sweating profusely when I stopped him, as if he'd been running. We didn't even know if the robber had been running, or had simply gotten into a car and driven away. And he wasn't carrying a gun when I frisked him. So I really had nothing on him, but he was all we had.

The detective had me put my suspect in an interview room. I asked the suspect which hand he wrote with, then cuffed his left, non-writing hand to an eye-bolt in the center of the table. While doing this, the detective entered, took a seat at the table, introduced himself to my guy, told him he appreciated his cooperation and that this shouldn't take too long, and then began chatting with him about family, high school, work, and Alabama–Auburn football—like a couple guys in a tavern might start a conversation over beers. I left to hit the men's room and get a cup of coffee.

When I came back I entered the little, darkened audio-visual booth between the two interview rooms and looked through the two-way mirror. The suspect was sitting in there alone. I took a seat in the hall outside the interview booths and sipped at my vending machine coffee.

When my coffee was all gone, I re-entered the little observation booth in time to see the detective rip open a wet-nap packet and gingerly wipe down the suspect's trigger finger and thumb, drop the wipe into a plastic bag, gather up his papers, then exit the room, saying he'd be right back.

He didn't come right back. I observed the suspect for a while as he sat cuffed to the table and fidgeted, gazing at the ceiling, shaking his head, his lips moving though no sound came out. Eventually I went back out into the hall to the more comfortable seat, switched my radio back on, and listened to my squad's chatter to find out what I was missing outside.

After what seemed like nearly an hour, the detective finally returned, carrying several sheets of official-looking forms on which information had been typed, along with the used wet-wipe in the plastic baggie, which I noticed now bore an "EVIDENCE" label, with the case number, the detective's name, and the suspect's name. I turned off my radio and slipped back into the observation booth.

"Sorry for the delay," the detective said as he settled in across from the suspect. "The guys in the lab took their time getting here, and then it took awhile to get the results."

The prisoner's eyes got slightly wider. "Huh? Whatcha mean, 'the lab'? What 'results' you be talkin' 'bout?"

The detective deadpanned, "The crime lab guys. Remember when I asked you about the gun, and you said—" He paused, flipping through his notes.

"Here it is, you said, and I quote," he cleared his throat, then, in his flattest hard-boiled white guy voice read, "'Gun? What I be needin'a muhfuckin' gun fuh? It ain't a reason in the worl' fuh me to be havin' no gun!' Did I get it right?"

The suspect nodded, utterly confounded about where this was going.

The detective then read from the two typed forms in front of him.

"Forensic testing indicates conclusively that residue captured from the swabbing of suspect's right index finger and thumb is consistent with gunpowder and gases from a firearm discharge no more than two to three hours prior to recovery of the sample."

Suspect's face dropped. Minutes later, he confessed.

The detective exited the interrogation room. "He's all yours. Take 'im to Metro. Robbery First."

"Wait! What 'crime lab'? There's nobody here tonight but me and you and the overnight property clerk."

He crumpled up the evidence baggie and forensics report and tossed them in a waste basket, smiling a broad, triumphant grin.

"I know that, and you know that. But numbnuts in there?" He nodded toward the interrogation room. "Muhfucka's clueless! All he knows is what he sees on *CSI*."

First thing I did was buy a two-hundred-dollar shoulder holster rig. Just like detectives Jeff Spencer and Stuart Bailey had for carrying their snub-nosed .38s on *77 Sunset Strip*. It looked so cool.

But a sixteen-round Glock is bigger and heavier than a six-shot .38. In a shoulder holster, which is tedious to put on every day and a little tricky to draw from, the .40-caliber semiauto is uncomfortable and just doesn't feel secure dangling from a strap against your ribs.

I realized I had seen only a couple of detectives in the department ever wearing one. One of them had been my old FTO, Portly Porter, shortly after he had become a detective. I ran into him at headquarters one day and remarked on his fancy rig.

"Cool, man! You look just like Double Oh Seven—except for the cheap suit, the crooked teeth, and thirty-pound beer gut."

"I can change my suit, fix my teeth, and lose weight, Pawpaw," he smiled. "But you can't ever get any younger."

Three weeks later I ran into him again and noticed he had gone back to the hip holster. I thought my teasing had shamed him into returning to the conventional hip carry. Now I realized Porter had simply learned what I had just discovered. The next day I took my shoulder harness back to the store for a refund.

Then I went to my locksmith, the guy who'd always cut a copy key for me at no charge whenever I was assigned a different squad car. (Ever since that time I locked myself out of my idling squad car with a cuffed prisoner in the backseat, I carry a spare key.) I inquired about the purchase of a small, discreet kit of lock picks—the kind that always gets the gumshoe through the door, any door, in seconds.

"Hollywood!" he harrumphed. I felt about as stupid as the robber who had fallen for the forensic gunpowder-on-trigger-finger "evidence." (If pick kits exist, my locksmith ain't sellin' 'em, even to a guy with business cards and a badge that say "Detective.")

Okay, a couple small missteps. Maybe real-life detectives, like real-life patrol cops, don't much resemble the Hollywood versions.

16

The New Squad

Prudence is a rich, ugly old maid courted by Incapacity. He who desires but acts not, breeds pestilence.
—William Blake, "Proverbs of Hell," from the poem "The Marriage of Heaven and Hell"

Welcome to First Precinct Investigations," he says, pushing his chair back from his desk and spinning a half turn to face me. He's wearing blue jeans. Not just any blue jeans, but frayed, ripped blue jeans, with stains that might be motor oil or ketchup. Dark blotches that have been there awhile and are set in the faded fabric. The jeans are complemented by a short-sleeved bowling shirt with the tails out and the name Earl stitched above the pocket. The kind of shirt the pampered one-percenters in my prep school used to wear with "irony." But something tells me this guy's idea of irony is something his mama used to do to his daddy's Sunday shirt.

He's probably thirty, and about that many pounds overweight. He has about an eighth-inch buzz haircut, and the day-old stubble on his unshaven cheeks is about the same length as the stubble on his head.

He smiles with his eyes as much as his mouth, and with a sweeping gesture like Vanna White displaying the lavish shelf space of a brand-new Frigidaire declares, "This is where the magic happens! That desk'll be yours. Earl Slocumb."

His thick paw envelops mine in a firm grip with a vigorous, pumping handshake.

I survey the quarters. The windowless ten-by-ten space, roughly the size of a two-man cell at Metro, has two desks pushed up against opposite walls, their wheeled chairs bumping back to back. Through-traffic with both chairs occupied would require an audible "Excuse me" to get the detectives to snug their chairs all the way up to their desks to allow a scrunched-up, sideways passage.

My new desk, a scarred and dented battleship gray with a faux-wood laminate top, is flanked by two four-drawer metal file cabinets that don't match each other, or the desk: one is a standard office beige, the other a bilious green. Slocumb's desk is equally battered but wooden and slightly larger, big enough to support a forty-inch monitor screen ("a seizure," Earl explains when he sees me comparing my standard-size monitor to his jumbo model) and a six-pack-size refrigerator. The walls above and behind Earl's monitor and dormitory fridge are decorated with an Alabama Department of Conservation calendar illustrated with tidal charts and fish, a snapshot of Slocumb holding up a string of fat red snappers, another of a twelve- or thirteen-year-old girl in a softball uniform and her nine- or ten-year-old kid brother wearing big sis's team cap, and a framed certificate proclaiming Detective Earl Slocumb Officer of the Year, 2010. Stuck in the corner of the frame is a snapshot of Earl accepting the certificate and a handshake from the chief. I've never worked with or even heard of Slocumb before, which surprises me, given this distinction.

"Officer of the Year! Impressive! How long you been on?"

"Three years," Slocumb replies.

"Really," I reply, tamping down my disbelief, thinking wow. This guy must be a police whiz-kid or the nephew of the chief—and he certainly is not the latter. I deduce this because I am a detective now. And our chief is black, which Slocumb is not.

Our two-desk suite adjoins another two-desk suite for two more detectives. There had at one time been a door between the two rooms, as evidenced by the surviving hinges on the frame. The door's removal was probably an anti-claustrophobia measure, I figure. Neither room has any windows, though each has a door. Theirs leads to the precinct's parking lot, ours to the center hallway.

Slocumb sees me looking at the other room, which is equally cramped with two battered desks and mismatched file cabinets.

"Lopez sits there. He was mostly in the Third 'cept for about a year or so up in Citronelle. Been on altogether five or six years. And that one's O'Malley's. He's a corporal. Did a couple years with NOPD before coming back home. He's got lotsa stories about policing the Big Sleazy. They both should be rollin' in anytime now."

I take it all in. It occurs to me that the space is less than half the size of my old office at United Way, yet is occupied by four men. And I used to think that my old office was modest, even by nonprofit standards. Slocumb seems to hear my thoughts.

"It's cozy in here, but we're all out of the office a lot, and most of us shower at least once a week, so it usually don't get too ripe in here." He spits a brown stream of tobacco juice into a plastic Dr. Pepper bottle half full of Levi Garrett–infused saliva.

The door to the parking lot opens and we're greeted with "Morning, bitches" even before a grinning, cherubic fella makes his appearance. It's the spittin' image of Barney Rubble, a uniformed leprechaun with corporal's stripes and a mean-looking scar across the top of his shaved head.

My presence startles Corporal O'Malley, who hastily retracts his irreverent greeting.

"'Scuse me, sir. Didn't realize we had company in here."

"He ain't company, Devin. It's just our new partner, Johnson. But he's old enough to be your daddy, so I think he deserves a little more respect than 'Morning, bitches.'"

O'Malley offers his hand.

"Devin O'Malley. I've heard about you. Didn't you use ta be, like, the Red Cross president or something?"

"Right, but United Way."

"Yeah, United. That's it. Same thing. That charity deal they give us the pledge cards for every year. United Fund. Yeah, I always sign up for a few bucks."

"So do I, but I never got any," Earl says.

"You retard!" Devin says, as if he believes Earl. "They take it *outta* your paycheck, they don't *give* it to you."

"Well I don't know why not," Earl protests. "I'm a single father of two. I don't make the big bucks corporals do, Devin. With my pay, I could get food stamps. Ain't the United Fund s'posed ta help the needy?"

"'Yes indeedy,'" I declare. "'We help the needy!' That's one of my favorite old campaign slogans. And I have no doubt you'd qualify, Earl. You should getcha some free groceries at the Downtown Pantry. Stretch those food stamps a little further."

"Problem is, if I went there for some a' that guv'ment cheese they givin' out, I'd probably get overbese and they'd hafta put me on the Michelle Obama diet and workout. Not to mention I'd end up arresting half the people standing in line with me," Slocumb says.

"Yeah, come to think of it, Earl, isn't that how you got Officer of the Year practically right out of the academy? All those arrests you made at the Sally and the Food Pantry?"

"You're just jealous 'cause you didn't think of it, Devin."

Now I'm not sure who's kidding and who's not.

"So how old are you, anyway?" Slocumb asks. "I've heard you're, like, retired already, and rich, and just doing this job like some kinda hobby or something?"

"Shit, Earl!" chides O'Malley. "You just tol' me I owe the man more respect, and now you're all up in his bidness, just like that? Where's *your* manners?"

"How'm I disrespectin' the man, Dev? I'm just bein' friendly."

"No offense taken," I say. "I'm fifty-six. Old enough to be your daddy— both y'all's daddy. I guess that's why they made me a detective. Puttin' me out to pasture."

"Don't let him fool ya, Earl," O'Malley says. "I've heard about this guy. Don't matter how old he is, he ain't no hobby cop. Man's been in patrol six years, all here in the First—that's like three times longer'n your whole police career, Earl—and he did it all in 12's beat. Man's a legend. He's the Dirty Harry of the First Precinct."

Before I could question O'Malley's sources or protest the flattery, the door opens and a little guy with tats on his arms who does not look Hispanic enters with the greeting, "Hola muchachos!" Then, to me, he says, "You must be the new *old* guy. Been lookin' forward to meeting you. Nash Lopez."

As we shake hands, Earl interjects, "Also known as 'Nashty.'"

"Or more commonly, 'Lusty,'" adds Devin.

Unfazed, Nash continues, and I quickly perceive whence cometh his monikers: "I bet you could let me have a couple of your spare Viagras, huh? I tried one once from a guy who's about your age: old. But that little blue pill? Aye Chihuahua! Coulda hung a wet towel on my pecker, y'hear me?

Got my nut three times in one night! Wife never knew what hit her. Poor girl couldn't walk straight for a week, know what I'm sayin'?"

Lusty Lopez, reporting for duty. I'm thinking "Kid Id" could be a good alternate moniker for him but refrain from mentioning it. "Id" would probably be mistaken as short for idiot, therefore insulting.

"I mean I played the whole repertoire that night! Tell 'im, Earl."

"Yeah, we got every detail of that night's playbook," Earl says, counting them off on his fingers. "Let's see, there was the Russian Trombone, the Meat Curtain Mudflaps, the Naughty Pirate, the Nasty Rooster, the Mexican Mustache . . ."

"What's a Russian Trombone?"

"It's pretty obvious," Lusty says. "She fills her mouth with vodka and your balls and hums while giving you a hand job."

Devin shakes his head and says, "It's the man's first day, Lusty. I think he's heard enough." Turning to me he says, "Don't even ask about the rest— especially the Meat Curtain Mudflaps, Mark. Trust me."

One of the cases I got in my first week as an investigator made headlines when we broke it and made two arrests several weeks later. Front page, above the fold. It was not a particularly remarkable case, nor was it solved by brilliant detective work. It was a collaborative effort, spanning three precincts, and the main break in the case was actually made by a colleague in the Third, Detective Roshunda Carter, a soft-spoken little wisp of a thing with less time in the department than me, but powers of observation and recall that surpass mine and those of many investigators. It takes all kinds to make a good PD, and Carter's kind is essential. I've heard several cops speak of her disparagingly, mostly about her quiet nature and small stature. Comments like "I don't know how she ever made it through the academy" and "I sure wouldn't want her backing me" were typical and understandable, but unfair.

"Say what you want, I never rode a beat with her, but she's a damn good detective" would be my standard response. This would invariably be met with a grudging shrug of acknowledgment (not to be mistaken for agreement). The department is and always will be a boys' club, and the sexual orientation of its capable females is a common topic of speculation.

My case with Roshunda was dubbed "The Wedding Crashers" by the *Press-Register*. At weddings all over town, in congregations of diverse races and classes, and denominations mainstream and fringe (Central African Methodist Episcopal Zion, Jacob's House of Blessings Assembly of God, Ebenezer Apostolic, Holy Name Catholic, Baltimore Street Baptist, even a Jewish ceremony at the swanky Country Club of Mobile), some enterprising thieves discovered that a common practice at weddings is for all of the bridesmaids to leave their purses, and often gifts for the newlyweds, in an unsecured anteroom somewhere near the sanctuary, ripe for the picking. In one particularly sad case, the newlyweds' passports and cruise tickets were stolen with the bride's purse, ruining their honeymoon.

Two such thefts occurred in my areas in my first two weeks. The others had happened in other precincts, primarily in Roshunda's beats in the Third, over preceding months. But I got lucky. My Jacob's House of Blessings church had security cameras that captured pretty good images of the thieves: a black male, late twenties to mid-thirties, and a black female, about the same age. They were both dressed as if they had been invited to attend the wedding. Nobody in the wedding parties knew who they were, but everyone had assumed they were friends or family of the bride or the groom. It's a good plan and worked well, over and over, even after the first couple of thefts were reported in the paper. The crashers were either bold enough or desperate enough to do two more even after their images were broadcast on local TV from clips of the footage at the Jacob's House of Blessings Assembly. Or, just as likely, neither of them (nor any of their friends or family) reads the paper or watches local TV news.

The Jacob's video had even caught the thieves departing from the church in a battered white Toyota with a dented trunk, though the tag number was not visible. That dent in the trunk proved to be their undoing, thanks to Roshunda's sharp eye and luck. She was driving to a call one day on I-65 and a battered white Toyota with a dented trunk passed her. It was driven by a black male who could have been the male half of the wedding crashers. She radioed in the tag, which came back to a residence in Citronelle, a small farming community forty-five minutes from Mobile. Then she called me, and together we went to Citronelle, where we were met by a couple local units who took us to the white Toyota, which was parked at the home of the female wedding crasher's grandmother. There we took the female crasher into custody, and she told us where we could find her boyfriend, at his mama's in the Bottoms neighborhood of the Third Precinct. We even recovered some of the stolen wedding gifts, still in their gift-wrapped boxes, in the barn behind granny's in Citronelle and in mama's house in the Bottoms.

It wasn't until the story broke on the arrests of the crashers that we received the call from the wedding party at the exclusive Country Club. Though the club is not in the First Precinct, I received the call from the mother of the bride, who knew of me from my United Way days and knew my wife, Nancy, through her circle of associates. She had not learned of the wedding crashers in the papers or on TV but by word of mouth. Then she had looked up the news stories online and was certain they were responsible for ripping off her daughter's bridesmaids. My first reaction was skepticism.

"With all due respect, Mrs. Finkel, I'm not doubting that some items may have been misplaced, or even stolen, at your daughter's wedding, but I'm not sure the people we arrested did it. I mean, have you seen their pictures? They don't exactly *blend* with your guest list."

"We *did* have several African Americans on the guest list, Mistah— excuse me, *Sergeant* Johnson."

"It's Detective, but just call me Mark, Mrs. Finkel."

"Certainly, and just call me Sarah, Detective Johnson. Anyway, as I'm sure you're aware, the club relaxed its guest policy and *even the membership policy* ye-ahs ago. And there were several black Afro Americans invited. But I understand yoah hesitation, as I'm sure you'll understand ours. Frankly their presence was a source of some consternation to our family as well as to that of the groom on the weddin' day. No one could *place* them at the time . . . but finally someone said they thought the girl was the daughtah of her housekeepah, who had helped out several times as a servah when they had entertained large holiday gatherins, and though they couldn't recall inviting the girl, they couldn't bring themselves to confront their housekeepah to ask her if the girl was her daughtah, so we all just let it go. Actually, even aftah I saw their pictures online, I couldn't be sure they wuh the ones who had worried us on the weddin' day. I just couldn't bring myself to believe it had happened to *us*. It took Mistah Jeffahson, who's in charge of the help at the club, to call me and inform me, when *he* saw their pictures in the papah, that he recognized them from our event, and I can't tell you how hard it hit us all. We're still recoverin' from the shock of it all. I hope you'll understand, we'd prefer not to heah from reportahs, or participate in the mattahs at the courthouse, if there's a way all that business can be avoided. I know you'll handle this with discretion, Sergeant Johnson."

The crashers had told me, in their interview confessions, that they had picked their jobs by simply checking the wedding listings in the paper and going to ones where they figured there was a good chance some black people would be among those invited. Neither of them had mentioned their grandest larceny in one of the grandest settings in Mobile during their interrogations. Why would they?

After the call from Mrs. Finkel, I went to Metro to reinterview the female crasher. She didn't play any games and admitted they had done the heist at the Country Club.

"How did you figure you'd blend in at a *Jewish wedding*, at the *Country Club*, of all places?"

"My auntie worked for the groom's mama her whole life. She wasn't there—she been real sick. If she woulda been there, we wouldna went, cuz she woulda knowed we ain't been s'posedta be there. But I knowed we could pass 'cause e'rbody would think we was there representin', know what I'm sayin'? An' they wouldn't say anything cuz those people don't be frontin' nobody out, 'specially at a fancy thang like that. And I was right. Nobody said nu'n to us. It was easier than a reg'lar church."

So easy that even after the theft, even after seeing the mugs of the perps in the paper and remembering that a couple of similar-looking folk of uncertain origin had been at the wedding, it had taken a call from *the help* at the club to prompt a call to the authorities. And even then, not just a call to the Second Precinct captain, in whose precinct the Country Club is located. The call was made only to a cop who could be trusted to handle the matter with discretion.

The Country Club had been a good lick for both parties: for the wedding crashers (until it wasn't) and for Roshunda and me. Though Roshunda deserves most of the credit.

17

Oedipus Wrecks

The sins of the father are laid upon the children unto the the third and fourth generation.
—Deuteronomy 5:9

About a year after finding and meeting Judy Culkin, I "escaped" the sales rep biz, thanks to a brutal termination that completely blindsided me. Nancy was seven months pregnant at the time.

I was selling *Better Homes & Gardens* cookbooks (as well as other lines of home repair, gardening, hobby, and craft titles) for Meredith Publishing Company out of Des Moines, Iowa, in the Rocky Mountain territory. It had been a step-up in salary from my stint with R. T. French Company out of Rochester, New York (makers of French's mustard, Worcestershire sauce, Big Tate instant potato buds, and a line of instant powdered sauce and gravy mixes) and (in my hopelessly hopeful way of self-deception) I believed it was a step closer to my true calling, since the cookbook people were, after all, *publishers*. Instead of supermarkets, I would be making sales calls on *bookstores*, way more befitting someone of my interests, education, and talents.

But I inherited a territory that had been vacant for over a year and was full of disgruntled customers. Pallets of dead, unsold Meredith books in bookstore backrooms all across the Rockies were awaiting return credit authorizations by a sales rep. My first six months of return credits had exceeded my sales; the home office was pissed, and the Big Guy came out from Des Moines to ride my territory with me. At the end of the day we were in the airport bar at Stapleton International in Denver, where I was to put him on a plane back to Des Moines.

He bought me a few rounds, then informed me that in his judgment, the problem with my territory was me. "You're an order taker, not a salesman," he said. He waved off my protests of backlogged returns, pissed-off customers, the need to rebuild confidence and trust in the brand. But I had a belly full of whiskey and a mouth full of bluster.

"I won every damn sales contest they had at French's. Set records, won a full set of luggage, a free vacation to San Francisco. You don't think I can sell?" I demanded, slapping the keys to the company car on the bar. "By God, here's your keys: fire my ass."

To my horror, he picked up the keys, said "You're fired," and drove my company car back to Des Moines.

After breaking the news to Nancy, I skulked home to St. Louis seeking solace, comfort, and encouragement from my folks. Dad told me to meet him for lunch at Busch's Grove, a clubby gathering place for St. Louis's old-money crowd, not far from his office at Monsanto and near St. Louis Country Day School, my preppy alma mater.

I still nursed a deep resentment for the betrayal I had felt when, after assurances by Mom and Dad that I wouldn't be forced to go to that stuck-up, all-boys, coat-and-tie school Ernie had transferred to from our public elementary in the fourth grade ("Just take the entrance exam to see how well you score," they had said), they had enrolled me anyway. There I rubbed shoulders with Danforth and Pulitzer and Budweiser scions who heaped scorn on me for my address out in the sticks and the JC Penney labels on my blazer and tie. As I got older and better able to return the scorn to the most loathsome of my classmates, my father's encouragement changed from "Toughen up" to "Think of the contacts for a lifetime you're making!" What I considered his blatant social climbing embarrassed me. Of course I later felt much (unexpressed) gratitude when, at the University of Colorado I was able to drink Coors by the pitcher and sleepwalk through classes by simply recycling my high school homework, thanks to that excellent prep school education.

After the waiter took our orders (mine including a midday Budweiser, which induced a scolding frown from Dad), I whined about the injustice of my termination from the cookbook company, criticized its stupid and shortsighted management, and declared, "Truth be told, I pretty much hate sales anyway, whether it's mustard or cookbooks." I took a swig from my longneck Budweiser and noticed my father's lips tighten.

"You could at least pour it into the glass," he said. "We're not in Boulder." I snorted through my nose at his bourgeois pretension and took another swig from the bottle. That was Dad's last straw.

"For goodness' sake, Mark, when are you going to grow up and take responsibility? Get on an even keel? You've got to quit blaming other people for your problems. You've got to buckle down—you're almost thirty, married now, about to be a father, and you can't hold a job. I guess we shouldn't be surprised. You dropped out of architecture, would've quit college altogether if I hadn't made you stay. You wanted to quit Country Day, would've even quit the Boy Scouts if I hadn't intervened. After all we've given you, the education, the contacts, I don't understand it. Most young men would be grateful for the advantages you've had, but you turn your nose up at it. I guess we spoiled you. By the time I was your age, I'd been in the navy, fought in a world war, worked my way into a good company, was building a career. Mom and I taught you better. I was never fired from a job and never quit a job unless I got offered something better. But that's always been your problem. You're a quitter."

I was stunned. Stung. And seething. So much for solace, comfort, and encouragement. I took another defiant swig of beer and watched my father cut his steak. I felt the urge to upend the table, make a big loud scene, and stomp out of the place shouting profanities. Instead I lit a Camel, contemplated my counterassault, and exhaled a long blue stream of smoke across his plate. He put his silverware down and glared at me.

"I'm sorry I'm such a disappointment to you, Dad. I guess I can't argue with most of what you said. But I will say one thing: I'm not a quitter. And I'll prove it to you. Remember, about ten years ago, when I asked you and Mom for information about my adoption, about how I could find out about whom I came from, and you said it was stupid, hopeless, impossible? 'No good would come from it anyway,' you said. Remember that, Dad? I was eighteen. Well, I didn't quit on that.

"It took me years, Dad, but I kept at it, and I found 'em. I found my *real* parents. And guess what? My mother's richer than anybody at Country Day, or anybody in St. Louis, for that matter. Her father had a seat on the New York Stock Exchange, owned companies, was elected to Congress, built hospitals and libraries that they named after him. Her brother, my uncle, owns an oil company in Dallas. And my father was a damn *war hero*, a Marine sniper in Korea."

Dad's eyes bulged. For a long moment he just stared at me.

That got him, I thought. Especially the word choice: *real* parents. *War hero*. A stroke of genius. Of course Dad heard only my highly edited, selectively excerpted version of the *real* parents but to great effect: he's got no comeback. I returned his gaze in stony silence, the subtlest evidence of a smirk at the corners of my mouth. I stubbed out my cigarette in my plate of untouched food.

"When did this happen?"

"Heck, over a year ago."

Dad made no reply. After a moment, he calmly pulled out his wallet, laid a couple twenties on the table, looked at his watch, said, "I have to get back to the office," and got up and left, leaving me and his full plate behind.

The ugly details and loose ends of the Tom and Judy story were best left unsaid. I hadn't actually *found* my *"real"* father yet. I didn't even know if he was dead or alive, for certain. Nor did I know if he was a "war hero" in Korea, just another grunt, or a deserter, for that matter. And I wasn't sure I wanted to find out, since it had taken me a few sessions with a shrink just to deal with Judy.

When Dad got home from work, it was clear he'd been drinking. This was unusual and concerned Mom, but she held her tongue. Dad barely spoke to her, said nothing to me, and headed straight for the bar, where he mixed himself a pitcher of martinis and began knocking them back as he watched the six o'clock news.

I had said nothing to Mom of lunch at Busch's Grove. Over supper, Dad alternated between distracted, silent gazes off in the middle distance and odd declarations apropos nothing Mom and I were chatting about:

"Margaret, I been thinking, we oughtta just sell this place and move to Hawaii. There's nothing keeping us here anyway."

"Stan! What has gotten into you? What are you talking about?"

"I mean it, Margaret! We got nothing here. If you don't wanna go with me, maybe I'll just go on by myself."

"I think you need to slow down the martinis, dear, and focus on your supper. I don't know what's come over you!"

"Whaddaya mean, 'come over me'? I've just come to my senses, is what it is. We've done our duty, worked our whole lives, put the kids through school. They're grown and gone now, got families of their own. Nothin' left for us here. We oughtta live for ourselves for a change. Just up and go." He was making grand, sweeping gestures, his voice loud and gruff, like George C. Scott's Patton, surveying the field of battle.

"Seriously! Where'd you rather go than Hawaii? California? 'Member how you thought San Luis Obispo was so pretty? We could take up golf, play at Pebble Beach. See movie stars. Or Europe! You always loved Paris, said you wanted to go back some day."

Mom was totally befuddled and knew better than to argue with him. She looked at me, but I clearly had said too much already, at lunch. I just shrugged.

Dad kept pounding down the martinis.

"Or if you'd rather, we could just go home to Oklahoma. Our folks're all buried out there, and we could be closer to your sister. Billye would like that I bet, and Bill and their kids, too. They're all still there, together, not scattered like ours, one off in Cleveland, the other in Colorado.

"You know, Margaret, we mighta all been better off if we'd just stayed in Oklahoma. But I still think Hawaii's best. We need to just get away. Or I do, anyway." Turning to me, he snarled, "Maybe I'll just do that, with or without you, Margaret. There's nothing for me here."

Mom got up and started clearing the table, muttering, "For goodness' sake, Stan," her eyes brimming, her mouth set. Dad pushed away his half-eaten supper, picked up his glass and the pitcher of martinis, and stalked off to his den. Moments later the smell of cigar smoke and the sound of Glenn Miller cranked up loud emanated throughout the house.

I went into the kitchen with a load of dinner plates and began helping Mom with the dishes. When I finished putting the leftovers in the fridge, I pulled out a cold can of beer.

"Now don't you start, too" she scolded, fighting back tears. "Why can't you two get along? What's going on between you? This started at lunch, didn't it? Why must you drink the way you do?"

I just shook my head and shrugged, popped the top on the beer, and lit a Camel. Mom left the room fighting back tears, and I could hear their raised voices from the den, but their words were drowned out by the band shouting "Pennsylvania six five oh oh oh."

Hours passed. Mom had given up and gone to bed. Dad was still smoking and drinking and playing his old swing music from the forties, now at a more civilized volume. I had called Nancy and told her what a disaster this trip had been and that I'd probably head back to Colorado in the morning to resume my job hunt. She wasn't particularly sympathetic or consoling. Maybe *I* should just light out for parts unknown, I thought, and popped another beer from the kitchen fridge.

Sometime after midnight I was sufficiently primed to confront the old man. I entered his den and sat in a leather wing-back chair opposite him. He wouldn't look at me, and we just sat there for a long while, smoking, drinking, listening to the music. My mind wandered back to Luling, my earliest memories, when he used to call me "Markie Doodle" and invite me to "wrassle" with him on the floor. And he'd take me to the plant to show me around; there were snapshots of him holding me, still in diapers, the plant in the background and a silver Lion Oil hard hat on my head. I remembered Boy Scouts, and Ernie's dad, my scoutmaster, who had reacted with disbelief when Dad had volunteered to spend two entire weeks at summer camp with the troop. Even the scoutmaster only traded off a couple nights at a time with the other fathers, none of whom committed to a whole week, much less two. And I remembered how Dad had attended every one of my high school football games, even that first year when I hardly played. I had been so caught up in my own embarrassment and frustration at being a bench warmer I had wished he hadn't come to the games. And there was that time he'd taken off work to drive across Missouri and halfway across Kansas to bail me out of jail in Junction City, where I'd been arrested for hitchhiking on Interstate 70. I'd been more embarrassed than relieved or grateful for Dad's unexpected rescue; the sheriff had called him, not me. I hadn't wanted the deputies or my cell mates to think less of me for whining to my daddy to come bail me out. "You're a lucky boy to have this man for a dad, son," the sheriff had said as he removed my shackles. They're in cahoots to make me feel as bad as possible, I remember thinking. And of course there had been the time he had flown out to Boulder to convince me to stay in school rather than enlist in the Marines.

What a shitty son I am! A flood of shame, guilt, and self-loathing overtook me as I studied him in his silent reverie across the room, but I was too drunk or stubborn or wrapped up in my own self-pity to find the words that needed saying.

It was probably too late for words, from me anyway.

Then he began, still not looking at me. "I think where I went wrong, was in stepping in too much. I probably should have just let you take your lumps, learn things the hard way. That's how my father raised me, and I didn't make the same mistake twice. I listened to my father, took his advice, even asked him for his advice, to avoid mistakes. I respected him—never argued like a smart aleck with him. I sure miss my dad." He took a sip from his martini and a puff from his Roi-Tan cheroot. I made no reply.

"Like when you wanted to quit school and join the Marines, it probably woulda been best. Apparently it was, for your 'real' father. A hero, you say, in Korea. This music reminds me of being in the navy: the danger, the pride, the camaraderie! We were at war! At sea! You just don't have any idea, Mark. Out in the middle of the Pacific, for months at a time. You don't know anything about sacrifice, or duty . . . or honor . . . courage. We saw ships wrecked, sunk! The whole fleet at Pearl Harbor . . . Jap subs stalking us for days. I was scared. We all were. But we pulled together and came through it stronger."

I'm thinking, wait a minute, Dad, you told me yourself that your hitch in the navy was more like *Mister Roberts* and *McHale's Navy* than *The Battle of Midway* or *PT 109*.

"I shoulda let you drop out and join the Marines, you mighta learned something about being a man—that is, if you survived. Afraid it's too late now . . . and y'know, I've wondered since then if that wasn't all just a bluff, anyway. If you'da really wanted to join, I doubt I coulda stopped you from it."

All my gushing sentimental guilt of mere moments ago ebbed, then vanished, replaced by welling, drunken anger.

"But I wasn't bluffing at dinner. What's to stop me from leaving? You're not the only one with options, you know. With alternatives. A man of my age and means has places he can go, interests, friends, companions. I've traveled all over the world and know places, people. I've got opportunities that none of you know about. You've obviously made your choices, for at least a year now. It's my turn to exercise my options, cut my losses. I can just disappear. Retire, move away, disappear without a trace, and be much happier . . . maybe start a new family."

I shouted, "What about Mom and Lynn!" and was on him, leaping across the room, raining blows, bloodying his nose. He joined the battle, rising through my flurry of fists with a punishing slam to my gut that knocked the wind out of me, doubling me over. I took him down with me as I fell forward sucking for air. Furniture crashed with us to the floor and by the time Mom came out to break us up it was already over and we both lay gasping and bleeding on the floor, wounded by shame and sorrow amid the broken glass and puddles of gin and beer.

18

The Chicken Comes Home to Pensacola

Though this knave came something saucily into this world before he was sent for yet was his mother fair; there was good sport at his making, and the whoreson must be acknowledged.
—Gloucester, *King Lear*

Now, gods, stand up for bastards!
—Edmund, the bastard, ibid.

A year later, having scrambled to keep the bills paid doing cowboy stories for the *Rodeo Sports News*, I finally landed full-time steady work. Better yet, I found it to be meaningful, challenging, and satisfying, something I could see making a career of. I was public relations director for the Pikes Peak United Way. Things were coming together for Nancy and me: our first child was born and we named him Peter. With Nancy's approval, I baptized him myself in Fountain Creek, the mountain stream that ran through our backyard.

At a weeklong management training program at United Way's national headquarters in Alexandria, Virginia, I skipped an afternoon session and took a cab to the Marine Corps archives in D.C. In just a few hours of poring over microfilmed lists of Korean Conflict KIAs, I was able to determine that no Tom Whitaker from Detroit had died in action in the summer or fall of 1951 or the winter of '52.

But there *was* a record of a Tom Whitaker from Detroit, riflery coach at Parris Island Depot and later Camp Lejeune, sniper in Korea, there awarded a battlefield commission, who had spent twenty years in the corps, the latter part as an aviator. He had done a couple of tours in Viet Nam flying cargo planes before retiring as a major at NAS Pensacola.

I had written him a letter, included a photograph of myself, requested a meeting. He had called me immediately upon receipt. He was all spit and polish.

"Before I say anything further in response to your letter, I want to be very clear with you that I have consulted with my attorney regarding estate law and matters of inheritance, and you have no standing per stirpes for any claim as a descendent of mine, assuming you could prove that you are in fact such."

I assured him I had absolutely no interest in *anything* of his. He didn't pick up on the bristling sarcasm of my words.

"Good. I didn't think you would. It's not something you would do, if you're a son o' mine. And I will further stipulate that, judging from the photo you sent, there *is* a strong possibility we're related." His voice then softened, becoming wistful, nostalgic.

"And I do recall, with no small measure of fondness, the cherry blossoms in the Tidal Basin in the late spring of '51 and a romantic picnic in Rock Spring Park with your lovely mother, Judith. If you'd like to come for a visit, son, you're more than welcome."

It wasn't going to work on me. No sir. None of this tough-but-tender warrior crap impressed me. And this generous "welcome, son" bullshit didn't fool me for one second, either. Not one second. And I didn't give a rat's ass if he had three sons and a daughter (more half-sibs) and a thirty-five-year marriage to a wonderful, understanding wife, and two decades of heroic, distinguished service to his country, or had given his goddamn left nut to save a fallen comrade, for Christ's sake. I know his game. Hell, I'm the *product* of his game. I'm *him*, and he ain't getting over on me.

It's almost dawn, and I'm nearing the end of another epic cross-country odyssey. My destination this time is the home of the Blue Angels, sugar-white sandy beaches, and a naval air station. The home of Major Tom Whitaker, USMC aviator, retired.

Though I lack the element of surprise (and control) that I had with Judy Culkin, I fully expect to inflict shock and awe with devastating fury. This time I'm heavily armored with advance intel, resolve, and purpose. There won't be any of that sad, weepy, huggy mother-and-child-reunion stuff. Nor will there be any longneck Buds or quarts of Beam, which nearly proved disastrous last time. It's been almost twenty months dry now, and I've even driven through the night with nary a hit of speed.

For this time, I'm no longer a bewildered boy seeking sweet comforts and excuses from a long-lost mother. I'm a man, and I'm on a mission: to avenge the honor of a woman betrayed, with all the righteousness of the denied, scorned, and abandoned bastard son.

I'm about three clicks out from his place on a bayou off Perdido Bay. When he opens the door, preferably in front of as many of his family as possible, I will

1. cold-cock the jarhead motherfucker, breaking teeth and nose,

2. knock his ass to the ground,

3. say, "This is from Judy" (and stomp a boot hard in his groin),

4. say, "And this is from me" (spit a cheekful of Red Man in his proud Marine face),

5. snap a smart middle-finger salute,

6. do a crisp about-face, and

7. never look back again.

Of course it only goes like that in the movies. Bad movies. Or in my twisted imagination.

Since Judy bore little physical similarity to me (a disappointing surprise), I hadn't given any more thought to physical resemblance. This proved to be a major miscalculation of my Major encounter. Rather than the crisp, choreographed vengeance I planned to dispense, I discovered that a close encounter, for the first time in my life, with someone whose face is an older version of my own, has a staggering effect. Staring at him in the doorway was like looking into a mirror from the future. My future. I was completely disarmed. All the righteous fury I had intended to visit upon his visage instantly dissipated, replaced by a jolt of recognition for which I was utterly unprepared.

For Tom Whitaker, I imagine the encounter was somewhat unsettling, but nothing like what rocked me. He had already seen my mug in the photograph I'd enclosed with the letter. Besides, he had three grown sons who favor him. They also look like me.

I knew I was finally at the right place when I saw the hand-painted sign proclaiming "Whit's End" posted at the curb of the oyster-shell driveway that curved through a dense jungle of palmettos, scrub oaks, and sago palms. A middle-aged woman in an apron, her hair pinned up in a loose bun, greeted me at the door. She was plumper, and about a decade younger, than my own mom (Margaret Johnson—Judy had asked me to call her Mom, but that title will always belong to Margaret).

Mrs. Whitaker's eyes got big and her mouth opened but nothing came out. I had been purposely vague about my arrival time, to grab what little control I could. I had insisted that I would find the place on my own. This had been a stupid, prideful mistake.

Whit's End is way out in the sticks on a bayou of Perdido Bay, closer to the Alabama state line than it is to downtown Pensacola—something you'd never know from a mailing address. I had left Colorado Springs on a Friday afternoon and flown to Memphis, where I borrowed a cousin's truck and headed down I-55 into the black Mississippi night. At Jackson, I left the interstate system to cut across piney woods and farmlands on two-lane blacktops, choked with slow-moving farm tractors and threshers headed to the fields in the misty gray predawn hours of Saturday. At Mobile (the first time I had ever been here, having no idea I'd be returning to settle years later), I hopped briefly onto eastbound I-10 to cross Mobile Bay, then slowly zigzagged my way south and east across rural Baldwin County behind more pokey farm trucks, finally reaching the Florida line by late morning.

Navigating Dallas in search of Judy Culkin had been a cakewalk compared to navigating Pensacola. Its roadways, conforming as they must to the irregular geography of coastal waters and bays, are a tangled mess. The Rand McNally was useless. (This was decades before GPS.) But calling Whitaker for directions was simply not an option, for reasons I chose not to examine. As a result, I spent almost as much time driving around Pensacola and its environs as it had taken me to get from Jackson to the Florida line. The whole 1,500-mile trek had required twenty hours by air and asphalt, then hubris had added three more hours of maddening drive time just circling around Pensacola.

By another measure, though, the journey had led me from Beaufort to Parris Island to New Orleans to Dallas to D.C.'s archives, then finally to this backwater bayou, and had taken thirty years to complete. What's a few lost hours driving backroads around Perdido Bay? I simply used the frustration to fuel the rage that had been simmering since hearing Judy's story two years earlier.

Mrs. Major Whitaker finally finds her voice. Without taking her eyes off me, she turns her head slightly and bellows, "Tom! He's here!" then recovers her southern hospitality and says, "Well, come on in, sugar. You must be plumb wore out from your trip!" and gives me a warm hug.

I stiffen at her embrace and hear Tom bounding up steps from a lower level. I ball my hands into fists. Then I see a fifty-year-old version of myself coming at me down a hallway. He stands next to his sweet-smiling wife and extends his hand and I see myself giving him the firm handshake my father had taught me and I know he's saying something, and so is Marilyn, and my own mouth might be moving in response but I'm not hearing any of it. There's a roar in my ears like the "white noise" setting on Nancy's sleep machine (a noise box she needs to sleep through my rip-snorting slumber).

Our handshake breaks and I feel myself straighten up, my chest swelling, my shoulders squaring, my stance widening, but I'm paralyzed, riveted by my own middle-aged face on this stranger.

That evening we feast on a bountiful spread of Marilyn Whitaker's home cooking, I meet two half brothers (the elder of whom looks even more like me than Tom), and all of us talk late into the night around the table, exchanging life stories and tall tales and family histories. Tom regales us all with war stories from two Asian conflicts, the first seen from frozen foxholes, the second from the air.

Marilyn's heard it all before. "Don't believe a half of it, Mark," she warns, shaking her head. Then with a laugh, "Tom never let the truth stand in the way of a good story, did ya, dear?"

Tom just frowns and shakes his head back at Marilyn.

"While you were galavantin' off halfway 'round the world, Major Whitaker, who do you think was back here runnin' this household fulla your kids with no daddy around? You wanna talk battlefields? It wadn't exactly Romper Room around here all those years." They're grinning broadly at each other.

Tom gets up and begins clearing the table. "Look at this, now, honey. Don't say I'm shirking my domestic duties."

I follow his lead and take my plate toward the sink, but Marilyn shoos us both away. "Go on now, y'all just git! Outta my kitchen. You'll only make it worse. You both got a lotta catchin' up to do."

Tom takes me downstairs to his den and shows me the family photo albums, starting all the way back when he was a boy in Detroit. We cover several generations of Whitakers in portraits and snapshots and lore; he tells me his father served in the navy, and if I'd like to visit him he's buried in the military cemetery right there in Pensacola.

He says I'd have had something in common with his dad. "He did PR for GM. Like you, didn't you say that's what you do with the United Fund? You're both wordsmiths.

"Me, I used to keep journals when I was overseas, thinkin' I might turn 'em into stories if I lived through it, but when I got back stateside and reread 'em, I thought, This is crap, and never did anything with it."

Around midnight we've worked our way over to the trophies and relics of his career in the corps. The rest of the Whitaker clan have long since shuffled off to bed. Tom shows me framed photos of the wreckage of a plane he crash-landed and walked away from in Viet Nam, his flight suit and pilot's goggles and mask, his steel pot and service .45 from Korea. He points out a nick in the pistol's barrel and explains that it came from the tooth of a North Korean infantryman who jumped into his sniper nest one night.

"I heard him just in time to roll away from his bayonet thrust. He was right on me, and there wasn't enough space between us to get my rifle around on him, so I pulled my sidearm and backhanded him across the face with it before firing five rounds into him at point-blank range."

Thinking back on that story years later, having had a few scrapes of my own as a cop, I have an idea of the impact that experience must have had on him. But that night, my response was to mutter something like "Wow. That was a close one" and let it drop. I was hunkered down in my own foxhole that night, too preoccupied with my own confusion and questions, struggling to muster the courage for my own confrontation.

I wish I'd asked him if he'd been scared or if it had all happened too fast for fear to even register; or if he had hesitated, even for an instant, before squeezing the trigger. Did he look into his enemy's eyes as he fired? Did all his rounds find their target, or had he shot wildly with the first one or two? Did he get the shakes during or after? Did he check the soldier's pockets to find out his name, see a snapshot of his family? Did he stay in that foxhole the rest of the night with his slain enemy, bracing to be overrun by more North Koreans, or did he hightail it out of there as soon as the smoke cleared? I wonder how long he had nightmares about it afterward.

Instead, after an awkward silence, I clear my throat and say, "I gotta ask you something, not about Korea or Viet Nam. I feel like we're kinda dancing here."

"I ain't much for dancing," Tom answers. "Shoot."

"Well, when I first met Judy, I asked her about you, and she said you were dead. Killed in action, in Korea. I asked her how she knew for sure, did she get something from the Marines, or the Pentagon. She said no, of course, she never got anything official because y'all weren't married, but she knew you were dead 'cause she got a letter from one of your buddies, a fellow Marine." I pause and study his face. He cocks his head but holds my gaze. "How did that happen?"

He frowns. "Hmmm. Guess that's why I never heard from her." He muses to himself for a moment. "That would explain it." Then he looks at me, and with a straight face tells me how there was a guy in his unit, a real oddball, eventually discharged on a "Section 8, mentally unfit" ruling, who they discovered had sent a whole series of letters to the families of other guys in the unit, with all kinds of crazy tragic stories about how their boys had been killed or were POWs or MIA.

"He caused a lotta uproar and needless heartache, you can imagine. Nuttier than a fruitcake, that guy. I guess he musta sent one of those letters to Judy."

"But how'd this guy get the names and addresses of everybody he wrote to?"

Tom doesn't skip a beat. "They investigated that. Discovered that he'd been getting into guys' footlockers, finding their mail from home. Figured he got the return addresses from the envelopes."

I'm thinking, is that the best you can do, Tom? You really expect me to buy this? A crazy guy sending bogus death notices to strangers? Besides, Judy was so pissed at you for denying paternity and skipping out to Korea, I *know* she never sent you any mail. In fact, didn't you just say yourself, moments ago, that you never heard from her? So from what letter sent to you by Judy did Mr. Section 8 Crazy Guy get Judy's return address?

I'm wondering, why don't you just tell me the truth? You didn't love her. It was a one-night stand. You were scared. You weren't ready to get married, be a father. You had villages to burn, commies to kill, teeth to knock out! You were only twenty. I get that. Just tell me the truth, Tom.

But I let it go. Why make the guy squirm? Thirty years had passed. He'd been a horny young man, itching to get in the fight. I understand, more so than I'd readily acknowledge, if I were in his shoes. How honorably had I behaved at that age with some of the girls I dated?

There's a long silence while neither of us looks upon the other.

Then he offers, in a lowered voice conferring confidentiality, "I hafta say though, and I don't want to offend you—I don't know how close you are to Judy—but she was a most enthusiastic lover. She was like no other woman I've known, before or since."

Another long pause. I can't face him. I'm remembering my own night of drinking and staggering with Judy, and Tom's disclosure doesn't surprise me. I feel torn between the urge to defend Judy—originally, my whole purpose for this visit—and a temptation to agree and commiserate with Tom. I just don't know what to think or feel or say, so I say nothing.

But I know this: I didn't want to hear this. It just might be the truth, but I wish I hadn't heard it.

Definitely didn't want to hear that about the woman who had given birth to me, even though "bastard son of a whore" had gotten me used to a bad image of my biological mother ever since the concept had been so rudely thrust into my imagination at that Boy Scout camporee so long ago.

But then, neither had I wanted to hear from her of his moral cowardice and duplicity in her time of need thirty years ago. Or maybe worst of all (or just the freshest of all my emotional wounds) to hear the outrageously, insultingly improbable whopper of a lie he'd uttered to my face only minutes ago. I feel like throwing up.

19

Thievin' Hoes, Prehensile Toes

You boys can keep your virgins. Give me hot old women in high heels with asses that forgot to get old.
—Charles Bukowski, *Love Is a Dog From Hell*

The best thing about being in patrol is the constant variety and the fast pace. About every forty-five minutes, a new set of players and circumstances is served up by Dispatch. But patrol's best feature is also its major frustration: you never really get to know how the story ends, much less anything about the players involved, beyond name, DOB, and the nature of the complaint.

Detective work allows a calmer, slower-paced interaction with the parties involved. The detective follows the case all the way through the court system, through preliminary hearings, deal making between the assistant district attorneys and the counsel for the defense, to trials and sentencing of the offender. Probably 30 percent of my time as a detective was spent at the courthouse.

One result of that was running into other cops there whom I had no opportunity to see when confined to shagging calls in my beat as a patrol officer: guys from my old academy class and others whose assigned units in the department require frequent court appearances. One I encountered often at the courthouse was the living legend, Tom McCall, who had shared with me his memorable observation about sheep and wolves, back before I had even started the academy and was working at the firing range. McCall had since switched to the Sheriff's Office, where he was working undercover narcotics—perhaps the most dangerous type of police work there is.

(And he was in his fifties by then.) His wife, like mine, was also a member of the Mounted Unit Auxiliary, and I'd occasionally see him at training events our wives and their horses attended at the police barn.

McCall looked even rougher to me than when we'd first met, partly the result of being undercover: unshaven, longish hair, dressed in jeans or fatigues with black Harley T-shirts and a vest with skull-and-crossbone insignia. He would always acknowledge me with a nod or a slight smile, but rarely would we exchange words.

Then shortly after Nancy quit the auxiliary, he spoke to me.

"Charlene tells me Nancy's hung up her spurs."

I nodded. We shook hands. His grip was as firm as the last time, at the shootin' house. I offered something about Nancy's increased workload, by way of explanation. She had started a new job as communications director for the County Commission. "But we're keeping the horse, of course. I ride him as often as she does."

"Good," he said. "He's a good one."

Shortly after Prince died, a couple years later, I ran into McCall in the courthouse elevator again. He offered condolences. It was still fresh with me, and painful. Putting down a horse is far more traumatic than putting down a dog, which is awful enough. But a horse is so much bigger. Especially a sixteen-hand Tennessee walker, with whom you've become one, in all kinds of places and circumstances. Nancy couldn't bear to be there. When the vet administers the fatal injection, a horse has farther to fall than a dog. It seems to shake the ground. And then he has to be pushed into his grave with a front loader.

My eyes clouded up in the elevator with McCall. No matter how stoic I aspire to be, my damn eyes always betray me. McCall looked away, squeezed my shoulder, and got out on his floor, mercifully, without another word.

Because the nature of investigations requires more interaction with offenders than the mere "cuffing and stuffing" of patrol work, the detective gets to know people and their backstories in more depth, which often makes it interesting, if not surprising. Over the weeks, or even months, of an investigation, a detective may talk to most members of a suspect's family: parents, siblings, girlfriends, children, homeboys, probation officers, even employers or coaches or neighbors. We get glimpses of personalities, causes, and conditions that the patrol officer never sees.

The story frequently changes as the stories evolve. The same person can seem reasonable and credible the first time, only to trip himself up with inconsistencies later. When these are pointed out, that "reasonable" person can explode in defiance or melt down in shame. Or both, alternately.

Based on who the players are and what kind of evidence we have, we stage our interviews with some forethought. Who and how many detectives are needed? Who plays what role? How much do we bluff? Where's the best setting? Will bringing his mama in help us or hurt us?

We even give some thought to the clothes we wear. Some people get more candid as they get more comfortable. A uniform or even just a white shirt and necktie can be off putting and stop an interrogation before it even starts. Alternately, sometimes a gray flannel suit and tie produce the desired effect. I once posed as an FBI agent called in on the case "due to possible federal charges," because I looked the part way better than any of my colleagues. The suspect was duly intimidated and became more cooperative.

Earl Slocumb's casual, rumpled, unshaven look is calculated and most effective. (It's purely coincidental that he's actually a slob in real life, too.) He's the champion of confession acquisition. He never leads with the Miranda warning and waiver. It's presented as an afterthought, a mere formality, after the guts start spilling. Earl will talk Crimson Tide or fishing or whatever he can get our guest interested in for as long as it takes to develop commonality and something akin to trust. Earl never raises his voice or shows anger. He reasons with them. They come to believe that Earl is offering a fair deal that allows them both to win. All the while the "guest" is handcuffed to a table and knows full well he's talking to a cop. I've had them refuse to even confirm their date of birth to me, only to see Earl emerge an hour later with a list of all the licks the suspect has hit, the names of all his homeboys who hit the licks with him or got rid of the stolen goods for him, and for little more than a Big Mac and a Newport, the suspect has agreed to take a ride with Earl through the 'hood to point out the specific houses he's burglarized in the last six weeks. It's astounding. It's why he has that Officer of the Year award adorning his office wall. If Earl applied his natural style to, say, sales, or contract negotiations, or consulting, he'd be living in a Gotham City penthouse.

Except then he wouldn't be Earl.

Lusty's style often begins with horny talk about bitches and hoes. Most guys, especially criminals, are more than willing to shoot the breeze about big-assed nasty women, and I've never met anyone who can articulate the id with the unabashed, unfettered, purely puerile enthusiasm of Lusty Lopez. But after a few minutes of booty banter, he abruptly switches to his unique style of Hispanic hellfire. Lusty gets into a rhythm, using the first name of the suspect in almost every phrase, as he describes with lurid detail the despair and degradation awaiting the suspect in prison:

"Listen to me now, Lamont, I'monna be one hundred wit'cha now, Lamont, this ain't no good cop–bad cop bullshit like you see on TV, Lamont, this is the real deal. I don't lie to you, you don't lie to me. It's big-boy time now, Lamont, no more juvie slap onna wrist. It ain't even Metro time, Lamont, y'feel me Lamont? This is the big house we talkin' 'bout now, Lamont. Huh, y'hear me? Listen to me now, Lamont: what we got on you, it's Atmore-for-shore, Lamont. And a young kid like you? Them fellas up in Atmore see you comin', they be lickin' they chops thinkin' a splittin' yo' sweet cheeks, Lamont. Them boys up 'ere be horny's three-dicked dogs, Lamont, for somebody just like you: a ass-virgin, Lamont, you hearda anal, ain'tcha, Lamont? They'll be the pitchers, you'll be the catcher. You 'n' yo' homeboys may think you rule 1010 Baltimore, but that's kiddiegarden compared to Atmore, y'know that don't you, Lamont? Kno'm sayin', brah? They spend all day long pumpin' iron and stroking they big cocks just dreamin' a sweet tight twenty-year-old ass like yours, Lamont, fresh from the projects. Fresh meat! Y'feel me, Lamont?

"And y'know what? That ain't even the worst part, Lamont. The worst part is how you gonna do your sweet ol' mama and your little brothers, Lamont. Mama's gonna be too ashamed to talk about you at church, your little brohs gonna get teased about you at school, y'feel me, Lamont? And you won't even wanna talk to them about your life up there in Atmo' 'cause you know you'll just start cryin' and if you tell them how you've become some big murderin' mothafucka's bitch and he makes you suck his cock every day and swallow his spunk, they'll just have nightmares and wanna die, so you can't tell nobody nu'n Lamont, 'cause you'll be wantin' a die your own self. Y'hear me? And you can just forget about all your homeboys and baby-mamas back at 1010 B'mo, 'cause you sure's hell don't want them to know you be takin' it up the ass e'ry day, Lamont. They be sayin' ol' Lamont gone sissy. 'You heard about Lamont up in Atmo'? Word is, he done gone sissy!' And who's to say that's even wrong, Lamont? Man's gotta do what he's gotta do, when his life's on the line. I ain't sayin' there's anything wrong with it, but it sure ain't for me, Lamont. And I'm pretty sure it ain't f'you either, Lamont.

"And don't forget, it don't end when you get out, 'cause then you'll be a convicted felon. Can't own a gun, can't hunt, can't vote, can't get a job. Can't even get into the army. Can't get any kinda scholarship. And they's a good chance you have AIDS, Lamont. AIDS up the ass. Ass-AIDS, Lamont: think about it. Ain't be getting any mo' sweet pussy when they all know you got the Bug, Lamont. Your life is totally fucked, Lamont.

"But it don't hafta be that way, Lamont, if you just do the right thing now, Lamont, the smart thing, Lamont. All you gotta do is man up, get one hundred wit' me right now, Lamont, and there's a good chance Atmore never happens, Lamont."

Lusty hits about a .350 average with this approach. Thirty-five out of a hundred Lamonts crack for Lusty. Which is about twice the national average, according to FBI stats.

Because I don't have a style, a rap, or a shtick like the others, most of the cases I worked in my first year were theft cases. I tended to devote more time to them because they're often easier to solve than burglaries: theft cases often come with suspects, because the victim knows the thief. Since there's so often an eyewitness, getting confessions isn't essential to clearing cases—it's mostly just a matter of tracking down the known suspect.

A theft involves taking someone's property without permission. A burglary requires unlawful entry into someone's premises, such as a garage, shed, residence, or business, for the purpose of committing a crime (usually theft) therein. A robbery occurs when someone's property is stolen from the *person* of the victim, or taken at gunpoint, or under direct threat of bodily harm. Often victims will say they've been robbed, when they've actually been burglarized, or a simple theft has occurred.

In Alabama, all robberies and burglaries are felonies. Robberies are more serious felonies than burglaries, because the victim is there, threatened, when the theft occurs. Robberies, though the most serious, are often easiest to solve, because there's always a witness (the victim) and often security video (in commercial robberies). Most burglaries occur when the victim is not present, but the violation of the victim's premises still makes the crime a felony. There are rarely witnesses or video of residential burglaries.

Some thefts, by contrast, are not even felonies. The gravity of a theft is determined by the value of the property stolen. If the value of the stolen property is less than $500, and it's not a firearm, a credit card, a motor vehicle, or a controlled substance, it's just a misdemeanor.

If a thief steals your lawn mower out of your backyard, and it's worth less than $500, you're out of luck, because it's just a misdemeanor, and there are probably no clues, and a detective won't even be assigned to it. If you had kept your old, used $100 lawn mower in a shed or garage, however, it would constitute a felony, even though it's worth less than the new $495 self-propelled Toro lawn mower that got stolen from your backyard, because the thief violated your building/residence to steal your beat-up old push mower.

A majority of felony thefts involve stuff stolen from inside a residence but which required no unlawful entry to steal the stuff—in other words, the theft is performed by someone who has a lawful presence inside the victim's house: a family member, ex-lover, a friend or neighbor who's been invited inside, the plumber who's been called in to fix the kitchen sink, the cable installer who's hooking up your new flat screen with surround sound. Except it's very seldom the cable guys or the tradesmen who've ripped off people's jewelry, or chrome .45, or new bottle of prescription Lortabs.

Usually the mere thief (as opposed to the burglar or the robber) is somebody who the victim thought was a friend. And when pressed by the reporting officer, or a detective, the victim will reluctantly admit that the likely thief is actually "that no good drug addict son of mine" or "my ex, my baby's daddy" or "that thieving sumbitch who lives across the street" or, as was the case with many middle-aged or older bachelors in my first year as a detective, "that goddamn whore I brung home from the Parkway Lounge last Saturday night."

The more timid, modest old bachelors would refer to them as just friends, or acquaintances or drinking partners, sometimes housekeepers, cooks, occasionally as lady friends or even sweethearts. They would be embarrassed to admit that they'd been snookered by the oldest game in human history, that they had been drinking with their big heads rather than thinking with their little ones. They would strongly deny that the girls were prostitutes, that there was any quid pro quo, and act insulted when I would suggest such a thing. But eventually they would admit that sometimes there was sex and that sometimes they would "help her pay the power bill ever' now an' ag'in."

Most of the victims did not even know the girls' real first names, much less last names, until I collected signatures from the credit card receipts. (As often as not, they'd sign their own real names, which were seldom compared to the male name on the stolen card by the clerks at the liquor stores, gas stations, and Walmarts where their sweethearts had run up hundreds of dollars in purchases on the stolen cards. If challenged, they'd simply claim the victim as their old man who'd sent them to the store for a six-pack and some smokes.)

I wouldn't have put much effort into solving these cases, figuring the horny old fools got what was coming to them, except that I was getting so many of these kinds of thefts. It was two or three a week. And it always seemed to be the same women whose names came up: Heather, and Victoria, and Kelly Ann. Sometimes more than one of them would be named by the same victim for the same theft: they had enticed the guy with a ménage à trois, which turned out to be a double-team bait-and-switch.

The ladies were well known in certain circles: the courthouse (where they had extensive histories of theft, soliciting, and drug arrests), the topless joints (where they had worked as waitresses and bartenders and even done a few turns at the pole), and of course among the habitués of the finer watering holes of the First Precinct. Places like Liz's Haven, the Ideal Lounge, Legends, the Zebra, and my favorite, the cleverly named Club Chez When (known to non-francophones—and most police dispatchers— as the Cheez Whiz). As a patrol officer I had often been dispatched to the Cheez for bar fights and disorderly drunks and had seen a few of the ladies working the place. Though I knew they had to be hustlers and hookers, I rarely arrested any of them, at least not for hooking. (Vice arrests are made by undercover cops working stings, not uniformed patrol.)

Occasionally, though, I'd see a girl flagging down cars, sufficient probable cause to arrest her for Loitering for the Purpose of Prostitution, a misdemeanor. I'd stop and check her purse for drugs, usually finding a joint or some pills or a rock and a pipe. But I'd just order her to toss the dope down a sewer, destroy the glass pipe with a stomp of her heel, and move to a corner in the Third or Second Precinct.

The first time I saw Mariah, she was at the Cheez Whiz. I was one of several backups who had been dispatched to an assault by one drunk with a pool cue on another. Both had fled before we arrived. Mariah nonetheless greeted us with a raucous "Thank God, it's the Law! I thought we'd never get you to *come*, officers!" Then she rose from her barstool and, stretching like a cat, purred in a husky tobacco-and-whiskey-thickened voice, "Frisk *me* first, Handsome!"

All of them were past their prime, and the hard roads they had traveled were etched in their once-pretty faces. Click "All Mugshots" on the Metro Jail web page for a particular female guest, and you get pages of full-color head shots, in one-inch square rows of three (full face, left and right profiles) revealing their declines into addiction, crime, and dissolution. The effect is disturbing. In a decade they go from smiling, healthy (if somewhat slatternly) young women to hollow-cheeked, gap-toothed, vacant-eyed zombies, like the FUCK MEN gal I had encountered with my FTO Porter on my first domestic. If they're meth addicts, their complexions are mottled with open sores, lips blistered with cankers or herpes. By the time I met the Parkway's professional companions they were too old to work the streets. Their looks wouldn't even slow traffic, much less stop any. They had to work harder for their money, relying more on their wiles than their wares. Their haggard forty-year-old faces looked more like mid-fifties, their hot-pink lip gloss only highlighting cracked lips and discolored teeth, their heavy mascara deepening sunken eyes and crow's-feet.

In my first interview with Kelly Ann, she was playing stupid and I wasn't getting anywhere. She probably knew I didn't have enough to hold her on, so she wasn't giving up anything.

I tell her I've already got enough to put her in Metro without even questioning her: my victim, a sixty-six-year-old Vietnam vet, his left leg a stump, has identified her by the name Kelly Ann and, based on his description of her (fortyish, kinda plain looking but not ugly, shoulder-length platinum blonde hair), which enabled me to find a likely suspect in our database. He picked Kelly Ann Kennedy's mugshot out of a six-panel photo spread without hesitation.

Kelly Ann has a few minor priors. All misdemeanors: a few theft thirds and marijuana seconds, although one drug charge started as felony but was reduced to misdemeanor drug paraphernalia in a plea bargain.

My victim Mr. Brock says that after Kelly Ann and her friend (a brunette whose name he can't remember) left his home, his wallet was missing, which contained most of his just-cashed VA disability payment for the month and credit cards. Kelly Ann doesn't deny "socializing" with "poor ol' one-legged Randy," but it was only because she felt "so sorry for him, being a crippled veteran and all." Of course she knows nothing about Randy's wallet, nor does she remember the name of the other girl, claiming to have just met her that night at Randy's.

"She was there when I got there. He called me over to party. I've known him a little while, been to his house a few times, sometimes help him with chores. I like to help people, Detective. He has my number in his cell, calls me when he needs me for something."

Kelly Ann's a little hurt, a little insulted that Mr. Brock would name her as a suspect.

"Randy's about half senile, anyway, and the other half's usually drunk. He probably just can't remember where he put his damn wallet, bless his heart."

I try another tack. I tell her I only want to help her turn her life around.

"Yeah, right, like you know anything about my life," she says. "Who says my life needs turnin' around? I've got a college degree and my own business. I'm a decorator. I take care of my half-blind eighty-three-year-old daddy. I cook his meals, give him his meds, do his nasty laundry, take him to the doctor, keep his house. You can ask anybody. They'll tell you: Kelly Ann takes care a her daddy."

"You're a decorator? What do you decorate?"

"I decorated the whole damn house. I'm an artist. You seen Daddy's mailbox? I did that."

I had driven by Kelly Ann and her daddy's place, on Scenic River Drive. Overlooking the wide part of the river with a hundred feet of waterfront and its own dock, the place was easily worth three-quarters of a million bucks. Daddy owns a string of dry cleaners. His mailbox, with some paint and plastic fins, had been transformed into a big-mouth bass. Not exactly a novel concept along Dog River. Or anyplace where there's water.

"I'm not disputing you take care of your father, or even that you have some artistic talent, Kelly Ann. But take a good look at yourself." I shake my head sadly. "You looked in a mirror lately?"

Her eyes flash, nostrils flare, but she remains silent.

I pull the "All Mugshots" pages of the last twenty years of Kelly Ann's life out of my file and slide them across the table to her.

"Pictures don't lie."

She thrusts her jaw out defiantly but allows her eyes to scan the twenty-odd thumbnails. After a moment she raises her eyes to mine and pushes the mugshots back across the table.

"Nobody looks good in a damned ol' Metro shot," she says.

"But you do, Kelly Ann. Or did." I pick up the second page and point to the bottom rows, her first few times as a Metro guest.

"Look at how good you look back here in your twenties. You were a really pretty girl, Kelly Ann. And you stayed that way, all the way up through the top of this page. A good-lookin' woman, into your early thirties. But then, on this page, I'm guessing that's when you started hitting the pipe, am I right? About your mid-thirties? Right in here, where you start to look like you been rode hard and put up wet—"

"I've had enougha your shit," she snarls, and snatches the mugshots from me, wads them up in a fury that startles me.

"If you ain't gonna charge me then we're done here."

I shrug and call for a transport officer to take her back to the Parkway Lounge where they picked her up for me. But I know I've hit a nerve.

I make it a daily routine to drive by Kelly Ann and her father's place. I write down the tag numbers of the numerous vehicles parked in her driveway, at all times of the day and evening. I run them when I get back to the precinct until I find one that comes back to a female whose DL photo matches the description of the "unknown" other female given by the victim. Heather Thibodeaux. Not unattractive, early forties, brunette. Obviously Cajun. I see that she's done a stretch in Tutwiler for drugs and theft offenses, and (ding ding, bonus!) she has an active warrant for probation violation. Probably failed a piss test.

I put Heather's DL mug on a page with five other dark-haired women in their forties and show it to poor ol' Randy, the stumpy Vietnam vet. He can't be sure but says it has to be one of these two (one of whom is Heather), but he just can't be sure, he had been drinking a bit, "and you know, wasn't all that focused on their faces, anyway, y'know what I'm sayin'?"

Yeah, I know what you're saying, bub. And what that means is I don't have enough on either one to make an arrest for stealing your wallet.

I decide to swing by Kelly Ann's and pick Heather up for the probation warrant if she's there. Maybe she'll confess, or at least put it on Kelly Ann. Actually, I'd prefer that she not confess, as long as she puts it on Kelly Ann. If I hafta charge Heather with the theft, then that turns her account of events into "codefendant testimony," which won't play in court, if I can even persuade the DA to take it that far. But Heather's going away for the probation violation anyway, and if she thinks I might put an additional felony on her, it could incentivize her to throw Kelly Ann under the bus, and I get a two-fer: both of 'em removed from my beat.

When I pull up to Kelly Ann's driveway, I see her talking to a dark-haired female in the same brown Corolla with the tag that had led me to Heather. Another female, auburn haired, sort of pretty, is walking down the driveway from the house toward Kelly Ann and the woman in the Corolla. Before I can even put out my location on the radio, I see the backup lights come on, Kelly Ann jumping back, and the Corolla coming at me in reverse. I slam my Crown Vic into reverse to avoid being struck and damn-near back into a passing pickup on Scenic River Drive. Meantime, the Corolla has jerked back into drive and Kelly Ann dives to avoid being mowed down by the Corolla as it ruts its way across Kelly Ann's daddy's manicured front yard, uprooting and wrapping an azalea bush around its axle before it disappears around a bend northbound on Scenic River. I hit lights and siren, jam it into drive, and slice a nice donut of my own into Kelly Ann's luscious green lawn.

"One-sixty-three, got one refusing to stop, northbound Scenic River, brown older model Toyota, Alabama tag 2Adam96Edward43. Occupied one time, white female, speeds 35 to 40."

Scenic River Drive is aptly named. Its narrow curvy lanes hug the bank of the river, sheltered by massive live-oak boughs dripping curly gray tresses of Spanish moss from the fern- and azalea-lined lawns of raised Creole mansions. Three bone-jarring sets of speed bumps (or "traffic calmers," as the Mayor's Office euphemistically refers to the damn things) precede its dead end at a 90-degree intersection with Clubhouse Road, which heads east from the riverside in a long straightaway with a dogleg left to Dauphin Island Parkway.

There are no other units anywhere near the lower parkway, and if I don't get her stopped before the parkway, or at least get right on her tail by then, she's got a pretty good chance of getting away in the parkway's four lanes of traffic.

It's my first pursuit in an unmarked detective car, and we're not really supposed to do pursuits in detective cars because of our limited, interior-mounted blue lights, none of which are visible from the side.

I've slammed my noggin three times on the roof of my car, which is now making a loud scraping noise from underneath (later found to be my dragging tailpipe), thanks to the mayor's traffic calmers, and I'm anything but calm. I'm almost caught up with her when she makes the right angle onto Clubhouse Road and stomps it. I'm right behind her, and my ten-year-old, 243,000-mile-old Crown Vic begins to shimmy and shake as we top 60 on a poorly paved two-lane in a residential neighborhood. If somebody pulls out of a side street or driveway, it'll be ugly.

Lieutenant Andrews gets on the radio and asks me the reason for the pursuit. I groan silently: Andrews is a notorious chase terminator. Gotta make this sound as serious as possible.

"Active 29 for probation violation, known suspect in a recent felony theft. Suspect attempted to ram my vehicle just before she ran, LT, so it's Reckless Endangerment, too."

I hold my breath. No reply from LT. Whew. I keep filling the radio with speed and location reports to keep LT off the air. We're nearing the parkway. Other units advise they're heading my way, but they're still north of I-10.

Heather blows right through a stop sign at Clubhouse and Gill, turning east onto Gill to avoid the red light at Clubhouse and Dauphin Island Parkway.

LT asks about traffic conditions and speeds. I lowball both.

"Approximately 45, approaching D.I.P. on Gill. No traffic."

Without even braking, Heather runs the stop sign at the end of Gill and crosses two (blessedly empty) southbound lanes of D.I.P. in a squealing 90-degree left drift that sends a northbound Buick bouncing up over the east side shoulder and into somebody's backyard at D.I.P. and Tallahassee. Unfazed, Heather zooms away northbound, weaving in and out of traffic.

I hafta slow and look both ways before following her and lose visual by the time I get northbound on the parkway. Other units are now approaching southbound on the parkway, and they're below I-10, so we've still got a pretty good chance to close in and cut her off. But then LT returns to the air.

"Did we get a tag number, operator?"

"Affirmative. 2A-Adam96E-Edward43, comes back to a brown '96 Toyota Corolla four-door registered to Heather Thibodeaux, active 29 probation violation."

"Terminate pursuit."

Damn! Another sixty seconds, we coulda had her, LT. I don't know who I'm more pissed at: Kelly Ann, for claiming she didn't know who the other female was at the victim's house, Heather Thibodeaux for nearly ramming her beat-up old Corolla into the front end of my beloved (but equally beat-up) old Crown Vic, or LT for being such a wuss.

Later that day I get a call from Kelly Ann. She's all apologetic and hyper. I'm thinking she just sucked the pipe before calling me.

"Did you catch her, Detective Johnson?"

"No. The lieutenant terminated the chase. 'Threat to public safety, too close to the school zone,' you know."

"Boy, I'll say! She was a threat to *my* safety, that's for sure. Did you see that, Detective? I had to dive out of her way or be *killed!* Isn't that, like . . . I don't know, vehicular . . . reckless . . . *aggression* or something? It's gotta be against the law, I know that much. I want to press charges. And what she did to my daddy's yard! That's property damage, right? We're gonna need new sod, and the azalea bush: there's nothing left of it! Just jerked it right out of the ground and dragged it off with her!"

"What was she doing at your place, Kelly Ann? I thought you told me you didn't know her."

"Well that's why I called you, Detective Johnson, to explain. I didn't want you to get the wrong idea, like I was aiding and abetting or something. She had just pulled up a few minutes before you got here. I had called her over here to talk her into turning herself in to you, I swear to God. I'm being honest. I was trying to help you and her both, but she saw you pull in and thought I'd set her up. That's why she tried to run me over. Anyway, I just called to tell you how sorry I am that all this happened, and I want to cooperate fully with you, if there's anything I can do. I was just trying to help, Detective Johnson, honest. I just like to help people who are down on their luck, you know? I guess I'm soft hearted that way. I knew she was just out of prison a couple months, and I was trying to get her on the right path, you know? But like they say, no good deed goes unpunished, I guess this proves it. So is there anything I can do to help, Detective Johnson?"

"Tell me where I can find Heather."

"There's no telling where she mighta run to, Detective Johnson. I know her mama lives across the bay, in Daphne. She took care of Heather's daughter while she was in prison. But I don't think her mama lets her come around much. Not a good influence for the child, especially if she's running from the law, and I certainly have to agree with that, don't you, Detective?"

Holy cow, I'm thinking, she's *totally* tweaked out. Undaunted by my silence (or perhaps encouraged by it), Kelly Ann prattles on.

"So there's really no telling where she might be. There's lotsa dealers and lowlifes she used to run with, and other girls, too, who'd put her up for a while. That's what I was trying to keep her away from, but we see how that turned out, huh, Detective Johnson? I bet you see this kinda thing all the time, and you think I'm a big fool for trying to help a drug addict fresh outta prison, don't you, Detective?"

"Who was the other girl walking down the driveway, Kelly Ann?"

"You mean Vickie? Yeah, that was Vickie, Heather's friend. Victoria Barnhart. They met in Tutwiler, but Vickie's been out for almost a year now. She was here to see Heather, too, 'cause she heard Heather got out. Vickie just had a short stretch. Drugs. But she's kicked. She wants to help Heather just like me, keep her outta trouble—she's really doing well, one of the success stories. Vickie and I were sure we could keep Heather out of the life, you know? With my, like, contacts and resources, and Vickie's example. You know, 'If we can do it, you can too kinda thing.'"

As Kelly Ann chatters on, I'm pulling up Victoria Barnhart's rap sheet on the Alacop database, and I see that she's also done time in Tutwiler. And she has an alias of Victoria Thibodeaux. Wait. Not just an alias, but a DL with that name on it.

I interrupt Kelly Ann. "Is Vickie Heather's sister? I mean, they both have dark hair, and I'm showing she has a last name of Thibodeaux, too."

"Well, no, Detective, they're not sisters. They're married. Got married in Tutwiler. But they're not really together right now. Vickie's going by her old name, and Heather's kinda mad at her since she got out. But I probably shouldn't gossip about their private business."

I'm silent, so Kelly Ann proceeds to tell me about their private business.

"The thing is, they both have hearts of gold, you know? I mean, really, in spite of what it looks like on their rap sheets. But I guess when Victoria got out, she kinda remembered how much she liked men, and she wrote Heather about her . . . mixed feelings, I guess you'd say, and Heather kinda took it hard like, and has been upset with Vickie since she got out, because she thought they'd get back together, bless her heart, and pick up where they left off, but it's not happening that way. It's, like, *complicated*, Detective Johnson, know what I'm sayin'?

"Anyway, I'll do my best to help you find Heather, and to help you clean up the whole damn parkway, for real. I'll call you whenever I hear anything, I promise, really I will."

Kelly Ann continued to call me a couple times a week with secondhand Heather sightings at all the usual places, and some new ones. She sent me to Mariah's place down on Fowl River. Kelly Ann said she'd heard from Bone, the crack man, that Heather's staying at Mariah's place off and on.

According to Kelly Ann, Mariah's "mostly out of the life now." She has an arrangement with a guy who works on one of the rigs in the Gulf. He's gone most of the time and gives Mariah a small allowance for when he's offshore. She feeds his dog and keeps the copper thieves from kicking in his door.

I drive out to Mariah's place. It's a ramshackle old cabin, up on pilings, junk cars and old boats scattered around underneath. No sign of Heather's brown Corolla, but that doesn't necessarily mean she's not inside. I knock on the door. Somebody peeks through the window shade and sees the white Crown Vic in the driveway. I hear "Just a minute" and the sounds of a flurry of activity inside.

Eventually, Mariah opens the door. There's the distinct smell of strong perfume, air freshener, and weed. She's about my age, curvy, and you could tell she used to be a looker. And she looks familiar to me, but until she speaks ("Can I help you?") I don't realize she's the "Frisk me first!" hooker from the Cheez Whiz. Mobile is a small town. And the circles cops run in are even smaller. But I don't let on that I've placed her, and she doesn't seem to recognize me.

I badge my way inside, look around as I introduce myself, and pull Heather's BOLO flyer from my jacket pocket.

"Know this lady, ma'am? I've been told she's staying here."

"Of course, Officer, er Detective. That's my friend Heather. But who told you she stays here? Nobody stays here but me and my friend Tommy, it's actually his place, but he's at work."

"Several people who are in a position to know said she's here. Mind if I check? You say there's nobody else home? Any weapons in the house?" I walk back to a hallway and glance in an empty bedroom, notice a closed door at the end of the hall. Probably the bathroom. Probably occupied.

Mariah has followed me, talking all the while. "I won't lie, Heather has been out here to visit a few times, but she's *not* staying here, I assure you. I had no idea the law's looking for her. What'd she do? Feel free to go on in, check the closet, under the bed if you want. If I'da known she was wanted, I woulda never let her set foot on the property, Detective. Does she have a warrant? What on earth did she do now?"

I'm more interested in the closed bathroom. As I start for the doorknob, there's a flush (no doubt the weed) and Victoria Barnhart-Thibodeaux comes out, brushing her hair, all innocent, and acting surprised to learn that there's a visitor. Her Tutwiler pics and DL don't do her justice.

"Oh, didn't know we had company, 'Riah."

"Mobile's Finest, Vickie. Just dropped in for a visit. And ain't he a handsome thang!" Mariah winks at me and thrusts her best assets the same way she did at the Whiz when I first saw her. Vickie shakes her head and smirks.

"Don't pay her any mind—uh-oh, look Mariah, I think you've made him blush! Just ignore her, she's always in heat."

"Says he's lookin' for Heather, can you believe it? Says somebody told him she's staying here!"

They both laugh at the preposterousness of my information, then Vickie holds up a finger, nods her head. "Wait. Could your Confidential Informant be a rich girl who lives on Dog River?"

"Kelly Ann!" they shriek in unison, laughing even louder than before.

"That girl's all the time stirring up the shit, ain't she?" Mariah says. "And now she's your CI! Not surprised she'd turn snitch for a handsome devil like you, Detective!

"Wait a minute! You're the one who tore up Kelly Ann's front yard chasing Heather a couple weeks ago, aren't you? You mean you haven't caught her yet? I want to be the first to know when you do, so I can stop worryin' about her comin' after me," Vickie said.

Mariah steers us back into the main room. "Have a seat, Detective. Can I offer you something cold to drink? I know you can't drink on duty, but we might have some orange juice or a Coke, let me check."

"No thanks, I'm fine."

"You certainly are!" Mariah says.

"Is that the last time you saw her, too, Vickie?"

"Yeah, haven't seen her since the great chase. Thought you'da had her locked up by now. She can't be that hard to find. Have you checked Bone's?"

"She's probably not that hard to find, but I do have other cases. It's not like we got a dragnet out for her."

"This is all about horny ol' one-legged Randy, isn't it?" Vickie says. "You know, I feel like that cheap bastard had it comin'. You wouldn't believe what he makes a girl do for beer money, for just, like, twenty bucks, if he feels like really livin' large." She catches herself. "At least, that's what I heard." She raises her eyebrows and makes her eyes real wide, grinning like a kid telling a whopper.

Mariah changes the subject. "Now I've got a question for you, Detective, if you don't mind?"

I shrug, and Mariah picks up a framed photograph from the coffee table and shows it to me. It's a snapshot of a curvaceous blonde, maybe mid-twenties, in a bikini bottom and a wet T-shirt, nipples pointing aloft. She's being presented a winner's trophy on a stage.

"Have you seen this woman?"

I study the picture a moment. The girl is really pretty hot.

"No ma'am, I'd definitely remember her if I had."

They both giggle. "Are you sure, Detective? Aren't you poe-leece s'posed to be trained observers? Look again."

I shake my head and shrug. "Why? She some kin to you? Missing person? Your daughter or something?"

Vickie hoots and Mariah scowls.

"Awww, come on, now! Shit. My daughter?"

She snatches the picture back from me and holds it up next to her face.

"Yeah, oh yeah, sorry. I see it now."

"Give it up, 'Riah," Vickie says. "He don't care about some old picture."

"First prize, at the Flora-Bama!" Mariah declares. "Aw hell, I gotta admit it was twenty years ago . . . but damn! I musta really let myself go."

"But you still got skills, babe," Vickie says. "Ask her about her toes, Detective."

"Shut yo' mouth, girl! He's gonna get the wrong impression of me!"

"Don't be modest, 'Riah!" Vickie says. Then, to me: "Mariah's the only woman I know can pick a man's pocket while flat on her back, *with her toes!*"

Now, that's a bona-fide *skill.*

On my drive back from Mariah's place on Fowl River, I wonder why Kelly Ann sent me out to Mariah's for Heather, if Victoria's hanging with Mariah, and Heather and Victoria aren't getting along. It hits me that maybe Kelly Ann Kennedy's a lesbian herself, with feelings for Heather. Now that Heather's been jilted by Victoria, Kelly Ann might be angling to get Heather to move in with her at the Kennedy compound on the river. I resolve to swing by the place whenever I'm nearby to check for Heather's old Corolla.

A couple weeks later I get a call at the precinct from a familiar husky voice.

"Remember me, Detective Johnson? It's Mariah. Hope you don't mind me callin' you, but I thought you might be interested in a little piece of information, as long as you don't let on where you heard it from. You still looking for Heather? I just came from Kelly Ann's, and she's there right now."

I head down the parkway and call for backup while en route.

20

Bad Bluffs, Slipped Cuffs

Police work is the only profession that gives you the test first, then the lesson.
—Mobile Police Department Training Academy

Mitch will be my backup at Kelly Ann's. That's a good thing: Johnny Mitchell's ex-military, got almost twenty years on the job, mostly riding the parkway. He knows Kelly Ann and her crew even better than I do; most of the theft reports involving them are written up by Mitch. He's a solid, no-nonsense cop who knows how to do what needs to get done.

I call Mitch on my cell while en route. He's waiting for me at Staples and Alba Club, right around the corner from Kelly Ann's.

"Got a good tip that my girl Heather's there, Mitch. The one that got away when LT canceled my chase a few weeks ago?"

"Ten-four. We'll just grab her before she gets close to the car, this time."

"Exactly. Thing is, I've got a warrant for her, but not at Kelly Ann's address. And you know Kelly Ann's gonna say she's not there."

"No problem. We'll just big-boy our way in. 'Specially if her ol' daddy's there, he'll cooperate."

"Right. I'll take the front, you drive all the way up around back. If she's there, she'll run, just like last time."

"I hear ya. Might could be some fun." I hang up with Mitch and reach for my Taser in the gear tote I carry on the passenger seat. The boxy old X26 barely fits, without its holster, in the left side pocket of my blazer.

Old man Kennedy opens the front door at my knock. He's white haired, bent and frail, and wearing glasses with lenses so thick his magnified rheumy eyes are big as silver dollars. I flash the warrant for Heather at him, knowing that all he can see is a blurry piece of paper. He seems surprised that I'm looking for someone other than Kelly Ann at his house.

"Heather, you say? Well I, I don't believe I know any Heather. It's just my daughter and me here, Detective," the old gentleman says. "But people do seem to come and go here. You're more than welcome to come in and have a look."

"He can't see a thing, Detective, you know that," Kelly Ann snarls. "Let me look at that. Heather hasn't been here since you both tore up our front yard. Daddy, this is the detective that tore up our yard."

I put the warrant back in my sports coat's inside pocket and motion to Mitch, standing at the backdoor.

"C'mon in, Mitch. Mr. Kennedy's given us permission. You take the upstairs, I'll check down here."

"Just a damn minute!" Kelly Ann says. "I live here, too. You don't have my permission to come in here. This is my house!"

Mitch is bounding up the stairs to the bedrooms while I glance around the great room and peek into a small oak-paneled den with built-in bookcases to the ceiling and twin tacked-leather wingback chairs. On a polished mahogany and glass table between the chairs is a cluster of cut-glass brandy decanters.

Kelly Ann is following me around ranting about her rights and demanding to see my warrant. I return to the great room and Mr. Kennedy.

"My eyesight isn't what it used to be, Detective, and for that matter, neither is my hearing," he says, smiling apologetically. "But I do think I would know if my daughter and I had a guest in the house."

"Yes sir, Mr. Kennedy, I'm sure you're right, but we just have to report to our sergeant that we gave the place a good once-over, you understand. It's just procedure."

"Of course, officer, of course," he replies, over Kelly Ann's protests. "Just let them do their jobs, Kelly Ann! It won't take but a minute, for goodness' sake. Why are you getting all upset, dear?"

"I must say that's a mighty fine library you have there, sir," I interject, before Kelly Ann gets a chance to blather on about her constitutional rights. "What's over here on the other side?" I say, walking toward the master suite.

"Oh, that's my bedroom. I can assure you, there's nobody in there, Detective," Kennedy says. His face clouds over. "I'm the only one uses that side of the house since my bride passed. We were married fifty-eight years!"

"That's quite an accomplishment in this day and age," I remark, entering his bedroom. I check under the king-size four-poster bed, then enter the master bath. It's massive, nearly as big as the bedroom. A large mirror runs the entire length of the double-sinked marble vanity. A chandelier hangs above a two-seater Jacuzzi. I check in the shower, which has a curved stone entry that precludes the need for a curtain, and is big enough to party in. Nozzles point from all directions but the floor. Finally I check the water closet, which has its own door. Inside, I find a gleaming black porcelain low-profile commode, complete with a mechanical seat-assist to help the user rise when finished, and to my surprise, something I haven't seen outside Europe: a matching bidet.

I hear Mitch's footfalls upstairs. His search is apparently about as successful as mine. I start to head back to the great room to call Mitch down to depart, when I notice the walk-in closet.

I switch on the light and open the door. Both sides of the large closet are lined with fine suits. It's quite an extensive wardrobe. I startle myself with my own reflection in a floor-length mirror on the far wall, and then I spy in the mirror the reflection of another: the backside of a female form, squatting tight against the wall behind one of Mr. Kennedy's summer seersuckers.

I pull the Taser from my coat pocket.

"All right, Heather. Let me see your hands, and come out real slow." Heather crawls from behind the seersucker on her hands and knees. I key my radio.

"Got her down here, Mitch, in the old man's closet."

"Ten-four. Comin' to ya."

The dispatcher comes over the air. "Hold all traffic, 163's taking one into custody."

I key the radio again. "You can release traffic, operator. Everything's 10-4 here." Then to Heather: "You dipped on me last time, bitch. Almost wrecked my car."

"I'm sorry Mr. Johnson, really, I . . ."

I hear myself say, "Please, just try something now, Heather. I'd love you to try it again. Been too long since I've tased somebody, and nobody needs it more'n you." The adrenalin's got me good. Do I really mean this? She is just a thief, and a female thief at that.

Heather seems even more shocked at me than I am.

"What? Why? I'm cooperatin', Detective, really I am. Don't shoot that thing. I surrender, Detective Johnson."

Mitch comes up behind me with his cuffs already out and snaps them on both Heather's wrists behind her.

Poor old Mr. Kennedy is mortified when we emerge from his bedroom with a woman he didn't even know was in his house.

"My God, Kelly Ann! What have I told you about bringing people here! And in *my* own room!"

He turns to me. "You might as well go on and take my daughter, too, Detective. I certainly won't put up with this kind of behavior here any longer!"

I look at Kelly Ann. "You know, he's right, Kelly Ann. We can take you for Harboring a Fugitive, Hindering Prosecution—not to mention how you've totally disrespected your father, *endangerin'* him with the likes a *her*."

"Boy howdy," Mitch chimes in. "I think that's Elder Abuse, don't you reckon, Detective?"

"Sure is, Mitch. Whadaya think? Take her, too?"

"It's your call, Detective. You da man," Mitch says.

We decide to leave Kelly Ann for now. We can always come back for her, depending on what Heather tells me.

Back at the precinct, Heather (predictably) tells me she was never even at "Stumpy" Brock's house with Kelly Ann, but she's more than happy to let me know who was.

"It was Victoria Barnhart did that with Kelly Ann. I wasn't even in Mobile that night. I was over at my mama's, in Daphne, visiting my baby girl. You can call them, they'll tell you I was there."

"Then how do you know Victoria was the one, Heather? Besides, Stumpy—Mr. Brock— picked your picture out of a photo spread."

From a file folder, I pull the spread, the one that Brock had been unable to pick from, for certain. Just before starting this interview with Heather I had circled her mugshot myself, anticipating her denials. I push it across the table.

Heather doesn't even glance at it. "I know because they were braggin' to me about it! They split the cash, it was about $300 apiece, and they bought everything they could on the card until Stumpy canceled it. Check the jewelry Vickie's prob'ly wearin' right now! She showed me! Got these big gold hoops for her ears, a couple bracelets, a necklace, all at Walmart on Stumpy's card, I swear!" Heather begins crying. "Check the cameras there, the Tillman's Corner store, if you don't believe me!" Her tears are real enough, but she seems more pissed off than sad or desperate.

Walmart has great security video. Their cameras hover over every checkout register, scan the parking lot, and record every customer at eye level coming and going through the entry doors. Heather knows this as well as I.

"You'll see it's Vicky, not me, buyin' all that stuff on Stumpy's card. And while you're at it, pull the video from the parkway state store. They put two liters of Stoli on his card there!"

"But if it wasn't you, why the hell'd you run from me, Heather? Try to ram my car? Besides, I've got a positive ID on you, from the victim himself. Why should I go runnin' all over town tryin' to get store video when I've already got what I need right here?"

"'Cause it wasn't me, Detective Johnson, I swear! I just ran outta habit, I guess. I know it don't make no sense. I knew my PO had already violated me, 'cause I missed my last few tests. Not 'cause I'd piss dirty, just 'cause I'm bad about missing appointments, and I been havin' car trouble, honest. Just put me on a lie detector, I'll prove it!"

Heather pauses, fixing her gaze right into mine.

"An' ole Stumpy Brock, all he sees when he looks at a woman is tits 'n' pussy, anyway. He's so drunk mosta the time he'd pick his own mama out of a lineup." She pushes my doctored photo spread back across the table. "This don't mean shit, an' you know it! I'm telling you who it really is, and you can take it to the bank! Why I gotta lie for?"

Heather's tears are dry now, and her composure regained. She takes a deep breath and makes her closing argument.

"Listen, Detective Johnson. You got me fair 'n' square on the Violating. I'm goin' back for that no matter what happens with this. I got nothing to gain or lose by just telling it like it is. I just wanna see justice done, don't you? This is what Vickie does, Mr. Johnson. I know her, believe me. Ask Kelly Ann. Hell, ask Vickie's own mama, she'll tell you: this is what Vickie does. And she's good at it. Been doin' it for years. With some o' the same men, over n'over. They get to where they don't even bother to report it, almost expectin' it when they take Vickie home. If you don't get her now, she'll just keep on doin' it, 'n' that just means more people ripped off 'n' more work for you."

Kinda compelling, I gotta admit (though I don't, not here and now, anyway). But I'm thinking: her estimation of my victim is right on, and I don't doubt that Vickie's caught up in this some way, too. Hmmm.

"Tell you what I'm'onna do, Heather. Gonna cut you a break. Can't do anything about your Violation. Warrant's already been signed by your PO. But I'm'onna hold off on chargin' you for Stumpy's thing. That doesn't mean it goes away. I can always charge you with it later. But I will look into your version a little more first."

"Thank you, Detective. You'll see I'm right about Vickie."

I tell Mitch to take her on to Metro for the probation warrant only. He gives me a quizzical look but doesn't say anything. Feeling a little sheepish, neither do I.

Back at my desk, I call Mariah.

"Didja catch her, Detective? She was there like I said, right?"

"I owe you one, Mariah. But listen: I need to talk to Vickie again. She there with you now?"

"No, haven't seen her for almost a week now."

"You got a number for her?"

"I think her phone's out of minutes, Detective. But I can call you when I see her again, I'm sure it won't be long. You trust me, don'tcha? I got Heather for you, didn't I?"

"Yes, you did, Mariah."

"We make a pretty good team, don'tcha think, Detective?"

"Yeah, I guess we do. Let me give you my cell number, in case you run into her after hours."

That night, my cell rings. It's not my week to be on call, but I get up anyway just to find out who the fuck is calling me at 2:30 in the morning. The cell is plugged in to the charger, on the bathroom counter.

"Johnson."

I hear a woman crying.

"This is Detective Johnson. Who's this?"

The crying subsides, and I recognize the husky voice. "Oh, Detective Johnson, I woke you up, didn't I? I'm so sorry, I didn't realize it's so late. Never mind."

"Mariah? Is that you?"

"Yes, Detective Johnson. I shouldn't have called, I'm so sorry."

"Forget about it. Just tell me what you called for. I'm awake now."

She starts to cry again but talks through it. "I just called because I . . . I did a rock again tonight, and I'm so disgusted with myself . . . and I don't want you to think bad of me . . . but I know you'll never put up with a woman who's a woman like me, and we could never . . . as long as I'm using . . . you would never . . ."

"Don't worry about it, Mariah. We all have our weaknesses. And we can all overcome them. So just get some sleep, that's best now, for both of us, all right?"

"All right, Detective Johnson. Thanks. I promise I won't call so late ever again. Please forgive me."

"You're forgiven. Let's just get back to sleep now, okay, Mariah?"

"Okay. Good night, Detective."

"Night, Mariah."

A day and a half later, Mariah calls me from the Parkway Lounge. The jukebox is playing loud in the background and I can hardly understand her. She goes into the lady's room to get away from the noise.

"Vickie's passed out in a blue Explorer in the back parking lot. Be sure to check her purse. I saw her steal Jordy Blankenship's credit card when he wasn't lookin'. Jordy's pretty wasted, and so is Vickie. But Jordy doesn't even know his card's gone yet."

I jump on I-10 from the precinct and head for the Parkway. It's not even noon yet.

Sure enough, in the front passenger seat of a battered old Blue Explorer behind the Parkway Lounge, there's Vickie, dead to the world. I walk up and peer in through the open window. She's got a crack pipe in her left hand, like a slumbering baby might grasp a pacifier. I reach in and snap a cuff on her right wrist, then hook her to the doorpost of the Explorer as she jerks awake and rattles the cuffs.

"What the fff—"

"Easy, Vickie. It's just your old friend the detective. Now, hold still while I check your purse for weapons, and if you would, please, hand me that stem in your other hand."

She slumps in her seat and surrenders the glass pipe, blackened with tarry residue from recent use. In her purse is a Home Depot credit card with the name Jordan Blankenship on it.

"How is it you have a Mr. Blankenship's credit card in your purse, Victoria?"

"He gave it to me 'cause he's too drunk. He wants me to pick out a good color to paint his living room with."

"Really? You want to rethink this a minute, Vickie? He gave *you* his card because he's too drunk to pick out paint, yet you're the one who's passed out behind the Parkway Lounge, and he's still vertical, inside the joint. How 'bout if I just ask Mr. Blankenship if he gave you his card?"

"I wish you would. I got no reason to lie to you, Detective Johnson."

I enter the backdoor of the lounge and blink my eyes to adjust to the gloom. I key my mike and start backup. "Got one in custody, white female, signal 68 [dope], possible 52 [theft], back lot of the Parkway Lounge."

At the end of the bar is Mariah, who signals me with a slight headshake and downcast eyes not to acknowledge her. I go up to the bartender, show her my badge, and ask her if there's a Jordan Blankenship in the house.

"You're shtandin' right nexta him, Officer," says a large fella to my immediate right at the bar. In Carhartt coveralls and a stained T-shirt, his leathery red face and heavy-lidded eyes topped with a bristly white flat-top crewcut, Mr. Jordy is at least as sloppy drunk as Vickie is wasted on crack in the parking lot. In front of him on the bar are his wallet, nestled among a pile of loose change, a couple empty longneck Buds, and an ashtray full of crushed Pall Mall butts. Conway Twitty intones "Hello darlin'" on the jukebox.

"You know a girl named Vickie Barnhart?"

"Sure I do," he says, swaying as he turns away to his right with a sweeping gesture. "She was right here minute ago. Hmmm, leastways, I thought she was . . ." He hangs onto the bar to steady himself as he looks around the room for Vickie. "Now where'd she go? Musta went to the little girls' room . . ." There's nobody else in the bar but Mariah, the barmaid, and me.

"I think I know where she is, Mr. Blankenship. I've got her secured outside. But tell me, is this your credit card? Did you give it to her to buy you some paint at Home Depot?"

"What the . . .? I'll be damned!" He sways in low to study the card, his unsteady face inches from the plastic in my hand. "Sheesh! Sure as shit . . . where . . . how'djoo . . . ?"

"I just took this out of Vickie Barnhart's purse. You didn't give it to her?"

"Aw, hayell no! That thievin' little . . . where's she at?" Mr. Jordy roars. He slams a huge fist down on the bar, making his empties and quarters dance. "Lemme at her!" he bellows.

"Hold on, Mr. Jordy," I say, putting a hand on his shoulder. "I got this." He shrugs me off, but the barmaid reaches across the bar and grabs one of the big man's meaty paws.

"Settle down, now, Jordy. Let the law handle it. He's already got your card back."

"Yeah, and I've got a unit on the way to take her straight to Metro."

A shout comes from the backdoor. A tall skinny fella, only his silhouette visible in the bright daylight flooding in behind him, is yelling, "Which one a y'all's the law? You got a lady out here just slipped outta some handcuffs, she run off thataways, to'rd them apartments!"

"Shit!" I dash past him out the backdoor. My cuffs are dangling from the Explorer's doorpost, but Vickie's nowhere to be seen. I look toward the apartments across the street, nothing. I stick my head into the barbershop next door.

"You see a white female, brunette, in a gray sweatshirt and jeans go by here?"

"She just got into a white van. I think a black guy was driving it. They went north on D.I.P."

Dammit! I get on the radio. "One-sixty-three, subject has escaped. Last seen northbound D.I.P. in a white van, unknown make, model, or tag. Possibly driven by a black male subject, unknown description."

All I can think is, it's gonna be hell trying to live this one down.

21

Solo Stakeout

Talk shit, get bit.
—Fritz, MPD K9 (if he could talk)

Three times in as many weeks, thieves had struck Theodore Aggregate at its sprawling thirty-acre complex down by the industrial canal on Hollinger's Island. The soaring price of copper was driving the larceny. At three bucks a pound, copper in any form became the new currency for drug addicts to support their ravenous habits. Copper plumbing and air-conditioning units by the hundreds were stolen every week from private residences, commercial buildings, schools, even churches. A $3,000 central air unit would be gutted, or carried off whole, for its copper components that might bring $100 at the scrap yard—enough for a shared pipe and a night of rough sex at a rundown motel with a willing crack whore.

But they weren't stealing air conditioners at Theodore Aggregate. They had found the mother lode: the fire-hose-thick power cables, almost entirely composed of thick braids of copper, which provide the juice to the elaborate, enormous network of conveyors by which industrial sands, gravels, macadam, and stones are moved from huge piles to waiting barges and tankers moored nearby in the industrial canal, ultimately to be shipped to construction sites worldwide, "to build the roads, side-walks, and foundations on which we live," according to site manager Roy Mullins, quoting from the company website as he gave me a brief walking tour of his operation.

A beehive of activity where everything is large, loud, and covered in dust, Theodore Aggregate employs a crew of a dozen or so men who are dwarfed by the company's mountainous piles of product and the machinery used to move it. Giant front-end loaders, with tires taller than me and buckets big enough to park a Toyota in, dump thundering multiton loads of crushed granite, sandstone, and limestone onto towering conveyors, longer than football fields, all clanking steel and hydraulics, themselves wheeled and powered by remotely activated engines in order to lumber from pile to pile fulfilling orders for the barges in the canal.

"With the cables cut, we can't move product. We're shet down," Roy said. "We've already spent over $50,000 to replace and splice the damage so far, just to keep at least one belt runnin' so's to keep my men workin', but this has got to stop." He spat a brown stream of Red Man into the dust. "We all got families to feed. I ain't gonna let some thieving sumbitches come in here and shet us down just to feed their dope habits."

It was the Monday morning after the third theft. Each had occurred over the weekend, when nobody was working, allowing the thieves the luxury of time and obscurity for a job requiring much hard labor and heavy lifting. The ten-foot lengths of cable, each weighing more than a hundred pounds, had probably taken nearly an hour each to cut by hand from the elevated conveyors. (Broken and dulled hacksaw blades had been found at the scene.) Then the cut cable had to be dragged at least a quarter mile out of the yard into the surrounding woods to be loaded into a pickup. The woods is a maze of old logging roads and two-tracks, providing multiple points of entry from Rangeline Road to the west, Hamilton Boulevard to the north, and a railroad right of way slicing diagonally across the northwest corner. After the first and second thefts, Mullins's crew had blocked off most of the roads into the woods with concrete barriers like the ones used around highway construction zones, but there remain a few overgrown two-tracks still passable and unblocked, and they lack the legal right to seal off the railroad tracks. The thefts continued. Mullins had begun to wonder if they were hauling off his cable on a boat from the canal and considered asking the Marine Police or the Coast Guard to get involved.

"I had half a mind to post up myself out here overnight, me and a couple of my men, with shotguns. But I decided I'd better let y'all handle it."

"That's the right decision, Mr. Mullins. This is a police matter. But your instincts, your tactics, are right on. It's gonna take somebody posted out here to catch 'em in the act. We've been checking the scrap yards, but by the time they take your cable there, it's just number 3 copper. We got no way to tie it back here. They strip it down, chop it up into smaller lengths, sell it all around so the weight doesn't give them away at any one yard. These guys know what they're doing."

"They damn sure do, and I can't help but wonder if somehow it's an inside job, Detective. Not many people even know we're back here, what we do, know anything about the cables on our conveyors. But I know my men, and I can't see a one of 'em doin' sech a thing as this."

"People will surprise you. The same thought occurred to me, but we're not likely to get a confession out of anybody by hauling each of your crew down to the precinct one by one. Besides, that wouldn't be nearly as much fun as catching the bastards red-handed out here, would it?"

Roy grinned, nodded, spat another stream of Red Man. "Reckon I'll leave it to you professionals," he said. "But I'll suggest this. If it was to be me out here overnight, I'd make sure to post some eyes up there in the tower. A feller can see the whole yard up there, but that tinted glass won't let anybody on the ground see inside. And the best thing: it's air conditioned. Though a thief might think it's strange if he hears the AC on in the tower at night when they ain't nobody here. If nothin' else, it'll keep you from bein' carried off by the skeeters." It was August, and hard to say which was worse: the heat, the humidity, or the mosquitoes.

Roy continued. "The light switches for the whole yard are up there, and there's even a loudspeaker you can use to tell 'em, 'Putcha hands up, gotcha surrounded!'"

He pulled a key ring out of his pocket. "This one here opens the lock on the front gate," he said. "This one gets you in the office, where you can use the bathroom or the Coke machine if you want. And this one here, not to be telling you how to do your job now, but this one here opens the door to the tower. Good huntin', Detective."

The centralized control tower commands the entire complex and remotely controls all the conveyors. It's tall enough to oversee the whole yard, taller than every pile of crushed stone, taller than the tops of the scrub pine choking the surrounding swamps, taller even than the bridge on Rangeline Road spanning the industrial canal. It seems like a good place to spend the night. Assuming I can get my captain to let me do this.

By Thursday I had been out to Theodore Aggregate twice, driving the rutted trails through the woods as far as the Crown Vic could take me without getting mired up to the hubcaps, and getting out and walking when necessary. I was looking for recent footprints or tire tracks, or signs of a staging or loading area. I found none but got a good sense of the lay of the land, parts of which were quite pretty. Families of wood ducks were gliding across the swamps, and a couple great blue herons stood motionless in tall grasses at the water's edge.

Friday morning I sprung the idea on my captain. He liked my initiative but said he didn't have the overtime in his budget to pay me for a night at the Aggregate yard. I told him I'd do it for straight time. He still balked. I told him I'd do it for nothing, unless I catch somebody, in which case I want to be paid for the time spent on the resulting paperwork. He shook his head at me, not refusing, but smiling at my stubbornness. "Make sure the shift sergeant knows exactly where you're gonna be, and knows how to get some units to you fast when you call for backup."

Nancy was a harder sell. Actually, I didn't sell her on the concept at all. She was pissed about my unavailability for supper and the movies on a Friday night and would've been doubly annoyed at my charitable volunteerism for the department. But she conceded to taking a snapshot of me before departure—standing proud and amused, shotgun at ready-arms, covered head to toe in camo—hardly different from the little boy dressing up like the mighty warrior. For Nancy, it was worthy of an eye roll, unhappy though she was to countenance what she saw as boyish excitement for a potentially deadly hunt.

On the way to my stakeout, I stopped at Walmart for a bottle of bug dope, some cans of Red Bull, peanut butter crackers, and a headlamp so I could use both hands for the shotgun, or the handcuffs, or whatever else I might need both hands for. Then I swung by the precinct just before shift change and gave the night-shift sarge my cell number and a dozen photocopies of my hand-drawn map showing the front gate to Theodore Aggregate, just past the railroad tracks about a half mile south of Hamilton Boulevard, and a rough layout of the yard, the canal, the conveyors, the tower, the railroad tracks, and the main dirt roads through the swampy woods leading off the property, where the thieves were likely entering and exiting. He said he'd distribute the maps and go over it with his squad at roll call.

At sundown I concealed my squad car in the mechanic's shed near the small cinder-block building that housed Roy Mullins's office and the crew's lockers, equipment room, and break room. From there I hiked a quarter mile to the control tower. There was no way to be quiet about it, every step a loud crunch on the gravel underfoot. But there was no need for stealth yet; I doubted the thieves would venture onto the property much before midnight.

The sweeping view of the brightly lit yard from the tower was perfect, and the control room wasn't too stuffy, even with the AC off. I sat in a comfortable chair at the control panel, found the loudspeaker switch and microphone, all the light switches—even a movable spotlight similar to but bigger than the one on my squad car—and settled in for the night.

Three hours passed, and the only movement I had seen was some stray dogs and feral cats trotting among the rock piles. At least I had developed a plan of sorts. I had never attempted to hold someone at gunpoint from a thirty-foot tower, and doubted it would work, not for long. Most right-minded, self-respecting thieves will bolt at the first inkling of trouble. I considered cranking open the tower windows so I could poke my shotgun out in a show of force, but the only windows that would crank open took awhile to crank, were blocked by screens, and allowed my barrel to point only north or south, whereas most of the conveyors were arrayed to my west. Pre-cranking the windows open and removing the screens in advance didn't seem to provide sufficient tactical advantage to discourage the bad guys from flight, much less sufficient reason to expose myself to the inevitable flight of swarming mosquitoes into my post.

If I used the PA system to order them to freeze, but they bolted, they'd melt into the woods before I could get down the tower stairs, and there was no way to keep eyes on them as I descended. I could tell them over the PA that we had canine units coming at them already from Rangeline and Hamilton, but they'd probably know I was bluffing when they didn't hear any barking in the woods. Best not to use the public address system at all, I decided.

Instead, I would radio for backup as soon as the thieves were visible, giving descriptions of the subjects and their direction of approach, and depending on the number of units available to respond, we'd set up a perimeter on Rangeline and Hamilton, looking for any pickup trucks parked along either highway or the railroad tracks. That way, if they heard my backing units approaching the tower and ran, I could at least keep eyes on them to know which direction they ran and alert the perimeter units. And maybe if they bolted, *then* I'd use the PA as a last-ditch bluff about canine units in the woods. It all depended on how busy the squad was, and how many units they could send to back me, and how far away they'd be coming from. If I can't get at least three units here within a half hour, I figured they'd probably get away.

I sat there in the tower sucking down Red Bulls, then tiptoeing down the steps to pee out the door, until 2 a.m. I figured that if they hadn't come by then, they probably weren't coming, because they wouldn't have enough time to cut much cable before sunrise around 5 a.m. I descended the tower and crept along the canal to the western edge of the yard, almost all the way to Rangeline Road, then circled north to the edge of the woods along Hamilton Boulevard, pausing to listen for voices or footsteps every dozen yards or so. Nothing. Finally, at a little after 3 a.m., I reached the mechanic's shed, fired up the Crown Vic, and went home.

Nancy woke me up a little past 10 a.m. Saturday morning with my cell phone in her hand. "It's a guy named Roy, from the Aggregate place. Says he really needs to talk to you."

"Detective? Thought you'd wanna know. Guess you couldn't get out there last night, 'cause they hit us again, but we—"

"What? You gotta be kiddin' me! I was out there till after three!"

"Well I guess they came after that. They cut the cable on the conveyor nearest to the tower. But we found what they cut hidden in a ditch beside one of those roads through the woods, right near the junction of the three main roads. We haven't blocked off one of those three yet, the one that comes out on Rangeline Road. That's probably the one they're goin' in and comin' out on. Guess they got tired, or got too late a start to drag 'em all out before sunup. I've called one of my guys in to help me block off that last road and to gather up the pile of cut pieces. We might can still use it for splicing—"

"No! Leave it there! And do not block that road. They'll be coming back for it tonight. Are you out at the yard now?"

"Yeah, I'm waiting for my guy to help me load this stuff, but if you think I shouldn't—"

"Leave it alone. Don't move it, don't even touch it. I'm on my way."

At sundown, I'm posted up in the woods near the crossroads where the thugs had dragged last night's load of cables and stashed them in a ditch without even bothering to cover them up with cut branches or weeds. Nine pieces of cable, each eight to ten feet long, raggedly hacked at each end exposing the braided inch-diameter copper strands encased within the rubber sheathing. They had duct-taped the cables into bundles of three to drag out of the woods and load into a vehicle. I had advised the shift sergeant that I would be setting up again tonight, but in the woods this time, over the stash at the crossroads from last night. I told him I'd most likely be calling on my cell if I needed backup, because I didn't want to risk spooking them or giving away my position with radio chatter.

I find a comfortable vantage point about twenty yards from the crossroads and four or five paces off the unblocked two-track coming from Rangeline Road, most likely the road they'll be taking, either on foot or possibly with a truck, to retrieve their stash from last night. I have a decent visual of the crossroads clearing from my spot while there's still daylight, but unless they're using flashlights or driving in on the two-track, I'll have to rely solely on listening to know when they're here after nightfall, especially if clouds obscure the sliver of moon. There remains just enough cover to conceal me after I cut away a few branches and bushes to allow me quick, silent access to the road, and I clear my path of sticks that might snap if I step on them.

I make myself a comfy pile of pine needles to sit on next to the trunk of a thick pine for a backrest. I douse myself in DEET, even spraying it on my camo pants and long-sleeved shirt and watch cap. And here I sit, sweating, itching, dripping, sucking lukewarm Red Bull poured into a squeeze bottle to avoid the pop of cracking open a can, eating jerky strips and chocolate Hostess cupcakes, pre-removed from their crackling cellophane packaging and swaddled in soundless paper towels. I'm basting in my own juices, sweat soaking through my shirt and pants, waiting, and dripping, as night falls and the mosquitoes swarm and whine in my ears.

Along about midnight, I jerk awake from dozing, having no idea how long I've napped. I nearly panic when I realize my legs and feet have also fallen asleep. If they're here now, or arrive anytime soon, I'm helpless. Slowly I stand and balance myself unsteadily against the tree, shaking one leg, then the other. As the blood rushes down and I begin to recover control over my rubbery legs and feet, I think I see a blink of light flash from the crossroads. My heart begins to pound and I can feel the veins in my forehead and temples throb as I strain to hear, to see. I'm shaky in the knees and feel my hands tremble as I grab the pre-racked 12 gauge leaning against the pine tree.

I remember to do "tactical breathing": inhale through the nose three counts, hold for three counts, exhale through the mouth for three, hold for three, repeat. After the third rep I feel steady enough to creep out to the two-track, silently, straining to see any movement, any dark silhouettes in the crossroads. Nothing. I think I see another flicker of light out of the corner of my eye, behind me. I spin and crouch, holding my breath, eyes bugging out, looking all around. Silence. Darkness.

I'm suddenly gripped by a sinking feeling that they've come and gone while I slept, and I'm certain the same thing must have happened right under my nose last night, I must have not even realized I'd been dozing up in the tower in that comfortable chair. I rise again, wheeling 180 degrees, and sprint for the crossroads, switching on my headlamp.

A wave of relief washes over me with the discovery of the stash of bundled cable in the ditch, just as I had last seen it at sundown. I breathe deeply and wonder if I'd merely glimpsed a lightning bug, or a refracted flicker of headlights through the piney woods from Rangeline Road? Dejected and puzzled, I trudge back to my hidey-hole to take up my post again after emptying my bladder in the pine straw a few steps behind my tree trunk.

Who do I think I am, I wonder. Rambo? I feel my ears burn with the recollection of the time I went turkey hunting up in Monroe County and set up next to a tree like this one, on the edge of a clearing, and dozed off, only to be awakened by a veritable *flock* of gobblers strutting right by me, literally within spitting distance. I had jerked upright and shouldered my rifle just in time to watch them flapping away in a wide spray and never even got one in my sights, much less squeezed off a round.

This is crazy, I think. And dangerous. At least the turkeys were unarmed. Who knows what these guys might be carrying, and how many of them there will be? I can hardly believe my captain allowed me to attempt this foolhardy stunt. And if there's more than two guys, I'm out of handcuffs. What then? I guess I can cuff the three of 'em together using the two sets of cuffs, so they'd trip all over each other if they tried to run. And I do have my Taser in case anybody resists. And my pepper spray, too, I remember. And they won't know I'm all by myself. I can get on the radio and they'll hear the chatter and think there's a bunch of us already out here in the woods closing in, and know the jig is up. I'm not alone, at least not for too long.

Yeah. I can do this, I decide. If I can just stay awake. I take a few long gulps of Red Bull, and sit still, and listen, and wait.

It's a little after three, and I'm thinking they're not coming back, at least not tonight. And I don't think I can do this again on Sunday night, even if Nancy doesn't object. I'm worn out and discouraged.

And then I hear them. Sounds like two different voices. They're not loud enough or close enough for me to make out what they're saying, but they're definitely voices. Coming from the crossroads. I key the precinct cell, Sarge answers.

"Got at least two at the crossroads," I whisper. "Start backup." I pocket the phone, rise, and creep to the road. The adrenalin dump begins. It's not really fear, exactly. (After all, I remind myself, I'm armored and armed and have the element of surprise, even if I'm outnumbered.) Whatever it is, it always happens, and the tactical breathing quells my quaking in seconds. Crouching down so they won't see my silhouette, I can make out theirs, twenty yards away, dragging the cable bundles up from the ditch onto the road.

I stand up and stride toward them and yell, "Freeze! Mobile Police!" as I shoulder the 12 gauge. I see the two silhouettes jerk upright. One drops a cable bundle and dives into the woods to the right. The other tosses what may be a backpack into the air and crashes into the brush to the left. Without thinking I point the 12 gauge up at a 45-degree angle and fire a round into the air. There's a long bright flash from the barrel and a really, really loud report. I had forgotten how damn loud the Remington 12 gauge is. We're always wearing ear protection at our yearly qualification with them at the range. And the kick: I still feel it in my shoulder. I rack another round into the chamber. I feel invincible.

I run to the crossroads, flicking on my headlamp, and pull my foot-long Stinger Streamlight from my belt, sweeping both sides of the road. Silence. So I know they gotta be laying down, and not too far off the road. Silently, slowly I retrace my steps looking for signs of entry into the woods: bent grasses, broken branches, a reflected flash of my beam from a pair of eyes.

Nothing. I stop and listen for heavy breathing, rustling leaves, snapping twigs.

Nothing. I walk all the way back down the road to my own path, from where I had just sprung out of the woods, without seeing any sign or hearing any sound from either of them. Was I seeing things? Am I dreaming? How'd they disappear so fast? I reverse direction and slowly, carefully approach the crossroads again.

A flash of reflected light from the ditch startles me but turns out to be just a discarded beer can. How did I miss this the first time? Another twinkle of light winks at me: shards of broken glass. Then I spot the knapsack that one of them had tossed and retrieve it from the ditch. This is not a dream, I think. The bag is heavy, filled with clanking tools, probably hacksaws. A step beyond that, my eyes are drawn to twin bright rectangles in the weeds, about the size of postage stamps, a foot apart. I step to the edge of the road to try to make sense of them. Whatever they are, they're made of reflective material. I continue to puzzle over them, my headlamp, Stinger, and shotgun trained on them.

With a start I realize I'm looking at little reflective squares of rubber on the heels of a pair of sneakers. Occupied sneakers.

"Let me see your hands!" I bark.

"Don't shoot! I surrender! Don't shoot" comes a muffled voice about six feet beyond the sneakers, deep in the undergrowth.

"I want you to crawl backwards on your belly, slow, like a snake, toward the sound of my voice. Keep your hands spread out wide and just scooch toward me, backwards, up to the road. You do anything stupid I will blow your ass off."

"Yessir! I'm comin'. Don't shoot, sir."

I stand back as he inchworms his way on his belly, up out of the ditch and onto the road, all the while sweeping the Streamlight all around in case his partner tries to spring out from somewhere while I'm focused on this one. I place a boot between his shoulder blades and order him to join his hands as if to pray, behind his back. He complies and I holster my Stinger light, sling the 12 gauge over my shoulder, and snap the cuffs on, then fill one hand with my Glock and pat him down with the other.

"I got nu'n on me, sir. You 'bout made me crap my pants when you fired that round, sir. Thought I was dead, honest to God, sir!"

"What about your partner? He got any weapons?"

"What partner, sir? I'm by myself."

I put more weight on the boot in his back, holster the Glock, and unsling the shotgun. "Don't even start with the lies. I saw the both of you. He jumped to one side, you to the other. And he didn't get far. Does he have any weapons, or should I just start popping off rounds in the direction I saw him jump?"

"I swear to God, sir, I don't know where he went. But he don't have any weapons on him, sir. We were just walkin' over to the canal to do some fishin', sir, I swear!"

I nuzzle the Remington's barrel to the back of his neck. "You fuckin' moron. 'Fishing'? Are you just *trying* to piss me off? 'Fishing,' with a sack fulla hacksaws and a hundred pounds of copper cable? Who's your partner, dickhead. What's his name?"

"Harley. Harley Draper. It was all his idea. He used to work here."

A flash of headlights is bouncing toward me along the two-track from Rangeline Road: my backup.

"Harley!" I shout. "Oh, Harrr-ley! Harley Draaa-per! Come out, come out, wherever you are! Your bro here just gave you up, Harrr-ley!"

Tyrone Anderson rolls up in a cloud of dust, followed closely by Heavy Harry Claggett, then Sergeant Edwards.

"Look at you, all ninja'ed up in camo with a headlamp on," Roney says as he gathers up the midnight angler to stuff into his cage.

"Your ghillie suit at the cleaners, Detective?" Claggett cracks.

"There's another one, jumped into the woods about here," I say. "He's gotta be layin' down, not too far in."

Harry and Roney set off to search the woods, while Sarge and I dump out the contents of the knapsack. Sure enough, among the hacksaws and pry bars that come clanking out is a wallet containing the Alabama driver's license of Harley Davidson Draper, white male, forty-three years of age.

"This should be all you need to sign a warrant on the one that got away," Sarge says. "That is if Claggett and Anderson don't flush him out."

"Yeah, but we can get 'im, Sarge. He couldna gotten far; I heard him crashing into the woods for no more'n a dozen steps or so, then quiet. He's probably got eyes on us right now. And this is the fourth lick these guys have hit at this place this month. Into 'em for over fifty grand already."

"Say no more," Sarge says. Then, into the radio, "One Sam Four, start canine unit to our location. We have one in custody, and one still at large in the woods. Advise units on Rangeline and Hamilton to hold the perimeter and switch to Tac channel."

The canine unit arrives about a half hour later, just as Claggett and Anderson come straggling back from bushwhacking through the woods, covered in brambles and sweat.

Heavy Harry's breathing hard, his pants slathered in oozing muck up to his knees. "Shit, Mark, you didn't tell me it's nothing but swamp back in there!"

"Sorry, Harry. I assumed you went in with a flashlight and could see what you were stepping into."

"You guys have been out tramping through the woods?" the canine officer demands in disbelief. "Dammit, you've fucked up my scene. Dog's trained to follow the freshest scent, and now that'll just be you guys! It's not even worth it to take him outta the car."

"You gotta be woofin', man," Roney says. "I'm tore up from the floor up, uniform's fulla stickers, spiders still crawlin' in my hair, and you ain't even gonna let the dog loose?"

"I got shit up to my knees and I'm covered in mosquito bites, mother-fucker," Harry says. "I say the dog gets a chance."

"I agree," says Sarge. Then, to the canine officer: "Let the dog do his thang."

The canine guy grumbles under his breath as he fetches the dog from his car. Fritz comes back straining at his leash, yelping and whining to get to work. Sarge offers Fritz a sniff of Harley Draper's backpack, and the animal bounds off into the woods, jerking the canine officer along behind.

"Har-ley, oh Harrr-ley!" I shout in a singsong voice. "Ollie ollie in free! Last chance before the dog gets ya!"

In minutes Fritz is going crazy and has bounded into a shallow pocket of swamp water. Snarling and thrashing, the canine has pounced on top of a prone, submerged figure, which rises struggling from the goopy water. Cries of pain fill the air.

"Bad dog! Down! Call him off! Get him off me! I surrender! Bad dog!"

Harry and Roney crash through the woods toward the yelping, growling, and screaming and return moments later with a handcuffed, waterlogged, muddied, and bloodied Harley Draper, who is unceremoniously tossed into Harry's cage as we all cheer the triumphant return of the muddy, dripping shepherd with lavish praise, shouting, "Good dog!" "Way to go, Fritzo!" "That's what I'm talkin' 'bout, take a bite outta crime!" singing, "Who let the dog out, who, who?" and doing coyote howls at the moon. Fritz joins in the merriment with his own howls and yelps, flinging swamp muck all over us as he shakes his fur and wags his tail.

"I'm amazed," the canine officer confesses. "The guy was completely underwater! Never woulda seen him. I had no idea what Fritz was after, but he went right in at a full gallop and the guy comes up screaming and fighting like a gaffed gamefish. Never seen anything like it!" There are high fives all around, and I give the last of my jerky to our four-legged hero.

Back at the precinct as the sun comes up, it turns out Harley Draper is the no-good ex-con brother-in-law of Aggregate manager Roy Mullins, who was shamed and enraged by the revelation. Harley had quit in a huff six months ago because he felt disrespected by Roy and was working at a better-paying job over in Pascagoula at the Exxon Refinery. What Roy didn't know was, Harley'd gotten fired from Exxon last month for failing a drug test and returned to Theodore to support his meth habit by scrapping copper cable cut from his old employer's conveyors.

To his credit, though, Harley manned up and wrote a full confession, including an expression of remorse and apology to Roy, knowing full well that this offense would violate the terms of his probation and put him back in Atmore for several more years.

As they were taking him away to Metro, Harley stopped and said to me, "That was a good piece of policin' out there, Detective. Don't know which is more dedicated: you or the dog."

I think it's one of the nicest things anybody's ever said to me.

During the next few months, I have three more solo stakeouts. Directly across Rangeline Road from Theodore Aggregate is an old chemical refinery that was shut down eight years ago by the EPA and declared a brownfield. As the Justice Department's lawsuit against McGrue-Tromax Corporation drags on, a skeleton crew of about a half-dozen dismantlers and salvage workers, as well as a couple of unarmed contract security guards, roam the sixty acres of rusting metal buildings, equipment sheds, and huge chemical storage tanks during daylight hours. After dark, there's a lone night watchman at the entrance guard shack. On any given night, four or five scrappers are on the grounds stealing whatever they can strip and carry off to the salvage yards.

My first night out there, I took two scrappers into custody at gunpoint. The second stakeout produced another arrest, but one (or more) of his accomplices got away. The third stakeout netted three scrappers. As I sat in my office back at the precinct typing up the paperwork on the night I hit the Tromax trifecta, Lieutenant Daniels came in and sat down in the chair at Earl's desk, behind me.

"Y'know, Mark, I'm concerned about all these stakeouts you've been doing down there on Rangeline Road. You really shouldn't be out there all by yourself." Daniels is a career cop, well liked and respected in the department. I stop typing and wheel my chair around to face him.

"I appreciate that, LT, but Captain authorized it. And I don't see anybody lining up to spend their nights out there with me. Besides, I've been pretty successful with it so far."

"Right—so far. That's exactly my point. Tonight, with three guys out there, y'know, there are so many ways it could've gone wrong. They coulda triangulated, and one of 'em coulda got around behind you, and—"

"Nah, don't worry, El-Tee, I wouldn't hesitate to use the 12 gauge at point-blank if I feel like I have to."

"I get that, I know you're capable and you can handle yourself. I know you'd do what you hafta do."

"Besides, these guys I been catching out there, they aren't exactly criminal masterminds, or they wouldn't be scrapping for a living. But I appreciate your concern."

"You're not hearing me, Mark. It's more than that. It's not sound tactically, and it's just not worth the risk. It's not like they're bank robbers, they're not endangering the public. Do you think those big corporations like Aggregate and Tromax don't have insurance? Frankly I think the captain's wrong to let you do it, and I'll tell him so if it comes down to that. You're one of the most conscientious officers I've ever seen in this department, and I admire you for it, Mark. And I also know how fun it is to go out there and make so many collars. In some ways it's like huntin' over a baited field.

"But it's not safe, and it's not smart, and unless you can get somebody to do it with you, I really don't want to see you go out there again. It's just not worth it, man."

Without another word, Lieutenant Daniels got up and left the office. I was grateful, because if he had lingered he might've seen my damn eyes moisten up.

22

Slocumb's Theorem

Like the dog that returns to his vomit, so a fool repeats his folly.
—Proverbs 26:11

Earl Slocumb was my informal FTO for general investigations. Informal because it was not officially designated by the chain of command or addressed in the department's General Orders, as it was with Porter in patrol. But Earl took me under his wing, let me shadow him, and shadowed me in my first few months as a detective.

Other than about eight classroom hours covering such topics as how to get your search warrants signed by a judge (be specific), how to get your arrest warrants approved by the DA's charging office (be thorough and complete), and how to tell when the guy handcuffed to the table is lying (basically, when his lips are moving), there was no training for investigations.

Earl never acts like a know-it-all, but he's generous with his accumulated wisdom, which is considerable. Though he's only about half my age and has less than half my time as a street cop, he clearly has a knack for detective work. That Officer of the Year plaque above his desk was awarded for just nine months' worth of investigating.

And well deserved it was. I've never known a more effective interrogator than Earl. (Excuse me, "interviewer." Today's kinder, gentler police don't interrogate, we "interview.") Earl develops near-instant rapport with victims, eyewitnesses, suspects (er, "persons of interest"), their accomplices (I mean "associates"), even with their mamas and baby-mamas ("mamas" and "baby-mamas") better than anybody I've seen. He's not above deception, manipulation, even intimidation, but mostly he just puts people at ease, talks their language, exchanges sports opinions or fishing stories like he's talking to a neighbor over the back fence, gets them to like him, believe him, trust him. No matter if they're white, black, young, old, tweaking, terrified, or full of attitude: Earl's an equal-affability investigator.

His modesty leads him to attribute his success simply to his informal outward appearance and laid-back style rather than any particular insight into the hearts of men or superior technique. He insists it's all about his faded Levi's and unkempt appearance. Says he's read professional studies that back him up. I don't doubt him, but there's no way I could emulate him, either in appearance or demeanor. According to Earl, my buttoned-down, coat-and-tie formality, my vocabulary, and especially my gray hair work to my disadvantage.

"You look like an authority figure," Earl said in my first week as an investigator. "Like a Clint Eastwood cop. Must be the boots and suits. I don't know, maybe you can get that workin' for you—e'rbody's got they own ways—but you sure ain't gonna pull off my ways. When they see you, no matter how you dress, they be thinking: Authority." (He said it with a long *y*, like the kid in the *South Park* cartoons.)

"Now, they see me, it's more like *anti*-authori-tye. They think, He got no agenda, got no evidence, no suspects, shit, he ain't got a *clue*. They're like, Here's somebody pays no attention to the rules, somebody I can relate to, mebbe he can understand my side a things. They think I'm just like their-selves: barely civilized.

"But I never really think about it much. I just come by it naturally, I guess."

Eventually, I learned that "come by it naturally" is more than just a figure of speech with Earl. As I got to know him better, he told me about his growing up around Brewton, Alabama, and the Florida Panhandle, one of seven kids in a family of rednecks (his word) on a hardscrabble farm.

"My daddy was a constable in Wetumpka, up in Elmore County, before I was born. Then the family moved down to Escambia County and tried farmin'. That didn't pay real well, either, so mostly he made a livin' mech-anicin', fixin' people's trucks and farm equipment. But we had horses, and some cattle, and chickens, and crops when I was growin' up. And daddy was all the time havin' run-ins with the deputies. Not for anything really criminal, but it seemed like he just couldn't get along with them, so they kept hemmin' him up on stuff I now know is bullshit, like animal cruelty because they thought our horses were too skinny, or not havin' a permit to build a pond, or the right zoning to fix cars. It coulda been *because* he'd been a constable, and knew they were fulla shit, and told 'em so, that they kept pesterin' him, I don't know. That's my theory anyway—some cops can be dicks that way, y'know? Anyway, he was killed when I was sixteen. Vehicular homicide.

"A family friend—I called him Uncle Dwayne, but he wasn't really my uncle—had just got outta prison, came back home to Escambia County. Dad was tryin' ta help him out, let him stay with us awhile. One night Uncle Dwayne got drunk, or high, I don't know which, and he stole my brother's car. Dad went out to try and stop him and got ran over by him. That was a long time ago. Matter fact, I think Dwayne's due to get out again early next year."

Earl's "uncle" Dwayne wasn't the only member of his family who'd spent time behind bars: there are cousins "and a no-good brother who oughtta be in jail, bein's he's nu'n but a con man and a cheat, all his life. Never paid a penny in taxes, scams people worse than a Clarke County Weaver, and collects disability checks even though he's in better physical shape than me."

Earl paused and patted his stomach. "'Course, that ain't sayin' much." He grinned his whole-face grin.

But Earl also has a brother on his second combat tour in Afghanistan, who's a sergeant with Escambia County's S.O.—the very same agency that used to bedevil his dad and sent Uncle Dwayne to the Florida pen.

"Nobody does just one burglary."

That's Slocumb's Theorem of Property Crime. Based on his own observations and life experience, he says, most petty thieves lack the imagination and entrepreneurial skills to think outta the box, change things up a little, throw us off.

"It ain't exactly science with these guys," Earl explained. "He'll hit a lick, usually right in his own neighborhood. Often as not, the first few houses he hits is gonna be his own people—a neighbor, somebody he parties with, maybe an old girlfriend, maybe even his own cousin or mama," Earl said. "Somebody who he knows the routines of: when they're at work, gone fishin' or whatever. He'll know the stuff worth stealin' in the house and where it's at 'cause he's been in that house, knows which window or door is easiest to get in.

"And he gets away with it. It's so easy: kick in the backdoor, wrap the shit up in a pillowcase, hide it in the woods till dark, sell it on the streets that night, or take it to the drug man for some weed or crack. Even if the victim suspects him, he won't usually tell us his name. Our victims don't trust us or like us any more'n the thugs do. And they don't wanna admit their friends or kin are thieves, or don't wanna be a snitch. Or they think they can handle it themselves. Which they can't.

"So it ain't long 'fore he does it again. Same neighborhood, same deal: somebody else he knows. Maybe same victim as the first time, or somebody else whose house he's been in, somebody who's got the stuff he knows he can move quick: flat screens, Xboxes and games, maybe a gun or some power tools.

"Sooner or later, he'll bring in a partner or two. That'll give him more good targets: the partners know other good houses with flat screens and guns, know their neighbors' work schedules, know other people who'll buy or swap for the merchandise. And now he's got somebody he can post outside with a cell to be lookout, and somebody who'll help him carry those big fifty-inch flats or that generator or power washer out of the garage. Before you know it, they're hittin' a couple licks a week, all in the same zip code.

"It's only a matter of time before they fuck up and get seen, or we lift a good print, or one of 'em gets ratted out by his baby-mama 'cause he gave some stolen bling to a new girl, but he ain't paid for her Pampers in a month, or they pawn something they can't sell or swap and we get a hit from pawn detail.

"So we look at who he's been arrested with before, for anything. Juvenile shit: fighting in school, shoplifting, loitering, or possession. Or maybe the baby-mama tells us all his homies' names. We pick them up, too. Bring 'em all in at once for questioning. Play one against the other, make shit up, do what we do, and one finally confesses to the lick. Now, at this point, most detectives are happy to make the arrest, clear the case, move on.

"But this is where the theorem comes in. Nobody does just one. Look at the open cases in the neighborhood over the past few months. Look at what's been stolen, time a day, day a the week, method of entry. Patterns. Check his pawn history, his baby-mama's pawn history, his family's and homies' pawns. Check the cars they drive, see if they match anything seen in the other cases. Then you tell him you know he did *all* the licks in the area. Word's out now that he's in custody, and we say we got people comin' to us from all these other cases in the area, sayin' they seen him cartin', off they TVs and weed whackers, wantin' they stuff back, or restitution. Whattawe gon' do about all this mess? But then we say, like we're just brain-stormin' that moment, 'Hmmm, Tyrone, mebbe there's a way we can he'p you out, but you gotta he'p us out.' And of course we can't make this offer for all his partners, but if *he* cooperates, he can be a *witness* 'stead of a defendant on all these other cases, and we can tell the DA he cooperated and deserves a deal.

"'Fore you know it, he's spillin' his guts and sellin' out his homies. And one case turns into a dozen cleared.

"Because nobody does just one."

I wouldn't have believed it if I hadn't seen it play out, over and over. One burglary arrest would lead to multiple confessions and case clearances. Eventually, I developed my own mojo, my own style, and it never felt better than the time I got a kid who had burglarized more than thirty homes over a two-month period, in an area that spanned my beats as well as Earl's. We both knew LaMarcus Pettway had done them, but we had nothing more than unreliable hearsay and circumstantial evidence: not enough to get a warrant signed for Pettway's arrest.

Earl had interviewed Pettway on several occasions, to no avail. Then I got a couple of cases that had Pettway's name all over them and brought him in for questioning.

"He ain't gonna talk," Earl warned. "Me and Lusty have double-teamed him twice: good cop–bad cop, claimed we had prints, said somebody ratted him out to us. That's after I spent a couple hours with him by myself. Pettway don't talk. He's just a fuck-'tard thug, too stupid to reason with and too hard to intimidate."

I didn't have anything to lose by trying, so my buttoned-down self went into the room and started talking. He was only nineteen years old but no small kid. Grew up in the B'mo Bricks, one of Mobile's toughest projects, been in trouble since he was fourteen and expelled from school. Six foot 3, 250 pounds, solid muscle, dark chocolate skin, LaMarcus looked like he could be a starting linebacker, replete with full gold grill and multiple tattoos.

I told him I had spoken with his mama and his grandparents earlier that day, and I could tell he came from a good family. His grandfather had introduced himself as Reverend Pettway, of Riverside Baptist. He had invited me inside.

"It's a nice house. Yard's kept up. He told me you used to cut the grass for him, that right?"

Pettway nodded but wouldn't make eye contact with me.

"That was my first job, too: cutting grass. Not just for my parents, but also around the neighborhood."

Nothing.

"Inside's real nice, too. Not like mosta the places I go in. Your folks have good furniture, keep it all real tidy. Saw the family portraits in the living room. Looks like you got some little brothers and sisters."

Pettway was still impassive, but at least he wasn't argumentative, or a smart aleck.

"Your grandfather told me they're all good kids, do well in school. Said you were like that, too, until those troubles with your father. When I told them why I was looking for you, they all three cried. I told them I had enough to put you in the same place as your father, for years. How you think your little brothers'll handle that, LaMarcus? Next to your grandfather, you're the man of the house, with your daddy being gone. Looks like you're fixin' to follow in his footsteps. Which means maybe your little brothers will follow in yours. At least that's what your folks are all worried about."

Pettway still avoided eye contact.

"My mama cried, too, when I was about your age, and I got arrested. My dad was really pissed, but I could deal with that. I even kinda liked it that I pissed him off so much. He and I butted heads a lot, and after a few years of it, he'd just had it with me. Called me a quitter, said I wouldn't think for myself, just always went along with the crowd. That made me so mad. Still does, just thinking about it. So I didn't care that I made him mad, and kind of embarrassed him, you know?"

To my surprise, LaMarcus Pettway seemed to be listening, and he nodded, though he still wouldn't look at me.

"But no matter how much trouble I got in, how many times I ended up in jail, my mama just cried but never gave up on me. I can still picture her in my mind, crying over me, even though she's been gone almost twenty years now."

I hadn't planned this out, hadn't thought I would be telling this stuff to a young (but accomplished) burglar, and wasn't sure how I got here or where I was going with it.

Worse, I had not anticipated the strength of emotion the memories would stir in me. I've always been an easy weeper, much to my dismay. I've gotten better at anticipating it, heading it off, disguising it. Nevertheless, occasionally my eyes still well up before I know it's coming. I looked down at the Miranda waiver form, filled in the date, time, and location, and signed my name on the line for Officer/Witness, then shuffled through Pettway's multipage rap sheet as if reminded of something I needed to check on, made some arbitrary notational scrawls and check marks.

When at last I brought my gaze back up to Pettway, I was startled to see him looking intently at me, blinking back his own tears.

"You can turn this around right now, LaMarcus. Stop your mama's tears. I can help you with that. We start with this case on Driftwood Drive. I know you did it, and you know I know. I got an eyewitness puts you at the scene, willing to testify. Didn't even need to talk to you today. Coulda just had 'em take you straight to Metro, but after I met your folks, I promised 'em I'd try to work with you. You're not like most of 'em I talk to in here, Marcus. You got a good family that still cares about you.

"So this is the deal: you get one hundred with me on this case on Driftwood Drive—and you might as well, 'cause I got you on it anyway— and you tell me about the others, too, on Delta and Greenwood and over on Bucker and Zula, too, then we can probably work something out. Now, I can't promise you anything, but you help me clear cases, I can talk to the DA and even the judge for you about getting a break. They the ones who make the decisions, but they wanna know what we think before they decide."

"You would do that for me? You could make some a this go away?"

"I could put in a word for you. How good that word is depends on how honest you are with me, how many names you give me, and how much stuff we can get back. That means you gotta tell me where the stuff went, and who all's involved. The more you tell me, the more you help yourself, and the sooner you put all this behind you, Marcus, and start fresh with a clean slate."

"What I gotta do?"

I pushed the confession forms across the table and gave him a pen.

"Start writing. Beginning with Driftwood and working backwards. I need names, addresses, I need to know as best you can remember what you got outta each lick, and who's got it now."

"But I don't know no 'dresses. I could show you on a map or something, but—"

"We can do better'n that. How 'bout we take a ride? You'll know the places if you see 'em, right? And we can get drive-through on the way. It's almost suppertime."

I left Pettway writing and went out to ask Earl and Lusty about checking out the undercover Tahoe with the dark-tinted windows. They couldn't believe I got LaMarcus Pettway to talk.

"Well, I did hafta promise him a Big Mac and large fries."

"Nah," Earl said. "I think it's that Clint Eastwood thing you got goin' on. It must be workin' for ya."

I sure as hell wasn't going to tell them how Marcus and I both got misty eyed over breaking our mamas' hearts.

LaMarcus Pettway confessed to three dozen cases and gave up three accomplices, who were also arrested on multiple burglaries. In addition, we prosecuted the dope slinger who received most of their stolen goods. Earl and Lusty and I executed a search warrant on the dealer's house and there recovered some $9,000 worth of stolen property as well as a bunch of marijuana and crack. Marcus was prosecuted for only five cases, sentences to be concurrent. He was back on the streets (on probation) in twenty months.

Within weeks of regaining his freedom, Pettway was shot in a predawn gun battle on Driftwood Drive. He and several others had attempted the armed robbery of a drug dealer, and the dealer won; he was found to be acting in self-defense and was not prosecuted for the shooting. Pettway's accomplices remain unknown, having sped away unseen. They left behind their homeboy LaMarcus Pettway, twenty-three, to bleed to death in the dope slinger's driveway.

23

Fool Me Once . . .

Ah, well, I am a great and sublime fool. But then I am God's fool, and all his works must be contemplated with respect.
—Mark Twain

It was just another garden-variety burglary: door kicked in, flat screen carried out.

But the lady across the street watched the whole thing through her front window blinds and called in the play-by-play to 911. As units sped to the scene from several directions, the eyewitness provided Dispatch with detailed descriptions of the faded gray Honda, its tag number, the black female driver with a blonde hair weave who sat in the driver's seat while her 300-pound black male passenger got out, kicked in the door, and emerged moments later with a fifty-inch flat too big to get in the little Civic's back-seat. The man finally laid it in the trunk with about a foot of it sticking out. They had nothing to tie the trunk lid down with, so they just let the lid flap up and down, banging on the unsecured jumbo screen, as they backed out of the driveway in a hurry.

At the end of the driveway, the Civic bounced over the curb and the screen shifted and slid halfway out of the trunk. When the blonde weave stopped to shift gears, the flat screen completed its exit from the Civic's trunk like candy from a Pez dispenser and clattered onto the asphalt. The burglars stopped for a second when they heard their load hit the street, looked back at the shattered hulk of high-definition home theater lying in the middle of Martinwood Lane, then sped away. When police arrived, they recovered the now-worthless jumbo flat screen from the street, but the little Civic was gone.

The Civic's tag came back registered to a black female whose address was just two streets away from the victim's, in the same subdivision. Police went to that location, found the Civic parked in the driveway, and knocked on the door. A heavyset black male matching the description given by the eyewitness came to the door and was taken into custody without incident. Blonde Weave came out yelling, demanding to see the arrest warrant for her boyfriend, demanding to know what the fuck was going on, yelling that she knows her rights, and taking cell phone video of the officers as they placed her boyfriend in the cage of a squad car.

This was convenient for police. When officers started to cuff her, she resisted. She was a big girl. It took two officers to wrestle her to the ground. Both were transported to the precinct, to be interviewed by me.

Ordinarily I would start with the female, because they're typically more cooperative and likely to rat out their accomplices. They have more to lose: they're more often employed and don't want to lose the job, have custody of kids whose care must be arranged if they go to Metro, and are generally not as hardened or experienced in the game as their male counterparts.

But given the circumstances of their apprehension and the volume of the bitch's complaints emanating from the interview room, I decide to start with the male. He's very polite, soft spoken, cooperative. Signs the Miranda warning and waiver form without hesitation. Has neat, legible handwriting. LaJuan Lawson is only nineteen, and despite multiple visits to Strickland Juvenile Center, his criminal history comprises only misdemeanor offenses like petty shoplifting, possession of paraphernalia and a couple of blunts, curfew violations, and the like. This would be his first felony, his first trip to big-boy jail.

Despite the gravity of the consequences he's facing, LaJuan confesses before I even ask him any questions.

"You got me, fair 'n' square, Detective," he says, looking me in the eyes, resigned to his fate. "I kicked in the door and took the flat, it ain't no point in lyin' about it. But I thought it was Kenyatta's."

Kenyatta is the blonde weave, still demanding her rights in the other room.

"She used to live with the girl at that house, and she said the girl changed the locks on her before she could get her flat screen out. I thought I was just doing her a favor, just getting her stuff back for her."

"You say you 'thought.' You think different now?"

"Yeah. When it slid out the trunk, I said, 'Oh, shit! Your flat's busted!' but Kenyatta just hit the gas and said, 'It ain't no thang, the bitch deserves it.' That's when I knew she done lied to me. But it's my own fault. I never shoulda been so stupid."

"Well, you aren't the first man to be tricked by a female," I say, feeling sorry for him. "And to your credit, you manned up, didn't waste my time with a buncha bullshit lies. I gotta say, I respect you for that, LaJuan."

"Yes sir. Thank you, Detective," he says. His earnestness is almost disconcerting.

"Unfortunately, there's no getting around the fact that a burglary was committed. I have no choice but to charge you with it, LaJuan, and Kenyatta, too, of course."

"Yes sir, I understand," he says. "You just got a job to do."

"But I promise you, I'll mention your cooperation to the DA. You're still young enough to qualify for Youthful Offender, and the DA'll probably agree to a plea deal, considering the circumstances, and your confession. Now, to bond out, it should only take a couple hundred dollars. Is there anybody you wanna call before they take you to Metro? Your folks?"

LaJuan lowers his eyes, shakes his head. "Nah. My daddy said next time I get in trouble, I'm on my own."

"What's his name and number?"

I call Mr. Lawson from my office and explain LaJuan's circumstances. He's pissed.

"That boy just won't learn, Detective. He refuses to listen to me. I've tried so many times with him, I cain't even remember how many times I've tole him not to run with those other little gangsters, how many times I been to Strickland for him. I couldn't even beat any sense into him, Detective. He just won't do right."

"I understand, Mr. Lawson. But at least he was respectful and honest with me. And I believe him about thinking he was just doing the girl a favor."

"Nahhh, you don't know him like I do. I'm finished with him. Metro is what he deserves."

"With all due respect, I think Metro would do him more harm than good."

"He's a big boy. He can take care of himself in there."

"He's big, all right. But that's not the kinda harm I'm talking about. I'm talking about the people he'll meet in there, the influence they could have on him. His bond's only gonna be a couple hundred."

"Shit. Even if I had a couple hundred, I ain't gonna spend it on no bond for that boy. He's a lost cause. I know him. He thinks he's grown now, let him sit in Metro with the rest a' them grown thugs."

"How 'bout if I split it with you? Could you come up with a hundred?"

An hour later I'm meeting Mr. Lawson at Bandit Bail Bonds. He's as bewildered as he is skeptical of our shared investment in LaJuan. I make him promise not to tell LaJuan or anybody else that his arresting officer chipped in to bail him out.

And Slocumb's Theorem is the furthest thing from my mind.

Several years later, we have finally persuaded HQ to allow us Facebook access from our precinct workstations in order to monitor its treasure trove of thug chatter. Devin O'Malley had been doing it from his personal computer for months and is current with the technology and the lingo of the website. More important, Devin's "down" with the culture of its habitués. He has valiantly taken on the hopeless task of teaching me, the avowed Luddite, how to navigate it.

Devin has created a fictional female named LaTonya Nettles, complete with phony bio that says she's a graduate of BC Rain High School, works as a server at Hooters, and grew up with the B'mo Boyz in the 1010 Baltimore project (thug central in the First Precinct). "Her" favorite quotes are from Michelle Obama ("Our souls are broken in this nation . . . as a black man, Barack can be shot going to the gas station") and favorite rap artists are Jay Z, Lil Wayne, Kanye, and local fave Rich Boy. "LaTonya" says she misses the (fictional) boyfriend she calls "my Boo" who's doing time in Atmore. The main attraction, though, that draws 'em like flies: non-identifying body shots displaying "her" tattooed cleavage and spandex-stretching booty.

Within hours, horny homeboys by the hundreds have "liked" and "friended" her and e-mailed LaTonya pictures of themselves posing with their stacks of Benjamins, their Gats and Nines, their smoke-billowing blunts. I'm incredulous at the bounty of criminal activity laid claim to, bragged about, and posted in snapshots on the Internet.

And then I spy a familiar face among LaTonya's wanna-be Facebook friends, in pictures posted from a smuggled cell phone inside Atmore Penitentiary. Dressed in prison whites, shirt unbuttoned to display a fully tatted chest and neck, fingers of both hands forming gang signs, is LaJuan Lawson. He's three months away from "touchdown"—the end of a three-year, split-to-serve-eighteen-month stretch for Burglary First Home Invasion.

I feel really stupid. I wanna throw up. Not only had I forgotten Slocumb's Theorem but also that stinging rebuke from my first FTO, Porter: "What *are* you, some kinda fucking *social worker?*"

Five months after seeing LaJuan's Atmore photo gallery through LaTonya Nettles's phony Facebook account, I'm looking at him face to face across a Metro visiting room table. He'd been arrested a few days prior for armed robbery of a Circle K. I didn't know much, nor gave a damn, about the specifics of the robbery rap. It had taken place out in the Fourth. But that case, resulting in LaJuan's arrest, made it much easier for me to locate him for questioning about a recent burglary report that had crossed my desk.

It had occurred the day before he was picked up for the robbery, and it had LaJuan Lawson's name on the suspect line.

He'd been out of prison less than six weeks, sleeping on a cousin's couch because he'd burned all his bridges. She had foolishly entrusted him with a house key. Four days ago she had come home from her job at the counter of a Long John Silver's to discover her flat screen missing. No forced entry, although the burglar had tried to make it appear so: a window had been broken.

But the window was too small for most grown men to fit through. And shards of broken glass were scattered on the sidewalk *outside* the window. It didn't take Sherlock Holmes to deduce that it had been busted from the inside out. LaJuan's cousin had named him as the suspect in her burglary.

"Remember me, LaJuan?" I say, shaking his hand when he enters the small Metro conference room.

His face lights up in a broad smile. "Detective Johnson! Sho' do remember you! You the one split the bond with my dad that time!" I cringe inside, wondering how many other people LaJuan's father has blabbed that to.

We sit down across the table from each other, and he seems genuinely glad to see me.

"You here about this thang they got on me? I ain't did it, y'know. Wadn't anywhere near no Circle K that night."

I wave him off. "I don't have anything to do with that, LaJuan. That's Robbery's case. You know me, I just work burglaries."

"Aw, man, I figured you'da been moved up by now! Dey oughtta had you on alla dem high-profile cases dey put on the TV!"

"Flattery won't do you any good, LaJuan. But I appreciate the thought. I'm here to ask you about your cousin Chandra's case. You musta heard about that—you were staying with her, right?"

"Aw yeah!" LaJuan frowns at the injustice of it all. "I sho' hope you find who done it, 'cause she good people—*family*—know'm sayin', dog?"

"Did you just call me 'dog,' LaJuan?"

"Sorry, man. Didn't mean nu'n by it, just da way I 'spress myself, Detective Johnson." He flashes his big pearly whites in a chastened grin.

"A'ight," I say, smiling. "Just clarifyin'. Anyway, what do you know about Chandra's flat screen?"

"I'ont know nu'n 'bout it, man. Wish I did—I'd put you on 'em in a heart-beat! Cain't belie'e some punkass damn niggas done her like dat. She good people, know'm sayin'? I jus' hope, when you catch 'em, you tell me who dem niggas is, 'cause I got a li'l some'in' for 'em my own self! Will ya do dat fuh me, Detective Johnson?"

"So you got no idea who stole Chandra's flat, LaJuan? You know, we lifted some decent prints from around the busted window."

"Good! I hope you catch 'em, Detective! 'Course, I was stayin' up in there, so my prints natchully be all over e'rethang a'ready."

"We realize that, LaJuan. Your prints wouldn't mean a thing. But there's something funny about that case. Whoever did it had a key. And Chandra says the only one 'sides her with a key—"

"Huh? Had a key? How you be knowin' dat? Den why dey busted open da winda' fuh?"

"That's what we were wondering. But now we're guessing they just busted the window to make it *look* like they broke in, to throw us off, cover the fact that they had a key. Pretty sneaky, huh?" I'm studying LaJuan's face, looking for telltale reaction. He's not giving anything away. But he's not saying anything either.

"But they weren't all that sneaky, really, because they didn't quite think it through, know'm sayin', dog?"

LaJuan says nothing but shrugs his shoulders, arches his eyebrows quizzically, awaiting my explanation.

"The busted window thing: know why they didn't quite think it through, LaJuan? The window was busted from the inside out. Broken glass all over the sidewalk, none inside. Whaddaya think a that, LaJuan?"

He shakes his head one time, then smiles. "I think it's a good thing fuh Chandra she got you on the case, Detective Johnson. If they's anybody can catch 'em, it gon' be you! But you need to be lookin' at summa dem niggas Chandra be talkin' to. She prolly ain't tell ya dat, but she be bringin' lotsa mens home wit' her, know'm sayin'? And it ain't nu'n to slip out wid a key and get a copy made at the Dollah Sto' right across the street."

I nod ponderously but say nu'n.

LaJuan takes this as his opportunity to change the subject. "You know the detectives on this robbery thang they got me up in here on? Could you mebbe talk to 'em fuh me, Detective? Tell 'em you know me, tell 'em to check out my alibi. I ain't did no robbery, Detective, you know dat! I mean, I just got out! Dey really think I'm 'onna be dat stupid, to get myself violated when I just got out? Will ya talk to 'em fuh me?"

"Sure, LaJuan, I'll put in a word for you," I say, rising to leave. I have no intention of going to bat for LaJuan Lawson with Robbery. Fool me once, shame on you. Fool me twice, fuck you—*and* your poor, hardworking, unfortunate cousin Chandra, "good people" though she may be.

When I get back to the precinct, I call Robbery and ask about LaJuan's case. It's a slam-dunk: an eyewitness picked him out of a six-panel photo spread, and there's pretty conclusive footage of LaJuan's 300-pound physique on the store's security cam.

"Good," I say. "Kid's nu'n but a thief, from way back."

"Yeah, we saw in his Compis file where you put a burglary on him a while ago."

229

"Uh-huh. But the judge granted him Youthful Offender, and they gave him a deal," I reply. "Wasn't too much later he gets sent to Atmore for the Home Invasion. He's a bad one. You guys need to really put dick to him this time." (Keeping my promise to LaJuan, that's the word I put in: dick.)

Then I call Chandra and tell her that although I'm as certain as she is that LaJuan stole her TV, without a confession all we have is circumstantial evidence, which isn't gonna be enough to win a conviction. She understands, is not surprised.

I offer her the consolation that Robbery's case is solid, so at least he'll be headed back to Atmore soon. "Of course, that won't get you your TV back, but it's something."

"That's good," Chandra says. "He won't be doin' it to nobody else, 'least for a while."

She thanks me for my effort before hanging up. She does sound like "good people," and that only makes me feel worse.

24

Bad Day on the Bayou

A fool gives full vent to his anger, but a wise man keeps himself under control.
—Proverbs 29:11

There had been six felony property thefts down the parkway over the past three weeks. Most of the stolen items were unsecured marine equipment, taken off boats and docks, big-ticket items like depth finders, radars and radios, a few trolling motors and outboard motors. Even a canoe, two kayaks, and a small wooden rowboat had gone missing. In addition, three misdemeanor thefts of the same kind of stuff, only of lesser value—tackle boxes, life vests, water skis, fishing rods, batteries, oil and gas cans, coolers, even tow ropes and mooring lines—had been taken from piers, boathouses, and gazebos along the same stretch of Dog River. And an alert citizen had reported seeing Wesley Colt driving what turned out to be a stolen John Deere lawn tractor down Riverside Drive yesterday morning.

All had occurred on the east side of the river and along that side's bayous and slues, all within a half mile of where Riverside Drive and Gill Road converge before dead-ending at the water's edge.

That alone—the location—was all I needed to know. Just past the Riverside/Gill convergence is the home of Little Ricky Stedman, seventeen, and his mama with the lazy eye who's not all there. She hasn't been right in the head, it's said, since her husband, Little Ricky's daddy Big Rick Stedman, had died in a fiery motorcycle wreck several years ago.

Big Rick had been a legendary wildman on the parkway. Though well liked and gifted with a wrench (he could build, fix, and race anything with two wheels, four wheels, or an outboard), Big Rick didn't leave his wife or Little Ricky much when he was cut down in his prime, so they took in boarders to make ends meet.

There was an ever-changing cast of drifters, grifters, dope addicts and slingers, thieves, tramps, and layabouts taking up temporary residence at the Stedman place, 3656 Riverside. They would hang around until the heat was on, we busted them, or they were run off by their own kind, only to be replaced by newcomers, or returnees who had done their time in Metro and had been released to wreak more havoc down the parkway.

Little Ricky's mama's house is, as you'd expect, a wreck, but the acreage it occupies is prime, graced with towering old live oaks in the front and a hundred feet of waterfront in the back. Many of the neighbors' homes, on both sides of the Stedman place as well as across the bayou behind it, still command high six figures and are equipped with all the pricey toys that go along with that lifestyle, despite the gradual but unremitting decline of the parkway.

A few short decades ago, the parkway had been one of the more prosperous, thriving commercial and residential areas of Mobile. The first blow was LBJ's closure of Brookley Field (home of twenty thousand good-paying aircraft fabrication jobs) shortly after Barry Goldwater carried Mobile in the '64 election. The final blow was the hurricane that took out the bridge at the bottom of the parkway, from Hollinger's Island to Belle Fontaine. This disaster had rendered the arterial's very name a misnomer, as you could no longer get to Dauphin Island by taking Dauphin Island Parkway. The lifeblood of the area was pinched off to a trickle, and blight, neglect, decay, and crime set in.

So now the parkway is a mix of vacant, abandoned, overgrown houses collapsing in on themselves as daily they are pillaged by copper thieves and squatters; modest, formerly tidy working-class neighborhoods that have become rundown pockets of federally subsidized housing favored by dope slingers and small-time gangsters; boarded-up businesses and empty strip malls sprinkled with second-tier chains and franchises like Burke's Outlet, Citi Trends Clothing, Checkers hamburgers, Shop 'n Save groceries, and pawnshops; and opulent waterfront homes nestled among the live oaks with $50,000 sailboats, trawlers, and yachts moored at their piers out back. A thief's paradise.

The most frequent boarders at the Stedman place are the Colt boys: Travis, twenty-one, and his brother Wesley, eighteen. Both are driven by fierce addictions and criminal inclinations, limited only by their modest intellects. The Colt boys stay at the Stedman place when banned (at regular intervals) by Grandma from the Colt family homestead on Gill Road, about a mile east of the Stedman place. Grandma Colt's daughter Brandy, in her late thirties, and Brandy's daughter Candy, nineteen, also reside there. Brandy and Candy are mother and sister, respectively, to the Colt boys. There's also another guy, Andy Colt, who is maybe a little older than Brandy and also appears to live at Grandma Colt's place. Andy keeps to himself, and the rest of the family doesn't seem to have much to do with him, either, but I always see him sitting on Grandma Colt's front porch or puttering around the yard when I drive by, and I see him walking around by himself a lot. Rumor has it he's a half-wit, but he doesn't look mongoloid or anything, and he'll say a sentence or two if you address him directly. Various accounts of the half-wit Andy have him as cousin or brother or nephew of somebody in the Colt clan. Whatever he is, Andy Colt's not a criminal, but he's not all there, either.

The mother-daughter team of Brandy and Candy Colt, though conniving and clever enough to stay out of Metro (for the most part), is nevertheless driven by the same demons as Travis and Wesley. Brandy and Candy usually manage to escape arrest by ratting out Travis and Wesley (and anyone else with the bad luck or bad sense to pass through their orbit), though as often as not, all four are equal participants in criminal enterprises that are usually hatched by Brandy and Candy in the first place.

A case in point was the theft of the $23,000 cash life savings of a sad old terminally ill alcoholic in the last month of his wretched life who had the additional misfortune to reside directly across Gill Road from the Colt clan. Brandy and Candy insinuated themselves into homebound Fletcher Gibbs's life by walking Gibbs's crippled old bulldog, Sarge, providing light housework and meal prep, running to the ABC state store and the Rite Aid to replenish his stocks of Crown Royal and Lortabs, and occasionally performing fellatio.

The girls introduced Travis and Wesley and Candy's then-husband, Troy, into the mix by convincing ol' Fletch that the boys' collective expertise in auto repair, home maintenance, and landscaping was critical to his well-being and to the value of the estate he'd be leaving his grown and distant heirs upon his imminent passing due to liver disease. Fletcher Gibbs's physician had estimated he had no more than six months to live and told him to get his things in order. Fletch's idea of getting things in order was to close his checking and savings accounts so as to keep a close eye on the $23,000 that he kept in fat wads of fifties and hundreds within arm's reach, under the cushion of his Lazy Boy recliner where he spent his days and nights drinking blended whiskey, chain-smoking Pall Malls, and watching old cowboy movies on the Turner Classic cable channel.

When Fletch came to one morning and discovered the cash gone, he still had enough sense to suspect the Colts but couldn't be sure which one and had no proof. The clerks at the state store and the Rite Aid confirmed to me that Brandy and Candy had been buying way more than their usual lately and paying for it all with crisp fifties and hundreds. The old parkway dope slinger Roosevelt Jenks, a favorite supplier of Travis and Wesley, confided to me that the brothers had recently been coming to him flashing rolls of Benjamins and acquiring his entire inventory every few days. And Candy's husband, Troy, had been seen wheeling around the parkway in a new (to him) '06 midnight blue Dodge Charger with dark tinted windows, fancy rims, and a paper dealer tag on the back. The owner of the car lot where Troy bought his muscle car recalled that Troy paid $5,200 cash for it, in hundred-dollar bills.

Poor Troy never should have married into the Colt family. He's the only one I was able to convict for the theft of the Fletcher fortune, because the Colts eventually put it all on him in written, signed, and sworn statements and convinced him to submit his own written confession to me. Troy told me he was doing so solely for the sake of his and Candy's infant son.

"Troy Junior's gonna need a family," he said tearfully. "He won't make it if we *all* go to jail for this," he declared with a sniff of noble self-sacrifice. Shortly after Troy went off to prison, DHS found Candy to be unfit and placed Troy Junior in foster care.

I was unable to recover much for Fletch. Troy wrapped the Charger around a concrete pillar on his way back from the casinos in Biloxi, totaling the car just six days after he bought it. It netted $150 at U Pull It auto salvage, after the towing and impound fees. And Candy turned over seventeen hundred-dollar bills to me that she said she found in one of Troy's hidey-holes.

When Fletch signed for the recovered cash, he was in a bad way. He told me his beloved Sarge had been missing for three days, and he was certain the Colts had kidnapped the crippled old hound. Fletch died a few weeks later, as much, I think, from sadness and despair as from cirrhosis and renal failure.

I had arrested Travis and Wesley several times in the past, and this latest rash of waterfront larceny had their names all over it. The Colt boys had been staying at Little Ricky's place since Grandma Colt and Brandy and Candy had kicked them out after the Fletcher fiasco. (I had tossed Grandma's place twice looking for Fletcher's cash, and Granny'd had it with the boys.)

I head down the parkway and radio for backup to meet me at the intersection of Gill and Riverside. I have no plan other than to look around the Stedman property for a stolen John Deere or boating and fishing equipment, and to arrest anyone on the premises for it—preferably the Colt brothers.

Veteran patrolman Frank Black meets me at the spot, near the Stedman place but not visible from it. Frank has patrolled the Parkway for more than a decade, has busted the Colt boys and Little Ricky at least as many times as I have, and has written a couple of the recent theft reports himself; he knows what we're there for.

"I walked up the driveway this morning when it was still dark, right after roll call," Frank says. "Didn't see any drivable cars around, so might not be anybody home. But that John Deere's parked up there right by the front door, sorta behind some bushes, so you can't see it from the street. Didn't go around back 'cause the dogs started barking. If anybody was in the house, I didn't wanna give 'em the opportunity to shoot me for a prowler. But I'm guessin' we'll find the boats and tackle back there along the bayou."

"Right. Well, let's just leave our cars here and walk on up there and knock on the door. If any of the boys answer, we hook 'em up. If Mama Stedman answers, we ask if we can come in to look for the Colt boys or Little Ricky. If nobody answers, we walk around back to see what we can see."

"Sounds like a plan, boss," Frank says.

There is no response to our knock on the door, other than the loud yaps, growls, and barks of the mutts inside. The John Deere is parked right where Frank had seen it; a busted left headlight and scratches in the paint on the mowing deck match the description from the report. We peer around the corner of the house and observe a yellow kayak, an aluminum canoe, and a wooden rowboat lying in the tall weeds along the bank of the bayou. A couple of blue tarps are also stretched over piles of unknown objects.

"Bingo," Frank says. "Shall I start the Impound truck to come pick this stuff up?"

"Not just yet," I reply. "C'mon, let's just walk back down the driveway like we think nobody's home. I wanna see if they come out after they think we're gone."

At the end of the driveway, no longer visible from the house, I tell Frank to wait for me there while I walk down the neighbor's driveway and peek through the slats of the fence to see if there's any movement from the house. I've done this before; the neighbors keep no dogs and they both work, so I can creep along their fence line undetected. I see no movement in the Stedman front yard. I continue around the neighbor's house to the backyard to get a look through the fence at the rear of the Stedman place. As I round the rear of the neighbor's house, I catch a glimpse of movement out of the corner of my eye and see a palmetto leaf waving among thick flora. I draw my weapon, approach the palmetto, and spy a blue-jeaned leg sticking out of the hedge row.

"Let me see your hands and come on out slowly. Is it Wesley or Travis?"

"Don't shoot, Detective Johnson, I'm comin' out. It's Wesley. Don't shoot, sir. I'm not gonna run or anything."

I cuff Wesley and pat him down, and we walk down the neighbor's driveway toward Frank.

"Why are you hiding under a bush in your neighbor's backyard, Wesley?"

"I was just scared, Detective Johnson."

"No need to be scared of the police unless you've done something wrong. What have you done wrong, lately, Wesley?"

"Nothin', Detective Johnson. I just ran outta habit, I guess."

"Wouldn't have anything to do with that John Deere in your front yard, or the boats in the back?"

"What? Whaddaya mean, Detective? I don't know anything about any of that. It must be Little Ricky's stuff, or his mama's. It's their place, Detective. I don't even live here, really. We just came over to chill, and maybe smoke a blunt, I'm bein' honest. I admit I smoke a little weed, Detective Johnson, I won't lie to ya."

"Who's 'we'? You said 'We just came over to chill.' Is Travis in the house?"

"Huh? Did I say we? I don't know who's in the house. I just got here before you showed up, and when I saw you I ran. I don't even know who's inside."

We meet up with Frank out by the road and put Wesley in the cage.

"Stay here with him, I'm gonna take one more look through the neighbor's fence."

I return to my first spot with a pretty good view of the Stedman front yard just in time to see Brandy Colt emerge from the house with Travis. She's telling him to hide in the rafters of the detached garage. I run back down the neighbor's driveway, tell Frank what I've just seen. We jump in his car with Wesley in the cage and roar up the Stedman driveway. Frank pounds on the front door while I check the garage for Travis.

To my surprise, he's not in there. Brandy comes to the door acting like she's just woken up and doesn't know what's going on.

"Don't gimme that shit, Brandy. I was on the other side of that fence just five minutes ago and I saw you telling Travis to hide in the garage. So where is he?"

"Okay. I'm sorry, Detective Johnson. But if he's not in the garage, I really don't know where he is."

"Mind if we check the house, Brandy? If he's not in the garage, he's in the house."

"Go right ahead, Detective. He's not in the house. I just came out of there. But feel free to search inside all you want. Just let me go inside and get the dogs out first."

"Right. How stupid do you think I am, Brandy? I'll come in with you for the dogs. Frank, go around and cover the back—I don't think Wesley's gonna try to kick out your rear window and escape."

"Let's just make sure," Frank says, and walks over to his squad car, puts a pair of shackles around Wesley's ankles, and straps him in with the seat belt. He mutters something to Wesley that Brandy and I can't quite hear, but Wesley's assurances that he "ain't about to try anything stupid, Officer Black, sir" are clearly audible.

Frank disappears around the corner of the house to cover the back. As Brandy and I enter the house I tell her, "You better control your animals, Brandy, or I'll shoot 'em, I swear." (A lie. I think I'd hate to shoot a dog, even an aggressive one, more than a person.)

The dogs who'd sounded so fierce and berserk earlier seem to consider me no threat when Brandy accompanies me inside. I toss the place pretty thoroughly, checking under every bed, inside every closet, even looking in the attic, the kitchen cabinets, the clothes dryer, and kicking my way through a waste-high mountain of smelly dirty clothes. No Travis. I did, however, make a mental note of the bong, some seeds and stems, and a glass crack pipe in plain view on the kitchen table.

We exit through the backdoor, and Frank and I check under the kayak, the canoe, and the rowboat in the tall weeds down by the water. Mired in the muck next to the bulkhead is a small, half-sunk sailing sloop that's been there since before Big Rick died. I step on board and shine my flash-light into its water-filled cabin. No Travis. Under the tarps, as expected, are outboard and trolling motors, marine electronics, life vests, tackle boxes, coolers, batteries, rods and reels and coils of rope, but no Travis.

I'm losing my patience. We check around all the overgrown clumps of shrubbery along both property lines and finally return to the front of the house. Wesley's still in the cage, and when I ask him about their hiding places, he only suggests places we've already checked. Brandy, of course, has no idea where Travis could have gone, nor how all that stuff in the backyard got there or who it belongs to; she feigns exasperation with her mischievous boys, remarking, "It looks like they've been up to no good again." She's become a chatterbox as, one by one, all the obvious hiding places turned out empty. She's not very effectively concealing her relief (or pride?) that her eldest has eluded capture.

"I guess he musta just ran off, Detective Johnson," she offers brightly. "I don't know how he dipped out so quick, but I promise you, when I see him I'll make him turn himself in to you."

"You will, Brandy? You'd do that for me?" I say.

"I swear I will, Detective."

"But I don't think you'll be seeing Travis anytime soon, Brandy." I grab her forearm and slap a cuff on her wrist. "Turn around for me, please. You're under arrest for Hindering Prosecution." I put the cuff on her other wrist as she wriggles and twists, sputtering, "What? What the fuck? Wait just a goddamn minute here! 'Hindering'? This is fuckin' bullshit!"

"Stop buckin' on the detective," Frank warns, "or he'll add the Holy Trinity: Resisting Arrest, Disorderly, and Failure to Obey."

"Not to mention the paraphernalia, weed, and rock on the kitchen table," I add. "Go ahead and put her in the cage with Wesley, Frank."

"Hell, no you ain't, motherfucker! You got nothing on me! That shit in the kitchen ain't mine! I don't even live here! This is Little Ricky's place! You ain't got shit on me! This is fuckin' bullshit!"

Frank pushes and pulls her to the squad car and opens the rear door. Even Wesley, cuffed, shackled, and strapped up in the cage, is yelling, "Mom! Stop it, Mom! You're makin' it worse! Just tell 'em where Travis is!"

"Hold up a minute, Frank," I say. Then, to Brandy: "I'll give you one more chance. Produce Travis in five minutes, or you're going to Metro with Wesley."

She starts yelling, "Travis! Traaa-visss!" It's ear piercing, her wail. "Travis, get your thieving ass here, now! Or they're takin me to jail! Traaa-visss, you motherfucker don't you dare put me in jail, you little bastard! Traaa-visss! I'm gonna beat your punk ass with a shovel if you don't come here right nowwww!"

Even Wesley joins in, from the cage: "Travis, I'monna kick your chicken-shit ass if you let Mama go to jail! Traaa-vis!"

They keep it up for the full five minutes. I time it with my watch. I didn't really think it would work, but Frank and I got a kick out of the pathetic display.

I tell Frank to go ahead on to the precinct with them. He drives off with a load of Colts in his cage, and I walk down the long driveway to fetch my car on Riverside Drive, pissed at myself for letting Travis get away.

Just as I turn the ignition and start to roll, I picture one place I failed to check, where Travis might be hiding. It's a long shot, but I radio Frank to tell him to circle back to the driveway and wait for me while I look in one more place out back. Then I retrace my steps down the driveway, around the house, and to the waterline.

I hop onto the top of the sunken sloop's cabin and step to the far edge, on the bayou side. Peering over the side, I look down into the murky water. To my shock—and his—I'm looking directly down into his face. Just his face, that's all that's visible. He sitting or squatting in the mucky bottom of the bayou, all but his face concealed in the brown water, his head cocked back so he can breathe, the water forming a ring around his chin, cheeks and forehead, so that his face looks like a floating Mardi Gras mask.

For a moment we just stare at each other, motionless, speechless. Then I draw my Glock and point it directly between his eyes as he slowly rises from the muck, both hands up. He had been crouching in water that barely reaches his waist when standing.

"Don't shoot, Detective Johnson. I surrender. Please, put the gun down."

"Step around the boat and come on out of the water," I say. "Don't do anything stupid." I feel the old adrenalin kick in. The thrill of victory. The rush of apprehension. Only, it's heightened, literally and figuratively, by my elevated position several feet above him on the dry white cabin roof of the sloop, in my charcoal gray suit and tie, my badge on my belt, in my polished black boots, poised in the ready-fire position, weapon trained on his center mass, as he unsteadily, haltingly emerges beneath me from the black primordial ooze.

The moment's all the sweeter precisely because it has taken so long to get here. We've been at this for more than two hours now since I first nabbed Wesley under the neighbor's palmetto. Then my sneaky spying on Brandy and Travis through the fence, all the searching, all the stolen loot recovered, the bonus bust of Brandy, with all its high-volume drama, and then, finally, when lesser men might have called it good, called it a day—and a good day it had been with two felony arrests and thousands of dollars in recovered stolen property—I go the extra mile, acting on instinct, on a wily hunch, switching from the mind of the predator to the prey to visualize the unlikeliest concealment, divining the ultimate hideaway, and *make the collar!*

I feel like Dirty Harry Callahan. I square my jaw and affect the Clint Squint.

"Please, Detective Johnson," Travis whines as he struggles to free himself from the sucking muck. "Just put the gun down, I surrender. Look, I'm trying to get to the shore."

"I'll put my gun away when I put the cuffs on you," I growl, Clint-like.

But then Travis pauses. I can see the wheels turning in his scheming criminal mind. He takes a step back, away from the shore, away from the sunken sloop.

"Don't shoot, Detective Johnson. I've got my hands up."

I can hear the synapses popping in the limbic system of his reptilian brain. Slowly he steps backward, away from the shore, away from me. Into the depths of the channel he retreats, the water slowly rising, now above his waist, all the while intoning, almost chant-like, "Don't shoot, Detective. I surrender. Don't shoot." He keeps creeping away from me into the bayou, his hands still up in the air.

"Don't be stupid, Travis!" I bark. "Come back this way, now!" My mind is racing. The conniving little shit knows I can't shoot him, not under these circumstances. For me to take a legal shot, he's gotta be a threat to me or somebody else. He's clearly no threat, he's just a petty thief, and he's getting away. And he's betting I won't come after him. Is that the little curl of a smirk I see forming on his lips?

"Don't shoot, Detective Johnson," he says, in the soothing, almost sing-song voice one might use with a snarling dog behind a fence. The little fucker's not worth ruining my suit and boots over, that's for damn sure. I've left my damn radio in the car, so I grope for my cell to call Frank and tell him to drive around to the other side of the bayou, where Travis is headed. The adrenalin is at full throb now, and I fumble with my gun-free left hand for the pesky little device.

Splash.

My cell disappears into the watery murk. I look back to Travis, now midstream and grinning broadly as he starts to backstroke away. He still calls out to me, "Don't shoot, Detective." In a fury, I decide to make a dash for my car in order to race around to the other side of the bayou myself. I slam the Glock into my holster.

Blam! A gunshot!

Instinctively, I crouch and scan my perimeter 360 degrees, then look back at Travis, who has stopped mid-stroke, equally stunned by the shot, trying to make sense of it. He raises both hands in the air. Where did the shot come from? It was fucking *close!* Loud as hell!

Then I smell the gunpowder and look down. There's a hole in the roof of the sloop's cabin, barely an inch from my right foot. Then I see my tattered pant leg. From the bottom of my holster, there's a ragged tear about six inches long, aligning directly with the hole by my foot.

My Clint Squint turns into a bug-eyed look of horror and shame. I have become Barney Fife.

25

Colt's Capture
and the Metro Amends

Man is the only animal that blushes—or needs to.
—Mark Twain

I'm hoping Frank hasn't made it back to the scene yet, hoping he didn't hear my shot. Then it'll just be Travis's word against mine, and Travis is probably on his way to Mississippi by now.

But Frank is waiting for me at the end of the Stedman driveway, on Riverside Drive, his cargo of caged Colts wild with terror, grief, and rage. Wesley is yelling, "He shot Travis! Mama, he shot Travis!" And Brandy is wailing and weeping incoherently. Clearly, my accidental discharge had been heard, and when they see me approach without a prisoner, Brandy and Wesley assume the worst. Frank is leaning against his hood, arms crossed, muttering to himself and shaking his head.

"They heard the shot and went completely bonkers," Frank says. "I can't do anything to settle 'em down."

I turn to Brandy and Wesley, who are rocking Frank's whole car in their hysteria.

"Shut the fuck up! I didn't shoot Travis! Settle down or I'll hit you with the pepper spray!" Then to Frank: "You got your pepper spray, Frank?"

"I do, Mark, but I'll be damned if I'monna get it all over my backseat." Then, to his prisoners, "I tol' you he ain't shot Travis! Now settle the fuck down! Detective Johnson prolly saved your boy's life back there, shootin' that water moccasin!"

Frank turns to me, just barely straight faced. "Ain't that right, Detective? I'monna nominate you for the Lifesaving Award myself."

I lock eyes for a moment with Frank, then grin back at him.

"Awww, that won't be necessary, Frank. But I 'preciate the thought. Now, let's get these bozos back to the precinct. I'll see you there in a few minutes."

On the way to the precinct, I make an important detour. I go home and change my pants.

The Colts have calmed down by the time I arrive at the precinct. Frank has them hooked to the interview tables in separate rooms. Wesley confesses tearfully that all the stuff by the bayou is the result of his and Travis's meth-fueled burglary binge. He insists his mama had no part in it, nor did Little Ricky Stedman or any of the other denizens of 3656 Riverside Drive. He puts all this in writing and begs me to tell the DA that he needs drug court, not regular court or jail, that he just can't kick his addiction without help, and that he's really not a bad person when he's straight.

Brandy is so relieved that I haven't slain her firstborn, she's willing to say or do anything. I offer to cut her loose for twenty-four hours to produce Travis for me. If she fails, she goes to Metro as an accessory to the boys' burglaries, as well as the Hindering charge for aiding Travis's escape. She swears she'll find him and drag him to the precinct herself, and I let her walk. I spend the rest of the day processing the recovered property, contacting victims, returning their stuff to them. At home, I tell Nancy nothing about my day and hope Travis is several states away by now, never to be seen around these parts again.

No such luck. About 4 a.m., I get a call from the precinct. They have Travis in custody and figured I'd want to interview him before they take him to Metro. Dammit, I think, wishing he'd gotten away. No doubt he's told whoever caught him about my Barney Fife moment.

"It was a pretty hairy collar," the officer on the phone tells me. I don't know him—he's from the Second Precinct. "Sumbitch damn-near killed Hawkins, in the parking lot of the Tides Inn out there by Highway 90 and Azalea."

I didn't think Travis had it in him. "Really? What happened?"

"Somebody—I think they said it was his mama—called in a tip that he was at the Tides, so me 'n' Hawkins go there to pick him up. We ran him first: he's got active 29s outta Baldwin County for Precursor and Manufacturing—he's a meth head, y'know."

I knew Travis was a meth head but didn't know he had active warrants. I realize with renewed shame that in addition to my many procedural and tactical blunders on the bayou, I hadn't bothered to check either of the Colt boys for active warrants. The number and nature of active warrants on a hunted suspect can provide a critical "heads-up" beforehand, indicating how likely he'll run or how hard he'll fight to avoid capture. No wonder my Dirty Harry triumph turned sour. No way was I gonna talk Travis to shore, not with active felony warrants on his head.

"So we knock on the door to his room," the guy from the Second continues. "This half-naked whore answers, she's all wasted and tweaking, and she says Travis just left to get some more beer and cigarettes. And we don't see the car he's s'posed ta be in, so we figure Mama prolly warned him after she phoned in the tip. We're about to leave, when who rolls into the parking lot but our boy. We order him to stop and get out, and he just sits there in the car. We approach, Hawkins on the driver's side, me on the other side with my Taser on him. He's just sitting there, like, frozen. We order him to turn off the car and get out, but he just sits there like a zombie, lookin' straight ahead. Finally, Hawkins reaches in to grab the car keys, and he starts fightin' with Hawkins. I fire my Taser but only one prong hits and it doesn't do anything. He slams it in reverse and I throw my Taser at his head, but it just bounces off and all of a sudden he's burnin' rubber backwards dragging Hawkins with him, his arm all tangled up in the steering wheel."

"Shit! Is Hawkins okay?"

"Aw, yeah. Arm's a little sore. Anyway, he drags Hawkins backwards about fifty yards, then puts it in drive. Hawkins breaks free, hits the pavement, and gets off a couple rounds at him as he peels out onto Highway 90, and the chase is on. We had units from the Second and the Fifth chasin' him all through Tillman's Corner, out Rangeline Road to Hamilton, and then some a your guys join up around D.I.P. and Gill. I guess your guys knew where he was headed 'cause one a your units was waitin' for him at a place on Riverside Drive. He drove right up the driveway and surrendered."

"Wow. No wrecks or anything? Nobody got hurt?"

"Nah. But now, a course, he's lookin' at Reckless Endangerment, Assault on an Officer, and Eluding, on top a the Meth warrants and whatever you got on 'im."

It's still dark when I pull in to the precinct parking lot about 4:30 a.m. There's a bunch of guys from the Second and the Fifth standing by the backdoor, smoking and joking and replaying the night's action with some of our guys from the First. They fall silent and part as I make my way between them to the door. Somebody says, "Make way for Da Man." There are snickers. "Mobile's answer to Dirty fuckin' Harry," another cracks.

There's that damn Clint Eastwood stuff again; I just can't seem to shake it. And this confirms that they're on to my delusions of grandeur: the frequent Clint references are not out of respect or admiration but derision. Like the moniker that stuck to me in high school football: "Mad Dog." I was a mediocre lineman at best: big enough in stature and stamina for the line, and I relished the repeated battering and collision required of linemen, but I lacked the quickness and agility to be a standout. In a one-on-one tackling drill one day, my task was to take down my buddy Gary, a receiver whose fancy feints and footwork had earned him the nickname "Dancer." I ran at him headlong, apparently growling, they say. (I don't recall growling—more likely it was mere *grunting*.) In any case, Gary did one of his signature moves, completely faking me out, and I ended up with a mouthful of turf as Gary flitted gaily around me. Much laughter ensued, and one of the coaches, Mr. Mussing, attempted to quell the guffaws of my teammates by saying, "That's all right, Mark. Good effort! He doesn't shrink from contact—he craves the hit! He went after the Dancer like a . . . like a *mad dog!*" Forty years later, at high school reunions, I'm still greeted by growls and barking and shouts of "Doggie! It's the Mad Dog!" They just won't let it go.

As I make my way down the precinct gauntlet of Dirty Harry jeers and jokes, somebody else says, "Your boy spun quite a yarn about you out there on the bayou," and there's lots of yukking it up all around.

I pause mid-gauntlet and look around at the guys, doing my best to affect insouciance.

"And y'all actually believe anything that lyin'sack a shit says? Sheesh." I smile and shake my head as if dealing with pathetic morons.

Inside, it's just me and Travis, across the table from each other. He's looking a bit rough: cuts and bruises color his face and arms. His lip is bleeding. His T-shirt is ripped and dirty and blood spattered. He was obviously "tuned up" a bit when taken into custody, which is de rigueur after a cop gets injured, and there's a vehicle pursuit.

I put my elbows on the table, clasp my hands at my chin, and study him. Aside from the scrapes, he's a healthy, good-looking kid with short, curly blond locks and blue eyes. I know from previous dealings with him that he's a little smarter than his brother Wesley—harder to manipulate or intimidate. We stare in silence at each other for a long moment.

Travis breaks the ice. "I'm sorry, Detective Johnson," he says.

"For what, Travis?"

This throws him off, and he doesn't immediately respond.

"For ripping off all your neighbors? For letting your brother take the whole rap? For letting your mama go to jail in your place? Which thing are you sorry for, Travis?"

He hangs his head, mute.

"Why apologize to me, Travis? It's your neighbors and your family you should be apologizing to. Or to Officer Hawkins, who you dragged across the parking lot. They told me about that whole thing at the Tides, how you damn-near broke his arm, almost ran him over, the shots fired and the high-speed chase all over town. You're lucky to still be in one piece."

"I know it, Detective Johnson," he says to the table, his head still hung down. There's another long silence between us.

"Well, sayin' you're sorry ain't gonna fix any part a this mess, Travis. You're totally fucked. In addition to your Baldwin County meth warrants, and the boat burglaries you did with Wesley—which by the way he confessed to in writing and put you in—there's all these new charges now, from the Tides and the car chase.

"And then there's the little matter of our shared encounter, out on the bayou yesterday," I say with a loud sigh.

Travis raises his head and locks eyes with me. "That's what I meant. I'm sorry for that, Detective Johnson." His eyes fill up, imploring. "I know I fucked up, but my mama had nothing to do with any of it. And Wesley—it was all my idea. Just put it all on me. I never shoulda hid from you, or started swimmin' away. And your phone, I'm sorry, Detec—"

"Yeah, you're sorry, Travis. You're so sorry, you gotta tell all those cops out there what happened between us. You're one sorry motherfucker, Travis. And if you think I'monna listen to any of your whiney bullshit, you think I'monna give your mama or Wesley a break, if you think for one second I'monna say anything to the DA and the judge other than 'Lock this whole sorry family up and throw away the key,' then you're as stupid as you are sorry."

I get up, march out of the room, and slam the door behind me.

A week later, I decide to visit the Colt brothers in Metro. I start with Travis.

Gone is the weepy supplication, the plaintive apologetics. In full Metro hard-guy mode, Travis swaggers into the tiny visiting room and slouches into a plastic chair across the table from me. I offer my hand, and he shakes it limply, eyeing me with suspicion.

"How you doin', Travis? Face is healing up pretty good, I see. Enjoying the baloney sandwiches?"

He gives me his best hard-guy sneer. "I got nu'n to say to you. I thought it was my lawyer when they said I had a visitor."

I ignore his posturing and begin.

"Sorry to disappoint you. I'm actually here today, not so much professionally, as on a personal matter, Travis. It really doesn't have anything to do with your cases. I'm not gonna Mirandize you or ask you any questions. It's just something I gotta do for me."

He remains sullen, skeptical, slouching silently across the table.

"I guess I'm here, really, to thank you, Travis. And to sorta make amends."

He cocks his head and narrows his eyes, trying to get what I'm up to.

"I don't expect you to understand, or even care, for that matter, but let me try to explain. First of all, I'm not nearly as different from you as I'm sure you think, other'n age-wise. I mean, I've had my own bouts with alcohol and drugs, and a few scrapes with the law, too. They always go together.

"But I managed to put all that behind me a long time ago, with a lotta help. Thing is, in order to *keep* all that behind me, I gotta do certain things, or I could real easily slip back into it. I gotta be grateful for shit that seems bad at the time—'cause that's the only way I can learn from it and keep from doing it again—and I gotta keep my side a the street clean, y'know? Admit when I'm wrong, do whatever it takes to set things right again. That's the amends part, what they call makin' amends. So that's what I'm here for today, with you."

Travis is listening attentively but is clearly clueless.

"That day out on the bayou, when I found you in the water behind the sunk sailboat? I gotta tell you, Travis, I felt like Clint Eastwood, know what I'm saying? Know who he even is?"

He gives the slightest of nods.

"I mean, there I am, up on that boat, my Glock drawn, and you're down there in the water and the mud. I've already got Wesley and your mama, got all that shit you stole, I've got my Glock on you, and, man! It went right to my head. I thought I was supercop! I mean, I was *da shit*. Wasn't I, Travis?"

There's the tiniest indication of a smile, and he nods again.

"Problem is, that's dangerous. It's dangerous for any cop to think that way. We can get cocky and take stupid chances, make stupid mistakes, know what I'm sayin'? But it's even more dangerous for a guy like me to get cocky, 'cause I can start to think I'm like ten feet tall and bulletproof, I'm God's gift to law enforcement. It's a way all addicts and alcoholics think, unless we learn how to change our thinking. And in my job, if I slip into that old way a thinking, I can get hurt, and other cops around me can get hurt, and even people I'm arresting, or innocent bystanders can get hurt.

"So, as embarrassing as that thing turned out to be for me that day, 'specially after you blabbed it all to the guys I work with, I gotta thank you for it, Travis. It was painful but necessary, to remind me not to take myself too damn seriously. We call that Rule No. 62. We're all a little safer, and I'm hopefully a little wiser because of it."

Travis keeps his eyes fixed on mine, lowers his head a little, arches his eyebrows in a quizzical stare, and doesn't utter a word.

"Now, as far as the amends: don't get your hopes up. All those charges on you are stayin' on you, and between Mobile and Baldwin County, you'll probably be going to Atmore for a spell. Nothing I can do about that, even if I wanted to. And I don't. Because that's not any harm I did. You did all that to yourself and to your victims, of course.

"But in spite of all this—I could be wrong—but I think you're probably not that bad a guy, Travis. You just act like one because a your drug habit. Mosta the people I arrest are addicts and alcoholics, no different from me, except they can't or won't stop, so they get caught doing stupid things against the law because they're too high to see how stupid it is, or because they're so desperate to feed their habits they take stupid chances, or because they been doin' so much dope for so long they've just fried their brains stupid, and they don't even know right from wrong anymore. But I don't think you're there yet. I think that if you could just stop it—and if I can, anybody can—you'd likely be a decent, law-abiding citizen. Like regular people, with jobs and houses and families.

"So I want to say to you that when you get out, if you wanna kick, and stay kicked, I'll help you do it. There's meetings, and programs, and people more your age I can hook you up with if you want. And I'm sorry I never said anything to you about this before now, before everything got so serious."

I push my card across the table to him. On it I've already written my private cell number. Travis picks it up, studies it in silence.

"Good luck, man. I hear they got meetings up there, inside. You should try a few, see if it makes any sense to you." I get up to go and offer my hand again. Travis rises and shakes it for real this time, with a firm grip.

On to Wesley, the youngest Colt. It's his first time in big-boy jail, which is a world apart from Strickland Youth Center.

I'm doubting I'll ever get a call from Travis, but Wesley's a little younger, a little simpler, a little softer than his big brother. I've had more contact with him than with Travis, because Wesley's still more of a criminal amateur. Most of Wesley's ventures into criminality have been petty crimes of opportunity: shoplifting, grabbing a pack of cigarettes and loose change out of somebody's unlocked car, stealing a friend's video games. And I've already broached the subject with Wesley once before, suggesting to him that his regular buffet of Lortabs, Adderall, Xanax, weed, meth, crack, and fruit-flavored Mad Dog 20/20 might have something to do with his poor judgment, lack of criminal success, and resulting frequent contact with police.

Wesley seems genuinely surprised and happy to see me. He affects none of Travis's tough-guy veneer. He couldn't pull it off even if he tried, though. He wears his hair short except for a long lock combed straight down in front like goofy Beatles bangs, and he has a spray of freckles across his cheeks. If Travis looks like Wally Cleaver trying to act like Eddie Haskell, then Wesley is definitely the Beave.

I touch on many of the same points with Wesley that I did with Travis. He seems genuinely surprised to hear of my own checkered past and readily agrees that his main problem is getting high.

But then his face clouds over.

"Thing is, Detective Johnson, I don't think I can ever kick. You know my family. Everybody does whatever kinda smoke or pill there is. I mean, even my Grandma—she's hooked on her prescription Oxys. 'At's why she keeps puttin' us out, 'cause we all keep stealin' her Oxys from her. Me and Travis and Candy been doin' it since I was in kiddiegarden. We'd do whatever shit Mom an' 'em left layin' around the house. Drain the last little bit a warm beer outta the bottles, smoke up their roaches in the ashtrays, eat whatever pills they'd leave layin' around. I'm a *born* addict. I ain't got a chance, Detective."

"But it *runs* in families, Wesley. Almost every alcoholic or addict has other ones in his family. I got it on both sides, I'm pretty sure. What about your dad? Is he still around?"

"Him? What about him? You've seen him. He's a fuckin' retard, Detective. I mean, I know he can't help it, but that's what he is and I'm gonna turn out just like him!"

Wesley's face contorts in pain, and he stuggles mightily to hold back. He swallows hard and clenches his jaw. His hands grip each side of the table. His knuckles turn white, but the sobbing begins.

I'm not clear what has upset him, what's going on, and try to keep him focused. "You mean that guy Andy? He's your dad? Is he Travis and Candy's dad, too?"

Wesley's sobbing so hard he's got that short, spastic kind of breathing that little kids often get when they cry hard. He can't speak and just shakes his head no, then nods his head yes, blubbering all the while.

"You mean Andy's not Travis's father, but he is yours and Candy's?"

Wesley nods again, still bawling. I avert my eyes and muse aloud.

"Hmmm . . . I guess . . . that's why you and Candy look so much alike . . . but not so much Travis."

Wesley's not looking at me, either. A moment passes. Finally, he takes a deep breath, gathering himself, and raises his eyes to meet mine.

"We're in-breds!" he sputters, his throat constricted, tears squirting out of his eyes in misery.

"What? I don't think you mean what you're saying, Wesley. You mean Travis is, like, your stepbrother, or a half brother. He's got a different father, but Brandy's y'all's mother, right?"

By now, Wesley's rocking in his seat, bellowing and shaking his head, then starts hitting his forehead with the heels of both hands.

"Or you mean, like, half-breeds, y'know? Mixed race or something? Half Indian? Neither a them is any big deal, there's lotsa half-breeds and half brothers, and it doesn't mean anything. Heck, I'm a bastard child myself, Wesley. I've got a buncha half brothers."

"I *know* what I'm sayin'," he cries, between hiccuppy gasps for breath. "We're in-breds, me an' Candy. And so is our father. That's why he's that way. He's our mama's half brother. Like, my half uncle, or cousin or something, *and* he's my father! We're all in-breds, 'cept for Travis!"

I don't know how to respond.

Wesley's crying slows, his breathing only occasionally hitched. "And Travis is our half brother—you did get that part right. And I ain't nu'n but a piece-a-shit in-bred. So's Candy, but at least she's a girl, and girls don't get in much trouble, that's just how it is for them. But me? I'm fucked."

"Well, listen to me, believe me, I know this firsthand: no matter how screwed up your family is, that doesn't hafta automatically mean you are, too, and you can't do anything about it. You know what's right and what's wrong, Wesley. You've just had some shitty examples, growing up. But you're not a retard, and you're not a thug, either—at least not yet. You hear me? This in-bred stuff's just a damn excuse. As long as you stay away from all that dope mess, you've got a chance. Keep doin' whatcha been doin', you'll keep getting the same shitty results. And you *will be fucked*. But if you wanna change, there is a way out. When you get outta here, you call me, Wesley."

I give him one of my cards, as I did with Travis. "In the meantime, they got meetings in here, right here in Metro, twice a week. Start goin' to those, and call me, or call one a the guys who bring the meetings in here, when you get out."

Wesley rises with me and grabs my hand, which I had not offered. I just want to get out of there.

"Thanks, Detective Johnson. I will, I promise. And wouldja do me a favor and call my mom for me? Ask her to come visit me, please; nobody visits me. I can only see Travis from across the room, they won't let us talk. And wouldja ask Mom to put some money on a canteen card for me here, so I can buy stuff and use the phone? Please?"

"Yeah, Wesley," I hear myself saying. "I'll tell her next time I see her. Listen, be careful and stay outta trouble in here. Good luck, kid."

At the pretrial hearing, Wesley sits on the other side of the courtroom in a row with the other guests of the city, in orange jumpsuits, cuffs, and shackles. He animatedly tries to make eye contact with me, but I don't want to look at him.

There's a pause in the proceedings while the court awaits the arrival of somebody's attorney. It's Judge McNaughton's courtroom, one of very few good ones. Most of the judges seem to actively dislike and distrust cops. They'll think nothing of nol-prossing a case if the cop is late but will make cops sit there all damn morning waiting for a defense attorney, only to grant the attorney's request for a continuance or reset. It's maddening, and I've come to understand why cops are required to check their weapons outside the courtroom.

But Judge McNaughton's a decent sort of fella. He and I had become acquainted one day soon after I had switched from patrol to investigations, and I'd gone to his chambers to get a search warrant signed.

I remarked on the framed picture in the bookcase behind his desk, a candid shot of hizzonner and the singer Jimmy Buffet hoisting brewskis together, in matching flowered Hawaiian shirts. The judge explained that he'd known Buffet since he was *un*known, back in the day when Buffet had been grateful to sing for free, in a rowdy little bar down on Duval Street, a joint owned by hizzonner before he became a judge.

Then it was the judge's turn to be nosy. "If you'll pardon the observation, Detective, you don't look like the typical cop. The gray hair, the coat and tie, the way you speak and carry yourself. What's up with that? What's your story?" I told him about my midlife career change, and his jaw dropped.

Since then, whenever I'm in his courtroom and there's a lull or a delay in the proceedings, he'll point me out from the bench and announce to all present, "Well, for goodness' sakes, there's Detective Johnson. Good morning, Detective. Do y'all know Detective Johnson? I bet you don't know that this man used to run the United Way here in Mobile. Did y'all know that? Raised a lot of money, millions, for the Boy Scouts, the Red Cross, the Sally, right? Penelope House, too, am I right, Detective? For the victims of domestic violence? But that was far too tame for him. So at the age of fifty, he up and quits, goes through the Police Academy and becomes one of Mobile's Finest! Can you imagine? From Penelope to policing! A remarkable story."

He does this routine again this morning, though all the court staff, the DA, and most of the defense attorneys have already heard it. And the people out in the peanut gallery, the ones waiting for their cases to be called, don't give a shit about some cop's story, even if it is one of the judge's favorite anecdotes.

This morning he concludes by asking me, "How long you been on the force, now, Detective?"

"It's getting close to a decade now, Your Honor."

"A decade! Is that right?" McNaughton asks, pondering for a moment.

"Are ya disillusioned yet, Detective?"

It's my turn to ponder. "Well, Your Honor . . ." I say, picking my words carefully. "With policing, no sir. But with the justice system? Now, that's another story."

Hizzonner chuckles and asks me what case I'm here for.

"Wesley Colt, Your Honor. It's actually several cases on him, but I expect we'll be bundling them together."

The DA steps in. "Your Honor, if I can have a word with the detective, I believe we may be able to dispose of these matters without a hearing?"

McNaughton nods his assent, and the DA tells me that Wesley's court-appointed lawyer will be requesting Youthful Offender status for Wesley, "and the Judge'll probably grant it, 'cause the kid's just a few months past eighteen and his juvie record's not all *that* bad, I mean compared to most we see in here, don't you think? And he confessed, and you recovered most of the stolen property, right? So his lawyer's proposing drug diversion, three years' formal probation, and restitution for whatever you didn't recover, in exchange for pleas to Theft third. Now I understand there's an older brother codefendant, correct? Who's really the primary player in all this, right? And he's facing multiple drug charges in Baldwin County, and some others here for endangerment and assault related to his arrest? He's the one we'll stick it to. So whaddaya think?"

I tell the DA I've got plenty of other things I could be doing, bigger fish to fry. And this is his arena, not mine, so I'll defer to his and hizzonner's judgment.

Then I just can't stop myself from adding, "Actually, I kinda feel sorry for the kid. He's the youngest in a really fucked-up family. If a deal means I don't hafta stick around to testify and be cross-examined on every little nuance, every rod and reel and tackle box, then let's make the deal."

The DA smiles, shakes my hand, and says, "Thanks, Detective. See ya next time." I exit the courtroom without looking back, trying in vain to drive my FTO Porter's accusation, Slocumb's Theorem, Marcus Pettway, and LaJuan Lawson out of my mind.

26

Folly Chases Death
(around the Broken Pillar of Life)

The only thing necessary for evil to triumph is for good men to do nothing.
—Edmund Burke

It's the first day of Mardi Gras season, Friday, February 3, 2012. The Conde Cavaliers will be parading tonight down Government Street before an estimated crowd of twenty thousand, and the revelry—and the overtime—will continue for another eighteen days.

Cops have a love/hate relationship with Mardi Gras. We love it because the overtime fattens our paychecks by several thousand dollars each year (more than enough to pay off the Christmas credit balance) and because those of us who enjoy combat get the opportunity to hone our skills and unleash our normally repressed aggression by breaking up the numerous brawls that erupt with ever-growing size and frequency as the season wears on.

But we hate it because we get worn out after the first week of fourteen-hour days, arguing with traffic-snarling tourists who insist they must be allowed to cross the parade route to get to their hotels. By the end of the second week, all the mirth has been drained out of us by our constant state of alert, scanning as we must the crushing, unpredictable crowds for violators and malefactors. As the season builds toward its climax, we're growing angered rather than amused by the pickled, privileged maskers swaying atop gaudy, slow-moving floats, imperiously fast-balling their damn Moon Pies, cheap beads, and trinkets at the screaming masses (and often slyly targeting weary, distracted cops).

By Fat Tuesday, when Folly chases Death around the Broken Pillar of Life with a flail of three dried, inflated pig bladders tied to a stick, we're rooting for Death to deal a mortal blow to Folly *and* the damn mule team they both rode in on. We've had it up to here with the whole nineteen days of public Bacchanalia, attended en masse not only by the local thuggage but by scofflaws, outlaw bikers, and gangbangers from far and wide.

For me, the season always begins with small but startling surprises, derived from the simple donning of the blues. As a plainclothesman for several years now, about the only time I wear the uniform anymore is for Mardi Gras duty. So I'm invariably struck, first, by the gear required of uniformed officers to carry, by its sheer bulk and weight—even though I carried it without complaint every day for six years in patrol. Now, as a detective, I just carry my duty weapon, radio, and handcuffs on my belt, my small switchblade clipped to a rear pocket, and when I remember it, a small flashlight in a pocket of my blazer. (Recently I've added—since receiving it for Father's Day 2012—a small seven-shot .380 "pocket pistol," or "Git back!" gun.) But uniformed duty, mandatory for Mardi Gras, requires me to be as fully equipped as a patrol officer.

This means the Belt, and more.

On my duty belt are two spare fifteen-round magazines of .40-caliber ammunition (for a total of forty-six rounds, counting the magazine in my weapon and the round in the chamber), a canister of pepper spray, two sets of handcuffs, a lead-tipped Monadnock expandable baton, a foot-long Super Stinger Streamlight (which can double as a baton, in a pinch), an old-style, big-boy M26 Taser with spare cartridge, my radio with remote shoulder mike, and my duty weapon, the Glock .40-caliber model 22. In my uniform shirt pockets are two ballpoint pens, a notepad, and a cell phone (as well as, in days past, a pack of smokes and a lighter, or more recently, a can of Skoal). Under the shirt, of course, is the "bulletproof" (except for rifle rounds) vest. All of this is rigged for quick accessibility and security with Velcro strips and "keepers" (leather snap-straps).

With this array of tools on my belt, it's critical to develop the "muscle memory" needed to quickly deploy—and holster—the appropriate tool for fast-changing circumstances. I must be able to draw (or holster and switch to) the appropriate tool without averting my eyes from whatever threat I face. Most cops keep the gun side of their duty belts uncluttered with other equipment to avoid accidentally bringing a knife (or a baton or a Taser) to a gunfight. This usually means that all the non-gun gear gets real crowded on the front, back, and opposite sides of the belt, sometimes forcing tough equipment choices for the fittest (or smallest) cops, whose trim waistlines offer limited belt space. It can also mean discomfort when seated for long periods (as in a patrol car for a twelve-hour shift), chronic bruising around the waistline, and periodic sciatica and lower back pain from the unbalanced weight distribution and pressure points.

(It also means uniformed cops require spacious, secure toilet stalls and must never delay a bowel movement, because a cop simply can't drop his trousers in a hurry. I learned this the hard way.)

In addition to the required equipment, most cops carry a variety of optional gear: backup guns, knives, folding Leatherman tools, and the like. The selection of optional gear varies by assignment. SWAT guys, for example, wear body armor more akin to flak jackets than to patrol's under-shirt vests, carry tourniquets and Kytostat bandages for spurting wounds, pack assorted flashbangs, smoke, and tear-gas grenades, and strap on much more ammo, for both assault rifles and sidearms. Optional gear is also driven by experience (or lack of it) and by superstition. Rookies will buy and carry anything that says "police" on it. As rookies become seasoned officers they will often shed all but the minimum required, until a scary fight or gun battle prompts the return or replacement of certain pieces of optional gear.

In my case, optional gear choices are probably due in equal parts to harrowing experience, unthinking habit, and dumb superstition. They include a backup ten-round model 27 "baby" Glock, which I carry Velcroed to the body armor under my shirt, below my right armpit (in the event that my right arm or hand is disabled), a fixed blade Ka-Bar knife in a boot, and my little pocket switchblade next to my main handcuff key. I carry tiny backup handcuff keys (in the event my cuffs are ever used on me) in other places. In the ceramic-plate-holding chest pocket of my ballistic vest, I carry a third knife, a small backup flashlight, a spare ink pen, and a dog-eared pocket copy of the Title 13A Criminal Code of Alabama.

To top it all off, for Mardi Gras crowd control, we're required to wear "hard covers" for all nighttime parades (to protect our noggins from thrown beer bottles or other airborne projectiles). The hard covers may be military-surplus Kevlar helmets (painted black) or city-issue riot helmets with plastic face shields—most of which are so scratched up that their use compromises vision.

All told, I'm twenty-seven pounds heavier, fully uniformed and equipped, than I am when dressed for plainclothes duty, and thirty-one pounds heavier than I am off duty, in jeans and a T-shirt (though I *never* leave the house, even for church, unarmed).

Even more surprising than the weight of all the gear that goes with the uniform is the mere sight of myself in it. In uniform, there's no mistaking that I'm a cop, though I'm still often startled to catch a glimpse of my uniformed reflection in the mirror over the bathroom sink. I'll pause a moment to regard my image, invariably struck by that same old curious mix of pride and doubt. As I gaze in the mirror, my first thought is who's *that* guy? Is that really *you?* Who do you think you're kidding, Markie Doodle? You're sixty years old and still playing dress-up.

I read somewhere that even bad cops—lazy, or cowardly, or corrupt or stupid cops—can, by their mere presence, inspire respect, restore calm and order, deter crime, even save lives. That's the power of the uniform. We're taught in the academy that the first level of the "Use of Force Continuum" is police presence. No physical force, not even spoken commands, is needed to produce compliance in most situations.

People see the uniform, and that's all they need to know. Rarely do they look at or evaluate the person wearing it, at least initially. I know this to be a fact, having on several occasions encountered people who know me personally—knew me before and since I became a cop—but failed to recognize me (despite face-to-face proximity in broad daylight) until I identified myself by name. All they saw was the uniform.

So when I catch a glimpse of myself in uniform again after a year in civvies, I banish my first thought ("impostor") by recalling the second one: nobody knows me, at least not at first, and not on the inside. Nobody knows my doubts, my fears, my wounds and weaknesses. Whew! I take a deep breath, swell up, stiffen my spine, fix my gaze. I may even practice a draw or two on my reflection in the mirror.

And off I go, where fools rush in.

(Do other cops have these thoughts? Hell if I know. Be damned if I'm gonna ask any of 'em, though.)

Since I've got eight hours of routine paperwork and neighborhood witness canvassing for some backlogged cases before fully suiting up for parade duty, I toss the vest into the backseat, to put on later. I'm a heck of a lot more comfortable without it, but its absence does cost me the backup baby Glock, which I normally carry strapped to the vest when in uniform. The baby G doesn't really ride well anywhere else.

Not long past lunchtime, I'm in my car down the Parkway writing up some case notes when I get a call from Bailey, a robbery guy, who asks if I'm familiar with a little thug named Donte Curtis, who's a suspect in some recent juvenile stickups he's working. Seems young Donte's been stealing the odd blunt, cash, and cell phones from neighborhood teens, at gunpoint. I'd seen Bailey's BOLO for Donte in my e-mail and been keeping an eye out for him myself.

"Yeah, I know Donte. In fact, I'm about a minute away from his mama's place right now. Got a warrant for him? 'Cause he won't come to the door when ya knock."

"He won't?"

"Nah. And both his mama and his sister'll lie to your face, say he doesn't live there, even though everybody who knows him tells me that's where he's staying."

"Hmmm. Well, I don't have enough for a warrant yet, that's why I'm hoping to bring him in for questioning, or at least do a knock-and-talk there at the house."

"Well good luck wi'dat, Bub. I'll meet you there if you wanna try—maybe your people skills are better'n mine—but don't get your hopes up."

"Thanks. I'm about five minutes out now. See if you can get one of your patrol units to meet us there, just in case we get lucky and need a cage for transport."

I call ol' Frank Black, who (predictably) knows Donte Curtis from several of his own encounters with the lad. The three of us converge on Merle Street, near the dead end of Riverside Drive at Dog River. There are no vehicles in the driveway or the yard; it doesn't look promising. Frank goes around to cover the back, I cover the west side where the bedrooms are, and Bailey knocks on the front door.

And knocks. And calls out, "Police! Mobile Police Department! Come to the door!"

I think I hear some movement in one of the bedrooms and pound on the window.

"We know you're in there, Donte!" I yell. "Don't make us kick in your mama's door!"

APPREHENSIONS & CONVICTIONS

Frank's peering in through a narrow gap in the curtains of a sliding-glass door in back and calls out, "Just saw somebody scamper up the stairs from the kitchen!"

We all continue beating on windows and doors, telling Donte to come on out, make it easy on yourself, we just wanna talk—the usual combination of bullshit and borderline harassment. Neither of which is working on young Master Curtis.

A crackle of static comes over our radios. The dispatcher's voice is taut with urgency and louder than usual. All of us stop our pounding and yelling for Donte.

"Hold traffic, all units hold your traffic to patch the channels."

This usually means a multi-precinct or even multi-jurisdiction car chase is under way. It could be a stolen car, a bank robbery, or just some terrified jerk with warrants for unpaid traffic tickets who can't bear the thought of going to jail for them. I wait impatiently for Dispatch to advise, and I know Bailey and Frank are doing the same, feeling the same anticipation for the signal as me, same as every other Mobile officer on duty. We listen intently to hear if we're close enough to get in on it, or if it's important enough that our distance doesn't matter.

It turns out, both.

"Signal 17 just occurred at Metro Jail, involving an officer. Time elapsed, two minutes. Officer down, signal 17, officer down. Subject has signal 51'd the vehicle of the signal 17 officer, last seen southbound on St. Emanuel Street from Metro sally port, in a marked MPD unit.

"Repeat, officer down, an officer has been cut at Metro jail, subject fleeing southbound at high rate of speed on St. Emanuel Street in marked MPD unit. Hold your traffic, all units hold your traffic, attempting patch with County . . ."

The three of us race to our cars, hit our lights and sirens, and spray Donte's mama's house with a scattershot of gravel and a cloud of dust. Frank's in the lead, Bailey's riding his bumper, and I'm bringing up the rear as we make the block and stomp the pedal eastbound on Riverside to Gill, down the long straight shot to Dauphin Island Parkway, hoping the bad guy will take I-10 westbound so we can get in on it as he nears D.I.P.

If he goes east through the tunnel to the Bayway and Baldwin County, we might as well turn around and go back to Donte's (although when he heard us peel out he no doubt skedaddled out the back to lay low with some nearby baby-mama for a few days).

"All units hold your traffic, County units in pursuit of Metro escapee, subject last seen southbound in a marked MPD unit on St. Ema . . . Correction, subject now westbound, Short Texas Street, hold traffic . . . Subject now southbound, Conception Street, County has lost visual."

A new voice comes over the air, one of ours, in pursuit. He's amped up, nearly shouting: "Three-twelve, I got visual on subject now southbound on Conception, crossing Texas . . . crossing Montgomery, I have two County units behind me . . . "

The shanker's headed for the Virginia Street on-ramps to the interstate, I'm thinking. Which way will he go? I'm betting westbound; to go east would require a hard left onto a tight cloverleaf to the right, but westbound would be an easier left, then a straight shot up and onto I-10, with better options beyond, like I-65 north to Prichard or Eight Mile, or staying westbound on 10, maybe running for Mississippi.

"Three-twelve, subject now westbound on Virginia! He's headed for the interstate! Do we have any units at either ramp? I've lost visual—"

A new voice, another one of ours, cuts in, shouting over the last one, "A unit runnin' code just 'bout hit me cutting onto the westbound 10 ramp, is that him or—"

"That's gotta be him!" 312 shouts.

The dispatcher tries valiantly to regain control of the airwaves. "Units crossing. All units hold traffic, 312 is in pursuit, 312, 10-9 your last?"

The second voice, ignoring the operator's instructions, walks all over her, yelling, "Subject now westbound 10 from Virginia! Westbound 10 from Virginia! Speed's approaching one hundred, I'm tryin'a get up behind him."

Dispatch tries once more to restore order. "Units crossing. Which unit's westbound I-10 from Virginia?"

"Three-seventeen, in pursuit of black male subject wearing light-colored shirt, in 51S City blue-and-white, westbound 10 from Virginia, speed's a hundred! He's weaving in and out of traffic! He's activated lights and siren, westbound 10 approaching Broad Street . . . crossing over Broad Street, speed now 110, 115, westbound 10 approaching Michigan . . ."

Behind 317's yelling, his siren and the roar of his Crown Vic can be heard, matching the roar and wail of my own as we zoom eastbound on Gill to the Parkway. I'm thinking, All right! He's coming right to us! If we can just make it up to I-10 in time, we might have a chance to do a rolling blockade, or to force him to scrape up onto a barricade or off-road into the ditch. At the very least we'll be in the chase.

Frank and Bailey are thinking the same: as soon as we hear he's headed toward us, they punch it up to 75, screaming eastbound on two-lane Gill Road. The three of us moving as one, tight, bumper to bumper, like the Blue Angels streaking low and fast in close formation over the beach on the Fourth of July. Pedestrians are fleeing the road ahead, cars veering off into yards as we blaze past. I feel the adrenalin dump and begin tactical breathing.

"Three-seventeen, I've lost visual ... I think he got off at southbound D.I.P. Advise any units behind me to continue westbound on 10, I'm getting off here . . ."

The dispatcher interjects: "Three-twelve, copy?"

"Read direct, continuing westbound 10," 312 replies.

"All units hold traffic for further . . ."

"Three-seventeen! He's southbound D.I.P.! Just blew the light at Old Military, southbound D.I.P., high speed, weaving, heading into the curve . . . I've lost visual."

Holy shit, I'm thinking. We'll be comin' up on him in less than a minute! How we gonna stop him head-on? Now I'm glad Frank and Bailey are ahead of me. We slow slightly to negotiate the 90-degree turn from eastbound Gill across D.I.P.'s two southbound lanes onto the northbound Parkway (exactly the route I'd taken in my ill-fated pursuit of the hooker Heather a few months earlier, before being canceled by Lieutenant Andrews as I closed the gap).

In the turn onto the parkway, everything not strapped down or boxed up inside my car—loose change, coffee cups, map book, case files—flies to the right, bounces off the passenger side door, and scatters all over the place.

Just as we straighten out and stomp it past BC Rain High School northbound, I see blue lights sweeping around the bottom half of the D.I.P. curve, coming toward us fast in the center turning lane. I hear Frank, in the lead, come across the radio. He's the first calm voice so far, even calmer than Dispatch.

"Three-nineteen, myself, 862, and 163 are northbound D.I.P. approaching Cedar Crescent, we have visual of the subject..."

Before Dispatch can respond, Frank continues, "Three-nineteen, subject just blew the light at Cedar Crescent, now eastbound on Cedar Crescent, and [his deep register softening] . . . I've . . . lost visual . . . momentarily . . ."

In an instant, all three of us have made the right-angle right from northbound D.I.P. onto Cedar Crescent. All the detritus from my preceding left turn now bounce back into my side of the cockpit and onto me. Cedar Crescent Drive is a long, gentle loop (hence the name Crescent) curving south through a residential neighborhood around the back side of BC Rain High School, with six roads shooting off toward Mobile Bay to the east, like spokes from a hub.

A new voice, even calmer than Frank's, a voice of reason (though betraying more than a trace of exasperation), says, "Operator, the subject's in 351's vehicle. Is that unit's automatic vehicle locator functional?"

"Ten-four."

"Advise subject's further locations from that unit's AVL."

I'm thinking, wow, why didn't I (or anybody else) think of that? All our marked units have trackers mounted on the trunk lids. Duh! Visual contact isn't even necessary to catch this guy as long as he's driving one of our units.

After a pause, the dispatcher, no doubt having just smacked herself in the forehead with the heel of her hand, says, "Ten-four, AVL now shows subject southbound Cedar Crescent at North Drive ... now at Shore Acres ..."

I see Frank peel off to his left onto Shore Acres. Did I miss her saying he turned onto Shore Acres? That must be what Frank heard. Our bad guy clearly doesn't know the parkway very well, I'm thinking, because Shore Acres dead-ends at Bay Front, which hugs the bay from there south. If he's not careful, the guy will launch himself right off into Mobile Bay. I visualize a spectacular splash like something out of *The Dukes of Hazzard*.

In front of me, Bailey slows but then continues south on Cedar Crescent. As I pass Shore Acres a moment behind him, I look to my left and see neither Frank's nor the bad guy's car and wonder, where'd they go so quick? Then I remember that little one-block connector, McVoy Avenue, which links Shore Acres with the next road down.

Just then, the operator reports, "Now showing at South Drive," and I see Bailey veer off to his left onto South Drive.

Am I missing something? I follow Bailey in a hard left onto South Drive but see nothing but Bailey zooming toward the bay. No bad guy, no Frank. I jam my foot on the brake pedal and all my interior debris, now including stuff for tonight's parade duty from the backseat, flies forward. My riot helmet ricochets off my base radio in the center console, my snack sack and vest in a tangle close behind.

The operator intones, "Now passing Seapines Boulevard . . . now turning south onto Jacksonville Drive," and I jerk the Crown Vic into a reverse whip back onto Cedar Crescent, then stomp the gas with tires squealing to Jacksonville Drive.

The operator says, "Turning west from Jacksonville onto Cedar Park," and a moment later I roll up on 351's idling cruiser, blue lights ablaze and siren still wailing, rutted in somebody's once-manicured front lawn. The trunk's popped up, obscuring my view of the interior; the driver door's wide open. It's a spooky-sick damn scene to behold.

Bad guy probably heard the chatter about his car's AVL over the stolen cruiser's police radio, heard his locations and maneuvers reported in real time, same as he performed them. Realizing his only chance was to put distance between himself and the GPS-tracked car, he musta bailed out and run. Or did he?

Wary of a trap, an ambush—he likely has the gun from the officer he cut—I approach the idling cruiser with my gun drawn. I crouch low to check for feet behind the open driver's door, or anyone squatting on the opposite sides of cruiser. Nothing, but he could be hidden by the front tires. Neither am I able to see (with the trunk lid popped up) if the car's occupied or not. Cautiously but quickly I "slice the pie" and get close enough to see, first into the trunk, then around the trunk lid all the way across the interior, next checking all the way down to the floor in the back, then down to the floor in front. Empty. I move back behind the trunk and circle around the far side, from rear to front.

Clear. I allow myself to exhale.

Dispatch comes over my shoulder mike. "Still showing Jacksonville at Cedar Park, subject may have bailed. Approach with extreme caution, subject may be armed."

I scan my 360, aware that the fugitive may have eyes on me right now, may be lining me up in his sights. With an electric jolt, I lock eyes with a terrified, middle-aged female in a house robe I somehow hadn't seen till now, standing wide eyed in the driveway next door, just beyond the abandoned cruiser I'd circled moments ago. She's just yards away from me, and I hadn't seen her! Tunnel vision, peripheral blindness, condition black: they told us about this in the academy . . . am I there? Is that happening to me?

She has one hand to her chin, her other holding a handful of envelopes. She musta just been walking back from her mailbox when the stolen cruiser jumped the curb and rutted to a stop in her neighbor's front yard. She stares at me, motionless and mute, mouth agape, then thrusts her hand with the mail toward the house across the street. I look where she's pointing, mimic her gesture; she nods vigorously, still waving her mail at the driveway across the street. I set out in that direction, as she finds her voice. Over the yowling sirens I hear her call out, "That way . . . . He dint look like no poe-leece, but he wa' carryin' a big ole gun he got from outta the trunk . . . He run up behine 'at house . . . . Wha's goin' on, Officer? Do I needs'a take cover?"

Without a word in reply, without putting out my location over the air, without grabbing my vest out of the car or my shotgun from my trunk, not thinking to check 351's trunk for *his* shotgun, without waiting for backup, without a thought in my mind beyond "I gotta get him," off I run in pursuit.

27

Shit Gets Real

Resist not evil: whosoever shall smite thy cheek, turn to him the other.
—Matthew 5:39

For it is written, Vengeance is mine, saith the Lord.
—Romans 12:19

Later that evening and over the days and weeks that follow, I learn from television and newspaper stories, written police reports, digital surveillance footage, and the firsthand, eyewitness accounts of the officers and detectives involved, that twenty-year-old Lawrence Wallace Jr. walked into a west Mobile Dollar General store on the morning of Friday, February 3, at 1113 hours. He was about as far away as you can get (without leaving the city limits) from the sad and crumbling subsidized rental houses and boarded-up commercial strips of the lower Parkway, where I encountered him a little less than five hours later. It's not a stretch to say that the North Schillinger Road Dollar store and its prosperous retail neighbors, as well as the comfortable middle-class subdivisions surrounding them, are a world apart from Dauphin Island Parkway south of the I-10 overpass.

Lawrence Wallace drove to the Dollar store that morning in his silver Toyota Camry. He entered the store wearing a black hooded jacket and blue pants. He walked around the store a few minutes, gathering seemingly random items, then approached the checkout counter and placed them (charcoal, lighter fluid, a longneck Bic lighter for barbecue grilling, and several knit caps) on the counter. As cashier Kayla Cunningham began ringing them up, Wallace exited the store, explaining he had to go get his money from the car.

When he returned moments later, he ordered the cashier to open her register and give him all the money. When Kayla Cunningham advised him politely that she couldn't do that, he began removing the articles Kayla had rung up for him from the plastic bag she'd put them in and demanded to speak to the store manager. Then he began squirting the lighter fluid all over the charcoal, the knit caps, and the counter.

Despite the old complaint about cops never being around when you need one, sometimes we are. Off-duty Mobile police officer Charles Wilson, shopping in the store at the time, had already noted Wallace with suspicion, even before he witnessed the confrontation at the checkout counter.

"He was walking around the store acting strangely, as if he was gonna commit some type of criminal act," Wilson told me. "You know what I'm talkin' about. You been on the job awhile. Sometimes we can just sense it with people, their vibe: something ain't right."

When the lighter fluid started to flow, Charlie Wilson ran out to his car for his gun.

Cashier Kayla Cunningham turned around and tapped her store manager on the shoulder. Tobias Smith was working the register next to her. "We have a problem here, Toby," she said.

"I turn around to see a guy squirting lighter fluid all over the place, clicking his Bic with his other hand," Smith said. "He says to me, 'Give me everything in the cash drawers and the safe, or I'monna burn this bitch down.' Then he walks around Kayla's counter over to mine and stands right next to me. I thought he was gonna squirt me and set me on fire, but instead he squirts the cardboard display of potato chips next to my register and lights it."

Charlie Wilson returned to the store just in time. He pointed his Glock at Lawrence Wallace Jr. and said, "Mobile PD. Get on the floor," according to his written account in the Incident/Offense Report.

"You can tell me the truth, Charlie," I said when he recounted the episode to me later. "I mean, how often do we get a chance like that, to hit a robbery in progress, catch the guy right in the act. You were psyched, I know you. What you really said, in your best Shaft voice, was 'Git onna ground, *now*, muhfucka!'"

Charlie laughed. "Well, I mighta used some colorful language. And yeah, I was pumped."

Charlie's a fifteen-year veteran, a motorcycle cop now. I used to work with him in First Precinct patrol years ago. He's a handsome six feet, 200 pounds, solid, dark skinned with blazing white teeth, and a no-nonsense demeanor about him, although he's quick to smile and joke around. He's really a gentle soul; I've always liked and admired him. But he can summon a fearsome command presence in an instant, and I can picture his eyes flashing fiercely with his weapon drawn on Wallace, the potato chips ablaze behind him, Charlie not knowing if Wallace's got a gun or not, and a terrified Tobias Smith and Kayla Cunningham within reach as potential hostages. Charlie was counting on his command presence—his stern countenance, the authority of his voice—to do the trick, or this could all go south in a hurry. It was Charlie's once-in-a-career Dirty Harry moment. Fortunately, his turned out better than mine. But Charlie's moment wasn't much like the movies, either.

If he'd been in uniform, it probably would've worked. Especially if he'd been wearing those shimmering black leather knee-high motorcycle boots he'd normally have had on. Those damn boots alone mean business.

(And they mean other things, too, if you believe John Balzer, who rides a PD Harley with Traffic now, too. He calls them his "fuck me" boots. "Women can't resist a man in these boots," Balzer swears, grinning. "Even when he looks like me.")

If Charlie'd been in uniform, if he'd had his radio on his belt and the microphone clipped to his shoulder, and Wallace could've heard the chatter of backup units being dispatched to the Dollar store on Schillinger, if he'd heard "robbery in progress, officer holding one at gunpoint," chances are Lawrence Wallace Jr. would have complied.

But Charlie was in his civilian clothes. He was off duty. Despite Charlie's intimidating size, his confidence, his fierce demeanor, and the authority of his deep voice and his .40-caliber semiautomatic Glock leveled directly at Lawrence Wallace Jr.'s center mass from a can't-miss distance of three strides, Lawrence decided to make a run for it.

Actually, backup was already on its way. Well, not "backup," exactly, but police *were* already en route to the Dollar store to respond to a robbery in progress. They were just expecting the gun toter to be the bad guy, not some weird little guy with lighter fluid and a lit Bic. Unknown to everyone at the time, an employee at a nearby service station had observed Charlie run out of the Dollar store to his car, grab his gun, and run back into the store. The alert citizen at Raceway Discount Gas called 911 and reported, "A black guy with a gun's robbing the Dollar store! I just saw him run into the store waving a gun! It's happening right now!" The good Samaritan's racial profiling aside, his call did the trick: the cavalry was coming, though Charlie—and Wallace and everyone else in the Dollar store—didn't know it.

"Sometimes, profiling works to our advantage, eh brah?" I said.

He laughed. "Yes it does. *No doubt* it does. And this ain't the only time it's worked for me, either, or probably for you, know what I'm sayin'?"

Wallace bolted to the rear of the store, entered store manager Smith's office, and attempted to close the office door behind him. But Charlie was right on his heels, his Glock stuffed into his waistband, and snatched Wallace back out of the office.

In the movies, Charlie would have just dispatched the bad guy with a single clean shot between the eyes before he could take a half step toward the back of the store, and it would've been ruled a righteous shoot by Internal Affairs because they'd have found a .38 in the bad guy's pocket. In real life, even though Wallace had already set the store ablaze (arguably placing people in danger), Charlie would've been in trouble for using lethal force at this point.

"A brief struggle ensued, which ended when I was able to control the subject with a series of body punches," according to Charlie's written account for the Incident/Offense Report. When I read this, I shuddered at the risk Charlie took by attempting to take a robber into custody—especially one who's actively resisting arrest—with his weapon just stuck in his pants, unsecured. What if the robber had made a quick, lucky grab for it? When Charlie told me how it *really* was, the hair on the back of my neck stood up.

"It was a real knockdown, drag-out, man. Messy. I mean, like one a those old cowboy movies where there's a fight in the saloon, dog. I had a holda him by his jacket, y'know? And he kept tryin' to wriggle out of it like they do. I was slingin' him by that jacket all over the store, we were knockin' down display racks, makin' a helluva mess. And this old white guy, a customer in the store, y'know, he jumps in, tryin' to help me. We were back in the shoe section, and this old man's whackin' the dude in the head with a shoe."

According to the witness statement written by fifty-one-year-old white guy Cornelius Jenkins (yeah, just fifty-one—really, Charlie?—"old"?), "I had cancer on my nose about six weeks ago, but I noticed a fight broke out and I helped the guard"—meaning Charlie—"subdue the thief and hold him down until Police arrived." We need more good citizens like Corny Jenkins, willing to risk life and limb and the cancer bandage on his nose to take a stand for justice.

Without the uniform, we're not Police, even if we have a gun and announce "Mobile PD." In Cornelius Jenkins's eyes, Charlie was a "guard." But at least Mr. Jenkins didn't mistake Charlie for the bad guy.

Cornelius Jenkins continues, "I removed his wallet from his back pocket, and he kept trying to put his hand in his left pocket and I did not know if he was armed or not."

I asked Charlie if Lawrence Wallace seemed high, or crazy. "I mean, what was he thinking? Like, 'I bet he's just bluffing with that gun, he won't really shoot me' or 'I can outrun this guy,' or 'I can take him, he doesn't look that tough.' He had to be high, or crazy, or really, really stupid."

Charlie shook his head. "If it's any of those, I guess it'd hafta be stupid, 'cause he didn't really seem crazy or high. But he didn't seem that stupid, either. I don't know. Probably just *young*. He was just inexperienced, naïve, y'know? Playactin' the badass, like he's seen 'em do on TV. He obviously had no experience in robbery: no plan, no weapon, no mask or partners. He wud'n no real criminal, he was just playin' one on TV. Lot of 'em are like that, y'know? Till shit gets real."

For Lawrence Wallace Jr., however, shit had not yet gotten real, if his televised perp walk is any indication. He was still playacting the badass gangsta two hours later, when he was walked out the backdoor of head-quarters by Officer Steven Green before a phalanx of TV news cameras and loaded unceremoniously into the cage for transport to Metro, on the very real charges of Robbery First and Arson First degree. For most people facing charges of that magnitude, on their way to Metro after two hours in police headquarters cuffed to a table in a cramped interrogation room with a robbery lieutenant, four robbery detectives, and an arson investigator, shit's gotten plenty real.

But not for Lawrence Wallace Jr. He strutted, sneered, and trash-talked all the way to Patrolman Green's cage, even pulling his cuffed hands around from behind his back to throw gang signs. "Y'all ain't seen the last a me," he declared with a snarl, playing to the cameras. "I ain't near done in da two-five-one," he said, referring to Mobile's telephone prefix. "Y'all gon' remember my name, y'hear me?" He smiled maliciously. "Fuck da Poe-lice! I ain't done in da two-five-one, y'all!"

According to the reports, Wallace was fully compliant, even polite, if somewhat unfocused at headquarters. "He was cracking jokes with everybody the whole time, even the secretaries we walked past," one of the Robbery detectives later told me. "Like this was his fifteen minutes of fame." He signed the Miranda warning and waiver and talked freely, fully confessing to his actions at the Dollar store. The interview and his confession to detectives were videotaped. Store surveillance video was also secured and viewed, which confirmed the accounts by Charlie Wilson and the others.

Wallace claimed to the robbery detectives that he had been forced to do the robbery by three unknown black males who had driven him to the Dollar store in a black Navigator and were waiting for him in the parking lot until, he theorized, they must have left when they saw police arrive. He had no explanation for the presence of his own silver Toyota in the parking lot but would not recant his "forced-to-do-it-by-three-bad-niggas-in-a-Navigator" story.

Officer Green, visible in the periphery of the television camera shots, climbed into the front seat of his cruiser after Wallace had his fifteen seconds of swaggering and transported his prisoner to Metro. Green, thirty-six and the father of two, had been a police officer for seventeen months. He had been one of several officers responding to the Dollar store after the 911 call, but another more seasoned officer, a sergeant with the tactical response team, had actually taken Wallace into custody. Green had transported Wallace from the Dollar store to headquarters. There Green had waited through Wallace's two-hour interrogation by the robbery lieutenant, four robbery detectives, and the fire department's arson guy.

At Metro, Green pulled into the sally port, which is essentially a cinder-block garage attached to Metro intake and booking, with large overhead garage-type doors on both sides of it.

You pull up outside and push a button to an intercom. "Control" is what you hear.

"MPD, one male prisoner" is what you say, what Green must've said, and Control pushes a button raising the overhead door and says, "Ten-four. Secure your weapon."

You drive into the sally port and the overhead door closes behind you. It's big enough to hold four cruisers, two in each lane. When Green pulled in with Wallace in his cage, there was another Crown Vic already there, the unmarked unit of a County Probation and Parole officer who had parked in the inside lane, all the way forward to the second overhead door, the one for exit. The PO had already taken his parole violator into intake for processing. Green pulled his cruiser up next to the PO's as the overhead entry door came down behind him. The intake area is to the left of the sally-port parking lanes, behind a heavy bulletproof door with thick bullet-proof glass that is locked and unlocked remotely with a loud buzz.

Green got out, popped his trunk, and secured his sidearm there, as he'd been reminded to do by Control over the intercom before entering the sally port. No weapons are allowed inside Metro, or any facility for incar-ceration, to preclude the possibility that a corrections officer or outside law enforcement officer could be overpowered and his gun taken from him by a prisoner, resulting in hostage taking, murder, mayhem, maybe even escape.

There are a few lockboxes for securing weapons by the intake door, but I've never seen anybody use them. Most of us prefer to secure our weapons in our cruisers. Those who drive caged units will sometimes just leave their weapons in the forward, uncaged half of their cars, locking the car behind them, unlike Green who put his weapon in his trunk. It doesn't much matter, security-wise.

My first FTO Porter would always slip his Glock surreptitiously from his holster and slide it under the driver's seat as he pulled into the sally port, before getting out and opening the backdoor to let the prisoner out, on the theory that the prisoner, whom we always keep away from our gun side, will assume he's still armed and not try any "funny stuff." If you get out and open your trunk before you unload the prisoner, Porter reasoned, he's gonna wonder what you're doing back there, watch you, see you put your gun in the trunk, and know you're unarmed, which might embolden him to try some "funny stuff," he explained. "Better to make him think you're still armed and you'll just pop a round in his ass" if he acts up. Maybe that's why nobody ever uses the little lockboxes by the intake door.

Of course, even though you don't have your gun, you're not exactly unarmed, I remember thinking. You still have your Monadnock knee-capper, your pepper spray, your Taser, and probably a knife or two to discourage any "funny stuff." But I've always done it Porter's way and slip my Glock under the seat.

I guess it can be argued either way. If you're not sneaky enough when you put your gun under the seat and the bad guy knows there's a gun in the car, it's theoretically more accessible to him there than in the trunk, because he could, I don't know, maybe smash the driver's window with the steel cuffs on his wrists—which would be a good trick with his hands behind his back, but possible, not to say *painful*—and then get the gun. Of course, he'd still hafta unlock the car door with his hands behind his back, and the little lock knobs, recessed down into the door when locked, are almost impossible to grasp even if you're not cuffed in back, and the remote unlock button is way down inside the door on the armrest, a stretch with your hands behind your back. And then there's the challenge of getting the weapon from under the driver's seat while handcuffed behind the back, too. Unless the bad guy's smart enough to snatch the disabled cop's car keys—and cuff key, which is rarely kept on a cop's key chain—to use on the cuffs, then on the car door or the trunk. Some thugs are skinny assed, long armed, and limber enough to maneuver their cuffed hands in the back over their boney little butts and around their feet to the front. I've seen it happen. It's plenty good reason to whack a handcuffed prisoner a couple times upside the head for "attempt escape." But any scenario—cuffed in back or cuffed in front, gun in the trunk or under the seat, and a prisoner who's really clever, quick, and a contortionist as well—requires the *big* assumption that the prisoner's "funny stuff" has somehow disabled the transport officer, thereby enabling him to go for the cuff and/or car keys, to get the gun in the trunk, or under the seat, or whatever, and then what? He's still locked up there in the sally port. And whatever he could have theoretically done to disable the transport officer would have been in full view of the intake officer just behind the bulletproof glass, to say nothing of the video cameras remotely monitored by corrections staff, who will instantly sound the alarm at the first sign of any funny stuff, sending jail guards swarming into the sally port, eager to put a good beatin' on the smart-ass before he can snatch any keys or weapons or anything else—it's all pretty damn academic, if you ask me. I'm sure every possible criminal scenario has been imagined, corrected, planned for, and prevented or defeated through tried-and-true, redundant security measures, architecture, engineering, and procedure relentlessly tested, reviewed, and implemented by experienced professional wardens, sheriffs, and chiefs all over the country.

So Officer Green locked his Glock in the trunk, got Wallace out of his cage, locked his car, stuck the keys in his belt, walked his prisoner over to the door, and signaled the corrections officer to buzz him in. But there was a delay. The intake space is small, and it was already crowded with Mardi Gras revelers who'd gotten a head start on the first parade's festivities scheduled for later that night, and inside there were also that PO and his proby violator being processed. It happens, especially during Mardi Gras. So Green and Wallace stood there side by side in the sally port, waiting patiently for intake to clear enough space to buzz them in.

Green stood with his right hand gripping Wallace's left arm, waiting. His empty holster was exposed to Wallace's view, but, all things considered, that was academic, anyway. Then Wallace scratched his nose with the thumb of his right hand but quickly put the hand back behind him. Green saw the nose scratch. Perplexed, Green leaned in toward Wallace, reaching behind him to grab Wallace's free hand, presumably to re-cuff him.

Quick as a Cassius Clay uppercut, Wallace punched Green in the throat with that loose right hand, staggering Green. Down he went. Wallace ran back over to the far side of Green's cruiser, as the stricken officer struggled back to his feet, his hand at his throat. Still in the fight, he stumbled after his prisoner, chasing him around the parked Crown Vics. But he was hurt, and not just from a sucker punch to the throat. Blood spurted through his fingers as he gave chase, and Green collapsed in a fountain of crimson.

Wallace circled the cruisers and returned to his victim. He snatched the keys from Green's belt, opened the trunk and grabbed Green's pistol, slammed the trunk, jumped in the cruiser, and crashed it through the sally port's exit door. A few seconds after the escape, the plainclothes PO and a few corrections officers can be seen rushing in to Green. They attempt to apply pressure to Green's wound, but it's already too late. Officer Green is beyond saving, having bled out onto the sally-port floor. His jugular had been severed, and he is gone.

My group at the firing range reacted to the Metro surveillance video as had every group preceding us: stunned, sickened silence. Stifled rage. Disbelief. And grief. The classroom lights came on, and our instructor, the same tactical sergeant who had first taken Wallace into custody at

275

the Dollar store months ago, told us to take a break and be back in the classroom in fifteen for a briefing from the intelligence unit on local gang activity. We filed out of the classroom wordlessly, as if from a wake.

Shit had gotten real.

My weapon still in hand, I hurry up the driveway on the north side of Cedar Park Drive, across the street from Green's cruiser, abandoned in somebody's front yard, lights and siren still going strong. I'm hunting a guy who has cut a cop, stolen his car, and escaped from Metro. Though Green is already dead, that word has not gone out on our radios.

I'm figuring Frank and Bailey can't miss Green's cruiser and mine right behind it. They'll be screeching up behind me any second, because Dispatch keeps saying, "AVL still showing Cedar Park at Jacksonville, subject may have bailed, subject may be armed . . . " and I'm counting on the lady with the handful of mail to point them my way.

I get to the end of the driveway and hug the brick house's rear corner, peering carefully around to scan the backyard—lotsa hidey-holes: a detached shed with an open carport coming off the back of it piled full of stuff, two junk cars in the tall weeds near the back, and a cement mixer, a couple of old gutted motorbikes and a rusty go-cart clustered nearby—all enclosed by a six-foot wooden slat privacy fence on all three sides.

I take a quick glance around the corner at the back side of the house before making a dash to the shed: no open doors or windows on the house, but he wouldn't have tried to go inside, anyway, not here, not so close. He's wanting to get the hell away from here to hide, as far away from here as he can get, quick, without being spotted by alert citizens or cops. He knows it's fixin' to get real thick here with cops, real soon, thanks to that cop car's damn tracking unit.

I figure he's probably still on the move but can't be certain, and I sure as hell don't wanna risk having him behind me, so I gotta clear the backyard. In a low fast-moving crouch, I run to the south side of the windowless shed, my eye on the shed door all the way. I see the door, on the shed's east side, has an exterior padlock on it, so he's not in there. I flatten against the south side of the shed, between the shed and the rear of the house, and move to the shed's southwest corner, slicing the pie around the corner. Nothing.

Creeping along the back side of the shed, in a narrow passage between the shed and the wooden fence at the left (west) side of the yard, I reach the next corner and slice my way around it. Nothing.

There's a loud squawk in my ear and I flinch. Damn Dispatch is repeating, "All units, hold your traff—" and I turn the blasted thing off, for silence at least till I clear this cluttered cluster of a backyard. Why creep around like a ninja if the damn radio's gonna give me away?

The open-sided carport on the north side of the locked shed is stacked with lumber, wheelless old bicycle frames, an ancient riding mower, plumbing fixtures, and barrels, buckets, and boxes. I creep through it scanning every spot big enough to hide in. Nothing.

A short distance away are the hulks of the two old cars, one on blocks, both nearly overgrown with weeds, and nearby are the scooters, the go-cart, and the cement mixer. They're all kinda out in the open, exposed, but I'm not gonna turn my back on 'em before going over the rear fence. I sprint across to the rusty hulks and scramble around them looking high and low, checking that their trunks are locked down, checking the engine areas under the hoods, checking inside front and back, checking underneath. Nobody. Behind the one closest to the rear fence, an old box-style Caprice, I crouch down and lean back up against it, my arms on my thighs in a triangle, both hands gripping my Glock. I do some tactical breathing to settle and try to figure out my next move. Where the hell are Frank and Bailey, I'm wondering. They'll be here any second, I answer myself. The main question is where the hell's the damn thug?

I'm scanning the rear fence looking for a good spot to clamber over it when I spot a gap near the corner that I hadn't seen from previous vantages. I push off from the old Caprice and creep up to it to study things more closely. Two slats have been pulled out, making a gap just wide enough for somebody not too plump to squeeze through. The torn-off slats are lying nearby, their nails sticking up, still shiny and slightly bent. They haven't been lying there long enough to rust or get cruddy. The fence's three cross supports—the horizontal two-by-fours that the pulled-out slats had been nailed to—are now exposed where the slats had been, and they're a clean bright blond on their inside surface, almost like fresh lumber, not weathered and darkened to a dull gray like their other surfaces.

Bingo! The bad guy's just gone through this fence, right here, I deduce.

I peek carefully through the gap in the slats and scan the empty backyard of the house directly north. No escapee from Metro is running around, and compared to the yard I've just cleared, this one's tidy and neat as a pin, although there are a couple places he could be hiding. There's a small windowless shed, at least from what I can see of it, to the left, some bushes along the west side chain-link fence line, and a car parked snug up to the back of the house by the backdoor, next to a central AC unit on a concrete pad. The house is raised up on cinder blocks, as are most down here on the parkway where flooding is frequent, but there's corrugated tin skirting around the bottom of the house, blocking off the crawl space beneath it, except for a three- to four-foot-wide gap near the air conditioner.

But even if I can squeeze my fat ass—made even wider by all the damn gear on my duty belt—sideways through this narrow two-slat gap in the wooden fence without getting shot at, there's a damn chain-link fence just inches beyond the wooden fence on the other side, the top of which doesn't match the height of the wooden fence's middle cross board, and is too far away from the wooden fence to straddle both at once. There's just enough room between the fences to stand with both feet in order to hoist myself over the top bar of the chain link, but it's gonna take some doing. Some contorting, and some luck.

And where the hell *are* those guys, Frank and Bailey, anyway? I could sure use a little cover as I try this, and maybe a shove to squeeze me through. I look back for the cavalry. Nothing.

Here we go. Putting my left foot on the lower horizontal member of the wooden fence, I grab the top cross piece with my left hand and attempt to straddle the middle cross piece with my right foot. This ain't gonna work, not one-handed anyway. I step back down and scan the yard on the other side of the fence one last time, reluctantly holster my Glock, and hoist myself up once more, grabbing the top cross board with both hands. I think for a second maybe I should just forget about squeezing through and climb on up and over the top. But I'd make an easy target at six feet off the ground. Best to keep a low profile.

I step up on the lower cross beam with my left foot, lean away from the fence sideways and feed my right foot and leg through the fence over the middle two-by-four and put my right foot on the bottom horizontal board, then sorta snake my way sideways through the fence, ducking my head sideways to get beneath the top horizontal two-by, my crotch—my 'nads—

just barely clearing the middle cross board and my spare mag pouch on the front of my belt damn-near hanging me up.

Managing somehow to clear the wooden fence, I step into the narrow space between it and the chain-link fence on the other side. I hafta place my feet parallel to the fences—there's not enough room to put them perpendicular—and I grip the top cross bar of the chain link after trying to sorta flatten those damn little triangular links that stick out above the top bar with the jagged-pointed twists sticking up to stab you in the wrist or the heel of your hand, and with a herculean effort I vault myself over the second damned fence into the next backyard.

Before I even get a chance to take a deep breath or to even glance back through the wooden fence gap and wonder, just what the fuck *are* Frank and Bailey doing all this time, a noise and movement to my right captures my attention.

A couple of guys have just come out of the house next door and are climbing into an SUV in the driveway. I bark, "Freeze! Police!" and draw my weapon, striding quickly toward them. They comply, putting their hands up high, their eyes popping. They're on the other side of the east leg of the same chain-link fence I just struggled over. No way am I gonna holster up and vault the thing again. I steal a glance to my left, to the north, and see the gate of the fence is open; that's how the car parked by the AC unit at the back of the house got there.

"Stay right there, keep your hands up and don't move," I command, not taking my eyes or my gun off them as I walk through the open front gate, round the fence, and approach them on the other side. Neither of them looks like a desperado just escaped from Metro after stabbing a cop, but I check the SUV they were getting into to make sure he's not crouched down in there having just ordered them at gunpoint to take him somewhere. The car's clear.

"What's wrong, Officer?" the older one, a guy about my age says. The other one is maybe thirty-five or forty, likely the older guy's son.

"You live here?"

"Yes sir," they reply in unison.

"Let me see some ID with this address on it. What the hell is this address, anyway?"

"F-ff-ffourteen eleven Daytona D-ddrive, three six six oh fffive," the old guy stammers, digging for his wallet.

"Never mind the ID," I bark. "You seen anybody come through here? Through that fence back there, maybe wearing a Metro jail inmate uniform?" (Sometimes they'll strip down a prisoner at HQ and dress him for Metro before transporting him there.)

They both nod vigorously. "We did just see a guy come from back there, don't know 'bout no Metro clothes, though," the older one says, excited. "He run across that yard there toward the front, didn't he, son?"

The younger one says, "Yeah he did, Pops. Musta went on up between them two houses . . . wudn't but a minute ago, was it?"

Old guy, still nodding, says, "He be damn sho in a hurry!"

I turn on my heel and begin jogging back toward the front of the house next door, saying over my shoulder, "Y'all need to go on back inside and lock your doors. And keep your heads down—don't be lookin' out your windows."

Circling around the front of the house, I scan the neighborhood in both directions, looking for somebody—anybody—running away, or crouching behind a parked car or at the corner of a house. Nothing.

But I'm incredibly relieved to see MPD officers, guys I know, some with combat rifles or shotguns, sweeping the area on foot and rolling up in cruisers. Some deputies, too, are rolling up in brown Crown Vics. I see one whom I FTO'd when he was a rookie, before he jumped to the County for better pay and less work. Blue and brown uniforms are saturating Daytona Drive.

I call out and gesture to anyone within earshot, "He came this way, from back there. Neighbors over there saw him runnin' between these two." I crouch to scan under the house next door, also raised up on blocks but with no skirting. I can see clear through the crawl space to daylight on the far side. Nothing.

Continuing on to circle around into the backyard I'd first landed in from the rear fences, I finally catch a glimpse of portly old Frank Black trying to squeeze his way through the two-slat gap in the six-foot wooden fence. He sees me and calls out, "I can't get through!"

"Don't even try, Frank," I yell. "Just come on around the block—we already got guys over here, an' he's prob'ly somewhere on across the street by now." Frank nods and disappears from the two-slat gap.

I spot the gap in the skirting by the AC unit that I'd first seen through the back fence, and throw myself down to the left side of it, behind a cinder-block footing. Lying flat on my belly, I peek around the cinder block and squint into the darkness, trying to force my eyes to penetrate the gloom, my weapon pointed in front of me.

About a dozen or fifteen feet directly ahead, about halfway into the shadowy crawlspace, I perceive what might be a wide pile of rags, maybe old sheets or a bedspread, spread out perpendicular to me in the darkness. It looks to be a tangle of something, maybe even crumpled-up old newspapers, I can't be sure. It's about six feet wide, maybe eight inches or a foot high, about a third the height of the crawl space, and I can't see its depth or anything that might give it definition. I crane my neck and stare hard, trying to discern what it is I'm looking at. There's just not enough light coming in from behind me through this three-foot-high, four-foot-wide opening in the tin skirting.

The winter sun is waning and the air has turned brisk. Downtown they're shutting the traffic down on Government Street, starting to form up the parade by the Civic Center: towing cars whose drivers have failed to heed the No Parking–Parade Route signs, lining up the marching bands and the floats, unloading the PD and SO Mounted Units; the vendors of funnel cakes and chicken on a stick are heating up their deep friers, the masker-flaskers are mounting their floats.

As I lay on my belly in the weeds, my eyes adjust slightly, and I can make out other cinder-block pillars spaced in rows at uniform intervals receding under the house into the dark, and I see narrow slits of light at the far-forward right corner, where the skirting is apparently composed of loosely laid bricks or blocks instead of long tin sheets, but the light there does little more than silhouette the unevenly stacked bricks. It does nothing to diminish the blackness that shrouds the center of the crawl space.

I wiggle back to my left, fully behind the cinder-block footing, and pull out my Streamlight, gripping it up near the neck where the on-button is with my left hand, my right hand still filled with Glock.

Behind the cinder block I roll onto my right hip and crook my left knee forward as a counterbalance to prevent rolling over to the right, out from behind the cover of the cinder block. I press my left forearm firmly against the cinder block about forehead high, further stabilizing me.

This is awkward, to say the least. And painful, for a guy with a right shoulder that's been frozen since high school, severely limiting that arm's upward and lateral range of motion. I work the Streamlight's lens around the corner of the cinder block with my left hand, lining it up parallel with the business end of the Glock, and then sorta scooch to the right and rock up onto my right elbow in order to see around the cinder block.

My right hand is now gripping the Glock at a sideways cant—but not as the gangsta boys do in the movies, thumb down and knuckles up, but the opposite, since I'm leaning hard onto my right elbow. Then I press the barrel-mounted on-button of the light.

Three or four ear-splitting cracks fill the air, and I roll back to my left for cover, thinking, what the fuck? Did that just come from under the house? I never even saw the muzzle flashes, much less whatever my Streamlight's beam may have revealed.

But there's not any doubt in my mind. That wasn't some old pile of dirty sheets. That was It. This is the Shit. And it just got real. The bastard saw my light and tried to take me out.

Guys are yelling at me, "Mark, pull back! Get outta there, Mark!" Nice of 'em, I think. Glad they're looking out for me, but I'm not real eager to move in any direction at the moment. The tin skirting to the left of the cinder-block stack isn't gonna stop a round. I'm best off laying right here behind this stack. I make myself real skinny and consider sticking the Glock around the corner to return fire blind. Suppression fire, I think they call it in the war movies. I could lay down a little suppression fire, just to rattle the sonofabitch a little, make him slither around on his belly in the dark like the damn serpent he is. I might even get lucky and sting the little snake, or at least brush him back long enough to push away from this narrow cinder block and get the hell outta here.

I raise my weapon to poke it around the corner and notice the raggedy, torn-up bottom of the Glock's grip. It's *all* gnarled up, *bad*, like it's been danced all over by a really dull drill press or hit by a . . . a *what*? I tip the barrel up and discover that the base plate of my magazine has been blown clean off. It has disappeared, along with—shit!—all my ammo!

All my bullets have fallen out. I look up into the empty magazine. Nary a round to be seen. I look on the ground and see a couple bullets among the blades of grass just a few inches into the line of fire. I sure as hell am not gonna try to reach over there and scratch around in the grass for them.

Oh well, I think. No worries. Things could be worse. I could have been wearing my usual civilian duds and I'd be shit outta luck. But not today. I'm in *uniform!* Fully equipped! Got two more full mags hangin' on my blessed belt! Thirty rounds, comin' at ya, muhfucka! Not countin' the one already in the pipe with your name on it!

If I could only get this damn empty mag out of the Glock, to replace it with a full one. I tug and twist, and pinch, and pry, and try to wiggle, then slap the useless, ruined, empty piece a shit out of the bottom of the grip, but hell. It's hopeless. FUBAR. I'm screwed.

There is still the one round in the chamber, thank God. Better not waste it in a blind pop around the cinder block. What if he's been crawling up this way and comes out blazing? At least I'd have one chance to drill him when his head sticks out of his dark lair. Better hold what I got and just get *real* skinny and push straight back an inch at a time, then make a run for it.

And that's exactly what I do. When I get far enough back from the house that I'm past the back side of the AC unit on the other side of the gap in the skirting, I draw my legs up under my chest and spring sideways over the line of fire and take cover on the ground behind the AC.

For about thirty seconds, anyway. Just until I realize the AC is really no better cover than the corrugated tin skirting. It's just a mostly empty, flimsy sheet metal box with a whole bunch of horizontal vent slits on every side; it may actually be *worse* cover than the tin skirting: it's already perforated. Whatever (and wherever) all those thicker mechanical things are inside the AC cowling, I don't know if they can stop a bullet.

Guys are still yelling at me to "Get better cover! Pull back!" and I decide that's what I need to do, so I roll over and spring back to the rear of the car parked next to the AC. Of course I'm not really safe lying on the ground, so I sorta crouch behind the trunk, thinking, it's only my feet and ankles at risk, and he'd need to be a pretty damn good or lucky shot to get me in the ankle.

But then I think of the base plate of my magazine that he blew all to smithereens, and I hightail it on outta there, back to the next yard over, behind the wheels of that SUV I had cleared before terrorizing the father and son setting out on some errands together, just minutes—but what now seems a lifetime—ago.

At a far safer distance, behind much better cover, with guys I know and trust who have working firearms and lots and lots of bullets, including armor-piercing combat rifle rounds, and grenades, and God only knows what all else, I take a knee next to none other than Captain Darby. Way back in the day, Darby had been my very first sergeant out of the academy, back when ol' Portly Porter was my first FTO, up in the Third. Three or four other guys are in the carport there, lined up along the rear wall of the house and crouching with me behind the wheels of the SUV.

Darby looks behind him, and I follow his eyes to see who he's looking at. To my surprise, it's the chief. But it shouldn't be a surprise, since this is a pretty major incident, and he's known to be out of the office a lot, riding around. I've seen him down this way several times. He lives down here off the parkway, in fact, right smack in the middle of my beats, not a mile from here. And besides, this is a cop convention. There's gotta be a hundred cops in a double perimeter around us, and I think I hear a helicopter circling above.

I nod at the chief, who doesn't acknowledge. He's looking very intently at Darby, kneeling next to me. I look back at Darby in time to see his eyes locked with the chief's. Darby nods slightly, signaling some unspoken but understood accord between them.

Then Darby speaks to me. "Good job finding him, Mark, but what the fuck took ya so long to get outta the line a fire? Could'ncha hear me and everybody yellin' atcha to pull back? We got plenty a firepower here, we can fuckin' *strafe* the blocks right out from under that house and bury him with it, but we couldn't do a fuckin' thing with you in the way."

"Sorry, Cap, but I got a little confused. My damn gun's all blown up." I show him. "All my rounds fell out, but I can't switch out for a fresh mag." I look around at the others nearby. "Anybody here got an extra gun for me? How 'bout one a you guys with rifles—gimme a Glock."

Captain Darby's looking in disbelief at the gnarled-up grip and the bottomless mag, then looks at me. "Are you all right? Are you hit? You been hit, Mark, lookit all that blood on your hand. No, the other one," he says. I had inspected my gun hand, figuring I must have caught a little shrapnel when my gun got hit. But that hand's clean. Then I see the thick red smear down my left palm. I wipe the blood off, looking for the wound, thinking I probably just stabbed myself in the hand on one of those jagged, spikey twisty things at the top of the chain-link fence.

But there's no puncture or tear on my left hand. I pull back my sleeve and realize the blood on my hand has run down from somewhere higher up my arm. I unbutton the cuff and start rolling it up my arm, and there's more blood, all over my arm, but still no wound I can see, although I now feel a kind of burn, or pinch, up past my elbow, but it's on the *back* side, the underside of my arm.

This makes zero sense to me, and I keep peeling back the sleeve higher until Captain Darby says, "Stop. Don't go any farther. There's a big bloody flap of skin you might pull off. Just leave it alone, Mark." Then, turning to the guys at the rear of the carport, he yells, "I need somebody to get Mark to an ambulance. He's been hit."

A couple guys I've worked with come toward me, but I wave them off. "Nah, it's nothing. Just a little scratch, prob'ly just snagged myself on one a those fences over there. Somebody just give me a damn gun."

Darby shakes his head at me and tells the guys to walk me out to the Rescue wagon on D.I.P. because Daytona Drive's so clogged with cruisers they'll never get any closer.

"Ahh, come on, Captain. Seriously. I'm fine."

"You're not fine, you're hit, and we don't know for sure how bad. Now, go with Fuller and Simmons. That's an order. I'm done fuckin' around with you."

At University of South Alabama Hospital's ER trauma center (after a long, maddening ride through streets clogged with Mardi Gras crowds), they've got my shirt off and a couple of doctors and a nurse are inspecting my upper left arm. The senior doc remembers me from a visit to the ER several years ago that I don't immediately recall. He tells the younger doc about it, trying to prod my memory.

"He and another officer came in with a prisoner to get checked before taking him on to Metro," he says. "I think it was a domestic you had arrested him for, and he had fought you," he adds helpfully.

"Well that really narrows it down, Doc."

"The prisoner only had a few scrapes and bruises, but I remember thinking you two looked like you'd gotten the worst of it because you were both covered in mud from head to toe," he says, and then I remember, but too late to cut him off, "and you had accidentally tased your partner in the fight."

"Yeah, that was me and LD Jones," I say. "Thanks for the memory, Doc."

They both have a chuckle, then he assures me that there's no real damage, it's just a flesh wound, I'm very lucky, and he'll be back to sew me up after Nurse Betty cleans out the wound and preps it for stitching.

Nurse Betty steps up, starts laying out bandages and sponges and little tools on a tray next to the bed, and says, "Have you called your wife yet?

Believe me, you don't want her to hear about this first on TV or anywhere else."

"You get really crappy cell signals in here, as I recall. Usually I can't get out at all from back in here."

"Yeah, it's something to do with all the equipment, they say. But you really need to let her know. Would you like me to call her for you?"

"Nah, they said this wouldn't take long, I'll just wait till you're done, and call her when I can get back outside for a good signal."

"You're making a big mistake, Detective. What time is it now? A little after five? Now, you know, she's probably on her way home from. . . . Does she work?"

"She works for the County Commission, at Government Plaza."

"Oh Lordy, the poor thing's probably stuck downtown in all that Mardi Gras mess, and you know she's gonna be listening to the news on her car radio. Trust me on this, Detective, you definitely don't want her to hear about all this, even if they don't say your name over the air, am I right? Just sayin'."

She's right. Nancy will shit a brick if she even suspects I'm anywhere near this cluster. "Yeah, I better not wait. How 'bout you just wheel me out closer to the door, or to a landline?"

She laughs and maneuvers my left arm up and back to get a better angle for scrubbing it or picking dirt out of it or whatever she's doing.

"Now, this might sting a little, or kinda burn," she says, not even acknowledging my request. "We'll be giving you a local in just a minute, honey, so it won't hurt for long."

"Oh, all right, I'll give it a try." I dig my phone out of my pocket and hit Aaanancell, the first one in my contact list. To my surprise, I get through, though it's breaking up.

"Mark?"

"Hey, first of all, I'm really okay, but—"

"Mark? You're breakin' up. You're really what? Can you hear me?

I raise my voice, as if yelling will strengthen my faulty signal. "Hey, I'm in a dead spot, but I'm okay . . . Nancy? You hear me?"

"Whaddayou me . . . ur . . . kay . . . at 'eans you're not . . . r . . . y . . . udn't . . . e 'alling . . . 'ere. R . . . ou?"

"Nancy, listen, listen to me, don't talk. I'm at USA ER, but it's no big . . . *Nancy*, can you hear me?"

Nurse Betty can take it no longer. She snatches my cell from me and walks out saying, "Oh for heaven's sake, I told you to let me do it for you. Lord only knows what she heard or what she thinks." Her voice fades as she hurries down the hall to get out to a clear signal before the call's dropped. "I just hope you didn't go and make the poor thing have a wreck."

By the time Nancy arrives, she *is* a wreck. She walks into my bay while I'm yukking it up with my sarge, my captain, the chief, and hizzonner the mayor. I'm feeling sorta buzzed and manic anyway, from the excitement of it all, I guess. It's definitely a giddy kind of high when it starts to sink in that you've cheated Death (yet again, in my case) and dodged a really close one; add to this the visiting Rank and Royalty, and it's all gone like a pop bottle rocket straight to my already volatile ego, and Whammo! It's like I've bumped a couple lines of quality flake and chased it with a slash of Jim Beam, or something.

But then shit gets real. The wisecracks and joking stop when my poor, worried, scared sweetheart enters the room panicked and fearing the worst. She walks right on in oblivious to all the brass and hizzonner, tears already streaking her pretty face, and when our eyes meet there's this moment of stunned silence and then the tears really start flowing and she comes to me, and as abruptly as my jovial banter stopped, my own eyes overflow. I'm a weepy damn pushover anyway, but I'm absolutely without defense when I see her cry. We both just choke out unintelligible sounds to each other, helpless to do otherwise, and for a few moments the rest of the world melts away.

28

Face of Fury, Search for Sense

Two police officers are shot every day in the United States. Every 54 hours somewhere in America a law enforcement officer dies in service to his community.
—Mobile Police Academy

The world reappears when Sarge clears his throat. "We'll be getting out of the way here, Mark," he says. The captain, the chief, and the mayor all smile and nod their good-byes to us.

"Wait a second, Sarge, how's the other guy? The one who got cut?"

Their smiles vanish. "He didn't make it," Sarge says, his head slightly lowered. I look to the captain, the chief, the mayor, and only then realize they hadn't rushed to the hospital to check on me.

"Oh my God," Nancy says softly.

"What? He *died?*" I scan their faces, back and forth. "I can't believe it! Who is it?"

"Steven Green," Sarge says. "He's in the Fifth. Only been on a little over a year."

"But I thought he was just cut, they just said signal 17 on the radio, not 19! I had no idea. Why couldn't they save him? I don't believe it. Where'd he get—"

"In the neck," Sarge says. "Bled out at Metro. There wasn't anything they could do."

"He has a wife and two young kids," Captain adds.

My wound tightly stitched, they wheel me to the ER door before they let me stand, and discharge me to Nancy's custody and care. Just before I step out the door, Sarge informs me that I have to surrender my weapon to him, even though I haven't fired a shot.

"It's procedure," he says. "ID has to examine and log in the weapons of everyone involved at the scene."

It doesn't make any sense to me, but I pull my weapon and lock the slide back, catching the ejected live round. I hand the single bullet and the now-safe Glock to Sarge. "Magazine's empty, what's left of it."

He looks at the torn-up grip and the gaping, mangled magazine. "Shit," he says. "They'll issue you a new Glock till they're done with this one. But I doubt you'll want this one back, 'cept maybe as a souvenir."

Nancy and I are walking to her car, when Sarge approaches from across the parking lot. He points to my empty holster.

"You want some protection until you can pick up your loaner? There were some of his family tryin' to bust through the perimeter down the parkway, making all kinds of noise and threats. I got something you can borrow if you need it."

"Sure," I say.

Out of the oversize pocket of his department-issue winter jacket, Sarge produces a holstered, chrome Smith & Wesson .357.

I feel honored. "Is this your backup gun, Sarge?"

"It sure's hell ain't my throw-down," he deadpans.

"Damn, Sarge, I don't wanna take your backup."

"Don't worry about it. I got others. Keep it as long as you need it, man."

Back home, we're greeted by my daughter, Kate, and her husband, Dave. When she sees me walk into the kitchen she hugs me tight and cries, just as her mother had, producing the same reaction in me that her mother had.

My cell rings, and of all people, it's Mariah, my ex-whore snitch, and she's crying, too.

"Oh, Detective Johnson! I just saw your picture on the TV and I was so scared! Are you all right? They said you were wounded and that other officer is dead!"

"I'm fine, Mariah, thanks for calling, but I've gotta get off now. I'm fine. I'll talk to you later."

There's a knock at the door. It's Sarge.

"If you're up to it, they want you back at the scene. Internal Affairs wants to get a statement from you while it's still fresh in your mind." He turns to Nancy and Kate. "Shouldn't take long, and I'll bring him right back," he says.

Fifteen minutes later we arrive back at the scene. It's almost 8 p.m. and cold. The house and its front, back, and side yards are floodlit like Friday night football. Everybody's breath is visible, except for Lawrence Wallace's. They've just pulled his body from under the house. I walk up close and bend over to get a good look at the man who had savagely thrust a shank into the throat of Officer Steven Green and tried to shoot me in the head from a distance of a dozen feet as I had peered blindly into his darkness.

It had been a stalemated siege for more than two hours. Two Ferret projectiles were fired to blow openings in the loosely stacked bricks skirting the northeast corner of the crawl space. Twenty-five tear-gas cartridges were fired under the house, and eight gas grenades were lobbed in. Multiple rounds of 12-gauge tactical slugs and .223 assault rounds were fired. But there had been no surrender. Nothing had emerged from underneath the house except gunfire. There had been several lulls, some as long as a half hour, interrupted by short, aimless bursts from underneath the house. At about the ninety-minute mark, two take-down dogs were sent in, only to return moments later without their quarry. Finally, two heavily armored tactical officers with ballistic shields and assault rifles crawled through the breached brick skirting on the east side of the house. At the north edge of the crawl space, beneath the middle of the front of the house, their barrel-mounted light beams revealed a crudely fashioned barricade composed of discarded lumber and scraps of corrugated tin. Using the rear of the concrete front steps to cover his back, he had burrowed behind this makeshift scrap-barricade to stage his last stand. He fired once at the tactical officers, who returned fired with a sustained volley, peppering the scrap metal and plywood. Then there were no more shots. They waited another fifteen minutes for any sign or sound of movement, then crawled on in and dragged him out from under the bullet-riddled house at 1413 Daytona Drive.

He lies on his back, shirtless and still, his brown skin mottled and smudged with the grayish clay soil of his earthen nest beneath the house. Though it's too soon for rigor mortis to stiffen his features, Lawrence Wallace Jr.'s face is frozen in a fierce scowl, his teeth bared, his brow furrowed, his empty eyes narrowed to slits. His countenance has a feral look to it, a face contorted

291

by fury, or pain. Or both. His upper torso, arms, and head are riddled with entry wounds, most of which are neat, nearly bloodless, perfectly round, and smaller than a dime. I stop counting at twenty. Somebody standing next to me points out the broken white band of adhesive tape on his upper left bicep. There's an inch-wide gap in the band on the inside of the upper arm.

"I'm guessin' that's where he had the blade that he used on Green." It's Hampton, one of the ID guys.

"But how'd he get outta the cuff, I wonder?"

"They found a cuff key in the backseat of Green's car. Musta had it in his sock or shoe and used it on the way to Metro."

I gaze once more at the terrible fixed grimace looking up at me, trying to interpret its meaning, the emotion behind it. It could be hatred, or defiance, or horror. Whatever it is, it's not feigned. It's not playacting. It's real. And I'll never forget it.

Back at work the following Monday morning, Devin, Lusty, and Earl are amazed that I don't milk the moment for at least a week, whether or not my injury is minor.

Devin calls his wife when I arrive. "Guess who just walked into our office, Honey? The man, the legend, right here in our midst. Who else do we know gets shot on a Friday and shows up Monday morning like nothing happened?"

Lusty wants to see the wound. It's still taped and bandaged up, so I show him a picture Nancy took with her cell phone at the hospital before they sewed it up. "Oh, that's not so bad," Lopez says. "Looks kinda like a little vagina, but with thicker meat flaps, y'know? Take a look, Earl, and tell me it doesn't remind you of pussy."

"Jeez, Lusty. Do you have, like, sexual Tourette's, or something?" Earl says.

"I'm just sayin'," Lusty says, then turns to me. "I gotta ask you something though, and don't take offense, but—"

"Lusty, after working with you, nothing offends me anymore."

"Okay. We all heard about the bottom of your mag bein' blown off, and all you had left was the one chambered round. But you were *right there*, man! Just a few feet away, closer than anybody else. You had the best shot. And the scumbag had just *killed a cop*, man."

"Nobody knew Green was dead till after it was all over," Earl interjects.

Lusty brushes Earl off and leans into me, the way I've seen him do with a suspect. "Yeah, right, but you *did* know that the cocksucker had just tried to kill *you*, in fact he'd just carved that split into your arm."

"He didn't even know he'd been hit, Lusty, till Captain Darby saw the blood on his hand. I was right there—you were somewhere on the outer perimeter. Quit yappin' about shit you know nu'n about, dickhead," Devin interjects.

"Y'all don't hafta keep answering for me," I say to Earl and Devin. "Lusty's got a good question. Why didn't I just lean around that cinder block and pop the shithead at close range, with my one round? It woulda been an easy shot, and we never woulda had that standoff. Even if I'd only wounded him, or missed, it woulda given him something to think about, a taste of his own medicine. He mighta surrendered. Believe me, I keep asking myself that, too."

"But I know you wouldn'a missed, man," Lusty says. "I been with you at the range. You'da taken him out, one shot. Bam. And you could be at Tattoo Town right now getting a teardrop on your cheekbone! Most of us will never get that chance, man."

"You're right, Lusty. It was a once-in-a-lifetime chance to kill a man, and one who needed killin'."

"Target acquisition, though!" Earl says. "The first rule of shooting."

"Yeah, Lusty," Devin says. "We can't just spray-and-pray like the thugs do. You know we gotta acquire before we fire—be sure of our target—and it was dark as sin up under that house. You couldn't see shit," Devin says, turning to me. "You couldn't be sure where he was, and for all you knew he coulda dragged a hostage up under there with him. And what if you fired and missed, what's behind him? Where would that bullet end up? You could hit a kid riding by on a bicycle, or another cop." Devin turns back to Lusty. "He only had one round and couldn't get good target acquisition, shithead. Quit Monday-mornin'quarterbackin'."

"All that's true," I say. "But to tell the truth, I didn't even consider any of that. Never thought he might have a hostage, never considered target acquisition or unintended victims. I kinda wish now I *had* squeezed off that one round, but I decided not to, and I'm not sure why. I remember thinking maybe I should save it in case I really need it, like if he comes out at me. And I knew the place was already swarming with cops, and everybody was yelling, "Pull back!" so I did. Simple as that. Figured, Let the guys with bigger guns and more bullets take it from here, my work is done."

Lusty has no more questions, apparently, which is good, because I'm sure Devin and Earl are out of answers by now. And I sure as hell don't have any answers. In fact, I have more questions, myself. But I'm not about to give voice to them.

"Have they set the day for Green's wake and funeral yet?" I ask.

"The wake's set for Thursday at 1700 at Radney's on Dauphin," Devin says. "Then the funeral's at ten Friday at his church in Prichard, and then the procession from there all the way out to Serenity Gardens, practically to the Mississippi line," Devin says.

"I'll be glad when that's over," I say.

"We'll all be happy to get that behind us," Earl says.

Cop funerals are big deals. Every state and local elected official, district attorney and judge, every chief and sheriff in the region, and hundreds of officers—including many from jurisdictions across the country—will be in attendance. Interstate highways (in this case, I-65 and I-10) will be shut down for the procession. The fire department will cross the fully extended ladders of two trucks over the highway to suspend a huge American flag. Strangers shake your hand and thank you for your service. The roads and overpasses are lined with officers saluting and well-wishers waving flags. And ordinarily stoic men are fighting back tears.

I've attended three such funerals before this one. They are emotionally draining, whether you personally know the departed or not. By the time the bagpipes play and the rifles crack and the color guard presents the folded flag to the widow, you're ready to spend the next couple days in bed, or drunk. Or drunk in bed. But of course, you don't. You report for duty. And as it happens for this one, duty means regular assignments, plus five or six more hours of Mardi Gras parade detail.

About four or five days after we put Green in the ground, I'm reporting to parade-duty roll call at Ladd Stadium as usual, after a full day of work, and Joey Broder, a detective from the Fourth Precinct grabs me.

"There he is! My hero! How's it feel to make the top-ten Most Wanted by the Black Foot Soldiers, Mark? I'll make that web page into your new screen saver, if you haven't already, man! I mean, that's like, better than a medal."

"Huh? The Black Foot who? What the hell you talking about, Joey?"

"Oh, man, you mean you haven't seen it yet? Wow! You're famous! Check this out, man." Broder pulls up the website on his iPhone and shows it to me. There's a full color portrait of the dead cop-killer Lawrence Wallace on the left side, and one of me, taken from the MPD website on the right side. Between us, over a background of a burning American flag, inch-tall flaming lettering declares, "FUCK racist mobile police regime terrorist MARK JOHNSON. —Mobile Black Foot Soldiers."

"I think it's a pretty good likeness. You got your Dirty Harry look on," Joey says. "Seriously, man: make it into a screen saver for the office. Or have it blown up into a poster, y'know, suitable for framing? I'm thinking maybe twenty-four by thirty-six?"

I read the copy below the blazing likenesses of Wallace and me:

Sunday, February 5, 2012
(BREAKING) Was officer Steven Green Acting White? Mobile Black Foot Soldiers praise Brother & Activist Lawrence Wallace in DARING Dollar General Reparations Protest, Condemn Green's Observance of "White Laws" denying Rights to Reparations; (PLUS) Racist Mobile Police Regime Terrorist Mark Johnson POPPED, Anti-Recovery Vigil Planned. "Although we know Johnson has been released from the hospital, let us continue our prayers against him, his family & his kind for the racial terrorism we face from him & his kind." —Mobile Black Foot Soldier Moses Abernathy.

I look from Joey's iPhone screen to him, a little pissed. "You are one sick motherfucker, Broder. Have your laughs about me, but you shouldna put Green in it. That's really poor taste."

"What? I didn't do this! You think I had nothing to do last week with the funeral and Mardi Gras and everything, so I just decide to fuck around on the Internet and invent the Black Foot Soldiers? This is real! Kimbrough over in the Fifth is the one who saw it first, and he showed it to me, and everybody's seen it. Check it out yourself, old man. You're not the only white cop in a gunfight they wanna burn down. They got the same kinda shit on cops all over the country."

I look at the iPhone screen again and scroll down. It continues:

*Mobile Black Foot Soldiers are reportedly mourning the loss of repa-
rations protester Lawrence Wallace as well as the loss of Mobile Police
Officer Steven Green. Green was reportedly stabbed to death by Wallace
after Green arrested him during an alleged reparations protest at a
Dollar General on North Schillinger. Many local soldiers now suspect
Wallace believed Green was acting white by attempting to arrest him in
a protest against the historically racist Dollar General Company.*
    (Developing Story)

After I get my parade assignment, I leave roll call and swing by the
precinct to log on. Sure enough, it's there, and as Joey said, they've got the
same kind of crap about wounded and slain white cops from all over the
country. I print out a couple hard copies of the Fuck Mark Johnson page
and call my old patrol buddy Richard Crudup who's in Intelligence now
and ask him where his parade post is. He's working an undercover, plainclothes unit that mingles in crowds and busts little gangster wannabes for
lighting up blunts or brandishing guns along the parade route. When I get
to his corner at Broad and Springhill, I show him the Black Foot Soldier
hard copy. He hasn't seen it yet either, has never heard of the Black Foot
Soldiers, but promises to run it through their databases and get back to me
in a day or two.

"It's probably bullshit, Mark. A made-up group by some racist nutjob
with a laptop and lotsa time on his hands. I wouldn't sweat it," he says.
"On the other hand," he adds (because he's Crudup, and he's like this),
"remember: consider all scenarios, watch your six, and stay in Condition
Yellow, even when off duty. And you might think about changing up your
route to and from work..."

"Thanks, Richard. You're such a comfort." I've known him since my
rookie days on third squad patrol at the First. Crudup's one of those cops
who is always vigilant, studies all the cop and gun magazines, goes to the
range every weekend. He and Balzer used to forty up with me when I was
right out of the academy during the slow, early morning hours of night
shift at Craighead (called Crackhead by Balzer) Elementary School and
he would drill me with scenarios: you've been shot in the gun hand, your
weapon's still holstered, and the bad guy's approaching to finish the job.
Quick, what do you do? (For that one, he taught me how to draw my gun
cross-body with my left hand, which places the weapon upside down in the
hand when drawn, but still fireable with decent accuracy when held upside

down with the weak hand, as long as you know how to do it.) They don't teach you that stuff in the academy, or at the range.

So it's at once comforting and a little disconcerting to have Richard looking into the Black Foot Soldiers for me.

Meantime, I'm more than a little jumpy. The next morning, after I've shaved, showered, dressed, and started the coffee, I go out like always to fetch the morning *Press Register* to read over a hot black cup. It's a little after 5 a.m., still dark, and cold. I notice an unfamiliar vehicle idling in my neighbor's driveway, directly across the street. I stop in my tracks and study the car, which doesn't look like my neighbor's, but the windshield is fogged up so I can't really make out who's sitting in it. My neighbor's never up this early, either. And what's he doing just sitting there in his own driveway, in somebody else's car?

I draw my weapon and dive for cover, rolling behind the azalea bed in my front yard. There is no blaze of assault rifle fire. Slowly I rise, Glock aimed at the dark blur behind the steering wheel, and command, "Get out of the car and let me see your hands!"

A long few seconds pass, and I'm wishing I had my radio to call for backup, but it's still on the charger in the house. I'm thinking, this azalea bush doesn't exactly qualify as "cover," and I decide I can drop back to the brick wall by my front door if it comes to that, when the car door opens, and old white-haired, retired Jim McClanahan slowly gets out, his hands in the air, and says, "What's going on, Mark?"

A couple days later, Richard tells me his first hunch was right. Black Foot Soldiers is a lone nutjob, not a network. It's a guy known to local police in Trenton, New Jersey, who does not represent any threat, at least not all the way down here in Mobile.

While this news makes it less traumatic to fetch the morning paper (for me as well as Jim across the street), it has no effect on the recurrent nightmares disturbing my sleep. I keep dreaming of losing my ammo as bad guys are closing in, then I wake up with a jolt. I doubt even Richard has a solution for that scenario.

After another week of fourteen-hour Mardi Gras days and sleepless nights, I call a friend of Nancy's, a woman she knows from being on the symphony board with her, who used to be a contract psychologist for a large metropolitan police department and still consults for departments around the country. (My department's free mental health counseling is unable to book me an appointment sooner than forty-five days out. Plus I don't trust them to keep my business confidential.)

On a moment's notice, Nancy's friend Leah tells me to come on over for coffee. We settle with steaming lattes on her back deck overlooking Rabbit Creek, and she's smart. With minimal chitchat and a sixty-second summary from me of the Metro murder, the siege, sleepless nights, and unformed questions since, Leah suggests I talk to somebody I trust and respect who's "been there": another cop who's survived a gunfight involving a fatality.

When I get back to the precinct, I ask Devin, who knows everybody in the department, and whose judgment and discretion I trust. He names a few guys who have been in gunfights, then eliminates them one by one for various reasons (he's an asshole, he's a bad drunk, he's stupid) until he snaps his fingers and says, "Pete Parsons. He was in that nightclub shoot-out up in the Third eight or ten years ago. He's a great guy, really 10-8. Give Pete a call."

Parsons and I meet for lunch at a Denny's. He's early forties, been a cop nearly twenty years (his first and only job, right out of the army and college) with two grown kids and an intact marriage to the same woman all these years. The latter is almost unheard of among cops. I appreciate Devin's wisdom in recommending Parsons to me.

Parsons tells me his story, which is a harrowing one: guy goes into an after-hours club, takes ex-girlfriend, her new boyfriend, the bartender, and a couple of random customers hostage at gunpoint. Begins killing people. Pete's the second in a four-man tactical stack that storms the club. Bad guy's waiting for them, up high—standing on a table, peeking over an interior privacy wall just past the front door. The tac stack fails to look high—and for the bad guy it's like shooting fish in a barrel. They eventually killed the shooter without further loss of life, but the first tac officer was wounded so badly, it ended his career, although he survived. Pete was hit in four places, and it took most of a year before he was back on duty.

Parsons credits his wife, family, pastor, and a few close friends (including a couple of cops) with pulling him through it. In addition to the months of physical therapy, there was the PTSD to deal with: the nightmares, the second-guessing, the survivors' guilt, the paranoia that we've all heard about. He assures me there's no shame in seeing a shrink and strongly recommends pastoral guidance. He gives me his pastor's name and number.

"But the best thing for me was what we're doing here, right now. I talked to guys who had been there. And lemme tell ya, unless you been there, you just don't know. The biggest thing I struggled with was when all the other cops—who had never been in a firefight themselves, either in the military or on the streets—would come up to me and say, 'Man, why didn't you return fire? If I'da been there, I'da emptied my magazine at him.'

"The fact is, I was a little preoccupied. Andy Andrews, the first guy in, when he got hit he fell back into me, then I got hit, and I'm bumping into Cotton behind me, and we're all in this narrow passage and none of us knows where the fire is coming from, we have no clue he's shooting down on us from above, we're just scrambling backwards for cover, dragging Andrews with us. For a while, I go through all that with guys who'd ask, and they're all 'Well why didn't you toss a flash bang?' or 'I woulda done this,' or 'I woulda done that,' and finally I just got to the point where I say, 'Well that's all fine and good, but brother, *you weren't there*,' and I just walk away."

That's exactly what I need to hear.

Fat Tuesday finally arrives and the season of wretched excess, of folly's triumph over death, staggers off to oblivion for another year. Kate and David are over for supper, and David takes his leave to head out for one of his meetings. He's also in recovery, although from a slightly different shade of fatal compulsion from my own.

"Want some company? I'm a little short on meetings myself, with all that damn parade duty."

"Heck yeah, Paw 'n' law. Come ahead on!"

En route to his meeting, located in the heart of Prichard, David asks, "So how are ya doin', *really?* I can't even imagine what all this has been like for you."

I start to minimize, to give him my rote response, the no-big-deal, I'm-good-to-go spiel, but stop. He deserves more; he knows bullshit when he hears it.

"To tell the truth, David, I've realized that I don't really know anything, for sure. I can't make any sense of it all. I didn't even know the cop who died. Met his wife and kids at the wake, and she recognizes me from the news. 'You're the one who found him, who got wounded,' she says to me. 'Thank you,' she says. With all she's dealing with, she thanks me. For what?

"And I keep picturing the face of that kid. It, like, haunts me. The kid slit a cop's throat and then tried to shoot me with the dead cop's gun. I mean, what the fuck's up with that? So I pull up his rap sheet: Lawrence Wallace Jr., twenty years old. He wasn't any badass gangbanger, that's for sure. Hell, *I've* been arrested more than he'd been. There's nothing in his jacket but a couple of minor drug charges: a weed second and a controlled substance—probably a rock or a pill—and that was it. No violence at all, at least on paper. I'm totally baffled. What happened to him? Did he just snap that day? I mean, what a bizarre way to rob a Dollar store! He probably coulda gotten a deal, it was so weird: probation and mandatory headshrinking. But then, at Metro, he slashes a cop's throat? The sheer fucking brutality of it makes me sick. But even after that, when he crashes through the door with the cruiser, he couldn't have known the cop was dead.

"So then, finally, under that house down the parkway, why didn't he just surrender when I lit him up? It still wasn't too late. He'd do some time, for sure, but he'd maybe get youthful offender, or plea insanity, get some kinda deal, and he'd get out eventually, and he'd be notorious, if that's what he's after. Was it a death-by-cop thing? Planned out all along? I seriously doubt he planned on dying like a trapped rat, under that house."

David and I roll off the interstate onto Wilson Avenue in silence.

"I don't know, David. My only answer to your question is, I got no answers. I don't know *jack*, other than I sure's hell need a meeting."

David makes no reply. I'm not even certain he's been listening. He seems to be trying to figure something out.

It's a rundown meeting hall in a former retail store on a rundown main street in the poorest community of one of the poorest states in the nation. Even the streetlights are busted. David and I are the only white faces in a rough-looking crowd of thirty or so people gathering to share their experience, strength, and hope in the face of seemingly insurmountable odds. I recognize a couple of familiar faces, "double winners" who occasionally attend the meetings I do, as well as this one. Though we're all applying essentially the same remediating steps to our own particular brand of insanity, this meeting is run a little differently from mine. Rather than people taking turns, or speaking spontaneously, a meeting chairman calls on them to speak. I'm glad for that, because I realize early on that I likely won't be called on to speak, and that's good. I feel depleted, like I got nothing to offer tonight. I just wanna sit back and soak up some gritty, practical, hard-fought Truth.

The chairman is calling on people he knows, people with some long-term, quality clean time. There's some Wisdom in this group. As the end of the hour draws near, the chairman calls on David, sitting right next to me.

"I've had it driven home to me in recent days just how fucking blood-thirsty our disease really is," he begins. "It is pure evil. It wants us dead." People voice their accord: "Yes!" "Uh-huhh." "Das right!"

David continues, his voice growing thick. "This disease will stop at nothing to inflict pain and suffering on me and whoever's around me. It doesn't give a damn who's in the way, who gets caught in the cross fire."

"Tell it, brother!"

"This disease almost killed . . . a member of my own family . . . just a few days ago," David says. "He's sitting right here beside me."

I'm thinking, that's a bit of a stretch, Dave. But I keep listening.

"We were talking on the way over here, and he said a name, and it sounded familiar to me. Just a few minutes ago I checked my phone list, and there it is. He's in my *fucking phone!*" David's choking now, but soldiers on. "He's a guy you all know, used to come to *this meeting*. He's in my phone 'cause he would call me for rides to this meeting. He's *one of us*. And he cut a guy's throat and tried to shoot my father-in-law! This disease is a *motherfucker!*"

Several months have passed now, and I've talked to the guys at the Dollar store who made the arrest, to each detective who talked to him, to the people at Metro who witnessed the slashing and the escape, and to the tactical guys who went under the house to finish him off. I've even grilled David about how good a program the kid seemed to be working: How much clean time did he have? What was his drug of choice? Did he have a sponsor? Was he hitting a lot of meetings? What step was he on? I've read and reread all the police reports, including the tox report from Forensics that says that traces of marijuana and opiate derivatives were in his blood. Probably a Lortab or a Z bar, I'm guessing. Not enough for a sudden psychotic break.

Something's still eating at me, something I can't even name.

I decide the only remaining place to get a clue is from his family. On a rainy late spring afternoon, I find the auto repair shop owned by the father of Lawrence Wallace, way out in west Mobile. At the bottom of the business sign is the proclamation "Jesus Loves You." The shop is just a stone's throw from the Dollar store.

It's a stand-alone shop, one of those all-metal prefab buildings, with a small office at one end and a couple of overhead doors to drive-in bays with hydraulic lifts inside at the other end. I notice a car parked in front of the office and check my watch. It's almost five, closing time. I decide to wait, to be sure any customers are gone.

A man and a woman come out of the office and dash through the rain to their car, as another man waves good-bye from the office door. They drive by me going out as I pull up to the office just before the man inside locks it up. I step inside and wipe the rain from my forehead.

"Hello, are you the proprietor here? The father of Lawrence Wallace?"

He nods, and I offer my hand. He shakes it with a firm grip. "We closed, but I can see by your car that you're not a customer."

"No, sir, I'm Detective Johnson. Mark Johnson," I say. "But I'm not really here on police business, at least not primarily."

"Oh, no? You're not here about my son, then?"

"Well, yes and no. I mean, I am here about him, but it's not official, really. I mean, I'm not working the case, or anything. I'm just here for personal reasons. If you don't mind, I'd like to ask you a few questions about your son."

I pause, trying to read his face, to gauge if it's too soon, too painful, to see if he feels threatened, or suspicious. All I can see is puzzlement.

"I'm the one who found him, down the parkway. The one he shot."

His eyes narrow, almost imperceptibly, and he takes a deep breath.

"I'm sorry about that, Detective," he says. "Are you all right now?"

"Yes, I'm fine. Thanks for asking. But I still don't understand it all, I just—"

"Lord, you and me both," he says. "Guess I never will."

"I checked his record, and there's really nothing there, compared to what I'm used to seeing."

"No, you're right. He had his little scrapes like kids do nowadays, y'know, but Lawrence never was in much trouble. He was a good boy."

"Did he have a drug habit? I did see some misdemeanor drug cases."

"Well, I ain't gonna lie, he'd been arrested for drugs, but like you say, they wasn't nothing serious, and it had been a while back. He wasn't no dope-crazy addict, if that's what you mean."

"Yeah, I didn't think so. In fact I heard he was goin' to those 12-step meetings."

"You've sure done your homework, Detective."

"What kinda student was he? Did he ever get in fights at school? Get suspended or expelled? Did he get decent grades?"

"He wasn't what you'd call a scholar, but he graduated high school and went to Bishop State after that. Got a diploma in jewelry makin'. He'd make the prettiest little rings, and bracelets and such. For his mama, and his sisters. And of course his girlfriends. But mainly he worked right here with me, at the shop. Matter fact, the day before all this mess happened, we took a trip together up to Montgomery, to get a car. Rode up and back together in the rollback truck, talked all the way, like normal."

"Was he just breaking up with a girlfriend, maybe? Something he may not have wanted to talk about with his dad?"

"He had his girlfriends, but no one special girl, 'least not one I knew about. He was more likely to talk to his mama 'bout that department."

"Would you mind, then, if I talk to your wife? Do you think she'd mind?"

"Well, I don't know. You're just gonna hafta ask her. See, his mama's not my wife anymore, hasn't been for some years now. We divorced when Lawrence was, lessee, twelve or thirteen. She's remarried, and he would stay mostly with them, when he wasn't at some girl's place."

"I see. That explains the different name." I've already run Wallace in the Relationships database and found a woman old enough to be his mother who has the same address.

"Yes sir. They stay right down the road from here, in that Deerwoods subdivision."

"I'll try to visit with her, then, too. But I'm wondering, Mr. Wallace, what about his other friends—not girls—but the guys he ran with. What kind of guys—"

"He really didn't hang with no boys. For Lawrence, it was the girls he was interested in. Not that he was some kinda ladies' man, neither. But with other boys, well, he wa'nt no loner, exactly, but I never knew him to, like, hang with any of 'em, never heard him talk about other boys."

"So it's not like he ran with a rough crowd or anything. Well, then, can you think of *anything* Mr. Wallace, anything about Lawrence—if it's not drugs, or girls, or the wrong crowd—*anything* different in Lawrence's behavior, or attitude, any little thing at all that might explain all this?"

Mr. Wallace cocks his head and thinks hard for a long moment. "I wish I did, Detective," he says. Then, in a softer voice that's almost wistful, he adds, "Y'know that day we took the trip to Montgomery, the day before he died. He had spent the night over at my place, with me and his sisters, 'cause we had to get up early to get on the road. And like we do every day at my house, we sit around the breakfast table, and hold hands, and say grace together. He was right there with us, holdin' hands and sayin' grace, like he always had, growin' up. I just don't know what happened, Detective. If you can figure it out, please let me know."

I go next to his mother's address. She's at work, but her husband, Lawrence Jr.'s stepfather, answers the door and invites me in. A tall, stout man with a proud bearing and a rich, deep voice, he introduces himself as retired Air Force, adding that he was formerly in the chain of command that controlled America's nuclear arsenal. "Had my finger on the button of forty missile silos," he says. And he has answers, an abundance of answers. He has *all* the answers.

"The boy had no structure, no discipline in his life. His mama spoiled him. He'd dabble at this, dabble at that. God only knows why he wasted two years of tuition—that I paid for—makin' jewelry! Of all things. He was never gonna make a living at that! But that didn't seem to matter to him. And why should it? He could always stay here rent free, or over at his daddy's, or with one of his little girlfriends. His daddy gave him a car to drive, his mother and I fed and housed him. Why should he grow up?

"I tried to encourage him to join the military. I did well by it. Made a career of it and didn't do too bad, either, as you can tell by this house and the cars in my driveway. But he'd hear none of that.

"I put him out several times, thinking maybe it would toughen him up, help him see the big picture, but after a while he'd just go to whining at his mama, and worm his way back in here."

Finally, I visit Wallace's mama. If Mama don't know, ain't nobody does. I call her at work and ask if I can meet with her briefly, privately. Her office is just around the corner from the First Precinct.

She rises from her desk and smiles sweetly as she shakes my hand. Her voice is high pitched, almost a falsetto, and she keeps smiling as we sit and I explain my purpose. She smiles and smiles and doesn't initiate anything, just responds to my questions with the briefest of sentences, barely uttered in the softest of whispers.

"His father told me he didn't know much about Lawrence's girlfriends, like if he had one in particular. I was thinking maybe he'd had a fight with a girlfriend. Maybe caught her cheating, or she caught him, or something like that that might've upset him? Mr. Wallace said he thought Lawrence confided in you about his love life."

"He did? He said that?"

"Yes, ma'am."

She smiles anew, and her eyes are unfocused, looking away from me, as if in a reverie. Maybe thinking of a fond memory. Who knows? Whatever she's thinking about, it's not my question.

"So, did he have a special girlfriend?"

"Oh, Lawrence had lotsa girlfriends. Not all at once. But it was usually more than one at a time. The girls, they loved Lawrence."

"Was he, like, in love with any one of them? Did he ever say to you, 'Mom, I think she's the one,' or anything like that?"

"Yes. Several times"

"So, he did have a special girl?"

"Yes."

"Were they getting along all right?"

"Who?"

"Lawrence and his special girl."

"He had lots of special girls."

"But I mean, the one special girl who he said, 'Mom, she may be the one' about."

"Who was that?"

"I don't know. That's why I'm asking you. His daddy said you'd probably know, 'cause he would talk to you about his love life."

"He would tell me about his girls, he would. Sometimes he'd ask me about them, too."

"You mean, ask your advice?"

"He'd say like Keisha, she's the prettiest, don't you think, Mama? But Syrentha, now, she's got a good job, her mama has a good house, but she already got a baby, and so what do you think, Mama? You know, that kind of thing."

"Well, had he asked you about one girl in particular lately? That he was serious about, but maybe having problems with?"

"Not just one, no . . ."

"So, it's not like he just broke up with a girl, or she broke up with him, or—"

"Which girl? No, I don't think so."

She smiles dreamily, not looking at me. I sit in silence for a moment, hoping maybe she's pondering my question, but knowing that isn't likely. She's gazing off somewhere over my left shoulder, still smiling.

"So, I guess it's your feeling that Lawrence wasn't having any girlfriend troubles. No broken heart, no breakup or fighting with a girlfriend . . ."

"I just don't know."

I pause again, consider rephrasing this line of questioning, but can't think of any way to break it down differently.

"Well, see, ma'am, I'm just trying to understand. This isn't an official investigation, I'm not trying to establish a motive for a case. It's not my case. There is no case, or, I mean, the case is closed. Was he not getting along with his stepfather? Had they argued lately? His stepfather said he thought—"

I stop. No point in stirring up a resentment between them. I'm trying to quickly think how to complete this sentence without revealing the stepfather's theories about Lawrence. But I can't think my way out.

To my relief (and simultaneous frustration) I realize it doesn't matter. I can't even be certain she's listening to me. Her eyes have dropped to her desk, and the smile is still there, but she offers nothing, and asks nothing.

"So, anyway, I . . . um . . . you saw none of this coming, is what I'm hearing. There was no change in his circumstances, or his behavior, or even in his moods, that seemed out of the ordinary? Nothing at all?"

"No, Detective," she says, with that frozen, forlorn smile.

I'm at a loss to extend the conversation or to even figure out what else to ask. I wonder, could she just simply be, *simple?* She couldn't be, and work here, in her own office. There's gotta be something going on upstairs, but I'm getting nowhere. Her lights are on, but nobody's home.

"Was Lawrence close to his brothers and sisters?"

"Oh yes."

"Was he closest to one in particular?"

"Yes, his brother, they're only a year apart."

"So Lawrence and his brother, they would talk, be together a lot?"

"Yes."

"Do you think his brother would mind talking to me?"

"I don't know. He works out of town a lot. Would you like me to ask him for you?"

"Yes, if you get a chance, yes, that would be—"

She's dialing the phone. I try to stop her. "You don't have to ... I didn't mean ..."

"Honey? How are you, it's Mama. I'm talking with a Detective, uh, Detective Johnson? And he asked me to ask if you would talk with him about Lawrence? Uh-huh. Oh. Uh-huh. When? All right. All right. I have it, yes. All right, then. Bye-bye." She hangs up, still smiling, and reports that big brother is out of town, but he'll call her when he's back in town, sometime next week, to get my number. I doubt that's going to happen, but it doesn't matter.

"Thank you. I didn't mean for you to call him right now, but thank you. I know this is hard on all of you. And it's very kind of you all to talk to me."

"He loved his baby brother. You know, he tried to go there to help y'all talk to Lawrence, but they . . . it was too late."

"Yes ma'am."

The smile is still on her face, though not as broad. Her eyes seem fixed on her desk.

There's a long pause that grows awkward, at least for me. I rise, and thank her for her time, and apologize for the intrusion, for bringing up a painful subject. She's gracious, and still smiling, and finally I get a clue—to her but not to her son—when she apologizes to me as I reach for the door.

"I know I haven't been much help to you, Detective. I'm sorry, but I just haven't been myself since Lawrence . . . ," she drops her eyes, but the smile remains, "since, my son passed. I hope you understand." Then she bravely lifts her eyes again, still with the frozen smile, though it has diminished now almost entirely.

"I do, and I'm so sorry for your loss."

"Thank you for visiting, Detective," she whispers.

I walk out feeling like shit. I feel like a voyeur, like a rubbernecker slowing for an accident on the interstate hoping for a glimpse of gore. A distant, sad memory has just popped into my head. The frozen smile, vacant gaze, and whispered words of Lawrence Wallace's mama have reminded me of the mother of a childhood friend of mine. My pal's mother was a close friend of my own mother's. She had the same fixed smile and disconnected demeanor as Lawrence's mother. Even at a young age I had picked up on it and asked my mom why Mrs. Barker was "so weird." Mom had explained to me that Robbie's mama "has a nervous condition, and her medicine makes her act like that." Mrs. Barker spent weeks at a time in one of the upper floors of Deaconess Hospital in St. Louis. When I was about eleven, she threw herself out of the hospital window. "I guess her medicine stopped working," Mom had explained.

I try to talk about it with my recovery sponsor, Red, and at the meetings. But my talking is as muddled as my thinking. I search for answers in my recovery literature and even in the Bible. But I don't know where to look. Even if it were indexed for topics and questions, I have no idea what to look up. I haven't a clue what's wrong with me, and there isn't much that seems right.

I thought about—and decided against—a visit to Green's widow and kids. His own squad and academy classmates are best suited to bring comfort. My only association with him, after all, was in the aftermath of something his family would prefer not to relive. And though this may be presumptuous, and may be giving Green short shrift, one thing I feel pretty sure in saying is, Officer Steven Green was not a mystery to me. He *was me*, more than not. Whereas, Lawrence Wallace was and remains a complete mystery to me.

The nightmares have long since ceased, and I'm sleeping okay. As months pass, the memory of Officer Green's brutal death and my small part in the capture and death of his murderer fades from the public—and even the police—consciousness, so there are fewer outward reminders of the event.

Then there's a more dramatic shoot-out between cops and four guys trying to rob a midtown Winn-Dixie that completely supplants the Metro murder and parkway siege. I'm forced to admit to myself, and to a few select others, that in a sick, twisted way I'm almost *jealous* of the cop who is gravely wounded in the grocery gunfight. He's getting way more public attention and sympathy than I did. And rightly so: for a while they weren't even sure he'd make it.

And then I learn that because he returned fire, the hero of the grocery gunfight will be awarded the Combat Cross in addition to the Purple Heart and Meritorious Service medals that I'll be receiving. I don't qualify for the Combat award, I'm told, because I didn't really engage in combat. I didn't return fire.

Shoulda shot that bastard with my last damn bullet, I think ruefully, simultaneously stricken with self-loathing and guilt at the recognition of my raging pettiness, my infantile self-absorption. Nevertheless, I think, Lusty's right: I shoulda shot him, I coulda got him, mighta killed him, and then I woulda got the Combat Cross, *and* the other two medals, *and* woulda earned the right to get a goddamn killer teardrop on my cheek from Tattoo Town.

Is this all it is? I wonder. Am I this damn childish, this much a narcissist? Uh, *yeah*. "No duh, Dad," as little Pete and Katie used to chime in unison at my frequent utterance of the obvious.

But it's gotta be more than this, I think. Because I wasn't firing on all cylinders even during my fifteen minutes of fame. It's not just this latest spike of jealousy and self-loathing (although there's plenty of that). I've been messed up since before the Winn-Dixie gunfight even happened, with a vague sense of admonition, a small but relentless misfire somewhere deep in the recesses of my brain, or my heart, or my soul.

The first disorder was likely some manifestation of PTSD, I conclude. It was all still fresh, jarring, a confused mix of survivor's guilt, and crazy nightmares, and "coulda-woulda-shoulda *meshugganah*" as I am wont to describe Nancy's uniquely tribal form of fretting.

Yeah, so it was just a mild case of PTSD back then, I figure, and it has pretty much passed. And the next affliction, the latest mortification, must spring from my pathetic envy of the grocery store hero's glory, I guess.

But that just doesn't cover it, because even after the hero of the grocery gunfight recovers, and even later, after a brief flurry in the press at the

Winn-Dixie robbers' trials, convictions, and sentencing, and even months after that, when we gather to receive our medals and commendations and grip-and-grins with the chief and the mayor, and I'm *really over it all*, absolutely done with all that, there's still a lingering *something*.

I don't even know if it's something I have, or something I lack. Something I did, or failed to do, or something I lost. Nothing seems to explain or relieve me of this nagging, nonspecific sense of admonition, or unworthiness, or duplicity. It seems to cling to me, like a crackhead's stink. I can't figure it out, and I can't shake it, or clean it off me.

29

(Can't Get No) Satisfaction

The united personality will never quite lose the painful sense of innate discord. Complete redemption from the sufferings of this world is and must remain an illusion.
—C. G. Jung, *The Psychology of the Transference*

Be yourself. No one else will.
 —Will Rogers, famous Okie oracle

It's Mardi Gras, 2013. It started early this year, kicked off by the Conde Cavaliers on Friday, the 25th of January, the eve of my sixty-first birthday, and the beginning of my eleventh year as a policeman. We're nearing the end of another season of mirth and mayhem. It's Saturday, February 9, and the Mystics of Time are rolling through the streets now. They've got the coolest floats: fully articulated, fire-breathing dragons. They've already made their first pass by my quiet post at Church and Washington, a block off Government Street, the main drag that they'll loop back around to for their last blazing belch of fire on the way to the float barns. The final pass of the MOT's fiery dragons means there are only three more long days of madness and fatigue until Folly chases Death once again, on the emblem float of the Order of Myths parade, on Fat Tuesday.

It's been a long day, with daytime parades starting at noon, running till three or so, with a three-hour lull till the MOTs roll, just after dark—the better to see the flames shoot forth from their dragons' maws. And tomorrow, Joe Cain Day, starts at the crack of 8 a.m. with the 5K Moon Pie Dash, followed at noon by the thousand-Harley procession from west

Mobile to Jackson Street, the Joe Cain parade at 2:30, and the Krewe de Bienville at five. I'm slap wore out, as they say here in Alabama.

But I'm grateful for my post. It's on a quiet residential street—befitting a cop of my advanced years—with friendly folks who live here and take good care of me, letting me use their bathrooms, feeding me, bringing me iced-down "Co-Colas" or steaming cups of strong, black coffee. They've been with me all Mardi Gras season, entertaining guests in their yards or front porches between parades. They stroll over to my barricade just before each parade rolls by, with grandchildren on their shoulders or at their feet, tall cocktails in hand, and sympathize with me over the long hours, the repeated idiotic questions from tourists, the drunk-and-disorderlies. Some of them even remember that I got wounded during last Mardi Gras and ask after my recovery.

But mostly I'm ready for this season to be over. And I've begun to wonder if it's time for this line of work to be over for me as well. The words of my father—shocking at the time—keep coming back to me lately.

Mom had arranged a small family reunion. Nancy noticed that my father didn't look well. "His face looks kinda ashen," she'd said. I didn't pay it much attention until Dad insisted (as always) that I play a few sets of tennis with him.

The game was his passion; he'd played it all his life. Though I was in my forties and Dad was in his seventies, he'd always kept me virtually scoreless with his blistering serves. But that day in the winter of '94, for the first time ever, I beat Dad on the court.

As the two of us sat on a courtside bench cooling down, Dad became uncharacteristically philosophical.

"Y'know, Mark, I wish I had retired earlier. I kept working, always thinking I had to make more money. Now I realize, I've got more than I could ever spend, over and above what I plan to leave you and your sister. Time matters more than money; you can't earn any more of it, or make up for any that you wasted."

This from a man who insisted, from my college days on, that at least once a year I spend an hour with him, just the two of us, going over his master ledger, his entire investment portfolio, reviewing with me the growth of his wealth, his increasing salary and net worth year by year and how much he had saved, how much he had spent, and how much and where he had invested it and why; the red-letter day when he had crossed the million mark and the inexorable march to the next; the importance of caution, prudence, patience, and diversification; the varying risks and rewards of blue chips, small caps, and emerging markets, commodities versus utilities, the dangers of some kinds of REITs and limited partnerships, the safety of Treasuries compared to municipal bonds, varieties of mutual funds and how to look for their hidden costs and fees, distinctions between the Dow Jones and the Nasdaq, the importance of saving and investing early and often, how to pick a broker you can trust, how to read a prospectus and a financial statement and the *Wall Street Journal* and Morningstar . . . until my eyes would glaze over, and he'd snap at me, "Now pay attention! You're gonna hafta to know all this after I'm gone. Even if you don't care about it now, you will someday, and it will be *your* responsibility for Mom's and Lynn's sake, do you understand?" and I'd say yes sir and force myself to focus.

I used to dread those sessions, in some ways like I dreaded his insistence that I play tennis with him. My attitude toward both sprang from my utter lack of aptitude for either. And of the two, the dullness and opacity of the investment game had the effect of anesthesia on me.

But there was more to it even than that. For me, those sessions with Dad and his ledgers were exercises in unworthiness. I had done little if anything to make my father proud, did not bear his looks nor share his temperament, talents, industry, or strength, and lacked even the most basic birthright, as a castaway bastard, rescued only by his whim or benevolence (or more likely Mom's saintly insistence). Not only did I not deserve what he would entrust to me, I was destined to be a poor steward of it. Upon reflection, I suppose a case could be made that Dad's insistent tutelage in matters financial or insistent play with me on the court were the only ways he could express paternal love. It's a nice theory, anyway.

Six months later, Dad was gone. He dropped dead on the court, at the tennis hall of fame in Newport, Rhode Island, where he had made a pilgrimage to fulfill a lifelong dream.

So lately I find myself wondering, do I really need to keep chasing thugs at my age? Why? To test myself, or my half-baked sociopolitical solipsisms? To make some kind of point? After a decade on the job, have I made my point, whatever it is? Have I made some kind of difference?

I had originally set out to be "a good cop," as I had declared to the TV reporter when I quit United Way and entered the academy. "The world needs more good cops," I had solemnly intoned, "and I aim to be one of 'em." Sometime during my first year on the streets, I had privately amended that aim to just being a competent cop.

Way back at the beginning, I had even entertained the notion of someday returning to United Way with my hard-won knowledge of the streets, to introduce a taste of Realville to the world of local philanthropy. But that grandiose notion is long gone, too; I haven't a clue what to do about the suffering I've witnessed almost daily.

To be sure, there remain plenty of thugs and countless victims, both in need of justice and mercy. But that's always been and always will be. As a well-known national figure recently complained, "What difference at this point does it make?"

When I catch myself agreeing with that sentiment, I know something's wrong.

"To whom much is given, of him much is required." One of Mom's favorite scriptures. She said it often, not to scold, but to remind me to be grateful, and not to squander my blessings.

But I wonder, is there ever any clarity, any satisfaction?

No. "Never. Never any." So snapped a friend of AA founder Bill Wilson, when Wilson asked the same question. As the story goes, Bill was well into sobriety when he became bedridden for weeks, so deep was his funk of grandiose self-pity. A Jesuit priest from St. Louis, Father Ed Dowling, had recently heard of this new fellowship bringing hope and recovery to hope-less drunken wastrels and traveled all the way to New York to meet the founder of this miraculous fellowship, whose principles he recognized from his own study of things spiritual. And he discovers Bill Wilson, whining and wallowing in depression, demanding the elusive "satisfaction." Father Dowling is best known in AA circles for the memorable quip, "If I ever find myself in Heaven, it will be the result of backing away from Hell." He knew that for certain kinds of people, satisfaction is code for complacency, for *self*-satisfaction, for sloth, and a slippery slope to intemperance and dissipation. I could use a good dose of Father Ed's brand of soul saving.

Eighteen months after Dad died, Mom left us. We had moved to Mobile by then and had brought Mom down to live with us because her health had been failing since Dad died.

"I wish your Dad had lived to see how well you've done, how well situated you and your family are here," she said not long before she died. I wish he had, too.

But by 2001, despite being "well situated" I was feeling restless, irritable, and discontent. I drove over to Pensacola to talk to Tom Whitaker about my idea of a career change to law enforcement. Not that I necessarily trusted his judgment, but what the hell. I met him at the FloraBama Lounge. He ordered a beer I was wishing I could drink, and I smoked a Camel he was wishing he could smoke. (By then, he was wearing a respirator about half the time, owing to his emphysema.)

"I think you'd make a great cop!" he wheezed. "And you oughtta get it out of your system before it's too late."

A year later, Tom died. His family invited Nancy and me to his funeral and insisted we sit with them as members of the family. When the Marines failed to synchronize the rifle salute, sounding more like three successive strings of firecrackers, Marilyn leaned over to me and said, "Tom would say, 'That's the Corps for ya: they can't even get a funeral right.'"

Shortly after that I joined the force.

After I'd been on a few years, I was invited to a small gathering of Dad's old buddies who were getting together in New Orleans to reminisce. Decades earlier, as young men, they had named their little group of chemical engineers the Onagers (wild asses; you can look it up). The old men were like uncles to me. Lonnie, and Fred, and Harry, and Frank: they were all from Texas or Oklahoma or Louisiana, had all served in the navy in the last good war, and had spent most of their careers working for Lion Oil, and then Monsanto. They had all come to both of my parents' funerals. Some of them had lost their wives by then; they all agreed each Onagers reunion could be their last. I drove over straight from work, still in uniform, and got there in time for their last round.

They all stood to toast "Stan's boy" when I joined them. They all remarked on how sharp I looked in uniform. And they all said, "We're proud of you, and we know your dad would be, too." I so wanted to believe them.

Still, I had my doubts.

So I went to visit the last survivor of my parents' generation, Mom's sister Billye. Her husband, my uncle Bill, had died several years before, and Aunt Billye had been taken in by her daughters, my cousins, who had moved to Albuquerque. They cautioned me that their mom is often "confused" and she might not know for sure who I am, even though they had been showing her pictures of me in preparation for my visit.

She knew my name when I walked in, knew that I was Margaret and Stan's boy. We talked for a while, catching each other up on family news, and she asked how things were with the United Fund. I reminded her that I had switched to law enforcement several years ago.

My cousin Susan prompted, "Remember Mama? We went to Mark's graduation from the academy. He was president of the class and gave the speech, and now he keeps the peace, just like Sheriff Andy in Mayberry."

"Oh, yes," Aunt Billye said, "how exciting it must be for you, Mark."

"Well, it has its moments," I agreed. "But tell me, Aunt Billye. What do you think Dad would've thought about my career change?"

Aunt Billye paused a moment, cocking her head. "That's a good question. Your father was a very opinionated man, and never shy about sharing them, either, but I think he'd be happy for you if it makes you happy, Mark. I know for certain that *Mayberry* was his very favorite TV show!"

It was all pretty inconclusive, at best.

The Mystics have just made their final pass at Washington and Government, and the crowd of mostly teenagers and a few grandmas with clusters of little kids is walking south on Washington, away from the parade route, toward home.

I'm facing southward, leaning on a portable barricade in the middle of Washington at Church. A sign on my barricade reads "Road Closed." You would think that the barricade, the sign, and the southbound flood of pedestrians filling the street would be sufficient to discourage northbound traffic on Washington, but it's not. That's why I'm there. I've just waved off my third driver, but this one is either clueless or an asshole. He just sits there, shrugging his shoulders and raising his palms as if helpless, despite my clear gestures indicating he should turn around or just put it in reverse. I guess I'm gonna hafta make it real clear to him.

"What should I do, Officer? I hafta get to a party on the north side of Government."

Through gritted teeth, in a polite and measured voice, I explain that he can back it up and take a big westward loop around the parade route and try to get to his destination from the north side, which will take about forty-five minutes, or he can park it here as long as he gets it off the street, and he can wait about forty-five minutes, until the crowds, barricade crews, the blower brigade, and the street-sweeper flotilla pass.

Neither alternative pleases him. I then explain that a third choice is for him to get out and walk, because I'm going to radio for a tow truck to impound his vehicle. He finally gets the idea and backs away from me.

I lean back on the barricade to watch the doofus recede into the sea of pedestrians when behind me I hear a chorus of screams in the crowd, followed by gunfire. And it sounds real close. I turn around and the crowd is parting like the wake behind twin Evinrudes and a kid about 5 foot 3, ninety-eight pounds, sprints past me like a wild-eyed jackrabbit, and seconds later another kid, a little taller, streaks by me close enough for me to trip, if I had realized what was happening quick enough to do it.

The second kid is firing repeatedly at the first kid from a distance of two or three strides. He's got his right arm extended with a full-size semi-automatic pistol aimed at the kid in front of him, and he's popping off rounds but not hitting his target, apparently, because the first kid rounds the corner from southbound Washington on to eastbound Church without breaking stride. My heart's in my throat with the horrifying thought that any number of innocents in the dense crowd may have already been struck. I draw my weapon and join the chase, yelling at the kid with the gun to "Stop! Police!" I think if I have to shoot on the fly, it would sure be easy to hit an innocent bystander myself in a running gun battle, and hell, even if I hit the shooter and don't injure anybody else, it will be just as sickening to kill some dumb-ass teenager.

Thank God the kid with the gun hears me after I've taken just a few running steps, and he stops. He turns, faces me, and freezes, his gun still in his hand but pointing up in the air. We stare at each other from a distance of maybe eight feet, my Glock in the two-fisted grip aimed directly at his center mass, and I order him to put the gun down.

It seems like the world goes silent: no more screaming crowd, no more marching-band-Mardi-Gras music. I can't even hear my own commands to the kid. And he stares at me, motionless, neither complying nor resisting, as if he's trying to comprehend the scene himself. He doesn't have Travis Colt's look of wheels turning in his head, that mental calculation that preceded Colt's leisurely backstroke across the bayou. This one is confused, and scared, and immobilized by it. I have since wondered, was there something different this time, in my face or voice? I was not smitten with my own delusions of a Dirty Harry moment of triumph, nor was I realizing (as Travis had calculated) that I couldn't really shoot in these circumstances. I doubt this kid gave any thought to the fact that I had grounds for a "righteous kill," that I could pull the trigger and blow a hole in his chest, pierce his teenage heart and lungs with a tumbling, fragmenting, slicing round of hollow-point .40-caliber law enforcement lead, and it would all be found justifiable in these circumstances.

I remember thinking, at this range I can't miss, but even if I hit him there's a good chance it'll go clean through him and hit some ol' granny or toddler behind him, and I really don't want to kill him, he's just a scared kid, what a helluva note to retire on, but I sure as hell am not gonna let him shoot me, or anybody else, and I start to squeeze the trigger.

Then I guess he has an epiphany or divine intervention or loses his nerve, because he drops to his knees and places the gun on the asphalt next to him. I charge, screaming, "Get on the ground!" and scoop up his weapon, stuff it in my belt, and put a boot between his shoulder blades. Holding my gun at the back of his head, about knee high, I radio for backup.

I know there's all kinds of backup within a block's radius of my location, but now the crowd starts to converge in around me, and they're on *his* side. They're mostly kids yelling at me, just boys and girls his own age, but I have no doubt some of them are armed just like the one on the ground had been, and I rip his gun back out of my belt and with both hands filled I sweep the crowd around me, keeping my foot on the kid's back, screaming, "Get back or I'll shoot!" They stop advancing, to my relief, but they don't retreat.

Then the cavalry arrives. Literally. Mounted cops on horseback gallop through the crowd and herd them away from me. Others on foot and in cars arrive and form a perimeter. They cuff my prisoner, and Sammy from my precinct takes the kid's gun from me, saying, "Mark fucking Eastwood! These punks picked the wrong corner today!" and a sergeant gingerly puts his hand on my gun hand, and says, "You can holster up and step off him now, Mark." They hustle my prisoner off to a paddy wagon.

I take a deep breath and a Sammy offers me a smoke, which I take without a thought. The others are getting witness statements, gathering up spent .45 casings in the street from the shooter's weapon, and doing reports for two people whose parked cars have shattered windows and bullet holes. Paramedics are called for an elderly female who thinks she may have been shot, but it turns out she only has abrasions from being knocked to the ground by the fleeing crowd. The shooter's target never stopped running, never looked back. I'm told to go sit in my car, chill out, and write a narrative of the event, then turn it in to the mobile Command Unit, a couple blocks away.

A half hour later, I go to turn in my paperwork and inquire about the shooter. The commander informs me that the on-call detective has already interrogated the fifteen-year-old shooter and he's been taken to Strickland juvie for discharging a firearm in the city limits, and no pistol permit. Both misdemeanors. I'm enraged. I tell the captain that I've just witnessed probably the most horrifying fifteen seconds in my decade of policing, and it wasn't any fucking misdemeanor.

"You don't have a victim," he shrugs. "Your victim never stopped running. Without a victim its nu'n but misdemeanor Discharging and No Permit."

I storm out of the Command trailer and drive with lights and siren to Strickland where I demand to interview the shooter. I read him his rights and he refuses to talk. He's full of cool attitude and nonchalance.

"Fine, you don't hafta talk, that's your right," I say. "But you're in custody, and you do gotta listen." I move in close, get right up in his face. "Do you realize how close I came to putting a bullet in you?" He betrays no emotion and looks away from me. "You came within a second of meeting Jesus, kid. I started to squeeze the trigger!" His eyes widen, and he faces me. "I'm old enough to be your granddaddy, and I'm fixin' to retire, and the thought of having killed you coulda really fucked up my retirement. That pisses me off!

"And you mighta not been the only dead person at the parade today. You coulda killed any number of grandmas and babies in that crowd, not to mention the kid you were shooting at. There's nothing any kid coulda done to you that's worth all that bloodshed."

My face is so close to him and I'm so furious I see little flecks of my saliva on his cheeks. He's more wide eyed now than he was when I had him at gunpoint. I back off and take a breath.

He starts to tell me about how he just did it in "self-defense," that the kid he was shooting at had shot and wounded his homeboy a few weeks ago at the movies, in an argument over a girl, and had been threatening them all on the Internet since then. I tell him that changes things, but he's gotta tell me who the kid is, and he says he only knows him by "Money," and he hangs in the "Bricks" (1010 Baltimore).

I head back to the precinct, get on Facebook, and find a little punk who calls himself Fat Money Goldmouth, whose page says he's from the B'mo Bricks and sports numerous selfies posing with stacks of Benjamins and guns. Cross-checking with his Facebook friends leads me to the real name of the sixteen-year-old jackrabbit who dodged a .45 round in his back. His rap sheet's three pages long, and I recall him as a suspect in several unsolved burglaries a year or so ago. By contrast, my shooter's never been in trouble with the law, although you wouldn't guess it from his Facebook page, where he calls himself D'thuggin Brown and strikes a menacing pose with a sneer and an AR-15 assault rifle. Both boys' Facebook poses include lurid snapshots with their little teenage girlfriends who are dressed like hookers, sticking out their barely covered booties and boobies, licking their gangsta boys' tattooed pectorals. They don't even have driver's licenses yet, these kids. They all still live at home with their mamas and attend high school. Where the hell are their parents, I wonder. To say nothing of their pastors, coaches, scoutmasters, aunts, uncles, grandparents, *anybody* with an ounce of moral fiber and sense of responsibility for these young savages, these feral kids.

Knowing the victim's name, I track him down. He doesn't wanna talk to the police, but I tell his mama and she makes him. They both thank me for saving his life. I secure his promise to testify and his written statement. As a result, the DA adds attempted murder to the shooter's charges. D'thuggin eventually pleads guilty and, as a juvenile offender with no previous record, gets sent off to state school, but he'll be back in time for the fall semester at his old high school if he behaves himself at Mount Meigs.

Epilogue

Time passes, seasons change. Things move slow and easy like the lazy waters of the bayous, with nothing much a bother but the 'skeeters. Parents neglect kids, kids shoot other kids; men rape, perverts molest; cops chase robbers and shoot shooters. *The wheels of justice grind slowly, but they grind exceeding small. All things work together for good to them that love God, to them who are called according to his purpose.*

Like hell.

To everything there is a season, and a time to every purpose under heaven: a time to be born, a time to die . . . a time to kill, and a time to heal. Blessed be the Lord my strength, which teacheth my hands to war, and my fingers to fight. Yea though I walk through the valley of the shadow of death, I will fear no evil, for thou art with me.

Yeah, that's what I'm talking about. Another half-second squeeze and I'da got me that teardrop from Tat Town.

But I say unto you Resist not evil; whosoever shall smite thee on thy cheek, turn to him the other also. Recompense to no man evil for evil. For it is written, Vengeance is mine, saith the Lord. Love thine enemy, feed him if he hunger, give him drink if he thirst.

Not always.

For the Officer is God's servant. The power of the Law is no empty phrase. He beareth not the sword in vain. He is the minister of God, the revenger to execute wrath, divinely appointed to inflict God's punishment on evil doers.

Yeah.

But what about the wars and fightings among you? Can't you see that they arise from conflicting passions within yourselves? You crave, you're jealous, envious, and in your exasperated frustration, you lust and kill. You are like adulterers, you only want to satisfy your own desires, and thereby become the enemy of God.

And the Lord visits the sins of the fathers on the children and the children's children unto the third and fourth generation.

So I turned my mind to understand, to investigate and to search out wisdom, and the scheme of things, and to understand the stupidity of wickedness and the madness of folly.

And yea, even as the fruit of fornicators' loins, he the inflicter of wrath upon distant tribes, and she an adulterer possessed of concupiscence, yet I do good works, only to find the works barren, naught but vanity. I find mine own self ill equipped to resist the sins of the father. What I resist, persists. So I resist not, only to be consumed by them.

Therefore then did I gird my loins and take up the sword, did I receive divine appointment to execute wrath upon the heads of evildoers. And I found it good, I found it satisfying, nay I found it thrilling to wreak holy vengeance upon man, yet did I grow troubled by the evil within mine own heart and I feared that which I did know would dwell therein unto the end of my days.

For that which has been is what will be and that which is done is what will be done, and there is no remembrance of former things, nor any remembrance of things to come. I learneth not, and like the dog who returns to his own vomit, so this fool repeats his own folly.

But if the truth be known by its fruits, doth not the sweet pear Pete and the tangerine Kate (to say nothing of sober decades, of heartfelt almsgiving, and of righteous vengeance visited by mine own hand upon evildoers) count for something? Yea, though the more I seek the truth the more vexed do I become. Wisdom eludes me. Is redemption an illusion? And so the song of the honky tonk doth ever and anon speak anew to me: I'd rather have a bottle in fronta me than a frontal lobotomy. Whiskey river, take my mind, I beseech thee.

False gods, idols, and mine own head speak in tongues to me, vexing me. But this I do know: verily, when I am disturbed, the problem is within me, and I am powerless to fix the problem because it *is* me. I am the least, the lost, the most, the ghost. The walking, talking paradox. The vanity of vanities. Alone, I fight that which I cannot change, am blind to that which I can change, and fail even to know the difference.

But finally, *what does the Lord require of me, but to do justice, to love kindness, and to walk humbly with Him?* Let not my heart be troubled, nor let it be hardened. By grace alone am I saved, not works, lest I boast. (And Lord knows I boast, in my heart of hearts.)

And so on I trudge, the Road of Happy Destiny.

I ran into ol' Tom McCall at the courthouse after word was out about my thirty-days' notice to the department. We were both going down, and at the ground floor we walked together to the gun lockers to retrieve our sidearms.

"True what I heard about you?" he asked.

"Yeah, Lieutenant. It's been a good run, but it's time."

"I didn't believe it when I heard. You know how rumors fly around here. I figured for sure this one was crap, because I know what the job means to you. Give any thought to comin' to the County?"

I shrugged, wondering how he knew what the job meant to me. "I just, you know . . . it feels like I've lived about eight of my nine lives, and I'm a little long in the tooth for this line of work."

McCall shook my hand and squeezed hard and looked right into my eyes and held his gaze, all of which I found a little unsettling, even after all these years. The man's a legend, after all.

"How old are you?" he asked, for the second time in twelve years.

"Sixty-two." I paused a beat, just like last time. Then, "You?"

He smiled, perhaps remembering. "Not far behind you."

"Haven't you had your fill yet of being shot at, and shot, and . . . ?"

He looked away and shook his head slowly. "Not yet, I guess, not quite yet. But I get it, I understand. Hate it though, that you're . . . you'll be leavin' a hole."

"Thanks, LT," I mumbled, averting my eyes.

As he turned and strode off, he said, "Ever need anything, call me. MCSO Narcotics."

A few months after leaving the department, I found myself back in the precinct after Devin O'Malley responded to my cell phone request to pick up a thief I had detained at a bank on Government Street. (There's a whole other story behind that, but don't ask. It's for another day.)

"We knew you wouldn't be able to stay away for long," they teased when I walked in.

And then I saw it.

Tacked on the wall above my old desk hung a photocopy of Dirty Harry gripping his .44 magnum, with my face photoshopped over Clint's. The block letters W W M D were taped above the picture. Though I didn't inquire as to the meaning, it was cheerfully explained that it stands for "What Would Mark Do."

But I already knew that. Because I figure things out: I'm a detective.

Additional Reading

Links to news reports of Mobile police officer Steven Green's death:

https://www.youtube.com/watch?v=c-8gWVES6eI

http://blog.al.com/live/2012/02/mobile_police_officer_fatally.html

http://blog.al.com/press-register-commentary/2012/02/death_of_police_officer_remind.html

http://blog.al.com/live/2012/02/mobile_police_identify_officer_2.html

http://blog.al.com/live/2012/02/policeslain_officer_steven_gre.html

https://www.youtube.com/watch?v=HwJgpTsGfkA

http://www.cnn.com/2012/02/04/justice/alabama-officer-killed/

http://www.reuters.com/article/2012/02/04/us-alabama-police-shooting-idUSTRE81301N20120204

http://blog.al.com/live/2012/02/slain_police_officer_remembere.html

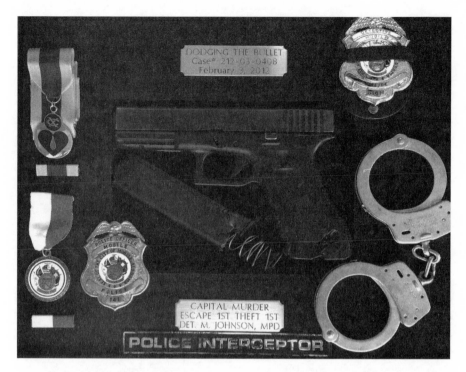

"Dodging the Bullet". Mark Johnson's damaged Glock and magazine, and the Meritorious Service and Wounded in Service medals from his confrontation with Lawrence Wallace, Jr.

Acknowledgments

Without the help and support of many, this book would never have been written, much less published. Special thanks to Nancy, for sticking by me through a lifetime of changes and challenges, and for serving as my primary proofreader, editor, and advocate, both on and off the page. Pete and Kate, both strong writers and sharp readers, provided criticism from their "millennial" perspective. Volunteer editors Jerry and Kay Friedlander, Tom and Nancy Dziubakowski, Craig and Chris Bogar, Greg and Connie Hetue, Phil Estep, Phil Norris, George Sinclair, Randy Moberg, Paul Kritzer, and especially Ernie Planck, provided encouragement and much constructive criticism.

Special thanks to active LEOs Adam Plantinga and Brian Overstreet, whose close reading and critical commentary kept the story squared-away and 10-8.

Friends and mentors Roy Hoffman and Charles Salzberg, long-published writers whose work I admire, generously shared their extensive experience, professional guidance, contacts, and navigation through the literary landscape.

The steadfast kindness, civility, and patience extended to me by Kent Sorsky and Jaguar Bennett of Quill Driver Books (to say nothing of their risk-taking, for giving me a shot) are much appreciated. Special thanks to Tom Swope, the only English teacher who ever encouraged me to pursue writing, and to editors Bill Crawford and Tom McClanahan of the *ProRodeo Sports News* and the *Colorado Springs Sun*, respectively, who actually paid me to write about ropers and bronc riders, freight-hopping hoboes, and long-haul truckers.

Finally, I owe a deep debt to the career law enforcement professionals who went out on a limb to hire me, especially Chief (now Sheriff) Sam Cochran, to the Academy staff and instructors who tortured, tutored, and trained me for the department, to the FTOs who prepared me to go solo on the streets, to the corporals, sergeants, lieutenants, and captains who led me, and to all my brothers and sisters in blue, too many to name, who had my back. They'd prefer to remain anonymous, anyway, but you're in here, guys, you know who you are. Thanks for all you gave me, and all you continue to give.

ABOUT THE AUTHOR

Mark Johnson grew up in Luling, Louisiana, and St. Louis, and graduated from the University of Colorado in 1974. Johnson served as campaign and public relations director for Pikes Peak United Way, executive director of United Way of Waukesha County, Wisconsin, and CEO of the United Way of Southwest Alabama.

After working for United Way for over two decades, in 2002 Johnson chucked it all for a badge and a gun and thirteen bucks an hour with the Mobile Police Department. He was fifty.

As a sworn officer—six years in uniformed patrol, six years as a detective—Johnson received numerous Chief's and Commander's citations for meritorious arrests, and received the medal for Excellent Police Duty, the Chief's Unit Medal, the Meritorious Service Medal, and the Wounded in Service Medal. He also received a handful of "performance observations" and citizen complaints, usually related to inappropriate radio traffic, car wrecks and demeanor issues.

Johnson and his wife Nancy have been married for forty years; they are the parents of two and the grandparents of five. They live in Fairhope, Alabama.

Index

"The new Bible for crime writers"
—The Wall Street Journal

WINNER OF THE
2015 SILVER FALCHION AWARD
BEST CRIME REFERENCE

400 Things Cops Know

Street-Smart Lessons from a Veteran Patrolman

by Adam Plantinga

400 Things Cops Know shows police work from the viewpoint of the regular cop on the beat—a profession that can range from rewarding to bizarre to terrifying in one eight-hour shift.

Written by a veteran police sergeant, *400 Things Cops Know* takes you into a cop's life of danger, frustration, occasional triumph, and plenty of grindingly hard routine work.

In a laconic, no-nonsense, dryly humorous style, San Francisco police sergeant Adam Plantinga tells what he's learned from 13 years as a patrolman, from the everyday—like how to drive in a car chase without recklessly endangering the public—to the exotic—like what to do if you find a severed limb in the street.

Part memoir, part practical advice and above all, a series of unvarnished truths about everyday life as a cop, *400 Things Cops Know* puts the reader into the middle of the police experience. Sometimes heartbreaking, sometimes hilarious, this is an eye-opening revelation of life on the beat.

"Essential for crime writers and anyone interested in the reality of police work." —George Pelecanos

---